OUR PRESIDENTS

BRIEF BIOGRAPHIES OF OUR CHIEF MAGISTRATES

THE MACMILLAN COMPANY
NEW YORK · CHICAGO
DALLAS · ATLANTA · SAN FRANCISCO
LONDON · MANILA
IN CANADA
BRETT-MACMILLAN LTD.
GALT, ONTARIO

STATUE OF GEORGE WASHINGTON IN WALL STREET, NEW YORK,
WHERE THE FIRST INAUGURATION TOOK PLACE

OUR PRESIDENTS

BRIEF BIOGRAPHIES
OF OUR CHIEF MAGISTRATES
FROM WASHINGTON TO EISENHOWER
1789–1958

BY

JAMES MORGAN

SECOND ENLARGED EDITION

NEW YORK
THE MACMILLAN COMPANY
1958

INTRODUCTION

WHILE the framers of the Federal Constitution were at their great task behind the bolted doors of Independence Hall in Philadelphia, alarming rumors ran about the streets to the effect that the fathers of the republic were plotting in secret to set up a monarchy. They were going to make the second son of George III King of the United States! They were going to import a Bourbon prince from France to rule over the infant nation! Kings yet ruled all the rest of the world, and naturally many Americans feared, many assumed, some hoped, that in their land a new king would take the place of the old king who had been overthrown.

Haunted by doubts and anxieties, the builders of the republic had to create a new model of government. For all the nations still were beneath the rule of princes. Although there are many more republics to-day than there are independent monarchies, many more presidents than sovereign princes, there still is no other President like ours. The President of France—like the King of Great Britain—only presides, and does not govern or administer.

One delegate to the constitutional convention merely ventured the opinion that the country ought, at least, to make the attempt to get along without a throne. Another conceded that in the end there would have to be a crown; but he wished that the unwelcome event might be postponed as long as possible.

Alexander Hamilton frankly proposed that the

President should serve for life. Oliver Ellsworth of Connecticut was doubtful if "the most eminent characters" could be coaxed to take the Presidency if they were to be "degraded" again to private citizenship! Gouverneur Morris of New York declared that it was not in the nature of man to be willing to "quit such an exaltation," and he favored a life tenure because, once a President was in, he would stay in anyhow by the power of the sword.

Fearing that it would be chimerical, James Wilson of Pennsylvania hardly dared to suggest that the people might be trusted to elect the chief magistrate. A scoffing Virginian exclaimed that it would be like leaving the selection of colors to a blind man. After a long experience, ours still remains the only country where the choice of a chief of state really is referred to the masses.

*   *   *

A Japanese having offended one of the officers of Commodore Perry's expedition for the opening of the ports of the hermit empire of Japan, the Japanese officials properly wished to make "the punishment fit the crime," and they proceeded gravely to investigate the rank of the American. First, they learned that he was under a commodore; then that the Secretary of the Navy was above the commodore, and next that the President was above the Secretary. Never having heard of a republic and having no conception of a democracy with a ballot box, naturally they expected to come to some one at the top, like the Mikado.

"And who is above the President?" they asked curiously.

"The people," was the American reply.

The simple chronicle adds, "Of this they could make

nothing." Of course not. That information must
have been as illuminating as if some voyagers from
Mars should alight among us with the statement that
the horses drive the wagons on that planet.

How the Japanese must have looked at one another
in their bewilderment! The people at the top? Surely
this strange, unknown land on the other side of the
world must be upside down!

* * *

Our Presidency actually was created under a strange
delusion. The makers of the Constitution frankly intended to set up a king in all but the name. They
really made him more than a king.

Thinking or pretending to copy the British monarchy, the fathers copied a system that had ceased
to exist, except on paper. Although the change had
taken place under their eyes, they failed to see, or
chose not to see, that parliament was fast absorbing
all the ancient powers of the king, and that already
he was hardly more than the figurehead on the ship of
state that he now is. By that queer mischance, the
elected chief of the republic was intrusted with more
power than any king is now permitted to wield.

A distinguished jurist once held—before the Czars
were overthrown—that only Russia and the United
States "represent the principle of political absolutism
and enforce it by one man's hand." Even the Mikado
of Japan has his elder statesmen and his parliament,
and every European monarch or president is under the
control of the ministers of a parliament.

* * *

"My Lord," Secretary Seward said to Lord Lyons,
as that envoy reported to the British government from
Washington in the Civil War—"My Lord, I can

touch a bell and order the imprisonment of a citizen of New York, and no power on earth except that of the President can release him. Can the Queen of England do as much?"

We saw in the course of the World War an answer to Seward's unseemly boast. While this country automatically passed under one-man power, Lloyd George succeeded only by a revolutionary stroke in reducing the British executive to five men, and that war cabinet was answerable to the House of Commons at its every sitting.

Without waiting for Congress at the outbreak of the Civil War, Abraham Lincoln decided by himself one sleepless night whether the Union should be defended or abandoned. Before calling the lawmakers together, he raised two armies and suspended the writ of habeas corpus. Without an act of Congress, he freed millions of slaves by a stroke of his pen. At the end of the conflict, he alone dictated the terms of peace.

In all national crises the Presidents have had to make the choice between peace and war. The most momentous decisions in the history of the country have rested with them. They have pushed the national boundary from the Mississippi River to the China Sea and taken the first step in the annexation of every foot of soil that has been added to the territory of the nation.

* * *

Only on impeachment for high crimes or misdemeanors can the President be called to account. He is subject to no other process by Congress or court. When Chief Justice Marshall summoned Thomas Jefferson to give testimony at the trial of Aaron Burr, the President only replied, "John Marshall has issued his subpoena, now let him enforce it." How could he, with the President in control of the army and navy and of every deputy marshal?

The person of this sceptered prince of democracy is inviolable. Constitutional students contend that even though he committed murder there is no power to arrest him. He is answerable only to those from whom he received his commission—to the people.

*   *   *

While Lafayette was paying his last visit to this land of his adoption in 1824-5, he was alarmed to see John Quincy Adams, the son of a President, elected to the Presidency. When he met young Charles Francis Adams at the White House, his patriotic soul took fresh alarm at the sight of that promising eighteen-year-old representative of the third generation of the Adamses. Taking the boy's mother aside, he earnestly begged her to caution him never to harbor the hope or wish to succeed his father and grandfather except at the free call of the American people. With difficulty Mrs. Adams saved herself from laughing in his anxious face, and when his back was turned, the family made merry over his absurd anxiety.

Yet even the philosophical Franklin predicted that the presidency would end only in a dynasty. As fiercely as ever he had arraigned the royal tyrant in the past, Patrick Henry denounced the presidential tyrant of the future, who would take the field at the head of his army, fasten his galling yoke upon the necks of the people and make one rush for the American throne.

Seemingly the makers of the Constitution did take a bold chance with tyranny when they gave such immense authority to the President. In reality they gave him so much that he has neither excuse nor wish to take more and become a usurper. Responsibility balances power in the presidency, and generally Presidents have wearied of the burden, laying it down with a sigh of relief.

Most Presidents have felt as Washington felt when he was accused of an ambition to prolong his rule. Jefferson describes him stalking the floor in a thunderous fury and, with words too harsh for the ears of school children, swearing that instead of seeking to be a dictator, he would rather be back on his farm than be emperor of the world.

*   *   *

Some Presidents have been dreary mediocrities; perhaps most of them have been only commonplace. But Americans boast, as well they may, that there never has been a President who has intentionally betrayed his great trust. People often wonder at this good fortune in the blindman's buff of politics. Seeing Presidents picked out of the crowd, seemingly at haphazard, they imagine there must be something in the tradition of the office itself which has the magic power to convert an unworthy man into a good President and save the country from the folly of popular elections.

The truth is, the great power of the Presidency has a sobering effect upon the people as well as upon the Presidents. President Hayes said that a Napoleon in the White House in time of war could do almost as he pleased. Possibly he could, but it is doubtful. Anyhow, the popular instinct has seen to it that no man of that stamp has approached the White House.

*   *   *

The Presidents themselves, taken as a whole, form perhaps a matchless line. It seems to Americans, at least, that no list of premiers, no other political succession since 1789 quite measures up to the presidential average in ability and character. Certainly no dynasty could afford to invite comparison. Neither the Hapsburgs nor the Hohenzollerns produced, in half a thousand years, two princes who are equals in world fame of Washington and Lincoln.

Kings are only accidents. If they rule by right divine, democracy cannot be led far save by the divine righteousness of character.

CONTENTS

		PAGE
An Introduction		v

GEORGE WASHINGTON (1789-97)

I.	The Man in the Making	1
II.	In Love and War	4
III.	First in War	6
IV.	First in Peace	9
V.	First in the Hearts of His Countrymen	11

JOHN ADAMS (1797-1801)

I.	John and Abby	14
II.	Our Unhappiest President	17

THOMAS JEFFERSON (1801-9)

I.	The Pen of the Revolution	20
II.	The First Progressive	23
III.	A Man Afoot	26
IV.	The Sage of Monticello	29

JAMES MADISON (1809-17)

I.	James and Dolly	33
II.	A Fugitive from the White House	36

JAMES MONROE (1817-25)

I.	The Triumphs of an Ordinary Man	40
II.	The Last of the Virginians	43

JOHN QUINCY ADAMS (1825-9)

I.	A Diplomat at Fourteen	47
II.	Our Only Non-partisan President	50
III.	A Glorious ex-President	53

ANDREW JACKSON (1829-37)

I.	An Immigrant's Son	57
II.	Hero of New Orleans	60

CONTENTS

PAGE

III. The Jacksonian Revolution 63
IV. Slaying Dragons 66
V. The Birth of the Convention 70

MARTIN VAN BUREN (1837-41)

I. The First Politician 73
II. The Heir Apparent 75
III. An Ill-Starred President 78

WILLIAM HENRY HARRISON (1841)

I. The First Westerner 81
II. President for a Month 84

JOHN TYLER (1841-5)

I. The First President by Succession . . . 89
II. A Political Revolution 91

JAMES KNOX POLK (1845-9)

I. The First Dark Horse 96
II. An Inglorious Victor 99

ZACHARY TAYLOR (1849-50)

I. Old Rough and Ready 103
II. The Second President to Die in Office . . 106

MILLARD FILLMORE (1850-3)

I. A Second-Hand President 109
II. Sowing the Wind 112

FRANKLIN PIERCE (1853-7)

I. New England's Third President . . . 116
II. The Second Dark Horse 118
III. The Prologue of a Great Tragedy . . . 121

JAMES BUCHANAN (1857-61)

I. A Bachelor President 124
II. The Most Tragic Administration . . . 127
III. Adrift in the Storm 129

ABRAHAM LINCOLN (1861-5)

I. The First American 133
II. In Politics, Love and Law 136

III. Awakened to His Life Mission 139
IV. Called to the Helm in a Storm 142
V. Lincoln's Valley Forge 145
VI. The Great Friend 149
VII. Lincoln in Victory 152
VIII. Lincoln's Last Days 156

ANDREW JOHNSON (1865-9)
I. The Only President Who Never Went to
School 160
II. Blowing on the Embers of War 163
III. The Great Impeachment 167

ULYSSES SIMPSON GRANT (1869-77)
I. A Failure at Thirty-nine 171
II. A Noble Conqueror 174
III. Grant in the White House 178
IV. Slings and Arrows 181

RUTHERFORD BIRCHARD HAYES (1877-81)
I. Another Dark Horse 186
II. The Only Disputed Election 189
III. A New Epoch 193

JAMES ABRAM GARFIELD (1881)
I. The Last of the Log Cabin Presidents . . 197
II. The Only President to See Himself Nomi-
nated 200
III. Assassination of Garfield 204

CHESTER ALAN ARTHUR (1881-5)
I. The Man Who Found Himself . . . 208
II. The Era of Reform 211

GROVER CLEVELAND (1885-9)
I. From Obscurity to the White House in
Three Years 215
II. The Democratic Moses 219
III. A Bride and Groom in the White House . 222

BENJAMIN HARRISON (1889-93)   PAGE
    I. The Second Harrison 227

GROVER CLEVELAND AGAIN (1893-7)
    I. The Only ex-President to Come Back . . 231

WILLIAM McKINLEY (1897-1901)
    I. The Man Who Waited His Turn . . . 236
    II. A Great Referendum 239
    III. A Strange Fortune 243
    IV. The Third Assassination 246

THEODORE ROOSEVELT (1901-9)
    I. The Strenuous Life 251
    II. The Square Deal 254
    III. The Big Stick 258

WILLIAM HOWARD TAFT (1909-13)
    I. Presidents Are Born, Not Made . . . 263

ANOTHER ROOSEVELT CHAPTER
    I. The Bull Moose 267

WOODROW WILSON (1913-21)
    I. A Professor in Politics 271
    II. Four Crowded Years 274
    III. Momentous Decisions 278
    IV. A World Tragedy 281

WARREN GAMALIEL HARDING (1921-3)
    I. The Sixth Ohioan 287
    II. A Bold Stroke 290
    III. A Fatal Tour 295

CALVIN COOLIDGE (1923-9)
    I. New England's Windfall 299
    II. The Homeliest Inauguration 304
    III. A Yankee Sphinx 308
    IV. "I Do Not Choose to Run" 313

CONTENTS

HERBERT HOOVER (1929–33) PAGE

    I. A New Road to the White House . . . 318
   II. An Engineer in Politics 323
  III. A Rugged Individualist 328

FRANKLIN D. ROOSEVELT (1933–45)

     I. Another Roosevelt 334
    II. The Man Who Was Born at 39 . . . 339
   III. History Made in 20 Minutes 344
   IV. The New Deal 352
    V. Roosevelt Revolution 362
   VI. Third Term Taboo Broken 366
  VII. Leading the World from a Wheel Chair . 371
 VIII. He Gave His Life for Peace 376

HARRY S. TRUMAN (1945–)

    I. Least Ambitious President 382
   II. On a Roller Coaster 387
  III. Biggest Election Upset 392

DWIGHT DAVID EISENHOWER (1890–)

    I. The Democratic General 399
   II. General in Politics 405
  III. Domestic Policies 416
  IV. Conciliator President 422

TABULATED HISTORY OF THE PRESIDENCY 431

INDEX 451

LIST OF ILLUSTRATIONS

Statue of George Washington in Wall Street, New York, where the first inauguration took place . . *Frontispiece*

FACING
PAGE

President and Martha Washington, by Stuart, with a photograph of an old print of Mt. Vernon . . .   2

John and Abigail Adams, with their son John Quincy at the age of sixteen   14

The Jeffersonian dynasty, with a photograph of Monticello by Holsinger—James Madison, Thomas Jefferson and James Monroe   20

John Quincy Adams, Andrew Jackson and Martin Van Buren, with the familiar portico of the White House which was added in Jackson's administration . .   48

William Henry Harrison, John Tyler, James K. Polk, Zachary Taylor and Millard Fillmore   82

Franklin Pierce and James Buchanan   116

President and Mrs. Lincoln with their sons Robert T. and "Tad"   136

Andrew Johnson and his wife who taught him his letters   160

Ulysses S. Grant, Chester A. Arthur, James A. Garfield and Rutherford B. Hayes   172

Grover Cleveland and his White House bride, Frances Folsom   224

Benjamin Harrison and William McKinley . . .   236

Theodore Roosevelt and William H. Taft, with a photograph of the south front of the White House . .   252

President and Edith Bolling Wilson   272

President and Florence Kling Harding 288
President and Grace Goodhue Coolidge 300
President and Mrs. Hoover 318
President and Mrs. Roosevelt 334
Harry S. Truman 384
Dwight David Eisenhower 400

OUR PRESIDENTS

BRIEF BIOGRAPHIES OF OUR CHIEF MAGISTRATES

OUR PRESIDENTS

GEORGE WASHINGTON

I

THE MAN IN THE MAKING

(1732) Feb. 22. Born near Fredericksburg, Va.—(1743) Death of father.—(1748) Began surveying in the West.

A LITTLE schoolgirl shouted with delight as she came running home: "Mother, the teacher told us about a man to-day, and he had a little hatchet, and his name was George!" Later in the year, she burst in again, full of a further discovery: "Mother, teacher told us about another man to-day, and he had an axe, and he was called Abe!" Character, patriotism, the great unheard-of past had been introduced to that child, as to generations of American children, in simple pictures that flashed upon her mind like motion films thrown upon a screen.

The useful, instructive myth of Washington's little hatchet is scorned by many writers who spare the more misleading myth that he was born with a gold spoon in his mouth. He was made of the same clay as most Americans who have won high leadership and, like them, he cut his teeth on the crust of poverty. Only four or five of our Presidents came from poorer homes than our first President, and he had less schooling than

1

four-fifths of his successors. He was, in fact, the only President in the first forty years who was without a college education.

Not starting to school until eight, Washington had to leave at fourteen to go to work. Thenceforth until the Revolution the woods and fields were his only schoolroom and life was his only schoolmaster. A bad speller and a worse grammarian, his English rapidly improved in contact with the educated men whom he commanded by the superiority of his character. His generals and his statesmen became his teachers.

We never can truly understand this man if we start with the mistaken idea that he was the product of wealth and aristocracy. His people really were only a plain, though always a highly respectable family, living on the outskirts of the cavalier caste which set up its manors in the James River region.

The greatest of Virginians made no ancestral boast, his great-grandfather having come out from England in the modest capacity of mate on a trading vessel. Mt. Vernon came into the family as part of the land granted to a Washington in reward for his services in transporting from English jails and almshouses one hundred indentured servants. George's own father, who at one time had been a sailing captain in the trade with the mother country, left his wife and children at his death five thousand acres of land, more or less unproductive, twenty-two slaves, a slender purse and a lean larder.

As only a younger son and the child of a second wife, George received but a small share of a modest estate. Being dependent on the bounty of his half-brothers, he passed to and fro between them as a poor relation and grew up mostly in their homes.

While at Mt. Vernon, which his oldest brother, Law-

PRESIDENT AND MARTHA WASHINGTON, BY STUART, WITH A PHOTOGRAPH OF AN OLD PRINT OF MT. VERNON

rence, had inherited, he learned the simple rudiments of surveying, and Lord Fairfax, who lived nearby, employed him to survey a vast estate in the Valley of Virginia. With that commission in hand, the sixteen-year-old boy rode away over the Blue Ridge and out into the wild west of that time, where he passed the next three years on the savage frontier of America.

Blazing paths in an almost trackless wilderness, the tall, lean, blue-eyed, young frontiersman built his fire at the end of the toilsome day, cooked his supper on forked sticks and ate it off chips in place of plates. Without seeing a bed for weeks at a time, he wrapped himself in his bearskin against the cold night and slept in his clothes on the hard ground, "like a Parcel of Dogs or Catts," as he said in his diary, which he carefully kept, "and happy's he that gets the Birth nearest the fire." Reckoning that "a Dubloon is my constant gain every Day and sometime Six Pistoles," he could smile at privations, as he jingled in his pocket those Spanish gold coins.

It was good pay, but he earned it. After one hundred and fifty years had passed since he ran his lines with the aid of a simple compass, the Government lately went over them with high-power transits and found them remarkably correct. So, too, the world has retraced the lines of his life and found them as true as those that he drew through the wild forest in his boyhood days.

The frontier ever has been a great training school in our new world. From Jackson to Lincoln, yes to Roosevelt, it has produced many rugged Americans, but its first graduate was Washington.

II

IN LOVE AND WAR

(1752) Washington inherited Mt. Vernon.—(1753) First expedition to the West.—(1754) Second expedition.—(1755) On staff of Gen. Braddock.—(1759) Married Martha Custis.

AFTER a youth of toil, which hardened the muscles of his character and body, Washington at twenty-one unexpectedly became by the death of his brother the owner of Mt. Vernon and free at last to give rein to his restless spirit for adventure in sports and politics, in love and war.

A foreign visitor once doubted the story that Washington threw a dollar across the Rappahannock. An American wit ventured to explain that a dollar went farther then, and a still wittier American argued that it was no feat at all for a man who threw a sovereign over the Atlantic.

From the bare soles of his feet, which called for No. 13 boots, to the crown of his small, well-formed head, Washington measured six feet, two. His enormous hands, with their knotty knuckles, required gloves specially made. Massive, yet lean, his sinewy frame always remained under two hundred weight.

A devoted sportsman, the new squire of Mt. Vernon once hunted for five days at a stretch, and in one period he chased foxes sixteen days in two months. He could clear the tallest fence without rising in his stirrups and shoot his musket straight to the mark with one hand.

In his young manhood Washington found his "inclinations strongly bent to arms." To softer arms than those of Mars the young militarist also was inclined. Through the grave manner he wore even in his laborious and anxious youth, he ever was ready to smile at a pretty girl and to sigh over her through the measures of a dance.

Prying posterity finds him at sixteen pining for a mysterious "lowland beauty," who would not have the penniless surveyor. He received also by his own confession a "cruel sentence" from a "Miss Betsy," and afterward was rejected by Miss Phillipse of New York. At last the oft-disappointed wooer came to the White House on the Pamunkey, and once more he lost his heart. The mistress of the manor, Mrs. Martha Dandridge Custis, was wise enough to keep it. A widow of seven years and the mother of two fatherless children, she was of plain appearance and simple origin, but with common sense and a solid character, with broad acres and shares in the Bank of England to boot.

When flying embers from the war fields of Europe ignited the savage forests of the New World, Washington was a militia major, and he was dispatched on a mission to the Ohio, a perilous journey of ten weeks through a wintry desolation. The next year he went again with a band of soldiers, for now the Seven Years' War had spread to America. His campaign was hardly a glorious failure, but he reported that he liked to hear the bullets whistle.

Now Gen. Braddock came out from England to scorn the colonial breed and show them how British regulars fought in proper, soldierly formation. The undrilled red children of the forest stubbornly refusing to fight on the European plan, Braddock fell amid his panic-stricken troops on the Monongahela. At the head of his grave in the wilderness the prayers for the dead were read by Col. Washington.

Although Washington had won no battles, he had

made a most important conquest. When the Seven Years' War came he was still an Englishman, and to him an island three thousand miles away still was home. In his contact with British officers he was shocked to find them aliens to him and his New World and himself only a colonial in their eyes. With native condescension they undertook to teach him his place, but with native independence he objected. They variously set him down in their letters and reports as "obstinate," "ungrateful," in "no ways like a soldier," and he returned the compliment to the "cowardly, dastardly behavior" of the regulars, who "broke and ran as sheep before the hounds."

By the time the Seven Years' War was over the colonial colonel no longer was an Englishman. That illusion was gone and had left Washington an American.

III

FIRST IN WAR

(1775) June 15, appointed Commander-in-Chief, aged forty-three.—(1781) Oct. 15, received the surrender of Cornwallis at Yorktown.—(1783) Dec. 23, surrendered his commission to Congress.

THE choice of Washington to be commander-in-chief of the Revolution is one of the mysterious but happy accidents of history. Nothing in the deeds of this militia colonel, who had lost every fight that he had fought, pointed him out as the one and only man to meet the armies of the greatest empire in the world. Nothing in the words of this farmer, who never had made a speech, inspired the Congress at Philadelphia to turn to him by unanimous consent as the leader of the young nation. Yet Patrick Henry testified that this silent member was "the greatest man" in an assemblage which Lord Chatham declared never had its superior anywhere in history.

When patriot orators raised their eloquent voices against the tyrant king, Washington offered to raise a regiment. "I will raise a thousand men, subsist them at my own expense and march them to the relief of Boston." When Congress was debating whether it should contribute another petition to the waste basket of George III, he simply put on his war clothes—his old blue and buff military uniform—quietly walked in among the able debaters and took his seat. But when his fellow members elected him commander of the army, he blushed like a schoolgirl and fled through the door.

As he went to the front, he met a courier on a lathered horse, bearing the direful news of Bunker Hill. "Did the militia fight?" was all he wished to know. "Yes." "Then the liberties of the country are safe." Although it is said that Washington never in his life read but one book on the art of war, he knew that if the people would only stand up to the king's regulars, they could lose every battle and still defeat an enemy who was three thousand miles from his base.

In these five-minute visits with our Presidents, there is no room or call for a history of battles and sieges. Anyhow, the only significant battle Washington ever won was his last battle at Yorktown. He never took a town after taking Boston. He let the British take New York, even Philadelphia, although it was the capital, and take all the towns they wanted. But he would not let them take him and his army, though five royal commanders in turn came out to entrap "the old fox" and chased him up and down the land six years.

The Revolution was not won by the sword of Washton, but by his indomitable character. It was his character, slowly built up by poverty and struggle, which had given him from the start the leadership over men who talked more; yes, and who knew more.

The invincible fortitude of a people, heroically embodied in him, overthrew the king's army and navy and his Hessians. The unconquerable spirit of the three thousand hunted, hungering, shivering, ragged Continentals of Valley Forge wrested from the British crown an empire greater than all the conquests made by Napoleon's grand army.

At the end, as the Americans leaped those last hurdles to independence, the British redoubts at Yorktown, Washington only said, "The work is done and well done. Bring me my horse." When he dined his vanquished foe and heard Lord Cornwallis toast "The King," he may not have added—"Of England; confine him there, and then I will drink a full bumper." But that traditional amendment would have been in keeping with his ready sense of humor, for which he receives too small credit.

The war was over, but the noblest victory was yet to come. Having received the surrendered sword of Cornwallis, Washington surrendered his own, unstained by personal ambition, to the people who had entrusted it to him and went back to his farm.

Eight years had passed since he left his estates only to attend a session of Congress and with no warning of the greater and longer duty that awaited him. Through all those years, while he was giving himself to his country without pay—not taking a cent above the exact amount of actual expenses in the field—his neglect of Mt. Vernon had lost him perhaps fifty thousand dollars, and now he must start all over again to build up his farm from ruin.

IV

FIRST IN PEACE

(1789) April 30, inaugurated first President, aged fifty-seven. October-November, touring the North.—(1790) August, visited Rhode Island.—(1791) Toured the South.—(1792) September, put down Whisky Rebellion.—(1793) March 4, inaugurated a second time. —(1793) April, issued Neutrality Proclamation.—(1796) September, Farewell Address.—(1797) March 4, retired.

WHERE the gray columns of the old Sub-Treasury in Wall Street stand to-day, in the financial center of the richest country of earth, this great nation was started without a cent in the treasury and without credit— doubted at home and scorned abroad. Its best visible asset was supplied by the fame and character of the tall man in a simple brown suit of Connecticut-made cloth, who stood on the balcony of the hastily improvised National Capitol, solemnly bowing to the crowd in the street as it caught up the cry of "Long live George Washington."

Foreign Powers, all of them monarchies then, had shown their contemptuous indifference by not sending one full-fledged minister to honor the birth of the first modern republic. So little did even the chosen senators and representatives care for their new honors that Congress had to wait four weeks for a quorum, and this negligence delayed eight weeks the first inauguration of a President.

As Washington kissed the Bible and lifted his grave countenance to the cheering throng in Wall Street, he was faced by problems more complicated than those which had confronted him in the Revolution. Without a working model before him, the whole machinery of a novel government must be created under his supervision almost in a day, and he had no experience in civil administration.

The only uncrowned chief of state in the world, people were puzzled to find the proper way of addressing him. The title of "His High Mightiness," was seriously debated in Congress, but a Pennsylvania German ridiculed the proposal with the objection that some successor might not be as high as Washington by a head. It was wisely decided in the end to call the President simply the President.

Being older, the States all thought themselves superior to the infant federation. Little Rhode Island, still doubtful whether she cared to belong to the United States of America, had not yet come in to complete the Union of thirteen states. The army consisted of just six hundred and sixty-six men.

Washington promptly went on the road for the new concern. From Portsmouth, N. H., to Savannah, Ga., he persisted in his laborious journeying over the muddy trails until he had personified before the people of all the jealous States the majesty of "the greater name of American."

This being boldly challenged by the famous "Whisky Rebellion," in Pennsylvania, the first President speedily vindicated the supremacy of the nation, and for two score years the ghost of revolt against national authority was laid. The French Revolution starting within five days of his inauguration, he gave to international history the first example of real neutrality.

No President has been more bitterly abused than the first. His Cabinet quarreled until Jefferson, his Secretary of State, resigned, and his next Secretary, Edmund Randolph, basely betrayed him. His Vice-President, John Adams, called him "an old mutton head," who had "not been found out only because he kept his mouth shut." "Treacherous in private friendship and a hypocrite in public life," Thomas Paine pronounced him. Because he refused to take the side of revolutionary France "ten thousand persons in the streets of Philadelphia"—then the capital—"threatened to drag Washington out of his house," John Adams tells us.

The target for all that mud-slinging succeeded generally in holding himself too high above his critics to be touched by their assaults. On rare occasions he slipped his superb self-control, as when he smote his dinner table with such violence as to cause the cups and plates to jump and rattle, or again when he cried out to his Cabinet that he would rather be in his grave than in the Presidency.

Notwithstanding all the outbursts of partisanship, he retained the confidence of the country to the last, when the people at the inauguration of his successor followed the retiring President into the street and left the new President all but deserted. The long task of the homesick exile from Mt. Vernon was done. He had found the Union a theory and he had left it a fact.

V

FIRST IN THE HEARTS OF HIS COUNTRYMEN

(1797) March, retired to Mt. Vernon.—(1799) Dec. 14, died, aged sixty-seven.

THE welcoming shouts of his slaves and the baying of his dogs at Mt. Vernon, no doubt, were more pleasing to Washington, on his retirement from the Presidency, than any public applause. For the second time he had come home with an empty wallet from an eight-year absence in the service of his country.

When he died, Washington was worth $530,000 above the value of Mt. Vernon and apart from Mrs. Washington's estate. But he was always land poor. When called to the Presidency he was behind in his taxes, even with his doctor's bill, and had to borrow the money to pay his way to the inauguration. As President, his steward and fourteen servants at the capital cost him six hundred dollars a month for their food and wages, and he gave away more money than his latter-day successors. Besides providing that his usual charities at Mt. Vernon should be continued, liberal charities in the Presidency were a serious drain on his official pay.

Without a child of his own, Washington always had a large family to support. He adopted or brought up nine children belonging to his or Mrs. Washington's relatives, and forty-one relatives received bequests at his death.

Although hating slavery, he had more than three hundred slaves; but he seldom sold one, his negroes growing old and helpless on his farm. Nor did this just man leave them to the mercies of another master after he was gone. In his will he freed them all, with a thoughtful provision for those who, because of age or infancy, could not shift for themselves.

Many a man does not look to the welfare of his brother as closely as Washington cared for his old bodyservant in the Revolution (purchase price three hundred and forty-three dollars), and in his will he remembered faithful "Billy" with an annuity. His war horse, "Nelson," fared as well. The war over, he pensioned this veteran of his campaigns, who never again wore a saddle.

Albert Gallatin said that Lafayette was the only man Washington loved. But Washington himself expressed his love for Gen. Knox and, in his loyal devotion to Gen. Greene, he offered at the latter's death to educate his fatherless son.

His devotion to his wife through forty years of married life was illustrated on his dying day. Although he awoke in the night with a chill, scarcely able to speak and breathing with difficulty, for fear that Mrs. Washington might take cold he would not let her get up to call a servant.

His life-long consideration of others lasted to the end. When he lay helpless and speechless, he made a feeble motion toward a chair for the servant who had been patiently standing at the bedside

The nations are united, as in no other instance, in honoring the memory of Washington. England competes with America in praise of the rebel who snatched from the British Empire its greatest possession. "As much one of our heroes as Alfred the Great is yours," Frederic Harrison has told us. "The purest figure in history," said Gladstone. "A life without a stain, a fame without a flaw," Thackeray declared. "The greatest man of our own or of any age," Lord Brougham acclaimed him. Byron ranked him only "Next to the Divinity." Southey bowed to "Washington's awful memory," and Lord Erskine wrote him, "You are the only being for whom I ever felt an awful reverence," a reverence that Green, the English historian, said "still hushes us in the presence of his memory." The tribute paid in Congress at the time of his death by "Light Horse Harry," father of Robert E. Lee, remains the most familiar: "First in war, first in peace, and first in the hearts of his countrymen."

JOHN ADAMS

I

JOHN AND ABBY

(1735) Oct. 19, John Adams born, Braintree, Mass.—(1755) Graduated at Harvard.—(1755-58) Taught School.—(1758) Admitted to the bar.—(1764) Married—(1770) Defended soldiers of the Boston Massacre.—(1774-77) In Congress.—(1775-85) On Mission to France.—(1785-88) Minister to England.

A SCHOOLGIRL complained that American history was so "littered up with Adamses" that she couldn't tell one from the other. Yet this most distinguished family in our national biography lived in America one hundred and fifty years before it broke into fame.

When the engagement was announced of John Adams of Braintree, Mass., to the daughter of Parson Smith of the adjoining town of Weymouth, people were shocked that Abby should marry so beneath her station. Was she not a Quincy and a Norton? And John, the son of a small farmer, was put down to fourteenth place among his twenty-four classmates, when Harvard catalogues were made up according to social rank. After that he taught school in Worcester to get enough money to study law, and the strictest of the Puritans looked on lawyers as ungodly.

Father-in-law Smith manfully stood by his daughter's choice, and tradition says that he preached down his gossiping parishioners from this well-chosen text: "John came neither eating bread nor drinking wine, and ye say ye hath a devil!"

JOHN AND ABIGAIL ADAMS, WITH THEIR SON JOHN QUINCY AT THE AGE OF SIXTEEN

Although she never went to school, this parson's daughter was by long odds the cleverest in the entire line of our President's wives. Her published letters form a delightful human document in our too often unhuman history. When John Adams joined the fathers of the republic in the great work of setting up the most masculine government the world ever saw, this mother of the republic stayed home to rock the cradle, cook and patch for four little Adamses and to tend the farm. Milking and churning, knitting and darning, teaching and praying, toiling and saving, she supported the family, inspired her husband in his progress to the Presidency, and reared a son to follow in the father's footsteps. To Abigail Adams alone belongs the glory of having been the wife of one President and the mother of another.

Although as a lawyer Adams defended the British soldiers on trial for shooting down the citizens in what is called the Boston Massacre, the patriots sent him to Congress, where he sprang the first proposal of Washington's appointment as commander-in-chief. Not that he ever was particularly partial to him. His real motive in proposing him was to interest the Virginians and the others in the yet conservative Congress to adopt the rebellious troops gathered about Boston, thereby committing all the colonies to the war, which until then had been only a local conflict in New England.

In the war, it fell to Adams to do picket duty in Europe. Congress sent him to France, with a thoughtful warning to put in the bottom of his dispatch bag plenty of lead or stone or other weighty substance to sink his papers. For his own neck no protection was proposed in event of the British capturing a signer of the rebel manifesto of July 4, 1776. Nevertheless, he took with him on the perilous trip his ten-year-old son, John Quincy.

On the next voyage, he carried not only John Quincy, but also his second son, and they were shipwrecked off the coast of Spain. Having to ride muleback over the mountains, they were three months on the road to Paris. Never mind; the boys picked up Spanish along the way!

After five long, anxious years of separation from husband and children, the mother herself sailed to Europe, and the pioneer American woman to appear at the Court of St. James' was Abigail, the farmer of Braintree. Her presentation costume, according to her own description, was white lutestring "covered with white crepe, festooned with lilac ribbon and mock point lace, over a hoop of enormous extent, and with a narrow train three yards long; also ruffle cuffs, treble lace ruffles and dress cap, with long lace lappets and two white plumes."

"You will be stared at a great deal," the Duke of Dorset kindly warned the Adamses. On the contrary, every back in the court circle was turned upon the Yankee rebels, and Queen Charlotte received Abigail with "contempt and scorn."

A man can defend himself always, as Abigail's husband did right manfully when it fell to him to be the first independent American to stand before the throne of England. George III venturing to infer from Adams' supposed dislike of France, a preference for England, his one-time subject frankly corrected the King: "I must avow to Your Majesty that I have no attachment but to my own country."

That was not an idle boast. It was the simple truth —the very corner-stone of the life of John Adams.

II

OUR UNHAPPIEST PRESIDENT

(1788) John Adams elected Vice-President.—(1792) Re-elected Vice-President.—(1796) Elected President.—(1797) Inaugurated, aged sixty-one.—(1798) Alien and Sedition Acts. Preparing for War with France.—(1799) Sent Peace Mission to France.—(1800) Concluded Peace. Moved from Philadelphia to Washington and opened the White House. Defeated by Jefferson.—(1820) Member Massachusetts Constitutional Convention.—(1826) July 4, died, aged ninety.

PROBABLY John Adams was the unhappiest man who ever sat in the Presidential chair. One of a dozen unwanted Presidents, who were taken only because the men that were wanted could not be elected, this humble rôle embittered all the remaining days of the proudest man in the line of our Chief Magistrates.

It was hard enough for Adams to be the understudy even of George Washington, while serving as Vice-President. When he became President it was maddening to his ego that he should be expected to play second fiddle to Alexander Hamilton, the master spirit of the old governing class, left over from colonial times, and which controlled the Federalist party.

The President made the fatal mistake of keeping Washington's Cabinet, which really had passed under the control of Hamilton, who presumed to direct the new administration. As Adams never had succeeded in ruling himself it was impossible for another to rule him.

Like aristocracies everywhere, the Federalists were thrown into a state of panic by the French Revolution and by the rise of the Jeffersonian democracy in our yet aristocratic republic. In their alarm they frantically rushed through Congress the Alien and Sedition acts, which became only millstones about their necks, sinking their party forever. Not satisfied with shutting the Revolution out of the New World, many of them were for joining the monarchical coalition against it in the Old World. In an uproarious quarrel with the absurd French Directory, the militia was called out and Washington summoned to command it, after which the President astonished the jingoes by suddenly throwing them over and returning to a pacific policy.

Long afterward, Adams said that he desired no other inscription than this on his tombstone: "Here lies John Adams, who took upon himself the responsibility of the peace with France, in the year 1800." It was a fitting epitaph, for in making that peace he dug his political grave, and he went to the election of 1800 foredoomed to defeat.

As he had been the first minister to England, John Adams was also the first President to take up his residence in Washington. As Mrs. Adams had been the wife of the first American envoy in London she was also the first mistress of the White House, if for only a few months. On the way from Philadelphia she and the President lost their trail in the wilderness, until a "straggling black" came to their assistance.

The Capitol was yet under construction, and out of a desolate bog, far off, the unfinished White House rose to view. There was neither a fence nor a tree about the structure, and the President's nearest neighbor dwelt half a mile away. Mrs. Adams had a hard time to get wood enough to keep her family warm in the big, bleak mansion, and she smiles at us still as her letters tell us of how she hung her washing to dry in the great East Room.

After sitting at his desk until midnight, hastily signing appointments, to forestall his successor, Adams

drove out of Washington at the dawning of the day
of Jefferson's inauguration.   He had no smiles to
bestow on the triumph of his rival, and few enough to
light his own pathway through his remaining years,
when he nursed for a quarter of a century the never-
forgotten grudges of his political life against Washington, Hamilton and his opponents.   With Jefferson, almost alone, he did make peace, thanks to the kindly
mediation of his wife.

After his brave, good helpmeet had been taken from
him, he lived on eight years more, lived to see what no
other ex-President has seen, a son in the White House.
At ninety, as he lay dying in the sunset of the fiftieth
Fourth of July, we are told that his thoughts turned to
the first and most glorious Fourth, and that his lips
murmured "Thomas Jefferson still survives."   The
author of the Declaration really had died a few hours
before, and in their flight from earth the spirits of the
two old patriots of '76 were strangely united again.

THOMAS JEFFERSON

I

THE PEN OF THE REVOLUTION

(1743) April 13, Thomas Jefferson born at Shadwell, Va.—(1761-2) At William and Mary's College.—(1765) Heard Patrick Henry. —(1767) Admitted to the bar—(1769-74) Member House of Burgesses.—(1770) Went to live at Monticello.—(1772) Married Mrs. Martha Wales Skelton.—(1774-6) Member of Congress.

THOMAS JEFFERSON, as much as Abraham Lincoln,

> was nursed at the breast
> Of the unexhausted West.

At the time of his birth beneath one of its foothills, the Blue Ridge of Virginia was the American frontier. The farm on which he was born had been cleared in the wild forest by his pioneer father when the smoke of a neighbor's chimney hardly could be seen from his cabin door.

Like both of his predecessors and so many of his successors in the Presidency, Jefferson was a widow's son. Losing his father at fourteen, as the eldest boy he inherited the farm and became the responsible head of the family of eight children.

It was not a large estate; for the Jeffersons, like the Washingtons, belonged more to the yeomanry than to the aristocracy who lorded it over tide-water Virginia. But Thomas Jefferson's mother was a Randolph and sprung from the class which found in her son the most unrelenting foe to its ancient privileges.

When he rode East, with his darling fiddle under his

THE JEFFERSONIAN DYNASTY, WITH A PHOTOGRAPH OF MONTICELLO BY HOLSINGER,
JAMES MADISON ON THE LEFT AND THOMAS JEFFERSON ON THE RIGHT, AT THE TOP,
WITH JAMES MONROE BELOW

arm, to be a student at William and Mary College, the tall, slender, sandy-haired, snub-nosed, freckled-faced, seventeen-year-old boy of the frontiersman never had seen a mansion, a church or a village of twenty houses, and he looked with a stranger's eyes upon the baronial pride and display of the old families who formed the vice regal court at Williamsburg. His light heart and his yet lighter feet made him welcome at the balls in the Apollo room of the Raleigh Tavern. His already curious mind won for the mere lad the remarkable fortune of a place in a small group of learned and traveled men who regularly gathered at the dinner table of Gov. Fauquier to discuss the literature and music, the science and the philosophy of Europe.

There over the roast and the pipes, the great world was opened to the silent, reflective youth. More than William and Mary's, the table of that unsuspecting royal Governor was the training school of the immortal rebel who indicted a king.

To support the large family of his mother on their too small farm, Jefferson turned to the law. In seven years at the bar he doubled his estate and increased his slaves to four hundred. Buying the little mountain at whose feet he was born, he built upon its summit from plans of his own drawing, with bricks of his own making, and with wood of his own cutting, the noblest house in all Virginia. There, at Monticello, he made his home ever after, and there at last, he died in sight of his birthplace, five hundred and eighty feet below. To that eyrie one wild, stormy winter's night he took his bride, the twenty-six-year-old widow Skelton, who brought him one hundred and thirty-five slaves and forty thousand acres, including the famous Natural Bridge.

Jefferson's law practice continued rapidly to grow until it produced an income of two thousand five hundred dollars a year, when he abandoned it forever to prosecute George III in the great and general court of mankind. He had heard the first call of the Revolution while a law student in Williamsburg. Its clarion had been ringing in his ears ever since he stood, an eager looker-on, in the door of the House of Burgesses. He saw Washington in his seat and he saw his own friend, Patrick Henry, a fiddling Virginian like himself, holding the floor amid cries of treason as he invited the king to profit by the example of Cæsar, who had his Brutus, and of Charles I, who had his Cromwell.

The sword, the tongue and the pen of American freedom were well met that memorable day. After the pen had waited twelve years for its turn to speak, Jefferson sat in the Congress at Philadelphia. The squire of Monticello was a silent member, as silent as the squire of Mt. Vernon. Opportunity and duty went straight to those two speechless congressmen as the needle leaps to a loadstone.

Although the great Franklin, and the able, ambitious John Adams also were on the committee to draft the Declaration of Independence, they left the task wholly to their youngest colleague, the thirty-three-year old, bookish, philosophic Virginian. When Congress was editing the manuscript, Franklin leaned over Jefferson to comfort him with a little story of a signboard which was to have read: "John Thompson, the hatter, makes and sells hats for ready cash," but which friendly neighbors, to save the cost of painting, cut down simply to the name Thompson and the picture of a hat.

By a miraculous escape, while a paragraph denouncing slavery was stricken out of Jefferson's draft of the Declaration, the assertion that "all men are created equal" was spared. That glittering generality surely would have been discarded if conservative members had foreseen what a blazing torch it was to become, lighting a Civil War that freed the slaves and ever leading men on along the endless road to justice and liberty.

II

THE FIRST PROGRESSIVE

(1776) Sept., Jefferson resigned from Congress.—(1776-9) Member Virginia Assembly.—(1779-81) Governor.—(1781) June 4, Fled from the British. Dec., Member of Virginia Assembly.—(1782) Sept. 5, Death of his wife.—(1783-4) Member of Congress.— (1784-9) Minister to France.—(1790-3) Secretary of State.

THE first and still the foremost progressive in American statesmanship often has been accused of taking his opinions from the French Revolution and of importing foreign ideas into this country. Any one who will read the Declaration of Independence and the bills written by the same hand in the same year of 1776 will find Thomas Jefferson already a revolutionist years before he saw France, attended the National Assembly, listened to Mirabeau and watched the fall of the Bastile.

After the Declaration had been adopted Jefferson hastened to Virginia to tear up by the roots that Old Dominion of kings and make it over into a free state. Abolishing entail, he pulled out the corner-stone, and abolishing primogeniture, he pulled out the foundations of an hereditary aristocracy. Disestablishing the Episcopal Church, he smashed a religious monopoly. Remaking all the courts and laws, he swept away the barbaric penalties of an old code. Could he have had his way altogether, the transformation would have been complete, with a schoolhouse at every cross roads, and with never another child born into slavery.

While he was wiping out the ancient system of primogeniture, a conservative member of the Assembly begged him at least to let the eldest son inherit a double share in an estate. The iconoclast refused, "unless the first born can eat and produce twice as much as any of the other children."

Although he abolished the slave trade, Jefferson wished to stop the coming of slaves from Heaven as well as from Africa, by freeing all black children at birth. Being thwarted in this purpose, he sighed ever after: "I tremble for my country when I reflect that God is just."

In the armed revolution, this revolutionist took no hand. Bold as a lion in council, he was a dove in war. When the British burst upon Virginia at the outset of the Yorktown campaign he was Governor. The best he could do to save the author of the Declaration of Independence from the Tower of London was to gallop down one slope of Monticello while the redcoats spurred their horses up the other side of the hill.

While Jefferson still felt after a year the sting or censure for the unpreparedness of the State, in the presence of that invasion, the great and lasting sorrow of his life fell upon him in the death of his wife. For four months he was not out of the sound of her voice, as she lay dying in their unique suite at Monticello, where their bed stood in an alcove between two rooms, so that on rising he could step into his room and she into hers. They were all the more a devoted couple for having been so often called to mourn together the loss of their children, four out of the six having died in infancy or childhood. The mother's last wish was

that the little girl she was leaving should never have a
stepmother, and she died content with the pledge which
her husband kept through the remaining forty-four
years of a life tenderly faithful to the bride of his
youth.

After weeks of despairing sadness, Jefferson turned
with relief from the haunted scene to re-enter Congress.
That body being engaged in casting off the pounds,
shillings and pence of England, he introduced the dollar as the new unit, with its dimes and cents. A happy
chance was missed forever, when the members rejected
his further proposal to start the young nation on the
basis of the decimal system in weights and measures.

From Congress he was sent as minister to the Court
of France. "You replace Dr. Franklin," the Count
Vergennes said to him on his arrival in Paris. "I succeed him," the new envoy happily replied; "no one can
replace Dr. Franklin."

France did not make Jefferson a democrat; she only
confirmed his native hatred of hereditary privilege.
Seeing the king and queen at Versailles, he called
Louis XVI a fool and Marie Antoinette something
worse. Visiting peasants in their hovels, where he
lifted the lids of the steaming pots and felt of the beds,
that he might see how the masses lived, he declared
that out of twenty million French people nineteen million were all more miserable than the wretchedest person in America.

Six weeks and a day after he had seen that old
France of the Bourbons crash beneath the walls of the
Bastile, Jefferson left Paris to become our first Secre-
tary of State. Taking his seat at the right of Wash-
ington he was face to face across the cabinet table with
Alexander Hamilton, the Secretary of the Treasury.

By nature and training the two were as opposite in

their political opinions as in their chairs, and they found themselves, as Jefferson said, "pitted like fighting cocks." As they fought and the feathers flew a great crowd collected behind each to urge on its favorite in that cocking main over which Washington had the unhappiness to preside. Quickly all the people in the land took one side or the other and formed themselves into the two political parties which, with changing names, and changing disputes, have divided the country to this day.

III

A MAN AFOOT

(1797-1801) Jefferson, Vice-President.—(1801) Inaugurated third President, aged fifty-seven.—(1803) Purchased Louisiana.—(1807) Enforced Embargo Act.

THE furious storm aroused by the combat between Thomas Jefferson and Alexander Hamilton, the greatest gladiators to face each other in the arena of American politics, makes our recent political campaigns seem like sunshowers. Hamiltonians scorned to eat and drink, to marry, and sometimes even to pray, with the Jeffersonians.

Nothing else so stirs the angry passions as a conflict of classes or of sections. This was both and doubly bitter. An almost solid South united with the Northern masses in a common dread of a strong government and in a common hostility to the old ruling caste in the Middle States and New England. The new parties called themselves Federalists and Republicans, but they denounced each other as Monocrats and Democrats, although Jefferson himself never accepted that latter term of opprobrium.

In the first battle, when those parties fought for the

chair of Washington in 1796, the result was so close that Jefferson came within two electoral votes of winning the Presidency against Adams. In the second battle, which was waged in 1800, he beat Adams, but an absurd provision of the Constitution, which was soon after amended, nearly lost him the fruits of his victory.

Under that old plan each elector voted for two men, the higher man becoming President and the second man receiving the Vice-Presidency as a consolation prize. Although the Republicans wished to elect Jefferson to the chief place and Aaron Burr to the second, they failed to do either, because both men received the same number of votes. This threw the choice of President into the House, where the Federalists in a blind rage struggled to elect Burr to the Presidency, not because they loved that unscrupulous Tammany politician more, but because they hated him less. For a week the House voted, and thirty-five ballots had to be taken before this most exciting deadlock was broken.

Contrary to the familiar story of his hitching his horse to the Capitol fence, Jefferson walked to his inauguration and afterward walked back to his boarding house, which was only a few hundred yards away. This man afoot, dreamer and theorist, quietly ushered in that day a more lasting revolution than a man on horseback could have wrought with a sword and a whiff of grapeshot. As a cannon rebounds, so a violent revolution begets a violent reaction. A peaceable revolution is less likely to go backward, and government by the old colonial aristocracy was buried forever.

Believing that revolutions should begin at home, Jefferson revolutionized the White House by casting aside the ceremonials which had been adopted in a

feeble imitation of kingly courts. Opening the doors
to all, without regard to social classifications and without order of precedence his rule was "first come, first
served."   Determined that the President, as he said,
should cease to be a personage, he stopped the custom
of celebrating a President's birthday; never made a
public tour; did his own marketing, and went and came
like any other citizen. Although no successor has
thrown a British minister into a fit of indignation by
receiving him in slippered feet, Jeffersonian simplicity
rather more than Washingtonian courtliness remains
the standard of Presidential conduct.

It was the strange fortune of this most thorough-
going pacifist to find himself at the helm in the midst
of a world at war. When the globe was bristling with
bayonets until it looked like a porcupine, President
Jefferson calmly announced that peace was his passion,
and started out by cutting down his little army one-
half and by talking of hauling up his seven warships.

His only interest in the Napoleonic struggle was to
keep out of it. "Palliate and endure," he counseled
his countrymen, "and put money in thy purse." Sometimes he made a somewhat comical motion toward his
empty scabbard, and again he tried to make the mar-
tial bullies of Europe be good by an act of Congress.
But his non-importation and embargo laws only bit off
the nose to spite the face.

Nevertheless while the military powers were fighting over little islands and provinces and drenching
Europe with their blood, this most unmilitary President, without firing a shot, gathered in far richer spoils
than the victors in twenty-five years of warfare divided
among themselves at the Congress of Vienna. As Jefferson's election was a bloodless revolution, his pur-

chase of the immense empire of Louisiana, which doubled the territory of the United States, was a bloodless conquest, the greatest peaceable annexation the world ever saw. Having made it, the flag was no more than hoisted on the farther bank of the Mississippi than he dispatched Lewis and Clark and Capt. Pike boldly to spy out the unexplored rivers and mountains of the new soil, so honestly won, and from which so many free States were to spring.

IV

THE SAGE OF MONTICELLO

(1809) Jefferson retired to Monticello.—(1826) July 4, died, aged eighty-three.

JEFFERSON is the only President who remained the leader of his party after leaving the White House. Indeed, the Democrats never have ceased to swear allegiance to his spirit.

Although elected for the first term only after the bitterest struggle in American politics, he was re-elected virtually without opposition, and for a quarter of a century the destinies of the country were intrusted to his guidance. President for eight years, he was the mentor of Presidents through sixteen years more of the Jeffersonian era. Both Madison and Monroe lived within a day's ride of his home. He shaped their studies in their youth, and they were to him like younger brothers or adopted sons.

More influential than any other of the ex-Presidents, this many-sided man was more fortunate than most of them in the variety of the interests and diversions that crowded his seventeen years of retirement from public

office He was surgeon enough to sew up a wound, tie
an artery or set the broken leg of a slave, and enough
of a mathematician to calculate an eclipse. He invented
a letter-copying press, a revolving chair and a folding
chair, a hemp machine, a pedometer to measure his
walks, a plow that won a gold medal at a French exhibition, and a light, two-wheeled vehicle for Virginia's
heavy roads.

He knew not only Greek and Latin, but also French,
Italian, Spanish and German. He wrote three books
and compiled his own edition of the Bible, leaving out
of the Scriptures everything except the precepts of
divine love, mercy and goodness.

His correspondence would daunt a man with a staff
of stenographers and typists to-day. Generally he had
to work from sunrise until past noon answering by hand
the flood of letters that never ceased to flow in upon
him.

In the finer arts, he was a musician, an architect and
a landscape gardener. Although he sprained his wrist
in Paris so badly that he could not again play his favorite instrument, the violin, he could still sing well, and
was forever humming tunes as he rode horseback,
which was his only sport.

He not only designed his house but laid out the
grounds of Monticello. He was also the architect of
the University of Virginia, and twentieth century architects agree that he produced a most beautiful college
group.

Domestic sorrows and poverty form the shadows in
the picture of his old age. Jefferson's wife and all but
one of his five children were taken from him, and after
nearly forty years spent in the service of the public, at
sixty-six he retired from the Presidency twenty thousand dollars in debt. For fear that some partisan foe

might even jail him as he left the White House, he borrowed the money to pay what he owed the Washington storekeepers.

Since he was thirty he had neither practiced law nor been free to look after his farm, and in his long absences the slaves had eaten up the neglected estate. Although a most systematic person, an efficiency expert by nature, he could not make his slender official salaries and his personal expenses meet at the end of the year. His twenty-five thousand dollar income as President fell eight thousand short of the outgo in one year at the White House.

To keep the roof over his head and a home for his always large family of grandchildren, grand nieces and grand nephews, he sold his cherished library to Congress. Soon he was plunged deeper into debt by the failure of a friend whose notes he had indorsed. Happily the hearts and purses of the people were touched by the spectacle of the author of the Declaration of Independence in want and in peril of losing Monticello. Only a few months of life remained to him, but these were cheered and freed from anxiety by an outburst of public sympathy and generosity.

As he lay dying an hour before midnight of July 3, 1826, he whispered, "Is this the Fourth?" To quiet him, the friend sitting by his bed nodded, and the sick man fell asleep with a smile on his face. Though he did not open his weary eyes upon the fiftieth birthday of the Nation, his heart still beat when the sunrise guns saluted the dawning and again when the noontime bells rang out. In a few minutes more it stopped.

His dust is mingled with the earth that was dearest to him, close by his house at Monticello. His burial place was chosen by him in his boyhood, when he planned and dreamed in the shade of a grand old oak.

There on a simple shaft the achievements of his manhood are set forth in his own words.

In this self-made tribute he does not record that he was Governor, envoy, Vice-President and President of the United States; they were only offices that he chanced to hold. That he added an empire to the United States by the Louisiana Purchase, he ignores as a mere real estate bargain which he happened upon. The three things in his life that Jefferson deemed worthy of remembrance were that he wrote the Declaration, was the author of the statute for religious freedom in Virginia, and the founder of the University of Virginia.

JAMES MADISON

I

JAMES AND DOLLY

(1751) March 16, James Madison born at Port Conway, Va.—(1772)
Graduated at Princeton.—(1776) In Virginia Legislature.—
(1778-9) In State Privy Council.—(1780-3, 1786-8) In Continental
Congress.—(1787) In Constitutional Convention.—(1789-97) In
Congress.—(1794) Married Mrs. Dorothy Payne Todd.—(1801-9)
Secretary of State.

As JAMES MADISON made a great name for himself
before entering the Presidency and added nothing to
it while in the White House, it must be that he was a
good deal of a man but not much of a President.

Like all the more famous Virginians, Madison was
not of the highest aristocracy, but the son of a plain,
well-to-do farmer in an outlying county. His whole
life was passed at Montpellier, the farm which his
grandfather had wrested from the Indians; from it he
drew his only private income and at last he was buried
in its soil. He was dependent on his father until he
was fifty, when the latter died and the place became
his own, with one hundred slaves, who continued always
to address him simply as "Master Jimmy."

Standing only five feet six and one-quarter inches, he
was, with Grant, the smallest of our Presidents. Naturally thin and frail, his zeal for study nearly wrecked
his health while a student at Princeton College, where
for months at a time he slept only three hours out of
the twenty-four. Physically unfit for military duty when

33

the Revolution came, he went to the Virginia Legislature instead. Yet this seemingly broken-down young
man was destined, with the single exception of John
Adams, to be the longest lived of all the Presidents.

When a candidate for re-election to the Legislature,
Madison revolted against the old Virginia custom of
setting up the drinks. His morality was mistaken for
stinginess and the thirsty voters flocked to the capa-
cious barrel of his opponent, who was elected. The
defeated candidate had to wait a dozen years for his
first chance to distinguish himself. Still no time was
lost; for, while he was waiting, he diligently prepared
to meet opportunity when it should come, by making
a close study of all governments, ancient and modern.

Although a shy, blushing little man, with a quiet, thin
little voice, which modestly sank almost to a whisper
at the end of every sentence, by sheer force of his wide
knowledge and sound judgment, he took first place at
once in the immortal assembly of wise men which met
to draft the Federal Constitution. Mere oratory
counted for nothing in that convention, which was held
behind locked doors, with no gallery to applaud the
orator and no reporters to play him up on the first
page.

Madison himself was the only reporter present; but
his report was not published until after he was dead
and until all his colleagues had returned to dust. Each
day unfailingly found this most illustrious member of
the reportorial craft in his place, down in front of
Washington, the presiding officer, where he made notes
of the speeches in a shorthand of his own, which he
laboriously wrote out in his room at night.

Having earned, by his constructive labors in framing it, the title of "Father of the Constitution," he took
a leading part in putting the principles of the conven-

tion into practice. As a member of Congress, he was the first congressman to rise and say, "Mr. Speaker!" He was the author of the first tariff and of the law creating the State, Treasury and War Departments, and he introduced the first ten amendments to the Constitution. With the rise of the parties, he took his stand by the side of Jefferson, who made him his Secretary of State, and his heir to the Presidency.

If Madison had not been crossed and blessed in love, posterity might not catch him on his human side at all and only yawn over this prosy, serious, studious, cool-tempered, unaggressive, weazened, little, great man. He was already a mature bachelor of thirty-two and a member of the Continental Congress, when a sixteen-year-old girl in his Philadelphia boarding-house was the first to touch a soft spot in his heart. A young clergyman who hung and sighed over her harpsicord cut him out, and he was painfully awakened from his first dream of love by a letter of dismissal which, for reasons unknown to this later generation, the young miss sealed with a pinch of rye dough. After two years had brought their healing, the jilted lover took part in another unsuccessful engagement, but no one seems to know who sent the rye dough in this second instance.

Madison was past forty, and well into his Indian Summer when he became involved in still another boarding-house romance at Philadelphia. Instead of a boarder, he fell in love this time with a landlady's daughter. Dolly Payne Todd, who was only twenty-six, had lost her husband and was living with her mother, "who received into her house a few gentlemen boarders." Among these was Senator Aaron Burr of New York. Madison himself was staying at another house, where he and two other future Presidents, Jefferson and Monroe, were living three in a room.

There the fame of the pretty young Quakeress trav‹ eled to him, and he asked Burr—they were at Prince‹ ton together—to take him to see her. The match flamed up in the flash of an eye, and Dolly and her son were borne away to Montpellier, where she proved her tactfulness and kindliness by dwelling in peace under the same roof with her mother-in-law thirty-five years. Whatever of evil may be justly chargeable to the account of Aaron Burr, that brilliant scamp must be credited with having united one of the happiest couples in the domestic annals of the Presidency.

II

A FUGITIVE FROM THE WHITE HOUSE

(1809) James Madison inaugurated President, aged fifty-seven.— (1812) June 19, war declared.—(1814) Aug. 24-27, in flight from the British. Dec. 28, Treaty of Peace.—(1817) Madison retired from Presidency.—(1826) Rector of University of Virginia.—(1829) In Constitutional Convention.—(1834) Denounced Nullification.—(1836) June 28, Died, aged eighty-five.—(1849) Death of Dolly Madison.

BUT for the smiles of his blooming Dolly, Madison's administration would be a desert without an oasis, over whose dreary expanse the weary biographer would wander athirst for human anecdote. Her bubbling spirits relieved the austerity of Jeffersonian simplicity and won her a popularity that has been equaled, if at all, among the mistresses of the White House only by Mrs. Cleveland.

The regal Dolly signalized the opening of her reign by holding the first inaugural ball, where she radiated in a gown of buff velvet, with a Parisian turban and bird of Paradise plumes, which had run the British blockade on its journey to her from Paris. Washington Irving, who was whirled from New York to another of her functions in "only fifty-two hours," as he said in amazement, has left us a picture of her as a "fine, portly, buxom dame" with "a smile and a pleasant word for everybody." But "as to Jemmy Madison —ah, poor Jemmy! He is a withered little applejohn."

Unless Grant must be excepted, Madison is the only President who found the Presidency an anticlimax to his career. One of the really great lawgivers of the Nation, he was without executive force; that is to say, without a knack for decisions and for choosing men to carry them out.

With a weak Cabinet, this gentle, sweet-tempered, peace-loving scholar found himself adrift on the turbid sea of the great Napoleonic wars. Perhaps it was no longer possible to keep us out of war when at last the United States was the only neutral left in the civilized world. Certainly it was no time for a fair weather sailor.

After twenty years of kicking and cuffing from both sides in the European conflict, bullied by England and lied to by Napoleon, the country was sore all over when the "warhawks" of Congress, under the youthful Henry Clay, seized the tiller of the ship of state from Madison's irresolute hand and recklessly pointed the vessel straight into the teeth of the storm. The seaboard East was more for peace, and at that time the militant section was the new West, where the Tennesseeans and Kentuckians, Indianians and Ohioans were lustily shouting "On to Canada!" Overborne by their rash counsels, Madison consented, as he said, to "throw forward the flag of the country, sure that the people would press onward and defend it."

Without competent civil or military leaders, without financial credit, without war equipment, the people could not press onward, as any history of the dismal War of 1812 will tell us. Even the capital was left undefended, and Madison, "in a little round hat with a big cockade," ran about in helpless bewilderment as the British marched upon Washington.

With the invaders entering at one side of the defenseless town, the President fled at the other. As he turned and saw the flames shooting up behind him, he flew the faster and the farther. While the British commander was blowing out the candles on his dinner table that he might feast in the light of the burning White House, its fugitive master was hiding in a forest hut twenty-five miles away.

After an absence of three days, a heavy-hearted, shattered, houseless President returned to view the charred walls of his official residence and of the Capitol. At every turn he was greeted by ugly mutterings of the general disposition to make him the scapegoat for all the national shortcomings in a war that had been thrust upon him. But with victory at New Orleans and the return to peace, the voice of the faultfinder was drowned in the hum of sudden prosperity. In the closing days of his administration, Madison was cheered by many assurances that his countrymen were not forgetful of the forty years that he had served them in pure devotion.

Like John Adams, he emerged from his retirement to sit in the Constitutional Convention of his State, where the aged statesman closed his active public life, as he had opened it, with a sentiment of humanity for the slaves. His long service still was to be crowned by him in his eighty-fourth year, when South Carolina and her policy of nullification aroused the venerable father of the Constitution and drew from him a ringing challenge to the spirit of disunion. After his death there was found among his papers a solemn warning for his country to look upon the secret enemy of the Union as "the serpent creeping with his deadly wiles into paradise."

As with the other Virginia farmer Presidents, Madison was land poor, and the threat of poverty hung over his last years. After he was gone, Montpellier was swept away in the dissipations of his stepson, Mrs. Madison's only child, who beggared his mother and left her without a roof of her own.

Returning to Washington, the widow passed her remaining years in a house belonging to a relative. Until Congress came to her relief by purchasing her husband's papers, she may sometimes have suffered want in sight of the White House. Although so poor as gladly to welcome an occasional market basket from her thoughtful neighbor, Daniel Webster, and to accept aid even from a former slave, she never lost the favor she won in her prosperity, but continued to the end, like a dowager queen, to draw about her a court of her own.

JAMES MONROE

I

THE TRIUMPHS OF AN ORDINARY MAN

(1758) April 28, James Monroe born in Westmoreland County, Va.—
(1776) Graduated William and Mary's. Entered the army.
(1782) In the Legislature.—(1783-6) In the Continental Congress.
—(1787) In the Legislature.—(1788) In the State Constitutional
Convention.—(1790-4) In the Senate.—(1794-6) Minister to
France.—(1799-1802) Governor of Virginia.—(1803-8) In the
Diplomatic Service.—(1809-10) In the Legislature.—(1811) Governor.—(1811-17) Secretary of State.

No OTHER President, with the exception of John
Quincy Adams, has served the country as long as James
Monroe and, without exception, none has had an official experience so varied. From 1776, when he was a
vigorous, six-foot, broad-shouldered, raw-boned boy of
eighteen and left William and Mary's College to enter
the Revolution, Monroe remained in the public service
until 1825, when he retired from the White House a
wrinkled, care-bent, impoverished old man. In those
forty-nine years, he had been a minor military officer
under Washington; repeatedly a member of the Legislature, a member of the Continental Congress and
of the United States Senate; twice Governor of Virginia; minister to France, England and Spain; Secretary of State and War at the same time and finally
President for two terms.

Without wealth or family influences; with a slow,
commonplace mind; with no gifts as a speaker; with a
modest, awkward presence and plain, unpolished man-

ners, this very ordinary man plodded up the ladder of ambition to its topmost rung. How? By sheer force of his rugged, courageous, industrious, honest, loyal character—a triumph of the homely, common virtues.

Although he failed in some of his most important tasks, Monroe's failures were forgiven because they were honest mistakes. The ridicule and the disgrace brought upon him by the most spectacular episode of his undramatic life would have buried forever a man more brilliant and less sincere.

That remarkable scene was enacted on the highly theatrical stage of the National Convention at Paris directly after the Reign of Terror and the fall of Robespierre, when France was an outcast among nations. At that moment, Monroe appeared as the envoy of the only sister republic. To let all the world see that the Revolution had at least one friend left on earth, the president of the convention melodramatically folded the rustic Virginian in his arms.

As an ardent believer in republicanism, it is true that Monroe had been specially chosen by Washington to soothe the savage breast of the Revolution. But in that fraternal embrace the new minister was somewhat infected by the Gallic fervor of his welcome. Regardless of England and other jealous monarchies, which were at grips with the revolutionists, he overstepped the bounds of neutrality by warmly applauding France and her armies. As if the two countries were open allies, he presented an American flag to be hung on the walls of the convention by the side of the tri-color—the red flag of revolt in that day.

Washington and the conservatives were outraged by the cordiality with which "Citizen Monroe" had taken the red hand of revolutionary France. Many were so unreasoning as to censure him even for an act of mercy which only did credit to his heart. Having found Thomas Paine in the shadow of the guillotine, he had taken that friend of our own revolution from prison into the American legation, where he nursed him back to health.

After two years he was recalled for his zeal and came home in a rage of indignation. Passing by the gate of Mt. Vernon without paying his respects to Washington, he paid them instead in five hundred pages that he published in defense of himself and in denunciation of the administration. Nevertheless, the discredited diplomat was sent to Paris again by President Jefferson in a few years, when he came away covered with success and carrying under his arm the treaty for the purchase of Louisiana—a fitting prelude to the Monroe Doctrine, twenty years later.

There is a most interesting souvenir of Monroe in Paris. Like Madison, he had fallen in love while a member of Congress and had married Elizabeth Kortright of New York. Two children having been born to them, one of the girls was placed in the famous French school of Mme. Campan, where she formed a friendship with Hortense Beauharnais that outlasted the many vicissitudes of the Empress Josephine's daughter.

Recently the notable figures in the court of the First Consul at Malmaison were modeled and grouped about Napoleon for a celebrated wax works show in Paris. In that brilliant galaxy of monarchs and dukes yet to be, Eliza Monroe, in girlish prettiness, is seen again by the side of the future Queen of Holland and the destined mother of Napoleon III.

After Eliza became Mrs. Hay, she loyally named her daughter for Hortense, who, as queen and ex-queen, always kept up a correspondence with her Amer *ican* schoolmate. To-day the two friends sleep but a few miles apart, Eliza having returned in later life to the scenes of her girlhood, where she joined the Catholic Church and at last was buried in the cemetery of Pere la Chaise at Paris.

After signing the Louisiana treaty, much of the prestige Monroe had won at Paris was lost by him in London, where he negotiated an English treaty that Jefferson repudiated. Once more he came home under a cloud, but soon emerged as Secretary of State in Madison's Cabinet. In the military chaos of the War of 1812, he took charge of the War Department also, and revived the dispirited defense of the country with an infusion of his own courage and vigor. Largely by his prompt measures Baltimore was saved, and the star-spangled banner continued to wave over Fort McHenry, as Francis Scott Key has testified unto all generations. At last, when the war closed with victory, Monroe rightly shared in the unexpected glory, because it was he who had ordered Jackson to New Orleans and had assembled there the forces which won the day.

II

THE LAST OF THE VIRGINIANS

(1817) James Monroe, inaugurated fifth President, aged fifty-eight. —(1823) The Monroe Doctrine.—(1831) July 4, died in New York, aged seventy-three.

MONROE's administration was the most serene and yet one of the most important periods in the life of the nation. It was an eight years crowded with glorious and lasting victories of peace, such victories as swords never can win.

By a mere exchange of notes between the United

States and England, those two jealous neighbors pledged themselves to disarm forever on the Great Lakes. After more than one hundred years of peace on that long watery frontier, this simple "gentleman's agreement" of 1817 stands before the world to-day the most successful example of disarmament. By a common-sense business transaction, Florida, which was of little use to Spain, but of much to the United States, was bought over the counter in 1820, a peaceable conquest that ranks second only to the Louisiana Purchase. By a civil notice to the Old World in 1823, the whole New World was set aside under the Monroe Doctrine as an immense preserve of international peace. By give-and-take in the Missouri Compromise of 1820, the North and South were bound together anew, though with false ties. Those four acts of constructive statesmanship, to the credit of Monroe's administration, cannot be outmatched by any other Presidency.

Monroe's two terms cover what is known as "the era of good feelings." The old Federalist party having given up the ghost, he succeeded to the Presidency as the last of the Virginia dynasty almost as easily as an heir apparent receives the crown of his father. With the exception of Washington, he is the only President who has been unopposed at the polls, and his second election would have been entirely unanimous had not a New Hampshire elector cast one dissenting ballot.

Yet that "era of good feeling" really was filled with many bitter feelings aroused by personal ambition and the quarrels of factions. But Monroe formed one of the strongest Cabinets in history, and, with John Quincy Adams, Wm. H. Crawford, John C. Calhoun, and William Wirt among its members, he succeeded in reconciling to his administration the most divergent elements.   In his desire for harmony, he would also have included Henry Clay and Andrew Jackson, but they declined.

One day the British minister glared across the White House dinner table and shouted to the French minister: "Are you biting your nails at me, sir?"   The Frenchman responded by drawing his sword and the two diplomats rushed at each other.   But as they were about to clash, the President drew his own sword between them and stopped the fight.

That little incident gives us a picture of the spirit of Monroe and his administration.   While he was in the White House, men and factions had to leave their quarrels at the door.

The quiet, modest President was not so successful in keeping the peace among the women of the official circle, and their disputes over social rank and precedence brewed many squalls about his head.   Having been with her husband at the courts of Paris and London, Mrs. Monroe and her daughter were accused of putting on semi-royal airs.   It was held to be beneath their Presidential dignity to return calls, to permit guests to sit in the presence of the President's wife or to receive any one not in ceremonial dress.   One poor relation of Mrs. Monroe actually was turned away because he came in the then new-fangled pantaloons rather than in proper knee breeches and silk stockings.

Although Monroe was the last President to cling to the ancient knee breeches, cockade and sword, he was as plain and easy as an old shoe.   When a newly arrived European diplomat saw a bald-headed, watery-eyed man in a striped seersucker coat, a dirty waistcoat spotted with ink, and with slippers down at the heel writing at a White House desk, he wondered that the President should have such a slovenly clerk until he was dumbfounded to find that he was in the presence of the President himself.

In the six years that remained to Monroe after retiring from the Presidency, he set himself, as an ex President, a high standard of conduct. Having received the supreme honor at the hands of all the people, he felt that his name belonged to them and he refused to lend it to any candidate or any party.

Unhappily, the country was not so scrupulous in meeting its obligations to him and neglected to pay a simple debt that it honestly owed. He had left the White House with hardly a dollar and without a ribbon—with nothing to show for a life spent wholly in the service of the country, save the badge of an honorable poverty and the Hessian bullet, which he had carried in his shoulder through the half century since the Battle of Trenton.

Feeble and alone after the death of his wife, Monroe sold Oak Hill, his Virginia farm, in the closing months of his life. With the feelings of an exile, the last of the Virginians left his native State to live with a son-in-law in New York City, where he died on July 4, 1831, the third President to pass out on the birthday of the republic.

JOHN QUINCY ADAMS

I

A DIPLOMAT AT FOURTEEN

(1767) July 11, John Quincy Adams born in Braintree, but in
what is now a part of Quincy, Mass.—(1781) Secretary of Lega-
tion at St. Petersburg.—(1787) Graduated at Harvard. (1790)
Admitted to the bar.—(1794-7) Minister to The Hague.—(1797)
Married Louise Catherine Johnson.—(1797-1801) Minister to
Prussia.—(1802) In Massachusetts Senate.—(1803-8) In National
Senate.—(1809-14) Minister to Russia.—(1814) Peace Commis-
sioner at Ghent.—(1815-17) Minister to England.—(1817-25)
Secretary of State.

AMONG the Presidents, John Quincy Adams holds the
record of having been the youngest and the oldest public servant. From boyhood, when he was a secretary of
legation at the extraordinary age of fourteen, until he
fell at his post in the halls of Congress in his 81st
year, he was in the service of his country fifty-five of
those sixty-seven years.

A President and the son of a President, all the other
fifteen Presidents from Washington to Johnson were
his associates. From the day he climbed a height near
his Massachusetts birthplace to see the Battle of Bunker Hill, fifteen miles away, he was a witness to nearly
every great event in the history of the nation until the
close of the Mexican War.

When John Quincy stood beside his mother watching the smoke of the first pitched battle for American
independence, he was not yet eight. At nine he heard
the windows rattle from the storming of Dorchester

Heights. Soon he stood again on the neighboring hill, looking off to Boston Harbor, where he beheld the glad sight of the British ships sailing away from the rebel town, which had been the first to defy and the first to vanquish the king.

The boy was aglow with patriotism. In the siege of Boston, a musket had been placed in his little hands by an officer of a company passing the Adams home to join Washington's army, and he went through the manual of arms. With crude drawings of soldiers and frigates, he covered the pages of his diary, which he began before he was nine and which he kept until the end, when twelve printed volumes were required to hold this most remarkable personal document in all Americana.

With John Adams in Congress, the child had to be the man of the family, and at nine he regularly rode his horse to Boston to fetch the mail. At ten, his father took him with him on his mission to France. By twelve, he had crossed the Atlantic four times, running the British blockade in leaky tubs and passing through the perils of shipwreck on the Spanish Coast.

At fourteen, the "mature youngster" was secretary of the American legation in Russia. By seventeen the youth had traveled over much of Europe, and he came home to enter Harvard. After graduation, he opened a law office in Boston. But business was only beginning when the young attorney was appointed by Washington minister at The Hague, where the government to which he was accredited fled before the armies of France and left him in the midst of the triumphant revolutionists. Meeting the daughter of the American consul in London, a Marylander, she and the young diplomat were married on the eve of his departure for Berlin, to which capital he had been pro-

JOHN QUINCY ADAMS, ANDREW JACKSON AND MARTIN VAN BUREN, WITH THE FAMILIAR PORTICO OF THE WHITE HOUSE WHICH WAS ADDED IN JACKSON'S ADMINISTRATION.

moted. As the first American minister to knock at the Brandenburg Gate, he was held up until a Prussian lieutenant was assured by a private soldier that there really was such a place as the United States of America.

Among his last acts as President, John Adams removed his son from office that he might deprive Jefferson of the malicious satisfaction of dismissing him. When the recalled diplomat was elected to the Senate he displayed his family trait of independence by taking sides with his father's hated rival and supporting the Jefferson administration.

The infuriated Federalists of Massachusetts savagely turned upon him as a traitor to his party and a renegade from his class. They drove him from the Senate, and when he came home he found himself in his Boston house, which stood where the Hotel Touraine now stands, a social outcast on a lonely island entirely surrounded by ice. The bitter feud was carried beyond the grave, and the old Brahmins of Beacon Hill bequeathed to children and grandchildren an unrelenting hatred of the man who had dared to break caste.

With his name erased forever from the Boston blue book, John Quincy was no longer a gentleman, and the Jeffersonians, who were not gentlemen, but only Democrats, took him up. By their favor he became minister to Russia, a negotiator of the peace of Ghent in 1814, and minister to England.

As it had been the unpleasant duty of John Adams to be the first minister to London after the Revolution and as it was to be the even more unpleasant duty of his grandson, Charles Francis Adams, to be the minister there in the trying time of the Civil War, it fell to his son John Quincy, to brave the frowns of the Court of St. James' at the close of the War of 1812.

But no other American ever was more ready and able to stand up to the critics of his country than this plain-spoken, single-minded, unflinching champion of America.

From London, John Quincy was called home to be Secretary of State in the Monroe administration. In that post, he played the leading part in obtaining Florida from Spain and in shaping the Monroe Doctrine.

In his retirement, John Adams had watched with fond admiration the rise of John Quincy until he was only one rung from the top. Although, in his crabbedness, he complained that "my son will never get a chance at the Presidency until the last Virginian is in his grave," fortune agreeably surprised the aged ex-President in next to the last of his ninety years, when he saw the scepter of the republic pass to a lineal hand.

II

OUR ONLY NON-PARTISAN PRESIDENT

(1825)—John Quincy Adams inaugurated sixth President, aged fifty-seven.

WITHIN the present limits of the Massachusetts city of Quincy the visitor may see what cannot be seen anywhere else: the birthplaces and the graves of two Presidents, side by side.

The chieftainship of every great nation still passed from father to son until the Presidency of the United States was created, when the first free-for-all race and an even start for the highest prize was opened to the sons of men regardless of the accidents of birth. In that fair test, new blood won every time for a hundred years, with but two exceptions, the Adamses and the Harrisons.

The result would be the same everywhere. Not a monarch in Europe to-day could have gained his throne in fair competition. Nature is a democrat.

Even John Quincy Adams did not win the race but was outrun at the polls by Andrew Jackson, the son of an immigrant. In bitter disappointment that he should not have been chosen by the people, rather than by Congress, he declared that he would refuse the office if he could only bring about a new election. Surely no other President ever stepped into the White House with so little gladness in his heart.

Political parties having disappeared in 1824, four men entered the contest and deadlocked the electoral college, which left the House of Representatives to choose from among the three highest candidates. That provision of the Constitution eliminated the fourth man —Henry Clay—who aided in the election of Adams and who received from the new President the appointment of Secretary of State.

Jackson denounced that transaction as a "bargain and sale." John Randolph poured out his scorn upon "the coalition of Blifil and Black George," the combination of "the Puritan with the blackleg." Notwithstanding Adams' stern uprightness was incapable of such a trade, the charge wore the ugly appearance of truth and long was believed by many.

The career of John Quincy Adams would be impossible in this day of organized politics. Without a party, without a faction, without an organized following, almost without a friend, this hermit among statesmen received the highest diplomatic posts, was called to the head of a Cabinet, won the Presidency and held a seat in Congress sixteen years.

The only non-partisan administration the country ever has had was not a shining example of success.

Uncompromising, alone, John Quincy stalked his solitary way, never once turning to the right or to the left from the straight and narrow path of independence. With no sense of humor to relieve his sense of self-righteousness, to light up his view of his fellows or to thaw his own icy virtues, it was impossible for his supporters to feel any enthusiasm for him, as Daniel Webster's brother Ezekiel said, "unless we disembowel ourselves like a trussed turkey of all that is human nature within us."

A rule unto himself in all things, John Quincy was defiant even of the conventions of dress. Notwithstanding he grew up in the courts of Europe, he was the most shabbily dressed man who has sat in the Presidential chair. It is a tradition at Washington that he wore the same hat ten years. "This the President of the United States!" was the involuntary exclamation of a stranger who saw him at Quincy in vacation time wearing a short jacket, striped jeans trousers and an old straw hat.

John Quincy surely led the simple life in the White House. Getting up at five, he built his fire, read his daily portion of the Bible and took his walk or swim while the Government clerks still slept. One morning, as he was enjoying himself in the waters of the Potomac, somebody stole his clothes from the bank. What must have been the surprise of a passing boy when a short, fat, bald-headed man, who was pacing the shore in a state of nature, shouted at him to run up to the White House and ask Mrs. Adams for a suit of clothes for the President.

One other innocent diversion brought trouble upon John Quincy. Fond of playing billiards with his son and secretary, he put a billiard table in the White House, for which the puritan President was denounced

as a gambler. Having also furnished the East Room,
he was held up by the Jacksonians as a spendthrift,
and the credulous folks out on the frontier were made
to believe that this most ascetic man was squandering
their money in a life of regal splendor.

When he came up for re-election he was easily defeated by Jackson, and he remained the worst-beaten
President until Mr. Taft touched a new low-water
mark more than eighty years afterward. Poor, discredited before the country and ostracised at home, he
found himself turned out of the public service in
which he had spent his life. Wrapping himself in his
melancholy, he left Washington, as he said, "to go into
the deepest retirement and withdraw from all connection with public affairs." Yet there stretched unseen
before this man of sixty-two, the most useful and brilliant years of his career.

III

A GLORIOUS EX-PRESIDENT

(1830-48) John Quincy Adams in Congress.—(1831) Presented first
petition against slavery.—(1836) The House adopted "gag rule"
against abolition petitions.—(1844) The "gag rule" defeated.
(1848) Feb. 23, death of Adams at the Capitol, aged eighty.

JOHN QUINCY ADAMS alone has solved the problem
of ex-Presidents. He forgot that he had been President at all and went to work like any other citizen.

Until John Quincy set this truly democratic example, people still looked upon Presidents more like Old
World kings than as New World servants, and ex-
Presidents were expected to bear themselves like de-
throned monarchs. Forbidden to earn their living and
required to keep up a semi-Presidential state, two of
our earlier Presidents were reduced to want in their

retirement and did not leave enough money to meet the cost of burying them.

With his houses in Quincy and Boston mortgaged and the income from his estate too slender for the support of his family, John Quincy heard the ominous bark of the wolf at his door as, in his gloomy fancy, he closed it upon public life in his sixty-second year. When some neighbors ventured to ask the next year if it would be beneath his dignity to represent the old Plymouth Rock District in Congress, this great American, who had been a senator, a minister at the courts of The Hague, Berlin, St. Petersburg and London, a Secretary of State and a President, replied that he was not above serving the people as one of the selectmen of his town.

Washington was aghast at the sight of an ex-President taking his seat in the hurly burly of the lower House only two years after leaving the White House. Without joining the Democrats or the Whigs, without any faction about him, John Quincy faced alone the Jackson administration which had supplanted his own, and alone he met a swarm of his old time critics on a level. Nor did he ever ask any special consideration for the high honors he had worn, because he had laid them aside.

Although not an anti-slavery agitator, he felt in duty bound to present the various petitions he received praying for the abolition of slavery in the District of Columbia or for the overthrow of the system everywhere. At first his action in the matter excited little attention. But as the abolition movement in the North grew more aggressive, the Southern members grew more sensitive. In its perplexity, the stupid House, like an ostrich, stuck its head in the sand to avoid hearing the rising outcry and foolishly voted no longer to permit the people to address their representatives on the subject.

That was a challenge to John Quincy's sense of justice and love of liberty and he boldly took it up. Thenceforth through eight stormy years he fought a hand-to-hand fight with the slave interests of the South and their allies, the moneyed interests of the North, which together controlled both political parties. Standing at bay, with his back to the wall, asking no quarter and never sparing a head, he struck right and left at the foes who beset him until, at last, he beat them off and saved the ancient right of petition, which he insisted should not be denied to the humblest, the poorest and the most wretched. The pages of our legislative history hold no other picture so glorious as that of this lonely "old man eloquent," his hands shaking, his feet tottering, his voice cracking with age, standing his ground like a gladiator day after day, year after year, as passion-blinded men assailed him from every side.

Defying the Speaker's gavel and the shrieks of rage rained upon his venerable head, he continued to rise and flood the floundering House with petitions against slavery. In the first two months of 1838, he presented more than five hundred papers only to have them "laid on the table." A still larger number was submitted by him on a single day in 1840.

"Expel him!" "Expel him!" his enemies cried in their fury. Even his assassination was threatened. On one occasion he breasted a wild tempest of debate for three days while the members talked of nothing else than the proper punishment to inflict upon him. The old lion cowed them with his courage. Although his censure was moved six times in the long course of those bitter struggles, the cowardly House flinched from facing the issue and no one of the motions was brought to a vote.

At the outset John Quincy's single-handed battle seemed hopeless. He grimly faced in his diary the probability that he would find himself in his last days "forsaken by all mankind." At one time most of the members of his committee resigned their places rather than associate with him. Nevertheless under his incessant pounding, the majority against the right of petition fell session by session until it disappeared entirely in 1844. He had won his long fight against the gag rule and his diary is lit up with his rejoicing in victory: "Blessed, forever blessed be the name of God."

His life was crowned. His work was done. Still he labored on. Although he fell in a Boston street under a stroke of paralysis, he insisted upon returning to his duties in Congress, where the members stood as he entered the hall and cheered him on his way to his seat. A year afterward, as he seemed about to rise to address the Speaker, he suddenly pitched forward upon the floor. Speaker Winthrop was on the point of putting a question, but was arrested by the startled outcry of "Stop! Stop! Mr. Adams!"

The veteran had been mortally stricken on the field. Although he lingered two days, he was not removed from the Capitol, but remained in a little room off the old hall of the House. There, still at his post, died this old and devoted servant of his country.

ANDREW JACKSON

I

AN IMMIGRANT'S SON

(1765) Andrew Jackson and his wife (Elizabeth Hutchinson), from Carrickfergus, Ireland, landed at Charleston.—(1767) March 15, their son, Andrew, born on border South and North Carolina.—(1781) Andrew taken prisoner by the British.—(1787) Admitted to the bar.—(1788) Went to Tennessee.—(1791) Married Mrs. Rachel Donaldson Robards.—(1793) Remarried her.—(1806) Killed Charles Dickinson in a duel.—(1813) Shattered for life in a fight with the Bentons.

ANDREW JACKSON, the unlettered backwoodsman, treading at the heels of John Quincy Adams, the most cultured in all the line, presents the sharpest contrast to be seen in the procession of Presidents.

The first President born in a log cabin, Jackson could not claim as his own even that lowly dwelling in the North Carolina forest but entered the world homeless and fatherless. Sprung from poor Irish immigrants, his parents had been in the country only two years when the father sank into an unmarked grave a few days before Andrew's birth, leaving his family without a roof or an acre.

With her two little boys who had been born in the old country, the expectant mother took refuge in the home of an invalid sister, where she served as housekeeper and brought up her children. It was her ambition to educate Andrew for the Presbyterian ministry, but small and poor was the schooling she was able to give him. The most he ever learned was from men rather than from books, the Vicar of Wakefield being the only work of literature that he is known to have read in the whole course of his life.

The first teacher to make an impression upon Andrew Jackson was the American Revolution, which filled his breast with a passionate devotion to his country and a flaming hatred of its enemies. Among the newly landed Irish and Scotch, who mostly peopled his part of the Carolinas, the great conflict became a furious war between clans, with raiding bands hunting one another through the wild forests and leaving behind them a trail reddened by blood and fire.

Into that mad strife between neighbors, Andrew was plunged at an age when most boys cannot qualify even for the mimic combats of the football field. At fourteen he was dashing about on his shaggy pony, "popping them," with his musket, as he said. Taken captive, he was scarred for life by the sword of a British officer, whose muddy boots he indignantly refused to brush. Thrown into a foul prison camp, he suffered from a virulent attack of smallpox that for a time left him a maniac.

No other among American leaders received from the War of Independence such a legacy of bitter memories as it bequeathed to Jackson. That savage struggle between Whig and Tory swept away his brave mother and both of his brothers; scattered his kindred and left him, at fifteen, utterly alone in the world.

A ragged, roving waif of the Revolution, he grew up wild as a weed. With no hand above him, his high spirits led him into temptations of his primitive world, whose social standards were two hundred years behind the time, and he went his way along a road that is not to be laid down on the map of conduct as a course to the White House.

Still the story points the moral that if a young man will only keep going he will leave the follies of youth behind him. Jackson's faults were the faults of his rough surroundings and they changed with changing circumstances. His simple virtues were drawn from the same rude environment, which molded him into a rugged, fearless man, who never forgot a friend and who never stooped to dishonesty.

Unhappily, his loyal nature could not forget an enemy either. As he rose from a chore boy and a saddler's apprentice to be a lawyer and a judge of the Supreme Court of Tennessee, he cast aside the manners of his careless youth, but he never lost the spirit of the clansman or subdued his ungovernable temper.

A bare catalogue of his quarrels and fights is too long to be given here. In most of them he was fired with the conviction that he was defending the name of his wife. This had been brought into question only by his own characteristic imprudence, when he fell in love with his landlady's daughter and rashly wed her without waiting to verify the mere rumor that her husband had obtained a divorce in a neighboring state. After two years of wedded life, the too hasty couple learned that the woman's first marriage had only just been dissolved and they had to go through another ceremony in order to be united in lawful bonds.

Because his own impulsive conduct had exposed his honest, devoted wife to the slanderous tongues of the gossips, Jackson was all the more sensitive to her sufferings. For sneering at her over a bar, one man was stood up at twenty-four paces and shot to death by the avenging husband, who kept his pistols in perfect condition through thirty-seven years, as Parton says, for anyone who dared breathe her name except in honor.

Even at the sober age of forty-six, Jackson plunged

into a tavern brawl at Nashville with Thomas H. Benton, afterward the distinguished Senator from Missouri, and was shattered for life by two balls and a slug which Benton's brother shot into his back. That was his last personal altercation. In a few weeks he was called from his bed of pain to take part in a public altercation between the United States and Great Britain and, with his arm still in a sling, he rose to do battle for his country.

II

THE HERO OF NEW ORLEANS

(1813) October, Andrew Jackson, general of Tennessee militia, led his forces against the Creek Indians.—(1814) May, appointed major-general in the regular army. September, repelled the British from Mobile. November, expelled them from Pensacola. —(1815) Jan. 8, won the Battle of New Orleans.—(1817-18) Put down the Seminole Indians in Florida.—(1821) Governor of the Territory of Florida.

WHEN fame knocked at Andrew Jackson's door it found him a storekeeper and a farmer on the Tennessee frontier, where he lived near Nashville in a four-room farmhouse which he had named the Hermitage.

The War of 1812 having aroused the Indians of the West, Jackson shook off his protesting physicians. With the bullet wounds of his tavern fight against the Bentons yet unhealed, he advanced upon the Creek nation, in Alabama. His arm was in a sling, leaving the left sleeve of his coat empty, and his shoulder was yet too sore to bear the weight of an epaulette. Squirming with pain, he could not climb into the saddle without assistance nor could he ride long without stopping to be washed from head to feet in solution of sugar of lead to keep down the inflammation.

In seven crushing victories in as many months, he broke the power of the savage allies of England. After one of the battles, a tender pity was awakened in him for an Indian baby, still clasped in the arms of its mother as she lay among the dead on the field. The squaws among his prisoners stolidly refusing to nurse it, he took the motherless infant to his tent and finally to the Hermitage, where the red boy grew up like a son of the family.

In his home no one could be gentler than this hard-hating, rough-fighting man, who gave his plain, simple, uneducated wife the chivalrous devotion of a knight and the happiness she had missed in her first marriage. Childless like Washington and Madison before him, he adopted one of Mrs. Jackson's nephews, who was rechristened Andrew Jackson, and brought up another who bore the name of Andrew Jackson Donaldson.

It was to fight the red foe and to defend the frontier that Jackson entered the war; but when he had fought his way through the Creek country, he found himself face to face with the white foe on the shore of the Gulf of Mexico. First repelling the British from Mobile, next he expelled them from Pensacola, where they had stolen into the territory of neutral Spain, and thence he marched to the defense of New Orleans.

With the banishment of Napoleon to Elba, England was left free to deal with her one remaining enemy, the United States, and an immense fleet, with twenty thousand soldiers and sailors, was hastening over the sea to capture New Orleans. The future of the entire West seemed to be at risk, and the Kentuckians and Tennesseeans rushed to Jackson's standard.

By blocking the Mississippi with a strong fortification, Jackson deprived the British of the advantage of their sea power and compelled them to attack the city by land, the decisive battle opening in the misty dawn of Jan. 8, 1815. The story that the Americans won the day from behind piles of cotton bales is a familiar myth. They had discarded them early in the campaign upon finding that the flaming cotton, ignited by the fire of the enemy, was more a peril than a protection. Mother Earth saved New Orleans. It was an early example of trench warfare that became so familiar in World War I.

The battle of New Orleans was remarkable in two respects. It was one of the most complete disasters in the records of civilized warfare, and was one of the most useless engagements ever fought. In twenty-three minutes the British lost 2,117 men to the Americans' thirteen—and the war had been over fifteen days! Yet it was not until Feb. 19 that Jackson heard of the treaty of peace, although it had been signed at Ghent on the day before Christmas.

Had there been an electric telegraph the battle would not have been fought; there would have been no hero of New Orleans, and Jackson never would have been President. The man was unambitious in politics. He had made only a single speech in his one term in Congress. Promoted to the Senate, he had not even answered the roll calls in that chamber and had resigned in a year. Afterward he resigned from the Supreme Court of the State also and retired from the law to attend to his store and his farm, where doubtless he would have been content to pass the rest of his days.

When people began to talk of making the victor of New Orleans President, he himself is said to have laughed at the proposal as an absurdity. When others laughed at it, he changed his mind.

Circumstances conspired to force Jackson into the White House. First, as major-general in the regular army, he invaded Spanish territory on a "hot trail" for hostile Seminoles in Florida and put to death two British subjects, who were accused of plotting with the Indians. That episode made him the center of a furious storm of applause and denunciation. The storm grew in fury when he became the Governor of Florida, after its cession by Spain, and when he proceeded to exercise all the despotic powers of a Spanish captain-general. In the end, his enemies more than his friends aroused his political ambition and incited him to seek the Presidency as a vindication from their bitter abuse.

III

THE JACKSONIAN REVOLUTION

(1828) Andrew Jackson elected. Death of his wife.—(1829) Inaugurated President, aged sixty-one.

JACKSON's electon to the Presidency almost deserves to be called the third American Revolution. The first in 1776 left the country still under the rule of the colonial aristocracy which, though liberty loving, distrusted the republic and hated democracy. The Jeffersonian revolution of 1800 called the masses into the court of public opinion, but the old governing class remained in exclusive possession of the offices everywhere, from President to selectman and village trustee. The Jacksonian revolution of 1828, changing the name of Jefferson's party from Republican to Democratic, threw open to all citizens the doors of the Government, and admitted Tom, Dick, and Harry indiscriminately to the sacred precincts of public honor and political power

The change logically came in the course of the nation's growth. For now there were eight or nine new States on the western frontier, where there was no aristocracy of birth or wealth, and where men were starting even in the race. This democratic spirit spread even to the old States, and in New England the village artisan and the poor farmer from the back road boldly rose up in town meeting to challenge the squire and the parson.

Jackson really was the first President to be popularly chosen. His was the first Presidential election to arouse the interest of the multitude, the people in nearly every village setting up a hickory pole and around it rallying to the support of "Old Hickory." At his inauguration, according to Justice Story, "the reign of king mob seemed triumphant," and the jurist saw with horror the White House invaded by "crowds of all sorts of people, from the highest and most polished down to the most vulgar and gross in the nation."

In derision of its fallen dignity in the eyes of the aristocrats, the "President's Mansion" or "President's Palace" was nicknamed "The White House" by Jackson's critics. To them it was no longer a mansion or a palace, but merely a house—and a whitewashed house at that!

Although the Government no longer was in good society, this first frontiersman in the Presidency was no social boor. He felt free to relax by stretching himself under the trees on the White House lawn, a corncob pipe in his mouth; but on proper occasion his manners were as courtly as those of any predecessor or successor.

James Buchanan, who once escorted an English lady to see Jackson, took the liberty of advising him to "slick up a little," and received this sharp rebuke:

"Buck-hannan, I knew a feller what got rich a mindin' his own business!" When the President came down to receive the visitor, she was charmed to be greeted by a gracious and stately gentleman in a ruffled shirt and swallow-tail coat, which had been quickly substituted for a faded dressing gown.

Unfortunately, the Jacksonian revolution imported from Europe the aristocratic system of official favoritism and patronage, which does not belong in a democracy. Adopting the slogan "to the victors belong the spoils," the new administration made more removals from office in its first month than were made altogether by the six administrations which had gone before.

In a simple, young country, still without big cities or railroads, without great industries, mines, corporations and monopolies and with an abundance of virgin soil, the American people needed little and asked nothing from their Government in Jackson's day. Having few measures to propose, his followers gratified their sense of power chiefly by turning out the old office-holding caste and by installing in the seats of the mighty new men of their own sort. Straightway our politics degenerated into a furious and often meaningless struggle for the spoils between the ins and the outs, an evil from which we have yet to recover.

In the passion of the hour for punishing enemies and rewarding friends, Jackson himself pushed the spirit of favoritism to an absurd extreme in his championship of Peggy O'Neal. Long before that gay and imprudent daughter of a Washington tavern keeper became the bride of the Secretary of War, Gen. Eaton, she had been the gossip of the capital, and the President attempted in vain to shut the mouth of Mme. Grundy. In his gallant but unavailing efforts to force the wives of his other secretaries to receive her into the official circle, he broke up his Cabinet, sent home his niece, Mrs. Andrew Jackson Donelson, who was the mistress of the White House, and made the social recognition of Mrs. Eaton a test of loyalty to his administration.

The President's sympathies were all the more easily aroused by the plight of "Peg" as he called her, because his own good wife had been the target of the scandalmongers, whose poisoned shafts at last, as he believed, had pierced her heart. After a campaign in which her name had been unjustly and shamefully dragged in the mire, Mrs. Jackson died between the election and the inauguration.

Jackson's hour of triumph was turned to a time of mourning for this devoted, faithful companion—"a being so gentle and so virtuous," as he recorded in her epitaph, "slander might wound but could not dishonor." Broken beneath the burden of his heavy loss—"twenty years older in a night"—he entered the White House a shattered and lonely old man, but yet with a zeal and a courage which were to crown his life with a great service to his country.

IV

SLAYING DRAGONS

(1830) Jackson's toast to the Union.—(1832) Vetoed Bank Bill. Suppressing nullification. Re-elected triumphantly.—(1833) Removed the bank deposits.—(1834) Censured by the Senate.—(1834-5) Brought France to terms.—(1836) The censure expunged.

JACKSON'S administration stands forth in the half-century between Jefferson and Lincoln because of two measures. One of these was the overthrow of the United States Bank.

That great institution, patterned after the Bank of England and the Bank of France, was an efficient but dangerous partner for a democratic Government. It was a money monopoly which could make or break any enterprise in the country; it held in its grasp the financial life of America; it received and disbursed all the revenues of the Nation, and half of its deposits were public moneys; but, with only a fifth of its directors appointed by the Government, it was not under public control.

When Jackson began his audacious fight upon the bank, it was at the height of its power. Against heavy odds, he vetoed the bill for rechartering it; took his case to the people in his campaign for re-election and scored a complete victory. On the strength of that popular verdict he removed the Government deposits and left the bank to a slow and ignominious collapse.

For this action the Senate censured him. After a bitter fight, in which Jackson's one-time antagonist, Thomas H. Benton, now a senator from Missouri, was his champion, the resolution was expunged by drawing about it in the records a heavy black line.

Unfortunately, nothing was provided by Jackson to take the place of the United States Bank. The Government moneys were scattered among "pet banks," as it was charged, and at length came the disastrous orgy of the "wild-cat banks." No substitute for the Bank of the United States was offered until the National Banks were improvised as a makeshift in the Civil War. For a real financial system the country was kept waiting three-quarters of a century, until the Wilson administration gave us the Federal Reserve Bank in 1914.

Jackson was equally bold and victorious in meeting

the threat of nullification, although it came from his own section, from his own party, and from his own Vice-President, John C. Calhoun. Shortly before his inauguration Congress passed the first tariff that was framed for the benefit of the new manufacturing industries which were springing up in New England. That bestowal of a special privilege aroused the jealousy of the agricultural South, and South Carolina had the temerity to talk of the constitutional right of a State to nullify an objectionable Federal law.

At a Democratic banquet in Washington in 1830, President Jackson rose and proposed this significant toast: "Our Federal Union; it must be preserved." Then Vice-President Calhoun got up and toasted the rights of the States. Thus the two highest officials of the Government joined issue across that dinner table on a question which great armies would fight out in another generation.

Two years afterward, a convention in South Carolina solemnly adopted an ordinance which nullified the tariff act in that State and forbade the collection of customs duties under it within the boundaries of the State. While recommending to Congress a modification of the offending tariff, Jackson appealed to the patriotism of the South Carolinians in a proclamation, which set all the North and much of the South ringing with cheers; ordered Gen. Scott to the scene of threatened trouble; reinforced the forts of the disaffected State; dispatched a naval fleet to Charleston Harbor and only waited for the first overt act of revolt to give him warrant for arresting Calhoun and the other leaders. But the nullifiers nullified their nullification, leaving the resolute and patriotic President riding a high tide of popular favor.

To show "the Yankees that a Democrat does not have horns," as he said, Jackson made a New England tour. And to the disgust of John Quincy Adams, Harvard conferred the degree of doctor of laws upon "a barbarian who could not write a sentence of grammar and hardly could spell his own name."

Another incident of the administration was amusingly characteristic. France had failed for years to pay the French spoliation claims, and King Louis Philippe kindly hinted that an earnest passage on the subject in the President's annual message might stir the Chamber of Deputies to make the necessary appropriation. The President took the hint, but some of his advisers feared that the threatening words he proposed to insert were too earnest for Parisian ears. "I know them French," he replied, and he insisted that a real dose of Jacksonian earnestness was just what they needed.

The French properly were indignant; they recalled their minister from Washington, gave our minister his passports and demanded "satisfactory explanations." Jackson would make none, and in the end this pioneer of shirt-sleeves diplomacy collected the bill without retracting or apologizing.

Jackson's pre-eminent service to the country was rendered in his battle with nullification. "The tariff was only the pretext," he said, "disunion and Southern Confederacy the real object. The next pretext will be the negro." Thanks to him, that irrepressible conflict had been postponed twenty-five years, until a great West should grow up to join hands with the East in saving the Union.

V

BIRTH OF THE CONVENTION

(1829) Jackson chose Van Buren to succeed him.—(1831) Called first Democratic National Convention. Van Buren nominated for Vice-President.—(1835) Van Buren nominated for President.—(1836) Elected.—(1837) Jackson retired.—(1845) June 8, died, aged seventy-eight.

JACKSON left the Presidential chair the most popular man who has ever sat in it, with Theodore Roosevelt the only retiring President to approach him in popularity. Since Washington and Jefferson, no other President whatever has been tempted with a real chance to prolong his power by a third election, and no other since his day, with the exception of Roosevelt, has dictated or could have dictated the choice of his successor. The almost idolatrous loyalty of his followers gave point to the common saying that fifty years after his death the Democrats still were voting for Jackson.

Jackson found politics in the parlors of the few and he left it in the corner grocery and the cross-roads post office, where it more properly belongs if we are to have a democracy. The new type of politician that arose was not always more selfish or corrupt than the old, but he was noisier and more open in his methods. Popular government cannot be carried on in a whisper and it is always an enemy to decorum.

The devotees of this passionate, self-willed idol of the people, laying plans to keep themselves in power by the prestige of Jackson's magic name after he himself should be gone, set up the first of our now too familiar political machines. "A Kitchen Cabinet," composed of the intimates of the President, was at the head of this organization, and a newspaper organ, fostered by Government advertising, was its mouthpiece.

Finally, it invented the National Convention, with a general system of nominating conventions, for the purpose of carrying out its objects.

The Constitution intended that the members of the electoral college in their wisdom should choose the President, free from all outside pressure or influence. But it was preposterous that this great office, with its immense powers, should be left at the absolute disposal of a few men in a secret conclave, and the electoral college never has been more than a Punch and Judy show.

At first the electors were nominated and instructed by little groups of managing politicians; next the nomination of Presidential candidates was made by Congressional caucuses and after that by State Legislatures. The Jacksonian revolution, in giving birth to nominating conventions, brought the choice nearer the people.

Not that the people even yet choose their Presidential nominees. A machine does that, but its manipulation is tempered by the latent power of the people.

Nevertheless the introduction of the convention was followed by a distinct decline in the quality of the Presidents it produced. The nomination of Lincoln seemed at last to vindicate and glorify it. Alas, the irony of that exception is that he, too, was nominated under the impression that he was a mediocrity in comparison with Seward.

Jackson had hardly more than seated himself in the White House than his favor for the succession fell upon his Secretary of State, Martin Van Buren of New York. "Matty," as the old President fondly called his political heir, was a clever politician, with ingratiating manners, and, being a widower without any women folk to complicate the situation for him, he was free to advance himself in the approval of his chief, by the ready social recognition which he bestowed upon Peggy O'Neal Eaton, when she was being cruelly tossed about by a tempest in a five o'clock teapot.

At first Jackson wanted only one term for himself, when he intended to give way to his favorite. As usual, when the time came, he was in need of vindication in the form of a re-election, and he decided to give Van Buren the Vice-Presidency as a stepping stone to the White House four years later.

The Legislature of the President's own State being opposed to Van Buren, the usual method of nomination by Legislatures was discarded. Moreover, there was need of obtaining some semblance of a more popular selection for this rubber-stamp candidate, and the first Democratic National Convention was called— "fresh from the people," as Jackson said—to nominate not a President, but a candidate for Vice-President. Four years afterward another convention ratified Jackson's selection of Van Buren as his successor in the Presidency, which was duly followed by a ratification at the polls.

The last President in seventy years to see a man of his own choosing succeed him, the aged leader retired to his Tennessee farm, the Hermitage, where he enjoyed through his few remaining years, though haunted by poverty and debt, such an unbroken continuance of the people's confidence and affection as has sweetened the retirement of no other President since Jefferson.

MARTIN VAN BUREN

I

THE FIRST POLITICIAN

(1782) Dec. 5, Martin Van Buren born at Kinderhook, N. Y.—(1803) Admitted to the bar.—(1807) Married Hannah Hoes.—(1808-13) Surrogate.—(1813-15) State Senator.—(1815-19) Attorney-General of New York.—(1819) Death of his wife.—(1821-29) United States senator.—(1829) Governor of New York. Secretary of State.

MARTIN VAN BUREN was the first machine-made politician in the Presidency, and he was more than that when put to the test. He was also the first of the Presidents to have been born under the American flag, rather than under the British, and he was first among the Presidents who was not wholly descended from inhabitants of the United Kingdom.

Sprung from Dutch families on both sides, Van Buren married into a Dutch family and was able to speak the language of his ancestors. He was born and he died in a little Rip Van Winkle village on the east bank of the Hudson, where his father was a farmer and incidentally a tavern keeper. Leaving school and entering a law office in his native town at fourteen, after the manner of most American leaders from Jackson to Lincoln, he picked up as he went along such education as he gained. Yet not one of our many lawyer Presidents has won a higher rank in his profession. While only a boy so small that he had to stand on a bench to address the jury, he scored his first success at the bar. At forty, he retired from practice, with money enough for a man with a Dutch thrift that was mistaken for stinginess by the less prudent Anglo-Americans around him.

Equally precocious in politics, Van Buren was chosen a delegate to a political convention before he was of age; was appointed a county surrogate at twenty-five; elected to the State Senate at thirty; appointed Attorney-General of the State at thirty-two, and at thirty-eight he was elected a senator of the United States. Already he was at the head of the "Albany Regency," which continued to run the Democratic machine in New York and to dominate the national counsels of that party for sixty years to come. His skill in political manipulation made him known all over the country as the "Little Magician," which a French traveler translated into a more doubtful compliment when he named him the "American Talleyrand."

Playing the game of politics only as a New Yorker can and as all New Yorkers in public life do, Van Buren was the first to make his way into the White House in gumshoes. Perhaps his caution as a politician has lost him the credit due him for his statesmanship, which he displayed in more than one grave emergency. A popular story reflected the general impression of his artful dodging. Once while he was a passenger on a Hudson River boat, an anti-Van Buren man said to a Van Buren man:

"I'll bet you the price of the passage that you can't go to him now and get a straight answer to the simplest question you can ask."

The challenged man, confidently taking the bet, went up to his favorite and inquired if he did not think the weather was fine.

"Well," was the carefully measured reply, "that is a relative term and . . . "

"By thunder!" the Van Burenite broke in, as he turned to this challenger, "You've won."

Van Buren became the pioneer national campaign manager when he made an extended electioneering tour for Jackson. Webster declared that he did more for the election of "Old Hickory" than any other ten men.

"Does the old gentleman have prayers in his house?" It was more as an adroit suggestion than as an inquiry that this propagandist of ninety years ago wrote to a man who was writing up Jackson for the campaign. "If so, mention it modestly."

In that fierce Jackson campaign, Van Buren took the party nomination for Governor of New York. Being elected, he resigned from the Senate, and then, after only two months in the Governorship, he resigned again to be Secretary of State in the new Cabinet. Thus he held within twelve weeks three of the highest prizes in public life and at the same time was heir-apparent to the Presidency itself.

II

THE HEIR-APPARENT

(1829-31) Martin Van Buren, Secretary of State.—(1831-2) Minister to England. Rejected by the Senate.—(1832) Nominated for Vice-President.—(1833) Elected.

BEFORE Van Buren had been in the Cabinet a year, Jackson publicly pointed him out as his successor in the Presidency and he remained through the eight years of the administration the first, last and only choice of his imperious old chief. In the idle gossip of history he is said to have won that high favor by his courtesies toward Peggy O'Neal Eaton when other officials were snubbing her.

It was easy and natural for Van Buren to be polite to Peggy since he could make up his calling list without having to consider any feminine sensibilities in his own family. For his wife had died ten years before, leaving him four sons and a memory, to which he remained loyal through forty-three years of widowerhood and until the close of a life free from the breath of social scandal.

There were more serious factors than Peggy O'Neal in the advancement of Van Buren. The choice lay naturally between him and John C. Calhoun, and the latter had given Jackson personal reasons enough for disliking him before his adoption of nullification added political reasons for that dislike.

To promote the candidacy of Van Buren, the President deprived himself of his counsels in the Cabinet after two years and sent him off as minister to England, where he would be removed to a safe distance from the enmities of domestic politics in a bitter period. But those enmities pursued him beyond the water's edge, the Senate refusing to confirm his appointment, professedly because of its objection to his policy toward Great Britain while he was in the State Department. The underlying motive was expressed in Calhoun's exultant words. "It will kill him, sir; kill him dead. He will never kick, sir; never kick."

This victim of senatorial hostility already was in London and frankly enjoying the life there, not the least of its delights being a coaching trip with Washington Irving, who was secretary of the legation. Learning of his rejection on the eve of a ball at Talleyrand's in London, he successfully masked his wounded feelings as he moved about the brilliant scene at the French ambassador's and received the more or less indignant sympathies of the notables. One of these, Lord Auckland, was prophetic when he assured the rejected minister: "It is an advantage to a public man to be the subject of an outrage." Before he had landed in America again Van Buren was nominated as Vice-President to preside over the body that had rejected him as an envoy to a foreign court.

The Vice-Presidency, to which Van Buren was elected in the great victory that swept Jackson into his second term, always is a blank page in a biography, but there is a story worth telling in this instance. The opponents of the administration were charging a passing financial disturbance to the withdrawal of the public deposits from the United States Bank. Henry Clay made a pretty play to the Senate gallery by imploring the Vice-President to go to the President and beg him to spare the poor country from ruin.

Van Buren followed the melodramatic outburst seemingly with the most respectful attention, listening with a guileless countenance as if anxious to catch every tearful word of the appeal and bear it to the White House. Leaving his chair at the close of the speech and with all eyes upon him, he walked down the aisle toward Clay, but not to discuss with him the message which he had been so solemnly charged to carry to Jackson. On the contrary, he only asked him, with a beaming smile and a sweeping bow, for a bit of his fine old Maccaboy. Having taken a pinch of the snuff from the box of the astonished senator, the Vice-President administered it to his nose with a mocking twirl of his fingers and then carelessly sauntered out of the chamber.

It was a smart and it may have been a fitting retort to Clay's theatrics; but in great public meetings Van Buren was gravely denounced as an unfeeling Nero. Sarcasm always is a treacherous weapon in politics.

III

AN ILL-STARRED PRESIDENT

(1837) Martin Van Buren inaugurated, aged fifty-four. Revolution in Ontario. Revolution in Texas. The Seminole War.—(1840) **The** Sub-Treasury Law. Van Buren defeated for re-election.—(1844) Defeated for nomination.—(1848) Free Soil candidate for President.—(1862) July 24, died, aged seventy-nine.

THE most notable event of Van Buren's administration was the occurrence of one of the great panics from which in the nineteenth century the country regularly collapsed every fifteen or twenty years, as in 1819, 1837, 1857, 1873 and in 1893. Those periodic prostrations always followed wild debauches in speculation, but since it is convenient and consoling to blame some one else for our own sins, the President invariably has been made the scapegoat in each period of hard times.

No doubt Jackson's removal of the public deposits from the United States Bank caused financial disturbances, and his distribution of the Federal surplus among the State treasuries also was disturbing. The Government, the banks and the people generally had all merrily joined in sowing the wind, whose harvest was the whirlwind of 1837.

The Nation had been indulging in the first of its big western booms. The river steamboat aided to open up new regions, where mushroom States, in ambitious emulation of New York and its Erie Canal, ran wild in appropriations for the building of canals. Van Buren was the first President-elect to ride in a train even part of the way to Washington, and the expansion of the steam railway system was beginning to inflame the national imagination.

When the day of reckoning and remorse came; when bread riots broke out; when laborers stood in line near

New York to get jobs at a wage of four dollars a month and board; when banks suspended payments in coin, and when business houses were tumbling into bankruptcy, the bankers and business men, who had always been violently anti-Democratic, turned upon Van Buren and pointed their accusing fingers at the White House. The foremost man of business in conservative New England, Abbott Lawrence, did not hesitate to hint to a public meeting in Boston the incendiary suggestion that the time might come for forcible resistance to the Government, when the crew, as he said, would have to mutiny and seize the ship of State.

Van Buren faced the gale without bending. He rose above political maneuvering and the temptation to flatter the mad passions of the hour—and preserved an attitude of masterful inactivity! In his philosophy of government, as in that of his opponents also, there was no solution of the pressing problems, and he bluntly warned the people not to look to the helpless Government for relief.

The President did call Congress in extra session, but only to recommend the adoption of the subtreasury system. The banks having failed, he proposed that Uncle Sam, like a timid old woman, should lock up his money in the bureau drawer. And the economic folly of the subtreasury was persisted in until the establishment of the Federal Reserve system.

It was squally weather all around, with the costly Seminole War dragging its slow course through the malarial everglades of Florida; with embarrassing revolutions on both sides of us, in the revolted Mexican Province of Texas and in the British Province of Ontario. Although Van Buren had appealed to the "sober second thought of the people"—a phrase which he popularized—they mistook his independence for indifference, and from mouth to mouth passed the false story of a cold and haughty aristocrat in the White House, eating from gold spoons and disporting himself with "English servants, horses and carriages."

With a New Yorker's more luxurious tastes, the White House did take on a somewhat different air during Van Buren's tenancy, but without the extravagances that were charged to him by his political opponents. Until his eldest son, Abraham, brought a bride to the mansion—a cousin of Dolly Madison—only the sons of the President lived with him. The best remembered of these, "Prince John" Van Buren, a really able lawyer and distinguished figure in society, coined an election day slogan that has carried more than one contest at the polls: "Vote early and vote often."

The defeats of the Democratic ticket in the off years plainly foreshadowed the ill-starred President's own defeat in his candidacy for re-election in 1840. No prophet was needed to write the refrain of the popular campaign song of the Whigs:

> Van! Van!
> Is a used up man.

Nevertheless Van Buren remained in active politics ten years, as will be recorded in later chapters. For still another ten years he lived on in retirement at Lindenwald, his country estate in his native village, where he died in the midst of the Civil War.

WILLIAM HENRY HARRISON

I

THE FIRST WESTERNER

(1773) Feb. 9, William Henry Harrison born at Berkeley, Va.—(1791) Entered the army.—(1792-6) Campaigning with Mad Anthony Wayne against the Indians.—(1797-9) Secretary of the Northwest Territory.—(1799-1801) Territorial Delegate in Congress.—(1801-14) Governor of the Territory of Indiana.—(1811) Battle of Tippecanoe.—(1814) Battle of the Thames.

ALTHOUGH William Henry Harrison was elected to the Presidency as the log-cabin candidate, in the first of our frenzied, parading campaigns, he was born to one of "the first families of Virginia," in a manor house on the banks of the aristocratic James. As a son of Benjamin Harrison, signer of the Declaration, with the blood of Pocahontas in his veins, and as a descendant of a Cromwellian colonel who had signed the death warrant of a king, no President has had a longer, more historic lineage. After the Adamses, the Harrisons were the next family whose name appeared twice in the presidential line.

In ability William Henry Harrison fell below the standard of his predecessors and properly is classed with the eight or ten mediocrities who have since had the greatness of the Presidency thrust upon them. He was elected not because he was a great statesman or a great soldier, but because he was thoroughly representative of the great new West, which was flattered to see in the White House for the first time a man created in its own image.

81

Among the few of our chief executives who were not bred to the law, Harrison was in Philadelphia, under the patronage of his father's friend, Robert Morris, where he was studying to be a physician when a desire for Indian fighting, so common to American boyhood, stirred his blood. He was only eighteen when he plunged into a twenty-year struggle to win the Ohio Valley for peaceable settlement by the white man. After campaigning with Mad Anthony Wayne, he was elected territorial delegate to Congress at twenty-six. There he took the lead in protecting the virgin soil of the great West from the landgrabbing lobby which had risen to exploit it. At twenty-seven he was Governor of the Territory of Indiana.

Although an ordinary man in his mental qualities, with no more physical courage than was possessed by the general run of adventurous men in the Western wilds, Harrison won his way to leadership by his downright honesty and by a sobriety of habit that was rare on the frontier. With no legislature to check him and no press to watch him, he exercised for years almost the despotic power of a Roman governor over all the vast country lying between the Western boundary of the new State of Ohio and the Rocky Mountains Tempting opportunities for personal gains came to him, among them an offer of half the land in and about St. Louis. But he left the office with hands as clean and pockets as empty as when he entered it.

Early in his term, there rose among the Indians a prophet, who spread abroad the welcome gospel that the Master of Life was himself a red man and was about to restore his people to their rightful supremacy over their white inferiors, who should be trampled under foot. By the side of this religious fanatic stood his warrior brother, Tecumseh. That pair of savage

WILLIAM HENRY HARRISON AND JOHN TYLER
JAMES K. POLK
ZACHARY TAYLOR AND MILLARD FILLMORE

crusaders were restrained for years from taking the warpath by Harrison's bold and skillful diplomacy and by the general faith in his word and his character.

The Indians were aroused at last by rumors of the approaching War of 1812, and they struck the long-delayed blow. But Harrison, with his eight hundred frontiersmen, got rather the better of them in a famous little skirmish at Tippecanoe, Ind. With the actual opening of hostilities between the Americans and the British, the savages became the allies of the British, and the entire future of the great Middle West was at stake.

At Harrison's request Oliver Hazard Perry was sent out to build and fight a squadron of ships. It was to the general that the victorious naval commander dispatched from the Battle of Lake Erie his celebrated message: "We have met the enemy and they are ours."

That naval victory was followed up in the Fall with an army victory at the Battle of the Thames, when Harrison drove the allied forces of the foe from the shores as Perry had driven them from the waters of the lake. With only three thousand men he had carried the war into Canada, Tecumseh was slain, and his ally, the British General, was put to flight; six hundred British troops and all the British artillery and stores in the West were captured.

The Battle of the Thames was a little battle, in point of numbers engaged, but was big in its effect. It gave the American army the control of Ontario and freed forever the Middle West from the ambitions of the British and from the dread of the Indians. It was one of the few bright spots on the American war map, and Harrison was received in triumph on his visit to the East. The people wildly hailed him as the victor in the most decisive military engagement of the war; but jealous politicians at Washington drove him from the army—and ultimately into the White House.

II

PRESIDENT FOR A MONTH

(1814) William Henry Harrison resigned from the army.—1816-19) Member of Congress.—(1819-21) Member of Ohio Senate.— (1825-28) United States Senator.—(1828-9) Minister to Columbia. —(1836) Candidate for President.—(1841) March 4, inaugurated, aged sixty-eight. April 4, died, aged sixty-eight.

SOME Presidents owe their election to their friends. Perhaps as many more are indebted to their enemies. William Henry Harrison belongs in this latter category.   By questioning and belittling his military victories, his critics succeeded only in magnifying them. By sneering at him as a man more fitted to adorn a log cabin than the White House, they gave him a popular symbol for his candidacy and made him the representative of the primitive West.

The first popular resentment for the slights placed upon this frontier general after the War of 1812 resulted in his election to Congress from Ohio, which State afterward sent him to the Senate.   But he cut a small figure in either House.   Although President John Quincy Adams made a wry face at him as "a political adventurer" of "shallow mind," whose "thirst for lucrative office is absolutely rabid," he appointed him minister to Colombia, but the incoming Jackson administration promptly recalled him from his remote post at Bogota.

Rigidly barred from Federal office thenceforth throughout the long Jacksonian era; honorably poor and without a profession; unable to make a living merely by farming his estate at North Bend, on the Ohio, a little way below Cincinnati, Harrison tried for awhile to eke out an income by running a whisky distillery on his place. But he reformed and became clerk of the Hamilton County Court. From that modest post to the Presidency is a long stretch, but he took it at a single step. It is the longest stride forward in the records of politics.

Jackson had blazed a new trail to the White House, and Harrison was the second to tread it. In the first forty years men became Presidents only after serving a regular apprenticeship. Jackson rudely broke that order of succession, and the country since has rarely selected its Presidents from among those who had any experience in high executive or diplomatic posts under the Federal Government. The rest have been picked out of the crowd.

At Harrison's inauguration, the Presidency entered an eclipse and was held for twenty years by secondary characters, who reigned but did not rule. With men of the eminence of Clay and Webster, Calhoun and Benton, more latterly Cass and Houston, Douglas and Davis, Chase and Wade, Seward and Sumner in the Senate, distinction and leadership passed from the White House to the Capitol. It was an ignoble period in our politics when both parties were dodging the irrepressible issue of slavery, and the smaller the candidate for President the better chance he had to dodge the question.

Thus Harrison, the county court clerk, outran Henry Clay in the Whig convention and outran Webster at the polls in 1836, when he himself was an unsuccessful candidate against Van Buren. Again, in 1840, the Whigs preferred him to Clay and made him the grotesque figurehead in a hippodroming campaign such as the country never had seen before and happily never since has seen. As proof of the impartiality of the Whig convention, it nominated John Tyler, a Democrat, for Vice-President, on the ticket with Harrison, and adopted no platform of party principles. Nevertheless,

Maine went, hell bent,
For Governor Kent

in the September election. Thenceforth, till November, a log cabin on wheels, with its coonskins and its barrel of hard cider, rolled noisily on to an easy, but empty, victory in the nation

For Tippecanoe and Tyler, too.

Elected without a party policy for his guidance, the President was expected by Clay and Webster to accept them as his guides. He invited both of those towering giants into his Cabinet, but only Webster accepted, taking the Secretaryship of State. To him was submitted the inaugural address for revision. After wading through its flowery rhetoric with a pruning knife, the great man was exhausted by his editorial labors and his anxious landlady was moved to inquire why he should look so wearied.

"Madam," Webster replied, "within twelve hours I have killed seventeen Roman proconsuls—dead as smelts, every one of them."

That was the first inaugural, by the by, to be borne to the country by a swifter messenger than the horse. The railroad sped it so fast that Philadelphia papers astonished their readers by publishing it on the very day of its delivery.

In the teeth of a piercing northwest wind, the old farmer President-elect, bareheaded and disdaining the protection of an overcoat, rode horseback to the Capi-

tol. After addressing a great crowd that shivered in
its shawls and furs, he insisted, though half frozen, on
remounting his horse and leading the inaugural parade
to the White House.

No sooner was this first Whig President in the chair
than the claims of faction and the clamor for patronage assailed him. Clay had declined Cabinet honors
—and labors—in the confident expectation of playing
the easier and more powerful rôle of the power behind
the throne. The imperious manners of the Great Com-
moner wounding the Presidential pride, he was requested to make his calls at the White House as infre-
quent and inconspicuous as he conveniently could.
Thereupon his total absence became embarrassingly
conspicuous.

The one clear mandate of the absurd election of
1840 was to turn out the Democrats and give the jobs
to the Whigs. Straightway a hungry horde fell upon
Harrison and literally devoured him. In a month to
a day he was dead of pneumonia, the first President to
die in office throughout the more than fifty years of its
existence.

That briefest of administrations is a pathetic little
story of a simple, lonely old man, lured from his farm
to be the sport of politics. Ailing in body and harried
in mind, he was without the care and companionship
of his good wife, Anna Symmes Harrison, daughter
of a New Jersey colonel in the Revolution, who became
one of the pioneer settlers of Ohio. Broken by the
hard toil of a frontier household and sorrowing for
the loss of eight of her ten children, this wife of one
President and grandmother of another, still was making ready to take up her duties as mistress of the White
House when the news of her husband's death came to
her.

The last of our Presidents to have been born before the Revolution, Harrison remains the oldest in the line. At sixty-eight he was too old to bear up under the onslaught of the office seekers, who have twice been the death of a President. For Harrison, no less than Garfield, must be reckoned a victim of the spoils system.

JOHN TYLER

I

THE FIRST PRESIDENT BY SUCCESSION

(1790) March 29, John Tyler, born in Greenway, Charles City County, Va.—(1806) Graduated from William and Mary's.—(1811-16) Member of Legislature.—(1815-21) Member of Congress.—(1823-25) Member of Legislature.—(1825-27) Governor of Virginia.—(1827-36) United States senator.—(1840) Elected Vice-President.—(1841) April 6, became President, aged fifty-one.

GREATNESS and the Presidency found John Tyler down on one knee, playing "knucks" with his boys in a pathway of his dooryard in Williamsburg, that stately old vice regal village of colonial Virginia. He had not even heard that Harrison was ill, until destiny, without steam, wire, or rail to carry it, sped to him from Washington by boat and buggy with the news that the President had been dead a day and that the empty Presidential chair was awaiting the Vice-President.

Rising from his game of marbles, the first problem that confronted this President by succession, was to get money enough to take him to the capital. He promptly received the offer of a loan from a money lender of the neighborhood. But since that thrifty man had coldly refused to take a similar chance on him a few months before, the favor was declined now, and personal friends supplied the needed amount to convey to the White House this sport of fortune.

It was the first time that a Vice-President had been called upon to discharge the one duty which gives that office its only excuse for existence—to fill a va-

89

cancy in the Presidency. People had all but forgotten the purpose for which the place was created. If those who nominated Tyler had given a thought to the possibility of his succeeding to the chief magistracy, he would have been about the last man they would have chosen for the emergency.

Tyler belongs among the third or fourth-rate Presidents. Although a clean-handed, kindly man of good presence and polished manners, he was a mediocre country lawyer and a narrow-minded politician, with a gift for getting offices that he had no gift for filling. Graduating at sixteen from William and Mary's, the only college besides Harvard to be the alma mater of three Presidents, he was elected to the Virginia Legislature at twenty-one, while his father was serving as Governor. At twenty-six he went to Congress; at thirty-five he was chosen to the Governorship and at thirty-seven he entered the Senate, to which he was re-elected for a second term.

His record of statesmanship in those various posts need not detain the reader a moment. It is a blank page, as with so many of our facile vote getters and place hunters. But for the accident of another's death, Tyler's name would have been buried with his dust in the oblivion of the grave.

A Jacksonian Democrat at first, Tyler followed John C. Calhoun off into nullification and to extremes on the dogma of States' rights and the protection of slavery. Rather than obey the instructions of the Virginia Legislature that he should vote to expunge the censure which the Senate had passed upon Jackson, he broke with the Democrats, resigned the senatorship and reappeared in the State legislature as a Whig member. He was also a delegate to the Whig National convention which nominated him for Vice-President.

Nevertheless he agreed with the Whigs only in op-posing Jackson and Van Buren. In the North, they were for protection and internal improvements; in the South, they were for the Union above all else, and Tyler was dead set against each of those policies.

Thurlow Weed and the Whig politicians understood this perfectly. To distract the North from the slavery question they nominated the log-cabin hero and to at-tract the slaveholding South they nominated with him a disciple of Calhoun. With a ticket facing both ways, they adopted no platform and stood for nothing except vote catching.

The scheme worked to perfection—at the polls. But in the hour of its triumph the Whig President died and his Democratic running mate was in the White House.

That unforeseen event served the Whigs according to their deserving. They had set out to fool the people and in the end they themselves were worse fooled. All they wanted was Tippecanoe, but they got Tyler, too.

II

A POLITICAL REVOLUTION

(1841) Aug. 16, Tyler vetoed Clay's bill for setting up a new bank in place of the Bank of the United States. Sept. 11, all the Cabinet, except Webster, resigned.—(1842) Ashburton Treaty signed. Death of Mrs. Tyler.—(1843) May, Webster resigned.—(1844) Feb. 28, explosion on the U. S. S. Princeton. June 8, treaty annexing Texas rejected by the Senate. June 26, marriage of President Tyler and Julia Gardiner.—(1845) March 3, Tyler signed joint resolution for annexation of Texas.—(1861) President of the Peace Convention in Washington. Elected to Confederate Congress.—(1862) Jan. 18, died, aged seventy-one.

As John Tyler stepped into the White House, its door closed against the party that had elected him only five months before. Death had turned out the Whigs after thirty days of power and caused a political revolution.

In vain the Harrison Cabinet, which was largely under the influence of Clay, proposed that Tyler should describe himself only as Vice-President and acting President. He rightly insisted that he was full President without qualification.

Clay looked upon this accidental President as a mere regent for the Harrison administration and for the Whig party. That impression of the senator from Kentucky was sharply corrected early in the extra session of Congress by a Presidential veto of one of his own bills—a banking bill.

The Whigs were wild with rage; the Democrats filled with glee. The Democratic senators hastened in a body to the White House, where they were patting Tyler on the back while a Whig mob out in the yard was making a vociferous but futile protest. When the next veto came in, Clay himself called the Cabinet together and the members, with one exception, agreed to resign.

The exception was none other than that of the Secretary of State, Daniel Webster. "Where am I to go?" the god-like Daniel thundered in his bewilderment. He held on for two years, until he had concluded the negotiation of the Ashburton Treaty, which fixed the disputed boundary between Maine and Canada, and then he, too, resigned.

Upon Webster's retirement, Tyler installed in the State Department his mentor and idol, John C. Calhoun, and thus completed the overturn. The Cabinet was now out-and-out Democratic and of the pro-slavery brand.

Although the President only stood true to the principles that he was well known to have entertained at the time of his nomination and election, great was the outcry. Nothing like it has assailed any other President except Andrew Johnson. The name of Tyler became a hissing and a byword in the mouth of every Whig in the land, and old women blamed him even for their rheumatic twinges, which they called "Tyler's grip."

A Southern States' rights oligarchy was enthroned in power in the first of a series of pro-slavery administrations. Secretary Calhoun proclaimed the ambitious policy of guaranteeing the security of slavery not only in the United States, but also "throughout the whole of this continent."

Texas had seceded from Mexico, which had abolished slavery, and its American settlers, who were facing the choice of slave labor or free labor in their new home, were anxious to be admitted to the Union. The slave holders of the Southern States wanted to expand their power over the vast Texan empire as an offset to the rapid expansion of the free States in the great West. But Northern sentiment was opposed.

At an opportune moment for the annexationists, the ubiquitous John Bull, with his omnipresent gunboat, appeared on the Texan scene as a mediator between the Mexicans and Texans. John was there for "business as usual," but he was talking in terms of freedom —also, as usual. His entry into the place gave the slave interests the needed villain for the play, and the cry went up that we must annex Texas to keep the British from grabbing it.

Nevertheless the Senate rejected overwhelmingly the treaty of annexation. Thereupon Tyler proposed to beat the devil around the stump, and Texas was annexed the last night of the administration by a simple joint resolution, rushed through the two houses of Congress.

The shadows of this Presidency were deepened by a tragic occurrence and then lightened by a domestic romance which flowed from the event. The President's wife, Letitia Christian Tyler, was an invalid and died in the next year after he had entered the White House. One day in 1844, as he was taking a party of friends down the Potomac on the U. S. S. Princeton, the explosion of one of her big guns killed two members of his Cabinet and three other guests. Among the latter was David Gardiner, the lord of Gardiners Island, New York, whose body was carried to the White House, followed by his two daughters.

While the widower President was consoling the daughters, he renewed his love making with Julia. She had been deaf to his proposals before but she listened now and yielded. For the suitor was qualified by his fifty-four years to take the vacant place of father to an orphaned girl of twenty-four.

John Quincy Adams, in his diary, revolted at the "indecency" of this enactment of "the old fable of January and May." The Whigs snickered at the nuptials, which were celebrated in New York in the still standing Church of the Ascension on lower Fifth Avenue, close by the town house of the bride in Lafayette Place. Despite disparity of years and partisan ill-wishes, the couple lived happily ever after, and one of their children was for a long time president of old William and Mary's College.

President Tyler deluded himself to the last with hopes of Democratic support of his election for a second term. The Democrats tossed him aside like a worn-out tool.

In his retirement, he was not above serving as a road overseer. He did not reappear in national politics until after sixteen years, when he acted as chairman of the abortive peace conference at Washington, on the eve of Lincoln's inauguration.

One of those infatuated political leaders who had sown the wind, John Tyler could not stop the whirlwind of civil war. As a member of the Confederate Congress and in revolt against the Union, over which he had presided, died this tenth President of the United States.

JAMES KNOX POLK

I

THE FIRST DARK HORSE

(1795) Nov. 2, James Knox Polk born in Mecklenburg County, N. C.—
(1806) Moved to Tennessee.—(1818) Graduated from University
of North Carolina.—(1820) Admitted to the bar.—(1823-5) Member Tennessee Legislature.—(1824) Married Sarah Childress.—
(1825-39) Member of Congress.—(1835-39) Speaker.—(1839-41)
Governor of Tennessee.—(1841) Defeated for re-election.—(1843)
Again defeated.—(1844) Nominated for President and elected.

JAMES KNOX POLK was the first dark horse to win the
Presidential race, and his figure remains among the pale
shadows in the procession of Presidents across the pages
of history. His personal biography being hardly more
than a catalogue of the offices through which he passed
without leaving a mark behind him, this must be mostly
a story of the remarkable circumstances whose creature
he was.

The Pollocks, whose name, from being slurringly
pronounced "Poll'k," came finally to be spelled Polk,
were among those immigrants from Ireland—like the
Jacksons—who took up in America the resistance to
British rule which they had carried on unsuccessfully
in their native island. The President's grandparents,
both the Polks and the Knoxes, were Irish born and
prominent in the revolutionary struggle in North Carolina.

When he was yet a boy, the family of James K.
moved to Tennessee, where he was too frail for frontier farming and was put to work behind the counter

96

of a cross-roads store. After a time in that excellent preparatory school of life he returned to his native State to enter college, and he graduated from the University of North Carolina.

Becoming a country lawyer, he was sent to the Tennessee legislature; married Sarah Childress, daughter of a well-to-do man of business, and went to Congress for fourteen years, in the course of which he became first the Jackson leader of the House and finally Speaker. Next he took his seat as Governor of Tennessee for a term. After having been twice defeated in his effort to obtain a second election to the Governorship, those defeats were immediately crowned with the Democratic nomination for President and with the highest prize in the lottery of politics.

Polk himself had no more than modestly suggested that he would like to be Vice-President. So far as known, no one ever had breathed his name in relation to the Presidency until within twenty-four hours of his nomination.

Martin Van Buren, seeking vindication for his defeat in 1840, was again the Jackson candidate. On the opening ballot he received a clear majority, and he remained the only majority candidate who failed of winning the necessary two-thirds vote and the nomination until three-quarters of a century afterward, when Champ Clark lost to Woodrow Wilson in another Baltimore convention.

After seven ballots had been cast, the Southern plotters against Van Buren obtained an adjournment for the purpose of hatching their plot in the night. In those days, when the States were called in their geographical order, New Hampshire was second on the roll, and the delegation from that New England State was craftily chosen to spring the name of Polk. Then came that now familiar convention maneuver which is called a stampede, with delegates wildly chasing the bandwagon.

It was in the first year of the telegraph. When the name of Clay was ticked off as the nominee of the Whig convention at Baltimore, those wiseacres of Washington, who still regarded Morse as an impostor, said that the trick was easy, since anyone could have guessed who the Whig nominee would be. Three weeks afterward, when the inventor at the capital spelled out, from the dots and dashes on a strip of paper, the name of Polk as the Democratic nominee, the doubting Thomases were convinced that he was a fraud. They scoffed at such an absurdity and were not persuaded of the truth until the arrival of a train from Baltimore.

The new telegraph also served to carry back from Washington Silas Wright's declination of the second place, to which that New York senator had been nominated as a consolation for the Van Buren men, and the convention had to choose another nominee for Vice-President.

The Whigs everywhere greeted the Democratic nominee with the derisive inquiry, "Who is Polk?" It stumped even loyal Democrats, like the steamboat captain who faithfully shouted, when told the news: "Hurrah for— What'd'ye say his name is?"

The obscurity of "Jim" Polk, which that snug, unsmiling, uninspired little man of respectable abilities had preserved even on the eminence of the Speaker's chair, was deepened by the shining fame of Van Buren, whom he had displaced at the convention, and of Clay, against whom he was matched before the people. Those two statesmen had taken it for granted that they were to be the champions of their respective parties. History suspects that they concocted, in a friendly visit, two letters which appeared suspiciously close together and which were suspiciously alike in discouraging the annexation of Texas at risk of war with Mexico.

Van Buren stood by his guns against annexation, going down in the Democratic convention under the displeasure of the Southern slave holders and the alarm of Northern dough-faces. Clay faltered in the campaign. Quibbling, qualifying and taking a back track, he went down at the election under the indignation of the abolitionists, who polled enough votes for their third ticket to cause his defeat.

Polk lost Tennessee at the polls, and is the only man, with the sole exception of Wilson in 1916, who has been elected without the vote of his own State. For several days the national election was in doubt, with the result hanging on a complete count in New York. At last it was found that Polk had carried the State by five thousand—thanks to the Liberty party, which had drawn away more than that number of votes from "the great compromiser." Henry Clay had compromised his last chance for the Presidency.

II

AN INGLORIOUS VICTOR

(1845) March 4, James K. Polk inaugurated, aged forty-nine.—(1846) July 17, Oregon question settled.—(1846-7) The Mexican War.—(1848) Greatest territorial conquest in American history.—(1849) June 15, death of Polk, aged fifty-three.

ALTHOUGH Polk's administration added more square miles to the map of the Union than any other, except Jefferson's peaceable acquisition of Louisiana, history and posterity continue to look that gift horse in the mouth. Why? Our deed to that immense territory is much the same as our title to all the rest of our coun try, which was taken from the Indians on the principle that land belongs to those who can and will use it.

What American to-day would wish that our settlers in Texas had been left at the mercy of Mexico, or wish that California, Nevada, Utah, Arizona and parts of New Mexico, Colorado and Wyoming still remained a huge, undeveloped, semibarbarous wedge of Mexican territory between us and the Western ocean?

Nevertheless, qualms of conscience over that conquest continue to disturb us. This is a wholesome symptom of national scruples. Even if the effect seems good, the motive was bad. For Polk was put into the Presidency solely because he could be relied on to push the boundaries of slavery to the Rio Grande.

The new President really went into the White House with two land claims to press. Besides Texas there was Oregon (including Washington), which was then our only foothold on the Pacific and which we were occupying jointly with the British. The American claim in that unsurveyed region took in what is now the coast of British Columbia, clear to Alaska, and the conflicting British claim ran down as far as Portland and the Columbia River.

Polk at once offered to compromise, but was rebuffed by the British minister. Thereupon he withdrew his offer, and the Americans demanded everything, the parallel of latitude to which they claimed being popularly expressed in the alliterative phrase. "Fifty-four, forty, or fight!" But when we found our hands full with Mexico, the Polk administration and the British Government agreed on the compromise which the President had first proposed, and the forty-ninth parallel became the permanent dividing line.

Although Congress and Tyler had hurriedly completed our part in the annexation of Texas, the very day before Polk's inauguration, and Mexico really had renounced the Lone Star State, the boundary still was open to question. The new administration insisted that Texas extended to the Rio Grande and promptly ordered Gen. Zachary Taylor to march to that river, with instructions to regard as invaders any Mexican troops on this side of it.

After a year of challenging by us, a Mexican general took up our challenge and a skirmish occurred. Thereupon, at Polk's request, Congress declared that war existed "by the act of Mexico."

It was not much of a war, as wars go. But few military campaigns have been richer in booty. Gen. Taylor had only five thousand and six thousand men in the most decisive engagements. Gen. Scott began his advance on the City of Mexico from Vera Cruz with twelve thousand troops. He did not have half that many effectives in his easy victories over a bankrupt, distracted nation, whose feeble governments tumbled down every time we gave them a tap.

The Mexican War was redeemed somewhat from its military one-sidedness and from its bad political motive by the daring exploits of American commanders. While Taylor and Scott were advancing with their armies, Doniphan with a brave band was marching across New Mexico to Chihuahua City, and Fremont, with a handful of men, raised the flag over California and kept it flying.

We had hardly less difficulty in conquering Mexico than in propping up a Mexican government long enough to give us title, in a treaty of peace, to the spoils of the war—522,568 square miles, for which we made Mexico a consolatory gift of fifteen million dollars. Add to that conquest, the great State of Texas and the great territory in the Northwest, which was confirmed to us in the Oregon settlement, and we have indeed a grand total of territorial gains under Polk's administration. Yet it profited the President himself and his party nothing, because their policy was tainted with the evil purpose to widen the area of slavery.

A grim, little, care-worn man, with clothes two or three sizes too large for him, Polk did not cut much of a figure in the Presidency. Although Mrs. Polk's straight-laced religion banished dancing and cards from the White House, her popularity and distinction of manner shone in contrast with the drabness of her husband's personality.

"Madam, I have heard but one opinion of you," Henry Clay said to her. "All agree in commending in the highest terms your excellent administration of the domestic affairs of the White House."

"Indeed," Mrs. Polk beamed in reply, "I am glad to hear that 'my administration' is popular. And I will say that if the country should elect a Whig next Fall, I know of no one whose elevation would please me more than that of Henry Clay."

Polk declined re-election, which he could not have obtained. With his always frail body broken under the heavy labors of his term, this luckless suitor of fame retired to his home in Nashville. There he died in less than fifteen weeks after leaving the White House, and there, within a temple of Tennessee marble, he was buried in his own dooryard by the wife who was to survive him forty-six years.

ZACHARY TAYLOR

I

OLD ROUGH AND READY

(1784) Nov. 24, Zachary Taylor born in Orange County, Va.—(1785) Removed to Kentucky.—(1808) Lieutenant in the regular army.—(1810) Married Margaret Smith.—(1812) Fighting Indians in Indiana.—(1832) In the Black Hawk War in Illinois.—(1836-7) In the Seminole War in Florida.—(1840-6) In command of the Department of the Southwest.—(1846) May 8, opening engagement with Mexico at Palo Alto. May 9, battle of Resaca de la Palma. Sept. 24, capture of Monterey.—(1847) Feb. 22, 23, 24, battle of Buena Vista. November, Taylor returned home.—(1848) Nominated for President by the Whigs.

ZACHARY TAYLOR was the first army man to be President, and the second was Gen. Ulysses S. Grant. Many of our Presidents, beginning with Washington, had seen war service, but only as citizen soldiers.

By birth, Taylor is one of the eight Presidential sons of the "Mother of Presidents." More properly he belongs, not to the Virginia group, but with the group of frontier Presidents. For in his infancy he was taken by his family out to Kentucky, where he grew up in a log cabin, with no other schooling than that received from a wandering Yankee schoolmaster.

At twenty-three he entered the army as a lieutenant, and he remained in it forty years, until he was inaugurated President. Yet he had seen only a little fighting with the Indians before his campaign in Mexico, where he commanded perhaps not many more than six thousand men and fought half a dozen engagements, rang-ing from the opening skirmish at Palo Alto to the battle of Buena Vista. In this last, his little army of raw troops was outnumbered four to one. But he spurned Santa Anna's demand for his surrender, and, "with a little more grape" from Capt. Bragg's battery, he defeated the Mexicans.

The commanders in the two Mexican campaigns, Zachary Taylor and Winfield Scott, were as unlike as their popular nicknames would indicate—"Old Rough and Ready" and "Old Fuss and Feathers." "Old Rough and Ready" remained throughout his army service a simple American soldier, a capable officer in peace and a resourceful one in war.

Obedient always to the civil authority, he retained a truly American dislike of military ceremonial and manners. With an unmilitary figure, his short, dumpy body was placed on legs so short that his orderly had to lift one of them over the flanks of "Old Whitney," whenever he mounted that war horse. He rarely put on a uniform, and Grant says that he saw him in it only once in the Mexican War, where he fought generally in the same clothes that he wore on his Louisiana farm.

He was as plain in his private life and with a wife as unaffected as himself. This devoted companion made her home with him in military stockades and tents, sending her children as they came along back to the care of relatives, but refusing to be parted from her husband.

When the second daughter was taken a willing captive by another Kentuckian, Lieut. Jefferson Davis, afterwards President of the Confederacy, Taylor was furious with the eloping girl and scornful of her husband, whom he vowed he would not "touch with a pair of tongs." In a few months the young wife died unforgiven. After years of estrangement, the disowned son-in-law found himself a colonel in Mexico under his implacable father-in-law. There he prudently kept out of the old man's way, until his reckless daring and brilliant success at Buena Vista melted the general to tears, and they clasped hands on the battlefield.

Taylor's reverence for the high office and for the great statesmen who had adorned it seemed positively shocked at the first proposal that he should be President. He frankly declared himself unfitted for its duties and unworthy of its honors. "Stop your nonsense and drink your whisky," he is said to have exclaimed with impatience when an oratorical visitor to his tent ventured to toast him as the next President. Mrs. Taylor agreed with her husband, preferring the artless pleasures of their own fireside (including her corncob pipe) to the formalities of the White House.

Like every man who has heard the seductive suggestion of his name for the Presidency, Taylor was not long in yielding to it. Revising his own poor opinion of his qualifications in the light of their higher appraisal by others, he came to regard himself as the people's candidate and he announced that he would run as such even if no party should nominate him.

The party preference of the old soldier was in doubt, with no other clue to it except his brother's illuminating remark that Zachary liked Henry Clay and American-made clothes. The Whigs nominated him without knowing where he stood on any question, and they made no platform for him to stand on. It was a merry game with the great problems that confronted the Nation.

After they had nominated Taylor, the Whigs became fearful for a time that the joke was on them. While they waited and no word came from their nominee at Baton Rouge, they took alarm lest he would not accept the honor from their party. But he had not received their letter of notification. For they had neglected to prepay the postage on it, at a time when the post office carried letters collect, and "Old Rough and Ready" was refusing to receive all unpaid mail!

II

THE SECOND PRESIDENT TO DIE IN OFFICE

(1849) March 5, Zachary Taylor inaugurated, aged sixty-four.— (1850) July 9, died, aged sixty-five.

IF the election of Gen. Zachary Taylor is one more proof that soldiers are popular, it is also one more proof that war is not popular in this country. In the midst of victory in the Mexican War, the party in power lost the congressional elections and, on top of a triumphant peace, it was turned out altogether. War never pays in American politics.

After boldly denouncing the Mexican War and tamely voting for it in Congress, the Whigs nominated for President one of its military heroes. Once more Webster and Clay were in high dudgeon to see an old soldier preferred to them. The Massachusetts statesman exploded with anger at the nomination of what he unfairly described as "a swearing, whisky-drinking, fighting frontier colonel." The Kentucky statesman sulked in his tent, where he hugged to his bosom the consolation which he had offered himself for Harrison's first nomination over him in 1836: "I would rather be right than President."

In his belated letter of acceptance, Taylor announced that he was a Whig, but he declared to the amusement of the country that he was "not an ultra Whig." On all the principal questions of the time he afterward candidly admitted that he had only "crude impressions."

The Whig candidate being a slaveholder and his opponent, Lewis Cass, of Michigan, being the first of the line of "Northern Democrats with Southern principles," the two old parties flattered themselves that they had effectually shut out the question of slavery. But the Free Soil party sprang into existence as a protest against this conspiracy of silence and nominated Martin Van Buren.

Webster said that for the leader of the "free spoil" party to become the leader of the Free Soil party was a joke to "shake his sides and mine." Many free soilers balked at Van Buren's nomination, in doubt of his sincerity. Nevertheless he was a disciple of Jackson, who had challenged the slave power at the outset of its aggressions, and he himself had always been under suspicion among the extremists at the South. He had broken with the Polk administration long before his nomination by the Free Soilers, the regular Democrats denouncing him and his followers as "barnburners," after the legendary Dutch farmer who burned his barn to rid it of rats.

In the election, Van Buren's "Barnburners" outran the regulars, or "Hunkers," in New York. With the same division existing among the Democrats in the other States, Taylor's success at the polls was a foregone conclusion.

For the second time the Whigs had elected a President; for the second time they had won with an old soldier who was too old to bear the strain of the Presidential office; for a second time they had gained power without a platform or any agreement among themselves; for the second—and last—time, they went to wreck on issues that they tried to dodge.

As Taylor's supposed superiors in statesmanship prepared the Compromise of 1850, this Southern slaveholder in the White House showed a most uncompromising determination to uphold the Union. Some Southerners telling him that they would secede if California was admitted as a free State, he bluntly denounced their talk as treasonable and warned them that if they attempted to carry their words into action he would put down their rebellion with a strong hand. The slave interests claiming all of New Mexico east of the Rio Grande as part of the slave State of Texas, they threatened to drive out the Federal troops from the disputed territory. With Jacksonian vigor, the President replied, "Then I will command the army in person and hang any man taken in treason."

This vigorous stand gave rise to the fear in Congress that the great compromise which Clay, Webster and the rest were planning might meet with a Presidential veto. Death intervened. Overcome by a long exposure to the blazing sun, at the laying of the cornerstone of the Washington Monument on the 4th of July, 1850, the President died four days afterward, having served only sixteen months, or just one-third of his term.

Webster believed that the death of the second President to die in office—and the last in seventy-three years to die a natural death—delivered the country from civil war. Possibly that catastrophe might have been forever averted by Zachary Taylor, as Jackson averted it when he boldly challenged nullification in South Carolina and nipped disunion in the bud.

MILLARD FILLMORE

I

A SECOND-HAND PRESIDENT

(1800) Jan. 7, Millard Fillmore, born in Cayuga County, N. Y.—
(1823) Admitted to the bar.—(1826) Married Abigail Powers.—
(1829-31) Member New York Assembly.—(1833-35, 1837-43)
Member of Congress.—(1844) Defeated for Governor.—(1847)
Elected State Controller.—(1848) Elected Vice-President.—(1850)
July 10, sworn in as President, aged fifty. Sent Commodore Perry
to open the ports of Japan.—(1852) Defeated for nomination.—
(1853) Death of wife.—(1855-56) Toured Europe.—(1856)
Nominated for President by Knownothings and Whigs, and defeated.—(1858) Married Mrs. Caroline McIntosh of Albany.—
(1874) March 8, died, aged seventy-four.

MILLARD FILLMORE, the second Vice-President to be
promoted by death, was the most commonplace President even in a twenty year period when the Presidency
remained at low-water mark. Tall and with magisterial front, but cold and hollow, he looked the part
which he played: the dummy of Northern trimmers in
politics and of Southern traffickers in slaves.

A fable of the day hit off the truth. The new President must have a carriage, and "Old Edward" Moran,
a White House attendant in many administrations, took
him to see a handsome outfit, whose owner was leaving
Washington and would sell it at a bargain.

"This is all very well, Edward," Fillmore mused,
according to the popular yarn; "but how would it do
for the President of the United States to ride around
in a second-hand carriage?"

"But, sure," argued "Old Edward," "Your Ixcel-
lency is only a sicond-hand Prisident!"

Fillmore was from New York, which is the unwilling mother of Vice-Presidents, with no fewer than ten in the first century and a quarter. Instead of big States bullying little States, as the fathers feared, our biggest State has been often disappointed in its ambitions for the Presidency. Most of the New York Presidents had to take the second place before they could get the first. Fewer of them have entered the White House by the front than by the side door.

In Fillmore we have another frontier President. For Western New York was an outpost when he was born there of New England parents. After receiving about the same kind of schooling as our other log-cabin Presidents, he was bound out to learn the trade of wool carder.

While serving that apprenticeship, there happened the most important event in his life until he suddenly found himself in the White House. As with the race of boys in general, he fell in love at nineteen with a girl older than himself. Abigail Powers was the village schoolma'am, and in his boyish admiration of her superiority he was spurred to read and to repair the defects of his education. The aspiring apprentice excited the interest of the village lawyer, who helped him to become a lawyer, and his marriage with the schoolma'am followed.

That is the one romance in the life of the thirteenth President. The rest is only a string of dates and a list of offices: member of the Legislature; member of Congress; defeated for Governor; elected State Controller. On the strength of his having carried New York for that modest post, the Whigs nominated him the next year for Vice-President, and fate made him President.

The one enduring act of the Fillmore administration was taken when it sent Commodore Perry to knock at the long-closed gate of Japan, and, with the gift of a toy railroad and a toy telegraph, to tempt the Japanese to come out of their hermit seclusion. The rest is politics, and that is a chapter in itself.

As American men struggled to rise from the bottom in the more primitive days of the country, their women often failed to keep up with them. By the time half of Fillmore's predecessors gained the Presidency, their wives were either dead, worn out or lagging behind.

Mrs. Fillmore, finding herself without strength or ambition to reign with her husband, her place was taken by a daughter. This girl of eighteen, Mary Abigail, was enough of a new woman to have insisted on fitting herself by a course in a normal school to earn an independent living. Being obligated to teach a certain length of time after graduating, she went on teaching school even after her father became Vice-President. She kept at it until her mother summoned her to preside over the White House, where she promptly induced Congress to install a library, the mansion having been until then a bookless desert.

A month after the end of her husband's term Mrs. Fillmore was dead. Next Miss Mary died of cholera, and then, after a tour of Europe, the pathetic loneliness of a retired President was relieved by a marriage with a wealthy widow.

Fillmore had tried to avert this retirement by an unsuccessful effort to be nominated to succeed himself. Four years afterward he attempted to break the retirement and return to the Presidency. Although he had both the Knownothing and Whig nominations, he ran third in the election. He lived on in his Buffalo home until another Buffalonian, Grover Cleveland, started for the White House by way of the shrievalty of Erie County.

II

SOWING THE WIND

(1820) The Missouri Compromise.—(1835) Anti-slavery matter excluded from the mails.—(1836) Right of petition on the subject denied by Congress.—(1850) The last compromise and the Fugitive Slave Act.—(1853-55) The Knownothing Movement.—(1854) Missouri Compromise repealed.—(1857) Dred Scott decision.

THE politicians who chose Millard Fillmore to be Vice-President and the political heir of Zachary Taylor builded better than they knew. They had found "Old Rough and Ready" more rough than ready. In the amiable, facile and respectable time-server who took his place they had a smooth and handy tool.

That was an ignominious era which opened with the accession of Tyler and closed with the inauguration of Lincoln. All through it, the politicians—yes, and the people, too—were only preparing the great tragedy of 1861-5. They foolishly thought they were averting it . . . but no one ever escaped trouble by running away from it.

As soon as the politicians saw that the people were afraid of the slavery question they began to prey upon the popular fear. While the Southern politicians were frightening their constituents into the false belief that only by expanding the territory of slavery and increasing its political power—in their hands, of course —could slavery be saved, the Northern politicians spread in their section the equally fallacious idea that only by concessions, compromises and by keeping still on the subject of slavery could the Union be saved.

The obvious truth was that unless the North resisted at every step, slavery would increase and spread. It was equally true, on the other hand, that slavery in the South never was in political danger; because even to-day the North has not in itself the three-fourths vote necessary to amend the Constitution. The slave States held the veto power on any Constitutional change, and the South still holds it.

With the Missouri Compromise in 1820, the slavery question was first made a football of politics. It was removed from the economic and moral realm where it belonged and where, as all enlightened Southerners originally believed, it would be eventually solved by a peaceable, gradual emancipation.

The pretended settlement in the Missouri Compromise only aggravated the problem. To stop the growing discussion of it, the Post-office Department permitted postmasters to exclude the subject from the mails, which necessarily increased the agitation by giving the agitators one more grievance to air. Then Congress denied them the right of petition, which straightway made Congress itself a forum for the agitation. Next came the too characteristically American resort to mobbings and lynchings, which inevitably increased the crowds and the tumult.

Following the Mexican War, with the annexation of more territory to be dedicated either to freedom or to slavery, the politicians staged the last compromise "to save the Union," making Uncle Sam a slave catcher. Federal officials were authorized to command the people of the North to join in hounding down runaway negroes and to throw into prison any white man who harbored the hunted things.

Every enforcement of that Fugitive Slave Act merely thrust before Northern eyes a moving picture of slavery in its most horrid aspect . . . with officers of the Federal Government dragging a fellowman through the streets in irons, to banish him from liberty and deport him into bondage. As a logical consequence, "the underground railroad" sprang into existence and organized and advertised better facilities than ever for the easy escape of slaves from the South into Canada.

When Clay and Webster sponsored and Fillmore signed that Fugitive Slave Act, the Whig party played its last card in the slavery game. Northern business interests, the mainstay of the Whigs, were faithful allies of the Southern business in slaves. But after the Fugitive Slave Act, those "cotton" Whigs of the North could no longer hold in check the "conscience" Whigs, and the party was split wide open.

This meant that a new party would have to be started. Naturally it would be an anti-slavery party, unless the public mind could be drawn away from the subject. That was easily done by raising a furious outcry against the foreigners. It is a familiar ruse. Whenever any wrong among ourselves is in danger of exposure, the first thing that its votaries are likely to do is to attempt to change the subject by appealing to the primitive prejudice against strangers.

To distract the Northern people from the slavery question, the losing Whig politicians took up with the American or "Knownothing" party. Its passwords, its secret oaths and mummeries and its cowardly mobbings of the laborious, unoffending Irish provided a timely, though happily a brief, diversion from the real question. Fears of the slave power at home were all but lost for a few years in fears of the Pope at Rome.

In the midst of that mad distraction the Missouri Compromise was easily repealed by the politicians of both sections. This left the free soil of the virgin West wholly unprotected against slavery for the first time since the Ordinance of 1787. The Supreme Court hastened to complete forever the work of destruction by declaring, in its Dred Scott decision, that neither Congress nor the States had power to keep slavery out of any part of the country.

From that judgment of the court of last resort there remained no appeal except to the sword. To that tragic pass the politicians in the White House, in Congress and on the bench—and the people as a whole—had brought the country at last. Politics utterly had failed to solve the problem, and that failure made necessary, made unavoidable a violent solution of it.

The spineless Presidents of that inglorious period were thoroughly representative of their generation, and they have conveniently served as scapegoats. But why blame Tyler and Polk, Fillmore, Pierce and Buchanan for doing the things they were chosen to do and for leaving undone the things they were chosen to avoid? They are dust. The American people still live. They ought to take their share of the blame as a warning against making the same costly mistake some other time on some other question.

FRANKLIN PIERCE

I

NEW ENGLAND'S THIRD PRESIDENT

(1804) Nov. 23, Franklin Pierce born at Hillsboro, N. H.—(1824) Graduated from Bowdoin College.—(1827) Became a lawyer.—1829-33) Member of New Hampshire Legislature.—(1833-37) Member of Congress.—(1837-42) United States Senator.—(1842) Resigned.—(1847-48) Brigadier-General in the Mexican War.

FRANKLIN PIERCE was the second dark horse and the third New Englander to enter the White House. He remained for more than three-score years the last President to be drawn from the six States which occupy the upper right-hand corner of the national map. Even he was chosen not as a representative of New England, but rather as an agent of the South, and New Hampshire debated half a century before it grudgingly set up in the yard of the Capitol at Concord a statue of her only President.

Franklin Pierce, the President, may have few friends; but Frank Pierce, the man, had more friends than most Presidents have been able to boast. One of his fellow-students at Bowdoin College was Nathaniel Hawthorne, and their lifelong friendship bridged the wide gulf between politics and literature. The author of the "Scarlet Letter" wrote Pierce's campaign biography, received from him an appointment as consul at Liverpool, and at last he died in the company of the ex-President, while the two friends were enjoying together a White Mountain vacation.

FRANKLIN PIERCE AND JAMES BUCHANAN

Hawthorne admitted in his campaign eulogy that Pierce was not distingushed for scholarship in the earlier part of his stay at Bowdoin. The unveneered fact is that the genial Frank was a roystering youth who did not let his studies interfere with his pleasures. When he discovered in his junior year that he stood at the foot of his class, his first impulse was to cut out college altogether rather than cut out his diversions. He absented himself from all the exercises for several days in the hope of expulsion or of suspension, at least.

After devoted friends had wrestled with him, he called off his strike and thenceforth did his best to make good in their eyes. For three months, Hawthorne tells us, the awakened youth rose at four and retired at midnight and gave to his studies all but four of the twenty-four hours. Once he had conquered the mind which had run wild so long, he could take his work easier; but he never again received a black mark, and he graduated third in his class.

Entering law and politics at a time when his father was a Democratic leader in New Hampshire, an easy path to promotion lay before this handsome, friendly young man. He declined as many offices as he accepted. Political honors gravitated to him so unsought that his ambition was dulled, and at last he was perhaps as unambitious as any man who ever gained the Presidency.

A member of the Legislature at twenty-nine, while his father was Governor, and twice a member of Congress, he was a senator of the United States at thirty-three. Resigning when his term had yet a year to run, he afterward refused a second election to the Senate and refused the Governorship and also the Attorney-Generalship of the United States.

Mrs. Pierce was the daughter of a former President

of Bowdoin College and a delicate, retiring woman, who passed her life in the shadows of the early loss of two of her three children. Shunning the glare of public station, she fled from Washington. Rather than be separated from his wife, her husband, who felt for her a chivalrous devotion, quit the Senate and declined a seat in Polk's Cabinet. In a little footnote to history Henry Watterson adds that the convivial senator was doing no good in Washington anyhow and that Washington was doing him no good.

The Mexican War tempted Pierce from his retirement and, as a brigadier-general, he served with Scott in the advance on the City of Mexico. Afterward there were partisan slurs on his military service, but his soldierly courage has been vouched for by no less an authority than Grant, who says that he knew him more intimately than any other of the citizen generals in that war.

Returning to his family and a first-class law practice at Concord, Gen. Pierce, at forty-three had no thought that any further public distinction awaited him. Yet the White House was only four years off.

II

THE SECOND DARK HORSE

(1852) June, Franklin Pierce nominated by the Democrats. November, elected. December, death of his only child, Benjamin Pierce.

THE country received the unheralded nomination of Franklin Pierce for President with as much surprise as when Polk was sprung upon it. "Hereafter," Stephen A. Douglas of Illinois indignantly exclaimed with a taste of sour grapes in his mouth, "no private citizen is safe."

A stranger in New Hampshire is said to have looked up in bewilderment from the newspaper headlines and asked his tavern keeper about the nominee. "Wa'll, up here," was the drawling reply, "where everybody knows Frank and where Frank knows everybody, he's a pretty considerable fellow. But come to spread him out over this whole country, I'm afraid he'll be dretful thin in spots."

New Hampshire Democrats were in the inner councils of their party from the inauguration of Jackson to the Civil War. Their hunker partisanship was as rock-ribbed as their granite hills, and from 1832 to 1856 the little State never faltered in its support of the Democratic ticket.

Granite State Democrats were special pets of Jackson, and there is a tradition that when he selected Van Buren as his successor, he slated Levi Woodbury of New Hampshire to succeed Van Buren. That slate was broken first by the defeat of Van Buren for re-election in 1840 and finally by the untimely death of Woodbury.

The Democratic convention of New Hampshire in June, 1851, indorsed Woodbury for the Presidency, but that associate justice of the Supreme Court died in the following September. Another State convention in January, 1852, substituted Franklin Pierce, but he positively forbade such a use of his name, declaring it "would be utterly repugnant to my taste and wishes." The earnestness of that refusal was not doubted, by the public at least. Apparently the proposal was dropped; but under cover loyal friends kept at work for Pierce's nomination.

When a political party is going wrong, or does not know where it is going, the first thing it does is to try to hide behind either a respectable or an unknown figurehead. After the Democratic national convention of 1852 had balked through thirty-three ballots at the nomination of such conspicuous leaders as Cass and Buchanan, Marcy and Douglas, the time came to trot out a dark horse. Virginia picked Daniel S. Dickinson of New York. But he was a delegate, who felt in honor bound to stand by Cass, and he put a stop to the movement in his own favor. Had he only sat silent in his seat or spoken with a double tongue he would have been President.

Senator Bradbury of Maine, who was at Bowdoin College with Pierce, had been persistently coaching his friend as the dark horse. Under the senator's timely inspiration the Virginians next cast their votes for Franklin Pierce on the thirty-sixth ballot. The little-known name did not start a wild fire. It was not until the forty-ninth roll call that the wearied delegations reluctantly nominated him in a perfunctory stampede.

Presidential honors were never less welcome in any home than in that of the Pierces. Washington was dreaded by Mrs. Pierce as a place of exile. When Benjamin, her little son, who was away at school, heard of the nomination, he wrote her that he hoped his father would be defeated in the election, seemingly having caught his mother's dislike of the capital and of public life.

The boy was not to keep his parents company in their unsought residence in the White House. In a train wreck between Boston and Concord, the month after the election, he was killed while traveling with his father and mother.

Afterward the railroad was sued on account of the death of another of the passengers on the wrecked train, and Pierce requested General Benjamin F. Butler of Massachusetts to defend the road from the charge of negligence. The reason he gave was a strange one. Mrs. Pierce was convinced that the company was blameless, because she looked upon the derailing of the train as an act of God. She was anxious not to be disturbed by a court decision that should run contrary to her consoling belief that a special providence had taken away from the President-elect his only child in order that he might give himself wholly to the duties of his great office.

The cynical lawyer did not attempt to prove that the accident was due to a supernatural cause, but he so cleverly upset the technical evidence of its mechanical origin that he cleared the corporation. With such comfort as she could find in that result of the trial, the bereaved mother dwelt her term in the White House under the pall of this domestic tragedy.

III

THE PROLOGUE OF A GREAT TRAGEDY

(1853) March 4, Franklin Pierce inaugurated, aged forty-eight.— (1854) The Ostend Manifesto issued. The Missouri Compromise repealed.—(1856) Pierce defeated for renomination.—(1869) Oct. 8, died, aged sixty-four.

FRANKLIN PIERCE was elected in a more sweeping victory than any other President has had since Monroe. He had the mandate and the opportunity to be President of the whole Union. With all his good qualities of head and heart, he was not broad enough to be more than the servant of a section; "of those who placed me here," as he expressed it.

The new President's appointment of Jefferson Davis to be Secretary of War identified his administration at the outset with the aggressive faction in the South.

Under its counsels, Pierce not only surrendered to the ambitions of the slave power for expansion over the North and West, but also for its expansion into foreign lands.

Slavery was in its last throes everywhere. Great Britain had abolished it in her West Indian islands. Mexico had abolished it next door to our own slave States. Even Spain was tending toward the freeing of the slaves in Cuba, when the American ministers to Great Britain, France and Spain met in Belgium and issued the "Ostend manifesto." That shameful document proclaimed the threat that if the Spanish Government should refuse to sell us Cuba we would take the island by force.

At the same time Congress at home was repealing the Missouri Compromise and wiping out the deadline against slavery, which had been drawn a quarter of a century before. That threw open Kansas to a wild scramble between settlers who wished the new territory to be free and those who wished it to be slave.

Then and there the Civil War began. "Border ruffians," as the North called the settlers who rushed in from Missouri and other slaves States, and settlers no less rough in their fighting, who poured in from the free States with Sharps rifles, quickly turned that primeval into "Bleeding Kansas." Rival territorial governments were set up by the two factions, and Pierce threw the weight of the Federal power on the side of those who were desperately striving to create another slave State.

The whole country was drawn into the struggle, and the Republican party sprang into life. At the election in the middle of his term, Pierce saw the Democratic representation in the House cut down one-half and the opposition sweep in with a big majority.

In spite of that warning, the President became a candidate for renomination, because he was very much in need of vindication. The selfish power that had used him had used him up, and it ungratefully turned to a new name less tarnished in its service.

The rest is the meager but pathetic story of a discarded President. The charm of a kindly nature continued to hold till the last the affection of friends, but public popularity was gone.

The Civil War, breaking out only four years after his retirement, served to deepen the shadows of Pierce's record. In January, 1860, he wrote to Jefferson Davis the encouraging prophecy that if the conflict should come, "the fighting would be not only along the Mason and Dixon line, but within our own borders and in our own States." In other words, that the North would not be united.

A few days after the firing on Sumter, he made a speech in which he took a stand for the Union. Unquestionably he had always been loyal to it in his heart. He had sacrificed even his good name in an honest but misguided effort to save it from the horrors of fraternal strife. But to its salvation by war he could give little faith and only a perfunctory support.

In the hot passions aroused by Lincoln's assassination, an indignant crowd marched to Pierce's house in Concord, with a noisy demand that he hang out the Stars and Stripes. The self-respecting dignity of his refusal to admit that his loyalty to the flag needed such proof awed the zealous into silence, and the eloquence of his sincere expression of sympathy with those who mourned the stricken chief sent them away with softened emotions toward the speaker. Though he lived four years more, that is the closing entry in the public life of Franklin Pierce.

JAMES BUCHANAN

I

A BACHELOR PRESIDENT

(1791) April 23, James Buchanan born in Franklin County, Pa.—
(1809) Graduated from Dickinson College.—(1812) Became a
lawyer in Lancaster, Pa.—(1815-16) Member of the Legislature.—
(1819) Tragic death of his betrothed, Annie C. Coleman.—
(1821-31) Member of Congress.—(1832-4) Minister to Russia.—
(1834-45) Senator.—(1845-9) Secretary of State.—(1853-6) Minister to Great Britain.—(1856) Democratic nominee for President.

JAMES BUCHANAN was the last President to wrap his
neck in a stock, as Monroe was the last to wear knee
breeches—and he was the last of an era. An age passed
away as he passed out of the White House.

After Buchanan's birth in a Pennsylvana log-cabin,
his father, who was an Irish immigrant, prospered as
a country storekeeper and was able to send his son to
college. But the college sent him back as a wild spirit
that it could not tame. The pastor of the scandalized
family begged and obtained another chance for the
wayward youth, who improved it so well that he graduated first in his class. Nevertheless, the still unfor-
giving faculty denied him the honors of his rank.

Buchanan always loyally credited his mother with
having exerted upon him the greatest influence for good.
Possibly the severe lesson which he received from his
stern alma mater may have been somewhat responsible
for the prosy propriety of his life ever after.

This would be but a dull story of law and politics were it not for a single tragic episode which cast a shadow over the whole after life of our bachelor President—the only President to die a bachelor. A young woman to whom Buchanan was engaged in early manhood, a daughter of the wealthiest family in the county, wrote him a letter of dismissal under the spell of a jealousy which had been aroused by gossips. Pride on both sides kept the two apart until their separation was made irrevocable by her sudden death—probably by suicide. In grief and horror the young lover wrote to the father of the dead girl begging the privilege of looking upon her remains and of following them to the grave. But the letter was returned to him unopened.

Four and forty years passed, and Buchanan went to his grave without ever having taken another woman to his heart. When his executors opened the papers which the aged ex-President had left in a bank vault, they found among them a little packet of treasured love letters from his sweetheart of long ago. But in accordance with the request written on the outside, those faded mementoes of his only love were burned without breaking the seal on them.

That old wound was torn open by a most cruel campaign lie when Buchanan was a candidate for President. In this atrocious attack, he was accused by the editor of the New York Herald, the elder James Gordon Bennett, of having gone out and hanged himself to escape the vengeance of a brother of his betrothed. Although he was cut down, according to the malicious yarn, in time to save him from a suicidal death, it was only necessary for Bennett to point the credulous reader to the way in which the candidate always carried his head tilted to one side, as proof that his neck had been permanently twisted in his attempt to commit suicide.

Everyone could not know that this familiar habit was due to an imperfect vision.

Buchanan was by no means a crabbed old bachelor. He remained always most courteously attentive to women, though with a perfect impartiality. Nor did he keep bachelor's hall. At Wheatland, his country place near Lancaster, Pennsylvania, he brought up from early childhood the orphaned son of one of his sisters and the orphaned daughter of another, who became, as Harriett Lane, one of the most admired mistresses of the White House. A monument in Washington to the memory of Buchanan will stand also as a memorial of the grateful loyalty of this niece, who left one hundred thousand dollars for its erection to a President who would otherwise go unhonored in stone.

After Buchanan had risen to top rank at the Pennsylvania bar, with a practice that brought him as much as twelve thousand dollars in a year, he entered politics. Starting as a Federalist, he became a Democrat only at the death of the party of his first choice. He was elected to the Legislature and to Congress; was thrice elected to the Senate; served as minister to Russia and Great Britain and was Secretary of State in Polk's Cabinet.

For twenty years an unsuccessful candidate for the Presidential nomination, the veteran politician had all but given up hope when, at last, it came to him unsought in 1856, on his return from a long absence as American minister in London. As he accepted it, he sighed that the honor had been denied him until he was too old to enjoy it, "when all the friends I loved and wanted to reward are dead and all the enemies I hated and had marked for punishment are turned my friends."

II

THE MOST TRAGIC ADMINISTRATION

(1857) March 4, James Buchanan inaugurated, aged sixty-five. March 5—Dred Scott decision.—(1858) Lincoln-Douglas debate.— (1859) Aug. 5, Completion of Atlantic cable. Oct. 16, John Brown's raid.

NO PRESIDENT has come to the discharge of his duties with a longer official training than James Buchanan, who had been forty years in the legislative, executive or diplomatic service. Yet no other has left behind him such a record of failure.

Only a great leader might have succeeded in those most difficult times when Buchanan failed. And office holding does not, cannot make a leader. It is more likely to unfit a man for leadership. Were not Washington and Lincoln among the least experienced in statecraft of all the men who have entered the Presidency?

Like the other Presidents of his futile generation, Buchanan was chosen not to lead on the slavery question but to mislead the country. He was selected because he had been on the other side of the ocean for three years while the politicians at home had been making bad records for themselves. Besides, he was nominated in the hope that he could carry his own State of Pennsylvania against the swiftly rising Republican party under Gen. Fremont.

In the political contests before the Civil War, Pennsylvania was in truth as in name the Keystone State. Holding its State election in October, whichever party carried it in that month was almost certain to sweep on to a victory in the country at large in November. That is why Buchanan was nominated and that is how he was elected.

The new captain, always an irresolute character, at

once surrendered the steering wheel to the most extreme faction in the South. Thenceforth he remained a helpless, bewildered passenger on the ship of state as it was hurled upon one rock after another in this most tragic administration. First came the Dred Scott decision, the very day after Buchanan's inauguration, when the Supreme Court held that all compromises were unlawful, that all political agitation for the restriction of slavery was in vain and that an owner had the same right to take a drove of slaves as a drove of horses into any State in the Union.

That decree left the Republicans, and the Douglas Democrats as well, appealing from the judgment of the court of last resort, with battle the only remaining tribunal. And the Lincoln-Douglas debate of 1858 heralded the impending, irrepressible conflict.

The fuse of civil war already had been lighted in Kansas and it continued to sputter throughout Buchanan's term. At last, it exploded a blast close by Washington itself, when John Brown of Ossawattomie carried the Kansan war to Harpers Ferry, West Virginia, but then in Virginia, in the wild dream of inciting the slaves themselves to rise in revolt against their masters. A peaceable political solution of the problem having been declared impossible by the Supreme Court, fanatics naturally came to the front and attempted to settle it by violence, by "direct action," as it is called to-day.

Although the Buchanan administration was the undertaker of a dead past, its sombre record is lit up by the first flash across the ocean of the submarine telegraphic cable. The conservative President was so doubtful of this new thing that he suspected the message of greeting to him from Queen Victoria might be a hoax. Before venturing to reply he cautionsly summoned all the members of his Cabinet. Against the advice of some of them he took a chance and finally sent his response to the queen. Soon afterward the cable broke and as not another message came under the sea for eight years the skeptics felt justified in their jeers at the imposture and the wild absurdity of the invention.

III

ADRIFT IN THE STORM

(1860) Nov. 6, Lincoln elected. Dec. 20, South Carolina seceded; Edwin M. Stanton entered Buchanan's Cabinet.—(1861) Jan. 1, the Cabinet broke up. Jan. 11, John A. Dix appointed Secretary of the Treasury. Feb. 1, six States had seceded. Feb. 4, the Southern Confederacy formed. March 4, Buchanan retired from the Presidency.—(1868) June 1, died, aged seventy-seven.

BECAUSE the drama of history, like that of the theatre, must have its heroes and villains, James Buchanan has been painted all black in the opening scene of the Civil War, loaded down with all the weaknesses and sins of his generation and banished forever into the wilderness. Anyone can see now, with the aid of hindsight, what Buchanan should have done, but not what he could have done.

Many have said that if Jackson had been President he would have stamped out secession as he stamped it out in South Carolina in 1832. But a blaze that a bucket of water may suffice to stop at the start may be beyond the control of a whole fire department when it becomes a conflagration.

The North itself, in the bewildering winter of 1860-1, was far from agreed that secession could or should be stopped by force. "Let the Union slide," the abolitionists said. "Let the erring brethren go," said Horace Greeley. "Wayward sisters, depart in peace," Gen. Scott would have said to the seceding States.

The poor, old, helpless President himself expressed toward secession no such toleration or resignation. Although he held that the Government had no authority to keep a State in the Union by coercion, he denied that the States had any right or any just cause to secede, and he ordered the commanders of Southern forts to defend them from seizure. That policy was continued absolutely without change by Lincoln when he came in.

Like every other form of injustice and special privilege, slavery was entrenched behind a wire entanglement of Constitutional dogmas, court decisions and legalistic technicalities. Men of all parties and of both sections, like flies in a spider's web, were caught fast in the political and legal metaphysics which sophists had been spinning ever since the republic was born.

In common with the politicians of his fast vanishing time, Buchanan clung to the idea that freedom rather than slavery was to blame for all the trouble. He had not gone with Douglas and the Northern wing of the divided Democrats in the campaign of 1860, but had sided with the Southerners and voted for Breckinridge.

When the first State seceded he was already within ten weeks of the end of his term, with a hostile Congress in front of him and behind him a country as irresolute as himself. As he saw the Union falling to pieces, he hoped on that it could be patched together again by another old-fashioned compromise. All the while, there were Southern members of his Cabinet who were staying in Washington only to ship Federal war supplies South and to aid in the preparations for destroying the Government.

Edwin M. Stanton of Ohio, although himself a Breckinridge Democrat, bluntly warned Buchanan: "You are sleeping on a volcano. The ground is mined all around and under you and ready to explode, **and** without prompt and energetic action, you will be **the** last President of the United States."

"Mr. Stanton," pleaded the feeble old man, "**for** God's sake, come in and help me."

The first day that Stanton took his seat as Attorney-General at Buchanan's Cabinet table he told the Secretary of War, Floyd of Virginia, that he "ought to be hanged on a gallows higher than Haman's" for having ordered Major Anderson, without the knowledge of the President, to stay in a defenseless old fort in Charleston Harbor, instead of transferring himself to Fort Sumter, as the major really had done in defiance of orders. The Secretary of the Interior, Thompson of Mississippi, protesting against such language, the new member of the Cabinet whirled upon him with the charge that he had been stealing public bonds.

Before the middle of January the Cabinet was reorganized and Buchanan was surrounded by stanch Union Democrats, who swept him along at a pace which sometimes left him breathless. The new Secretary of the Treasury, John A. Dix, quietly reported one day that he had sent to New Orleans his now famous message, "If any man attempts to haul down the American flag, shoot him on the spot."

"Did you write such a letter as that?" Buchanan exclaimed.

"No," Dix replied, "I telegraphed it."

Had Buchanan been a man of iron instead of putty, probably he could have done no good in that chaotic interregnum between the election and inauguration of his successor. If he had taken any step which should have hastened Virginia and Maryland into revolt, there would have been no national capital on March 4, 1861.

The retiring President would only have made heavier, perhaps impossible, the task which he wearily laid upon a stouter soul when he transferred the Presidency to Lincoln and sadly tottered into the shadows.

ABRAHAM LINCOLN

I

THE FIRST AMERICAN

(1809) Feb. 12, Abraham Lincoln born near Hodgdenville, La Rue County, Ky.—(1816) Moved to Indiana.—(1818) Mother died.—(1819) Marriage of his father and Mrs. Sarah Bush Johnston.—(1830) Moved to Illinois.—(1831) Went to New Salem, Ill.—(1833) Postmaster of New Salem.—(1835) Death of Ann Rutledge, his first love.

OTHER Presidents than Abraham Lincoln have risen from a log-cabin to the White House; other Presidents also were of humble birth; but none other has moved so humbly in high places. No honor, no power, could exalt him above his native simplicity; a common man who could

> walk with kings—nor lose the common touch.

Lincoln was cast in a new mold. The first President born beyond the boundaries of the thirteen original States, with no traditions of a colonial or Old World origin, he was in truth,

> New birth of our new soil, the first American.

Although he is asserted now to have been descended from the New England Lincolns, so far as he himself ever knew—or cared—he entered life in a Kentucky log cabin, "unprivileged, unancestried, unknown," with his mother's arms his only cradle, the lonely forest his playground. His father—"a wandering laboring boy"—

133

learned to write his name and to spell his way through the Bible only from his wife. Nancy Hanks, a poor orphan like himself, who sank into an early grave under the crushing hardships of home-making in the Indiana wilderness, to which the family had moved. The good woman who came to take her place and who sanctified the name of stepmother found that the ten-year-old boy, growing up like a weed, had forgotten how to write and that there never had been a book or a newspaper in the cabin.

Lincoln never attended school a year all told. Life was his school and he was his own teacher, doing his sums with a piece of charcoal on a wooden shovel and borrowing all the books for many miles around. Reading while he plowed, he recited to his horses and declaimed from a tree stump to his fellow field hands.

A youthful giant in strength and stature—he was six feet four at nineteen—he was hired out by his father to more prosperous neighbors. He swung the ax and the scythe, wielded the flail, slaughtered hogs or poled flat boats on the great rivers. But already he stood apart and alone in the midst of the crowd with whom he toiled and joked. His thoughts and dreams had borne him out of their forest world and far away from the day's work.

Going with his father to the newer frontier in Illinois, he helped him build another log-cabin, clear another farm and he split the rails for fencing it in. He was now past twenty-one, and he started out in the world for himself, with an ax over his shoulder and all his belongings tied up in a red bandanna handkerchief. Mauling rails, flatboating, surveying, captaining a company in the Black Hawk War, keeping store, choring about New Salem, a log hamlet on the Sangamon River

—where, for a time he was postmaster with his hat for a postoffice—he remained a homeless man of odd jobs until his twenty-eighth year.

The sympathetic hearts of New Salem had been touched by a great sorrow that came to him in the death of his sweetheart, Ann Rutledge, an auburn-haired daughter of the tavern keeper. Lincoln grieved until his friends feared for his mind. He confessed that he did not dare for months to trust himself with a pocket knife. Slowly he emerged from his despondency, but the shadow lingered.

He remained ever a primitive man in his emotions and sympathies, never rising superior to the pangs and appeals of the heart. He could always cry.

Although New Salem reckoned him a failure, he had always paid his way and ever had stood ready to help others, whether it was to put his powerful shoulder to the wheel of a stalled wagon; to cut firewood for a widow; to watch with the sick or to rock the cradle for a weary mother. Through his seeming shiftlessness, a moral dignity shone, and to all the villagers the quaint, jesting, clean-living, kindly man was "Honest Abe."

The bustling planners and builders of New Salem did not suspect that this dreamer who loitered in their lanes was planning and building for all time and that their village would be remembered only because it had chanced to be a station in his progress. For like Peter the Great, who stepped down from his throne and in disguise went to work among the masses, Abraham Lincoln in those apparently aimless years was in reality, though unconsciously, an apprentice in the leadership of the people whose life he was living. There out of poverty and toil and sorrow, the character of the man was woven.

II

IN POLITICS, LOVE AND LAW

(1835-43) Abraham Lincoln in the Illinois Legislature.—(1836) Declared for woman suffrage.—(1837) Moved to Springfield, Ill.,
and became a lawyer. Took his stand against slavery.—(1842)
Nov. 4, married Mary Todd.

ONE day, while he was a storekeper in New Salem,
Lincoln's long arm fished out of a barrel of odds and
ends a copy of Blackstone's Commentaries. Over its
fascinating pages he pored day after day as he lay on
the ground outside his now neglected store, with his
feet resting high against the trunk of a shade tree.
The volume finished, he began to borrow other works
on law from a lawyer in Springfield, and people remembered in all after years the picture of the tall barefoot
student intently reading as he walked the twenty miles
of dusty road.

Before he became a lawyer, Lincoln's neighbors
elected him to the Legislature, which was like a university for this unschooled man, who never had lived in a
town or associated with educated people. Neverthe
less he straightway became a leader of the Whigs and
finally their candidate for Speaker.

There are just two items in the record of his eight
years as a legislator that are worthy of remembrance
—first, his declaration for woman suffrage, long before
that question was an issue anywhere; second, his stand
against slavery, though only one other member joined
him in his bold dissent from the otherwise unanimous
action of the Legislature, in denouncing the abolitionists instead of the lawless mobs that were persecuting
them all over the North.

After Lincoln had become a rising young lawyer in
Springfield and while Mary Todd, daughter of a nota-

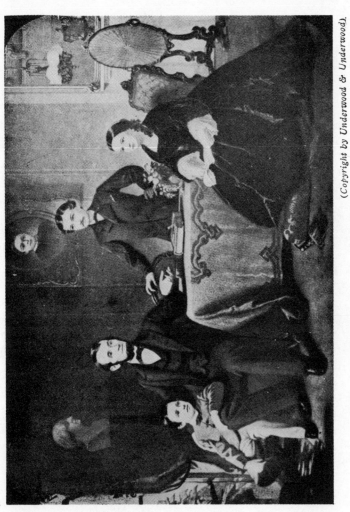

PRESIDENT AND MRS. LINCOLN, WITH THEIR SONS,
ROBERT T., STANDING, AND "TAD," SEATED
(From a photograph of an old picture)

ble Kentucky family, was visiting the prairie capital, that pretty, high-spirited little woman accepted the shy railsplitter in preference to even such a graceful courtier as Stephen A. Douglas. But on the wedding day the bridegroom failed to appear, for some reason that remains in dispute; probably from a correct presentiment that they were ill-mated in temperament.

Once more Lincoln was so tortured in his melancholy soul that friends anxiously watched over him, and he consulted by mail a Cincinnati physician, to whom he described his love sickness in the past and in the present. In the end his sense of duty or an ideal of chivalry triumphed over his forebodings. As if determined to take no more chances with his wayward moods, he and Miss Todd married in such haste that the bride had to wear a borrowed wedding gown. If either repented at leisure, neither ever gave voice to the repentance.

At least, Lincoln's knightly honor, single-minded. patient devotion were well matched by his wife's inspiring admiration of his abilities and her prophetic faith in his greatness. Careful as the husband was of the feelings of others, he innocently offended Mrs. Lincoln's sense of propriety . . . forgetting the special knife for the butter or impulsively getting up from his favorite position on the floor when the bell rang and, instead of waiting for the busy hired girl, going to the door, perhaps in shirt sleeves and slippers, to welcome ladies who came to make a fashionable call.

Lincoln's law partner also found his informality a trial. Their office was to him only a shelter and his desk a footrest. He wrote on his knee; he kept no books and he filed his papers in his tall stove-pipe hat until it was full, when he dumped its contents in a pile and wrote on top of the pile: "If you can't find it anywhere else, look in this."

Better than home or office he enjoyed the gypsy life of a lawyer on the circuit, over which he rode in a rattletrap buggy to attend the courts of a dozen counties. A hearty welcome awaited him at any farmhouse where he stopped for dinner or as he alighted before the village tavern, with a queer old carpet sack in one hand and a faded green umbrella in the other; with a twenty-five cent, low-crowned palm hat or a high, shaggy beaver on his head and a suit of dusty, rusty, shiny bombazine hanging on his enormous frame, the suspenders, perhaps, fastened to the trousers by sticks which he had whittled to take the place of missing buttons.

Yet this cheery, companionable man really had no companions. Those who knew him best saw only a whimsical, simple, helpful friend and neighbor, who milked his cows, bedded his horses, carried his boys pick-back in the streets, went to the market with his basket on his arm or sat on a box at the foot of his office steps, telling stories to a group of street loiterers They caught only baffling glimpses from time to time of another man who walked the street wrapped in solitude, or who brooded in his office far into the night. This was the mystic, the inner Lincoln, poet, dreamer, idealist, prophet, who pondered within the outer Lincoln and guided him on to his high duty.

III

AWAKENED TO HIS LIFE MISSION

(1847-9) Abraham Lincoln in Congress.—(1849) Unsuccessfully applied for appointment as commissioner of General Land Office and declined Governorship of Oregon Territory.—(1854) March 4, aroused from his political indifference by repeal of Missouri Compromise; his first debates with Stephen A. Douglas.—(1856) His name presented to Republican National Convention for Vice-President.—(1858) June 16, his "House Divided Against Itself" speech. July 24, challenged Douglas to the great debate. November, defeated for the Senate.—(1859) Spoke in Ohio and Kansas.—(1860) Feb. 27, his famous Cooper Union address in New York. May 18, nominated for President by the Republican National Convention at Chicago.

THE iron-throated cannon of Washington Navy Yard, breaking the stillness of a March dawn in 1854 with its one hundred exultant roars over the repeal of the Missouri Compromise, awakened Lincoln to the great mission for which his whole life had been an unconscious preparation. After a single term in Congress, where his criticism of the Mexican War in the midst of that conflict had left him unavailable for a second term, and after providentially failing to obtain the snug berth of commissioner of the General Land Office, he had retired to his dingy law office in Springfield.

The wiping out of the dead line against the spread of slavery in the Missouri Compromise aroused him from his indifference to political questions and drew him from his retirement. "I know there is a God and that he hates injustice and slavery," he said simply to a friend. "I see the storm coming. I know His hand is in it. If He has a place and work for me—and I think He has—I believe I am ready."

The cannon that called Lincoln to his duty also was the signal gun that heralded the birth of the Republican party. Joining the new party, he became at once its leader in Illinois; to his own surprise, the second man in the balloting for its candidate for Vice-President in 1856 and its candidate for senator in 1858 against Stephen A. Douglas, the author of the repeal.

While Lincoln made ready for that campaign, as always in every hour of decision, he retired within himself. He consulted no one and gave no hint of his line of attack until he called together a dozen friends and, in a private rehearsal, read to them his opening speech, which began with these immortal words: "A house divided against itself cannot stand. I believe that this Government cannot endure permanently half slave and half free. . . . It will become all one thing or all the other."

Every man in the little group warned him that the speech would defeat him for the Senate. "If I had to draw a pen across my record and erase my whole life from sight," he quietly replied, "and I had one poor gift or choice left as to what I should save from the wreck, I should choose that speech and leave it to the world unerased."

The Lincoln-Douglas debate is the old story over again of David and Goliath. Although physically Lincoln towered above the "Little Giant," who was hardly five feet four, Douglas had all but forgotten the country lawyer that he had left so far behind in his swift climb up the steeps of fame, and the brilliant senator patronizingly dismissed his antagonist now as a "kind-hearted, amiable gentleman, a right good fellow, etc., etc."

Lincoln modestly admitted that he had been a "flat failure" in the race of ambition on which the two men had started in Springfield twenty years before. "I affect no contempt," he added, "for the high eminence he has reached. So reached that the oppressed of my species might have shared with me the elevation, I would rather stand on that eminence than wear the richest crown that ever pressed a monarch's brow."

Lincoln was transfigured by the great issue that had taken possession of him. Forgetting in his earnestness stage manners and platform tricks, his gestures were as simple as the words that he spoke in his high tenor voice, which sometimes ran almost into a piping falsetto or again softened into music.

Douglas carried a few more Legislative districts and was re-elected, but Lincoln led in the aggregate popular vote. As the defeated candidate was going home in the rainy election night he caught himself as he was about to lose his footing and, in his superstitious vein, he drew from the incident an omen: "It is a slip and not a fall."

Lincoln had met his Bunker Hill. The great unknown, who had dared to cross swords with the foremost champion of the repeal, piqued the curiosity of the country. Accepting an invitation to speak in New York, his Cooper Union address established his intellectual and moral right to lead the Nation.

Nevertheless when zealous neighbors had first entered him as a candidate for President, he protested that he was not fit for the place. Until the convention of 1860 actually met in Chicago, his name seldom was mentioned for the honor outside his own State. Two-thirds of the delegates really favored the nomination of William H. Seward, but, as so often happens in politics, the very pre-eminence of the New York senator made him unavailable. In the end Lincoln was nominated largely because he was the least-known man on the list of candidates.

As they reluctantly turned from Seward to cast their

ballots for Lincoln, some of the delegates actually shed tears for the great man that had fallen. Few dreamed that a greater had risen.

IV

CALLED TO THE HELM IN A STORM

(1860) Nov. 6, Abraham Lincoln elected President. The vote: Lincoln, Republican, 1,866,452; Douglas, Northern Democrat, 1,375,-157; Breckinridge, Southern Democrat, 847,953; Bell, Constitutional Unionist, 590,631.—(1861) Feb. 11, Lincoln left Springfield. Feb. 23, arrived in Washington.

AFTER a campaign in which he remained silent in Springfield, except for a merely formal acceptance of the nomination, Lincoln received the news of his election to the Presidency with the bitter anguish of the nation's jeopardy in his heart and in his face the shadow of his awful responsibility. For Southern leaders had warned the country that the triumph of a minority candidate and of a sectional party, which did not put out a ticket in ten States of the South, would be the signal for breaking up the Union. The Republican party, falling far short of a majority, had won a four-cornered contest only because the Democrats had divided their votes between Douglas and Breckinridge, with a large remnant of the old Whig party voting for Bell.

As State after State made good the threat by withdrawing its representatives from Washington and by entering the Southern Confederacy, a moral, financial, and industrial panic shook the North. There rose a frantic clamor for letting the South go or for compromising with it again. Seward and a large section of the Republicans began to trim sails, and not less than forty measures for patching up a truce were proposed in Congress.

From the new captain came the clear command, "Hold firm as a chain of steel." While so many other Northern leaders were buffeted about like corks in a surf, Lincoln steered his steady course in the storm by two beacon lights: the Union, and the mandate of his election, which was to stop the spread of slavery beyond its existing boundaries.

Office-seekers and statesmen flocked to the simple village home in Springfield, where the President-elect— in "snuff-colored, slouchy pantaloons and open black vest with brass buttons"—let them in and talked with them while his two little sons noisily clambered over him. But he kept his own counsels. Without consulting any one or confiding in any one, he completed the outlines of his Cabinet, as he sat in the excited hurly-burly of the telegraph office election night. When the time came to write his inaugural, he retired into the solitude of a bare room over a store.

One day, as he and Mrs. Lincoln were busily unpacking some purchases which they had made in Chicago for their journey to Washington, and as he thought of the public fears that the rising tide of secession would engulf Virginia and Maryland and cut off the President-elect from the capital, the humor of the grim situation brought a twinkle to his eye and a pucker to his lips. "Well, Mary," he said, "there is one thing likely to come out of this scrape, anyhow. We are going to have some new clothes."

On the eve of his departure he made a journey to the home of his stepmother. He was loyally caring for the good woman who had brought sunshine into his desolate boyhood, whose faithful hands had clothed him and who had given him a chance to go to school and learn his letters. But her enjoyment of his visit was clouded with gloomy forebodings that his enemies would kill him and that she never would see him again.

He had his own dark presentiments. On the day of his nomination he saw two reflections of himself in a mirror, one of them a pale shadow, and the superstition always present in this primitive man was aroused. On the night before he started for Washington, as he was sadly leaving his old law office for the last time and saying good-by to his partner, he foretold the rate that awaited him, that he would never come back alive. The people who had gathered at the railway station the next morning to say good-by to him, saw him, as long as his train remained in sight, standing on the platform of his car, a melancholy figure, wistfully looking back at the vanishing little town into which he had walked a barefoot law student and where fame had sought him out.

An instance of the simple nature of the man, which occurred in the course of his journey, caused many smiles and as many sneers. Having adopted the advice of a little girl in a New York town, who wrote him a letter begging him to grow a beard on his hitherto clean-shaven face, he called for her when his train stopped at her station and told her, as he kissed her, that he had made the change at her request.

At Philadelphia there was a more solemn incident, touched with a tragic prophecy. In the unwonted emotions evoked by Independence Hall, where he spoke on Washington's Birthday, he was moved to declare that if the Union could not be saved without giving up the principles of the Declaration of Independence, he "would rather be assassinated on this spot than surrender it."

As the Presidential train neared Washington, Lincoln was met by a messenger from Seward and also by Allan Pinkerton, the noted detective, with the warning

of a plot to mob him in Baltimore, where in those times
all through railway cars had to be slowly hauled across
the city by horses.   Although he disliked to steal into
the capital, as he said, "like a thief in the night," he
accepted the advice of those around him and quietly
left his party at Harrisburg.   Accompanied only by
Pinkerton and another loyal Illinois friend, he finished
the journey unobserved in a general sleeping car.   Arriving in Washington at dawn, the three men hailed a
station hack, like any other strangers, and were already
settled at their hotel when the capital awoke to
the startling news that the President-elect was in the
city.

V

LINCOLN'S VALLEY FORGE

(1861) March 4, Abraham Lincoln inaugurated President, aged fifty-
two.   March 15, advised by the Cabinet to surrender Fort Sumter.
March 29, he determined to provision and defend it.   April 1,
because of his supposed unfitness, he was asked by Seward to relinquish to him his powers and responsibilities.   April 14, Fort
Sumter surrendered.   April 15, Lincoln called for 75,000 volunteers.   July 21, The Union army routed at Bull Run.—(1862)
July 1, McClellan retreated from before Richmond.   Aug. 2,
second defeat at Bull Run.   Sept. 16-17, victory at Antietam.
Sept. 22, Emancipation proclamation.   Dec. 13, Union defeat at
Fredericksburg.—(1863) May 2-4, disaster at Chancellorsville.

SEVEN stars already were gone from the blue field of
the flag at Lincoln's inauguration, and still others were
fading away.   How to keep more States from seceding
and how to win back to the Union those in secession was
the heart-wracking problem which he faced while standing on the steps of the Capitol to register in heaven, as
he said, his vow to preserve, protect and defend the
Constitution.

When he sat down at his desk in the White House
the next morning he found lying on it a report that the

loyal garrison which was besieged in Fort Sumter in Charleston Harbor had food enough to last only a few days more. Gen. Scott assured the new President that it was impracticable to attempt to provision the fort, and all except one member of the Cabinet agreed with the veteran soldier.

When the commanding general recommended that still another fort be given up, there came to Lincoln a sleepless night, through which he watched by the rended Union in its mortal crisis as the shadow of dissolution lay upon it. The morning found him fixed in his determination to save it. The forts should be defended.

He had kept his own counsel in all the soul-torturing struggles of that first decisive month of his term. While the inner Lincoln walked alone under his awful burden, the outer Lincoln shuffled along good naturedly through the daily routine. As Cabinet and leaders, not one of whom had known him a year, watched and measured this quaint, simple-mannered man, smiling and joking as he met the biggest and hungriest swarm of office seekers that ever assailed a President, they were puzzled or disheartened. After four weeks, Seward, the Secretary of State, bluntly proposed in writing that the new President should leave statesmanship to him and continue to amuse himself only with handing out jobs.

Without betraying the least resentment but with a firm hand, Lincoln put Seward in his place so effectively that in a little while the Secretary was writing to his wife, "The President is the best of us." At the first test he had established his moral supremacy over the eminent statesman whom he had defeated for the nomination.

The arrival of the Federal supply ships at the mouth of Charleston Harbor was the signal for the Confederate bombardment of Fort Sumter. The South had struck the first blow, and the people of the North rallied to the support of the Union.

When Congress met in extraordinary session on July 4, the President already had enrolled three hundred thousand volunteer troops. In a few days, he started the first army toward Richmond, the Confederate capital, but only to see it hurled back in wild disorder from the banks of Bull Run. Slowly gathering a second army, he sent it forth under McClellan, who was repulsed at the very gates of Richmond and driven back in retreat down the James River. Then he launched a third army southward under Pope, but it was stopped again at Bull Run.

Emboldened by its successes, the Southern army advanced northward, but McClellan stopped Lee in Maryland. Five days after that first victory for the Union at Antietam, Lincoln met his Cabinet with a humorous story by Artemus Ward, and then, suddenly turning from the ridiculous to the sublime, he gravely announced that he had promised God to free the slaves if the arms of the Union should win the battle. Thereupon he drew from a drawer the emancipation proclamation which he had originally prepared in such complete secrecy that history has been unable to discover where and when he wrote the momentous document.

The darkest winter in American history since Valley Forge was yet to come. A fourth army that Lincoln hurled at Richmond met with disaster at Fredericksburg and Chancellorsville, and the Western army under Grant seemed to be floundering hopelessly in the swamps of the Mississippi.

"My God! My God!" Lincoln cried in broken tones, as he held in his hand the direful message from Chancellorsville. "What will the country say? What will the country say?" All that night he paced the floor.

of his office. When the clerks came in the morning they found him eating his simple breakfast at his desk and beside him the instructions to the Army of the Potomac that he had thought out in the long, silent watches he had kept alone on the bridge.

Lincoln never became a great or an efficient administrator. Except for a term as village postmaster, he came to the Presidency wholly without executive experience, never having had a clerk under him, and as chief executive he made almost every possible administrative mistake.

The greatness of this man is to be found only in his simple humanity, his unshakable faith in the right and in his leadership of the people. In the first dark year of the conflict, these gifts of his had made possible and probable the ultimate victory, by winning to the Union the States of Delaware, Maryland, West Virginia, Kentucky, Missouri and the eastern section of Tennessee. Himself born among the people of that borderland, he knew them and, with his finger on their pulse, he had slowly, patiently led them away from the South and into the path of the Union.

The secret of his leadership everywhere was the same—his kinship with the people, who never failed him. When statesmen fell away from him—they talked of forcing him to resign after Chancellorsville—the people pressed forward with the shout, "We are coming, Father Abraham, three hundred thousand more."

The faith, the spirit, the soul of Lincoln was the fortress of the Union whose stout walls withstood every assault. Even when he confessed, in the general gloom of the Winter of 1862-3, that he was nearly as inconsolable as he could be and live, he sat down and wrote out this secret pledge to himself: "I expect to maintain this contest until successful or till I die or am

conquered or my term expires or Congress or the
country forsake me."

VI

THE GREAT FRIEND

Lincoln's children: Robert Todd, born Aug. 1, 1843; died July 25, 1926.
Edward Baker, born March 10, 1846; died in infancy. William Wallace,
born Dec. 21, 1850; died Feb. 20, 1862. Thomas, born April 4, 1853;
died July 15, 1871.

THE stone walls of the White House no more shut
Lincoln in from his fellows, from their hopes and sorrows and pride, than did the unhewn logs behind which
he shivered in the cabin home of his youth. One night
he dreamed that he was in a crowd, when some one recognized him as the President, and exclaimed in surprise, "He is a very common-looking man." Where-
upon he answered, "Friend, the Lord prefers common-looking people. That is the reason he makes so
many of them."

Lincoln liked people, and he always kept in touch
with the mass. He did not have to take the word of
politicians or newspapers about what the country was
thinking. He went to the source. In truth, he needed
only to look within himself to find a mirror of the
popular mind.

As he finished his daily wrestle with senators and the
big-wigs, he plunged with zest into what he called his
"public opinion bath." Seated in his chair, with one
leg thrown over its arm, he received the motley crowd
that poured in through the wide open door of his office.
Those who approached him in awe found themselves
at ease in the presence of a friend, whose manner said
to every one what he said in a speech to a regiment: "I
happen temporarily to occupy this big White House.

I am a living witness that any one of your children may look to come here as my father's child has."

The man fairly exhaled democracy, fraternity, equality. Frederick Douglass said that Lincoln was the only white man he ever met who did not show consciously or unconsciously that he recognized his color.

Sympathy flowed in a constant stream from its fountain in this great heart. A mother's tears, a baby's cry, a father's plea, a crutch or an empty sleeve seldom failed to move Lincoln. "If he has no friend, I'll be his friend," he said as he stopped the shooting of a soldier under sentence of a court-martial.

"My poor girl," he said to a woman who pleaded for the life of her soldier brother, "you have come here with no governor or senator or member of Congress to speak in your cause; you seem honest and truthful and you don't wear hoops, and I'll be whipped if I don't pardon him."

He hated Friday—"butcher's day," as he called it— because that was the usual time appointed for carrying out death sentences in the army. "They are shooting a boy to-day. I hope I have not done wrong to allow it." "There are already too many weeping widows; don't ask me to add one to the number." On one pardon he wrote, "I think this boy can do us more good above ground than under it." And here is another characteristic message: "If you have not shot Denis McCarthy, don't."

Even the coward had a friend in this brave man. "If God Almighty gives a man a cowardly pair of legs, how can he help their running away with him?" A pigeonhole in his desk was stuffed with these "leg cases," as he labeled the papers regarding men condemned to death for "cowardice in the face of the enemy."

A soldier, whom he had spared a dishonorable death before the firing squad, was found dead on a battlefield, and in his pocket was a photograph of his deliverer, inscribed "God bless President Lincoln." Like this is the oft-told story of the sleeping sentinel. True to the man, if only a legend, is the pardon of that Vermont boy, who repaid him in his first battle by swimming a river under fire again and again to carry the wounded to safety until he had given his life for his comrades.

This native democrat never put on Presidential manners. He did not need them. His inborn dignity protected him. "Good morning," he surprised a passerby at the White House gate at six o'clock. "I am looking for a newsboy. When you get to the corner I wish you would send one up this way."

The hard muscles and steel nerves of the railsplitter enabled this President to bear responsibilities, labors and annoyances such as would have broken perhaps any other man in the Presidential line. He still could grip an ax by the end of the handle and hold it out even with his shoulder.

His sense of humor was his safety valve. "If I couldn't tell these stories I should die," he explained to a solemn congressman who impatiently protested that he had not come to the White House to hear jokes.

The man who kept all great decisions to himself could not enjoy a little joke alone. John Hay depicts him stalking the White House corridor in night shirt and bare legs to read to young Nicolay and Hay, his secretaries, a punning conceit from Theodore Hook, "unconscious that he . . . was infinitely funnier." Here's another snapshot by John Hay: "He read Shakespeare to me, the end of 'Henry VIII' and the beginning of 'Richard III,' till my heavy eyelids caught his considerate notice and he sent me to bed."

Lincoln's office was almost his prison cell through four terrible years. The shouts of his two little boys at play always were welcome notes of joy to their care-

weighted father.   He never objected to their noisily
bursting in upon him, and often he joined the children
in their boisterous games in the White House grounds.'

In the dark days when the nation itself was at death's
door, one of the boys died. For weeks the grieving
father strove in vain to win a spirit of resignation, dropping his work for a day at a time and surrendering to
his sorrow. Doubtless the fortitude he gained at last
in that wrestle with himself became part of the heroic
faith which lifted him above the general despair when
the fortunes of the Union sank lowest.

After Willie's death, the other boy received a double
share of paternal affection. Tad was in the habit of
going to his father in the evening and making a report
of all that had happened since morning, usually falling
asleep in the midst of his prattle. Laying the little fellow on the floor by the side of his desk, Lincoln returned to his heavy tasks until his own long day was
done, when he took his sleeping boy on his shoulder
and carried him off to bed.

VII

LINCOLN IN VICTORY

(1863) July 1-3, battle of Gettysburg. July 4, Grant took Vicksburg.
Nov. 19, Gettysburg address.—(1864) May 4, Wilderness cam-
paign opened. June 8, Lincoln renominated. July 10, Confed-
erates in sight of Washington. July 16, gold rose to $2.85.
Aug. 23, Lincoln forecast his defeat in the election. Aug. 31,
Democratic National Convention declared the war a failure.
Sept. 2, Sherman entered Atlanta. Sept. 19, Sheridan won battle
of Winchester. Nov. 8, Lincoln re-elected.—(1865) Feb. 3,
Hampton Roads conference. March 4, second inauguration.
March 22, Lincoln arrived at Grant's headquarters. April 4,
visited Richmond. April 9, returned to Washington.

THE country lawyer in the White House, who never
had set a squadron in the field, turned at last the tide

of battle when it had been running for two years against the Union. As Lee's army swept northward, after smashing the Federal forces at Chancellorsville, Gen. Hooker, the Union commander, proposed to stay behind and take Richmond. Lincoln's common sense rejected that absurd plan, and he ordered the army to follow Lee. But after beating the Confederates at Gettysburg, it let them retreat in safety, and the President impatiently exclaimed: "If I had gone there, I could have whipped them myself."

The next day after Gettysburg, Grant took Vicksburg, and that was another victory which Lincoln made possible. He had stood by Grant, whom he never had seen, when that general had hardly another supporter in Washington. "I cannot spare this man," he insisted; "he fights."

The President expressed in these few words the significance of the fall of Vicksburg: "The 'Father of Waters' again goes unvexed to the sea." A few months afterward he compressed the high, world-wide meaning of the whole struggle into the few simple sentences of his noble Gettysburg address.

After more victories by Grant around Chattanooga, the victorious general was brought East, and, under his command, Lincoln started his fifth drive on Richmond. Then came the darkness before the dawn of the final triumph, and 1864 was in some respects the most trying year of the war. A Presidential election was at hand, and leading Republican politicians were for "anybody but Lincoln." Some were for Grant. "If he takes Richmond, let him have it," said the President.

Above the whisperings and plots of the politicians, the voice of the people rose in a chorus for the renomination of Lincoln. Finding themselves without followers when the Republican convention met, the leaders clamored only for the chance to second the popular motion. The President modestly accepted the uprising for him simply as evidence that the country did not believe it "best to swap horses while crossing the river."

Even Lincoln's faith in the people was shaken in that summer of despair. He doubted if they would go on longer beneath the crushing burden. A shudder of horror ran through the land at the frightful slaughter under Grant in the Wilderness. "I cannot bear it," the President said, as he turned his saddened face away from a long line of ambulances. Nevertheless he did not flinch, in the midst of his campaign for re-election, from making the staggering demand for five hundred thousand more recruits. A Confederate army boldly advanced within sight of the capital and where the President himself saw the enemy. A gold dollar was worth in July $2.85 in greenbacks.

Under the thickening clouds in August, Lincoln wrote and sealed a forecast of his own defeat in the November elections and also his resolve to co-operate with McClellan, the Democratic candidate, as soon as the latter should have been elected. Equally certain that the President was in a losing fight, the Democrats adopted a platform which declared the war a failure and which called for peace by negotiation. But in two days more Sherman was in Atlanta and in two weeks more Sheridan won the battle of Winchester.

The war was not a failure, and Lincoln was a success. Carrying all but three of the States that took part in the election, he could yet say in truth to the serenaders at the White House, "It is no pleasure to me to triumph over anyone."

Victory in the war was to call out the noblest qualities in the man. No sooner was he assured that the

Union was saved than peace and forgiveness became his ruling passion. In the hour of assured success, he did not hesitate, for the sake of stopping the bloodshed, to go into conference at Hampton Roads with the leaders of the doomed Confederacy. After his return from that fruitless parley, he wrote a message to Congress, proposing to pay the slaveholders four hundred million dollars for their slaves if the South would only cease fighting. All the Cabinet objecting, with a sigh he put the message in his drawer.

"With malice toward none, with charity for all," came forth from Lincoln's soul like a chant at his second inauguration. As the curtain was lifted in the spring for the closing scene of the great tragedy, the voice that never had faltered in the dark days of the war pleaded at Grant's headquarters, "Can't this last bloody battle be avoided?"

Richmond fell, and the conquerer who had hurled so many armies against the stubborn defenses entered the conquered capital afoot, leading his boy Tad by the hand. He had not come to triumph over a vanquished foe, and as he sat in the "White House of the Confederacy," from which Jefferson Davis had fled thirty-six hours before, he said in reproof of a man who cried out for vengeance against the fugitive chieftain of the South, "Judge not, that ye may not be judged."

As the Presidential boat returned to Washington, and the white dome of the Capitol swam into the horizon, the haunting shadow of dread revisited Mrs. Lincoln's face. "That city is filled with our enemies," she said.

"Enemies!" Lincoln protested, as if the word had no place in the new era of peace. "We must never speak of that."

VIII

(1865) April 11, Lincoln's last speech. April 14, shot by John Wilkes Booth. April 15, died, aged fifty-six. April 21, the funeral cortege left Washington. May 4, the burial at Oak Ridge, Springfield, Ill.

WITH the winning of the war, Lincoln turned at once to bind up the wounds of the Union. The South having surrendered to force, he wished to conquer it forever by magnanimity. He would not hold the States together with bayonets and erect a rebellious Ireland within the borders of the republic.

Unfortunately, many Republican leaders, who had not been so much in the thick of the fight, were unable to calm the passions aroused in them by the long struggle. A clamor arose for wholesale hangings and confiscations and for ruling the Southern States as conquered provinces.

It was the same conflict that follows every war, the conflict between a healing peace of reconciliation and an armed peace of vengeance. The radicals of Congress had no faith in Lincoln's idea of a reunion of hearts. They demanded that the rebellious States of the South be held in subjection indefinitely and that the ballot be given to the newly freed slaves, whom Lincoln preferred to admit to the suffrage gradually.

On the second day after the surrender at Appomattox, in an address from a White House window, the President spoke of a new announcement to the people of the South. But that was to be his last speech.

At the Cabinet meeting, on the closing day of his life, he rejoiced that Congress was not in session to interfere with peacemaking and reconstruction, and he was confidently hoping to re-establish the Union before it met

again. As to Jefferson Davis and the Confederate
leaders, he declared with much feeling that no one need
expect him to hang them. "Frighten them out of the
country!" he cried in excited, high-pitched tones. "Open
the gates! Let down the bars! Scare them off!
Enough lives have been sacrificed. We must extinguish
our resentments if we expect harmony and union."

With those accents of a generous statesmanship ringing in their ears, the secretaries went away from the
last Cabinet meeting. Secretary Stanton sent, later in
the day, to ask permission to arrest Jaocb Thompson, a
Confederate emissary in Canada, who had slipped into
the United States for the purpose of escaping to Europe from Portland. "Well, I rather guess not," the
President replied. "When you have an elephant by the
hind leg and he wants to run away, better let him run."

An unwonted ease and happiness seemed to rest upon
Lincoln that tragic day. Although he had dreamed the
night before that he was in a strange ship, moving
toward a dark and indefinite shore, he took it as a good
omen. Had not the same dream come to him before
the victories of Antietam, Gettysburg and Vicksburg?

In the evening he sat in a box at Ford's Theatre,
enjoying a comedy, when John Wilkes Booth stole upon
him. That handsome but ungifted young actor, who
was a prey to dark moods and whose mad hostility to
the Union had upset a never well-balanced mind, peeped
through a hole in the door of the box and observed the
position of his illustrious victim. Could he have looked
into Lincoln's face with its simple benignity, his better
nature might have turned him back from the threshold
of his crime.

While the curtain was down between the acts, the
President and Mrs. Lincoln fondly talked over plans
for the future, when they should be free from the heavy

cares of the White House. As they planned the travels they would enjoy, he said, "There is no place I should like so much to see as Jerusalem." Those were his last words. The play began again and the assassin, noiselessly opening the door of the box, fired his cowardly shot. Lincoln rose from his chair under the impulse of the shock and then sank back into it, his head drooping and his eyes closed, not to open again this side of that mysterious shore toward which he had sailed in his dream ship.

The frenzied murderer pushed his way through the bewildered party in the box and leaped over the railing. But the folds of the flag that draped it tripped him and he fell upon the stage. Although the fall had broken his leg, he rose with the melodramatic cry of "Sic semper tyrannis." Making his escape from the stage, he rode away through the night, but only to be shot down two weeks afterward as he stood at bay in a Virginia barn.

To spare the stricken President a ride over the cobblestones to the White House, he was carried to the simple home of a tailor across the street from the theatre. There his giant strength battled with death until the morning. Then the great heart stopped, and Stanton hoarsely whispered, "Now he belongs to the ages."

No other death ever touched so many hearts. Millions mourned a friend. As the body was borne back to Springfield, sorrowing hundreds of thousands along the way looked upon the face which had been the mirror of a people's sacrifice and of a people's hope.

At Springfield simple men and women brought from humble homes in the countryside their tribute of tears, not to the dead President, but to the good neighbor who had helped them in counsel, in the field, in the forest or on the highway, when he shared with them the crust of poverty.   In the place of honor behind his funeral car in the procession to the tomb walked "Old Bob," the faithful horse that had carried him on his travels around the law circuit.   Above his prairie grave a lofty monument was raised and, out of the earnings of their free labor, thousands of freedmen, whose shackles he had broken, contributed to its building.

ANDREW JOHNSON

I

THE ONLY PRESIDENT WHO NEVER WENT TO SCHOOL

(1808) Dec. 29, Andrew Johnson born at Raleigh, N. C.—(1818) Bound out to a tailor.—(1825) A runaway bound-boy.—(1826) Opened a tailor shop at Greenville, Tenn.—(1827) May 17, married Eliza McCardle.—(1828) Elected alderman.—(1830-33) Mayor of Greenville.—(1835-39) Member of Legislature.—(1841-3) State senator.—(1843-53) Congressman.—(1853-57) Governor of Tennessee.—(1857-62) Senator.—(1862-5) Military Governor of Tennesseee.—(1864) Elected Vice-President.

NEVER has there been a change in the White House so untimely and unwelcome as when, in the flash of Booth's pistol, the Presidency passed from Abraham Lincoln to Andrew Johnson. That sudden shift in pilots was dreaded by all the people, South and North, except for a radical faction in Lincoln's own party, which confidently hoped to see his noble watchwords of "Malice Toward None," and "Charity for All," replaced by the slogan which the Vice-President had been sounding, "Treason Must Be Made Odious."

Although a Southerner, Johnson had always been at odds with the slaveholding aristocracy, which frowned on the rise of a penniless youth who had been bound out at ten to a tailor and who had been advertised at seventeen as a runaway "bound boy."

A fugitive from his native State of North Carolina, he crossed over the mountains to Greenville, in Eastern Tennessee, and there he nailed above the door of a

160

ANDREW JOHNSON AND THE WIFE WHO TAUGHT HIM HIS LETTERS

two-room house the sign upon which the weather beats to this day:

A. JOHNSON, TAILOR

No other private occupation did he ever have. From the table on which he sat cross-legged as he worked at his trade, he stepped directly into Congress, and he remains the only President who could describe himself as a hand-craftsman. He continued most of his life to make his own clothes, and when he was Governor of Tennessee he complimented the Governor of Kentucky by making a suit for him.

Johnson's tailor shop was also his only schoolroom. He never was in any other, even for a day. But he was not his own teacher. That post was filled by Eliza McCardle, who had chanced to see the North Carolina boy walking into town and had giggled to her companions, as so many giggling girls have done: "There goes my beau!" In less than a year, though the bride was only seventeen and the groom not yet nineteen, they were married and keeping house in the two-room tailor shop.

Johnson already could read a little and could painfully form the letters of the alphabet. But his wife became his first teacher, reading to him while he plied his needle or guiding his hand while he practiced writing. Her eager pupil was most apt in oratory, and soon his shop became the forum of a debating society, where other ambitious workers joined the tailor in wordy combats.

Before he was of age, this village Demosthenes was elected an alderman on a workingman's ticket, and in two years more he was mayor. Then for eight years he was in the Legislature; for ten years a representative in Congress; for two terms Governor of Tennessee, and finally he was elected to the Senate. His worthiest monument as a legislator is the Homestead law, which opened the great national domain to the landless poor, a measure that he introduced and that he perseveringly championed against a lobby of land-grabbers.

No one ever questioned Andrew Johnson's honesty any more than his courage as he rudely forced his way up the ladder, rung by rung, in hard-hitting, rough-and-tumble contests. He neither gave nor asked quarter. It was a poor school in manners, taste and temper. His triumphs over those who boasted their descent made him boastful of his own ascent, and this self-made man never forgot his maker.

The bold self-reliance of Johnson became heroic in the eyes of the Nation when, alone among the twenty-two Southern senators, he breasted the wave of secession which engulfed his section and which swept out of the Union even the State from which he held his credentials. He not only fought secession in the Senate, but he challenged it on its own ground in Tennessee, where he faced a cloud of deadly threats. Pulling out his pistol at one place, he pointed it at his muttering audience and defiantly shouted: "If any man has any shooting to do, let him begin now." No one venturing to second that motion to a hip pocket, Johnson laid his weapon on the table and opened a vocal bombardment of the foe.

By Lincoln's appointment, he was made military governor of Tennessee, where his dauntless, fiery soul became the very breastworks of the Union in the midst of the enemy's country. It was from that outpost at Nashville that he was called to the Vice-Presidency, and in a month more he was President.

Exiled from his home and family as he had been, his house seized by the Confederacy as the property of

"an alien enemy," the long struggle had been indeed a
civil war to Andrew Johnson, and it left him in a most
uncivil mood toward the Confederate leaders.   Yet
through it all he had remained as stubbornly a Southerner and a Democrat as he was a Union man.   It was
as a War Democrat and a Southern Unionist that he
was nominated on the ticket with Lincoln in 1864, when
the partisan designation of Republican was laid aside
for the broader name of the National Union party.
What his course would be now that he had taken the
wheel was the riddle of one of the most anxious and
pregnant hours in American history.

II

BLOWING ON THE EMBERS OF WAR

(1865) April 15, Andrew Johnson took the oath as President, aged
fifty-six.—(1866) April, Congress overrode his veto of the Civil
Rights bill. August-September, his "swing around the circle."
November, Republican victory in Congressional elections.

A LOUD rapping on his hotel door in Washington awakened the sleeping Vice-President to the startling news
that the President had been mortally shot.   Even before Andrew Johnson took the oath the next morning,
strong men were laying plans, with unseemly haste, to
have him reverse Lincoln's generous policy toward the
conquered South.

Secretary Stanton turned directly from the death bed
of his chief to order the imprisonment of Jacob Thompson, the fleeing Confederate emissary, whose arrest
Lincoln had refused to sanction only the evening before, and he offered a reward for the capture of Jefferson Davis as an accomplice in the President's assassination.

At the same time radical Republicans in caucus at Washington were hailing with unseemly rejoicing the change of leaders. "By the gods! there will be no trouble now in running the Government," exclaimed Senator Wade of Ohio, as he grasped the hand of the new President.

Meanwhile, as the Southern people saw a "poor white" of the South enthroned over them, they sank to a still lower level of despair than when their armies had surrendered. When Davis heard of the monstrous charge that he had conspired with Booth, he made the bitter retort that there was at least one man who knew it was not true: "Johnson knows that I would have preferred Lincoln to him."

Power quickly cooled the vindictive passions kindled in Johnson by his long, bitter feud with the Southern leaders, and he returned to Lincoln's policy of reconciliation. Wisely no one was punished for treason. Happily vengeance for a great war was not wreaked on any individual.

The radicals, who had secretly rejoiced in Johnson's accession, turned upon him furiously. It was easy for them to excite the doubt of the North in this Southerner and to estrange the Republicans from this Democrat.

For the first time even the sobriety of a President was called into question. Johnson's unfortunate condition at his inauguration as Vice-President had shocked Charles Sumner into starting a whispered discussion of his enforced resignation. When he became President his intemperance in speech lent color to exaggerated reports of his intemperance in drink.

It is an unanswerable question in history whether even Lincoln could have mastered the rising opposition to him in Congress and restored the Union on the plan which he had adopted. That plan had small chance of success in Johnson's hands, with his lack of Lincoln's good-humored tact, modesty, forbearance and hold on the public confidence.

For two years before Lincoln died, the radical leaders had been insisting that Congress, not the President, should fix the terms of peace for the Southern States. They had angrily denounced him as a despot, an autocrat and as a usurper because of his policy of reconstruction. And Congress had persistently refused to admit the senators and representatives from the States that he had reconstructed on his liberal plan.

The conflict was forced to an issue on the last day of the session in 1864, when Congress adopted a reconstruction plan of its own, under which it was to be the final judge of the State governments in the South. But Lincoln defeated the bill by a "pocket veto"; that is to say, he took no action on it before adjournment, which left it lifeless.

With the ending of the war, Lincoln was hoping to complete the work of reconstruction before Congress met again and could renew its interference with him. Instead the assassin intervened, and when Johnson attempted to carry out the same policy, with the approval of Lincoln's Cabinet, which he retained, Congress broke into open revolt. He appealed to the people to stand by him, but his "swing around the circle," as he described his tour of the East and Middle West in 1866, destroyed the last shred of his influence in the North.

Face to face with hostile, jeering crowds, he cast aside Presidential dignity and let loose the fiery passions of the Tennessee mountaineer. Gen. Grant, who unwillingly accompanied him, had to step forth to quiet a riotous crowd in Lincoln's own town of Springfield. The general recalled the disturbers to a sense of propriety simply by waving his hand toward the target of their hootings and saying, "The President of the United States." In the presence of a still wilder mob at Indianapolis, Grant felt it prudent to order the President to retreat. For he had been greeted with a storm of bullets, although they were probably fired in the air.

Apart from the Republican politicians and a mere faction of extremists, the North probably was in favor of Lincoln's moderate policies. But when it became a question between Johnson and the radicals, the radicals won overwhelmingly in the Congressional election of 1866.

With a two-thirds majority in the new House and Senate, the Republicans overrode the President's vetoes, and Congress took command of the Government. The reconstructed States were outlawed. The South was divided into military provinces. The ballot was thrust into the unready hand of the illiterate, penniless freedmen, notwithstanding it was still denied the negro in all but six States of the North. At the same time a large class of Southern whites was disfranchised for disloyalty in the war, which left several States to pass under the corrupt government of Northern "carpet baggers" and Southern "scalawags," who gained power by manipulating the ignorant black vote and who held it by force of federal bayonets.

As Northern "fire eaters" pressed to the front, on one side of the Mason and Dixon line, Southern "fire eaters" took the lead on the other side. By night the Ku Klux Klan rode their sable horses, in a campaign of terrorism to frighten the blacks from using the ballot and from presuming to set themselves above "Old

Massa." And the "bloody shirt" began to wave from the political stump in the North.

Party and sectional politics, North and South, still was the marplot of the Union. As it had fostered disunion before the war, it was doing its worst to prevent reunion, now that the war was over.

III

THE GREAT IMPEACHMENT

(1867) March 2, Congress passed the Reconstruction act over President Johnson's veto; also the Tenure of Office act. Aug. 12, Johnson removed Stanton.—(1868) Jan. 13, Senate refused to consent and Stanton returned to War Department. Feb. 22, the House impeached Johnson. March 5 to May 26, the impeachment trial before the Senate, and Johnson acquitted.—(1869) March 4, Johnson retired from the Presidency.—(1872)—Defeated for congressman-at-large.—(1875) March 12, senator from Tennessee. July 31, died, aged sixty-six.

ANDREW JOHNSON'S Presidency began with a great tragedy and came near ending in another. With a two-thirds majority in Congress, his opponents overrode his vetoes, seized control of reconstruction, stripped the President of authority to dismiss a postmaster or get rid of an enemy even in his own Cabinet, and bound him hand and foot.

Although the President faithfully executed the reconstruction laws that had been passed over his vetoes, he asserted the right, which never before had been denied a President, to choose his own Cabinet advisers. When he tried to dismiss Secretary Stanton, Stanton turned the War Department into a fort, and for weeks held it, night and day, while he slept and ate at his post.

Emotion having supplanted reason, the House hastened to declare that "in the name of the House of Representatives and of the people of the United States we do impeach Andrew Johnson, President of the United States, of high crimes and misdemeanors." Although there were twelve counts in the remarkable indictment, no crimes were specified and the misdemeanors that were alleged consisted almost wholly of the President's attempts to remove Stanton without the consent of the Senate.

That most important trial in American history began on March 5, 1868, with the Senate chamber crowded and Chief Justice Chase of the Supreme Court in the chair. "Andrew Johnson, President of the United States!" cried the sergeant-at-arms; "Andrew Johnson, President of the United States!" But the defendant remained in the White House, wisely leaving his case in the hands of able counsel.

The President had few friends left in Washington, but fortunately the Presidency itself had more. Johnson's abler lawyers, with their better case, tore to shreds the impeachment and the arguments of its advocates. When one of them, William M. Evarts, was chided for working on Sunday in the preparation of his defense of Johnson, he replied, "Is it not written that 'if thine ass falleth into a pit it is lawful to pull him out on the Sabbath Day'?"

There was a general expectation that the Senate would convict, no matter how flimsy the case, and crowds of eager partisans flocked to Washington to enjoy the spectacle of a White House eviction—to see "Andy walk the plank." Senator Ben Wade of Ohio was confident to the last that he would be called on, as President of the Senate, to take Johnson's place. His inaugural is said to have been written and his Cabinet selected, with Gen. Butler of Massachusetts for Secretary of State. Mrs. Wade was no less forehanded than her husband. She was surrounded at her hotel and in the Senate gallery with her women guests, who had come on from Ohio to assist at her installation as mistress of the White House, and they had provided themselves with becoming gowns for the great function.

As the roll of the Senate was called, amid a hushed suspense, the Republican senators all voted for conviction, until the Chief Justice asked, "Mr. Senator Fessenden, how say you? Is the respondent, Andrew Johnson, President of the United States, guilty or not guilty of a high misdemeanor as charged in this article?"

"Not guilty," answered the distinguished senator from Maine, who had been in Lincoln's Cabinet. The party alignment was broken and it was again broken in another moment by Senator Grimes of Iowa, who had been stricken with paralysis under the strain of the trial, but who managed to struggle to his feet when his name was called. Trumbull of Illinois, an old friend of Lincoln, was another man of ability and distinction among the seven Republican senators who broke away and joined the Democrats. Yet there were thirty-five votes for conviction against only nineteen for acquittal, just one less than the two-thirds necessary to convict.

Johnson himself had expected to be convicted and was packed up in readiness to leave the White House. But instead of meekly resigning himself to such an unexampled humiliation, he was eager to battle for his vindication at the hands of the people, an effort which was only postponed the few months that remained of his term.

When less than seven years had passed since he had been put on trial in the Senate chamber, Johnson walked into that forum of his enemies and took his seat as a senator from Tennessee. It must have been to him a sweet triumph, but he bore it becomingly.

In his only speech in the Senate—he died in four months—he did not indulge his old passion for recrimination. On the contrary, he begged the senators, in courteous, but earnest terms, to forget what had gone before and to lay aside party feelings for the sake of reunion.

The Southern Unionist only sounded the keynote of his whole life when he pleaded, "Let peace and unison be restored to the land! May God bless this people and God save the Constitution!" That had been the true object of his unfortunate administration, and history has rendered the verdict, which offers a useful lesson, that in trying to do the right thing Andrew Johnson failed, because he tried to do it the wrong way, in a wrong spirit.

ULYSSES SIMPSON GRANT

I

A FAILURE AT THIRTY-NINE

(1822) April 27, Hiram Ulysses Grant born at Point Pleasant, O.—
(1839) Enrolled at West Point Military Academy as Ulysses
Simpson Grant.—(1843) Second lieutenant, United States army.
(1846) First lieutenant.—(1846-8) In the Mexican War.—(1848)
Aug. 22, married Julia Dent.—(1853) Captain.—(1854) Resigned
from the army.—(1854-8) A farmer in Missouri.—(1858-9) Adrift
in St. Louis.—(1860) Moved to Galena, Ill.—(1861) Colonel of
Twenty-first Illinois Volunteer Regiment of Infantry.

A TANNER'S boy, who was born in a two-room house
on the banks of the Ohio, was named at his birth Hiram
Ulysses Grant.   Although simple and modest by nature, ' he yet preferred classical Ulysses to homely
Hiram, and so he parted his name in the middle.   As
he was starting for West Point he became fearful that
the hazers would nickname him Hug, and he turned H.
Ulysses around, making it Ulysses H.   On his arrival
at the military academy, he found that his name had
been changed again by the congressman who appointed
him to the cadetship, this neighbor of the family having
guessed that Ulysses' middle name was Simpson, because his mother was a Simpson.   Since the Government never corrects a mistake, U. S. Grant he had to
remain ever after.

Cadet William Tecumseh Sherman was struck by
those suggestive initials when he first read on the Academy bulletin board the name of the newcomer, and all
the cadets straightway hailed the shy, stumpy, freckled-

faced, blue-eyed, brown-haired, big-headed plebe as Uncle Sam, until familiarity reduced it to Sam. And Sam he was to them always after, even when some of them grew up to be generals with him or generals on the other side in the Civil War. Not being a prophet, Cadet Simon Bolivar Buckner of Kentucky had no idea that one day this silent little fellow from Ohio would send him a letter under a flag of truce at Fort Donelson, which would arouse admiring millions to rise up and call the writer Unconditional Surrender Grant.

Before becoming a cadet, the boy's schooling had consisted mostly of hard work . . . hauling and sawing wood, plowing, harvesting, tending horses and cows and driving stage. Yet he insisted in after life that it was better training than West Point gave him. It taught him to see a thing through, to stick to a job till he had finished it. And that was all Grant ever knew.

Grant's first conquest, after entering upon a military career, was of the heart of seventeen-year-old Julia Dent, a sister of one of his classmates. But he did not reveal his conquering powers in the Mexican War, which interrupted the courtship. Going in as a lieutenant, he came out a lieutenant.

After the war there was a wedding and then a parting, with the young husband exiled to barrack life in far-off Oregon and California. Idle, lonely, homesick for wife and baby, and indifferent to books, this man, whose life and speech were as clean as a woman's, found the only possible excitement in the bottle.

In those days, when the best was no better than the worst west of the Missouri and where there was little to do by way of amusement except to raise a thirst, hard drinking was the common diversion of army offi-

ULYSSES S. GRANT AT THE BOTTOM AND ABOVE IN ORDER,
CHESTER ARTHUR, JAMES A. GARFIELD AND RUTHERFORD B.
HAYES.

cers at the dreary frontier posts.   Their legs may **have** been hollow, but Grant's were not, and these betrayed him so badly that his captain gave him the choice of resigning or facing a court-martial.

Grant resigned—to Jefferson Davis, Secretary of War—and sailed for New York. Landing broke, he would have had to sleep on a bench in Park Row or on the Battery, if his classmate, Simon Boliver Buckner, had not opened his purse to this forlorn captain out of a job.

On a little piece of wild timber land in Missouri, which Mrs. Grant had received from her father as a wedding gift, Grant built a log cabin—it is now proudly exhibited—and he gave the place the well-deserved name of Hard Scrabble. He hauled into St. Louis and peddled around town the fire-wood he cut and the little grain he could raise. But his false, seductive friend, the bottle, still dogged his heels, and, drifting away from the farm, he turned first to a real estate agency in the city and next to a precarious little government job.

As it would at least save express charges on the money that his father was remitting to him, he went to Galena, Ill., where the Grants were prospering in handling hides. Arriving there in an old, faded, blue army overcoat, he became a clerk under his younger brothers. The Union was already breaking up; but he wrote to a friend that he liked his new employment and was sanguine of success in the hide business.

When Lincoln's call for troops came to Galena next spring, Grant still was known to the town only as the silent man in the old army overcoat. By that token of his military experience, he was called to preside over the meeting to raise a company of volunteers, and he went with it to Springfield.

Officers' commissions were going where the pull was

strongest, and Grant did not know a politician at the State capital or in Washington. The only use the politicians in Springfield had for him was to hire him at three dollars a day to do the "paper work" of the political majors and colonels.

When one of those colonels fell down in handling an unruly regiment, other political aspirants shied at it as a tough job, and Grant got it. To impress the roystering youngsters who had broken their commander, two political spellbinders were sent along to introduce the new colonel, who had not yet succeeded in borrowing the money with which he finally purchased his first uniform. While the orators ran the scales of bombast, he writhed two long hours in his own oratorical inferiority, as he sat there on the platform wondering what in the world he could say. When at last, with an eloquent flourish, he was presented to the curious soldiers, he took a step or two toward the front, and then there rang out in the quiet but clear tones which had won admiration on the campus at West Point, Grant's first command in the Civil War: "Men, go to your quarters!"

II

A NOBLE CONQUEROR

(1861) June, U. S. Grant colonel. August, brigadier-general. September, took Paducah, Ky.—(1862) February, took Fort McHenry; took Fort Donaldson. March, suspended from command. April, fought Battle of Shiloh.—(1863) July 4, took Vicksburg. November, commanded in the battles about Chattanooga.—(1864) March, lieutenant-general in command of all the armies. May, opened his campaign in the Wilderness.—(1865) April 9, received Lee's surrender at Appomattox Court House.

A FAILURE at thirty-nine, at forty-one Grant was the most successful soldier of his generation. War was his element, but he had not suspected it. On the contrary, he hated warfare, was bored by army life and never read books on the military art. In the Mexican War he had been content to be side-tracked from the fighting line in the Quartermaster Department. That experience inclined him to be a contractor for supplying bread to the army at the outset of the Civil War, when the politicians refused to make him an officer.

The first time Grant came in sight of the enemy in the Civil War, his heart jumped into his throat. "I had not the moral courage," he said, "to halt and consider what to do; I kept right on."

That is the whole story of how Grant got to Appomattox: he kept right on. Starting without a friend at his back, and with only a long, unbroken trail of disappointments behind him, he never asked for promotion, an assignment or a favor; yet this unambitious man rose to be general-in-chief.

While some of our generals, posing as Napoleons, were parading, reviewing, polishing up brass buttons and patting down entrenchments, Grant went at once to taking towns and forts, to the dismay of his armchair superiors. Halleck took away his command in the midst of his victories. McClellan even suggested his arrest. It was easy for any envious desk-soldier to cast suspicion on the personal habits of an officer who had once been forced out of the army for drunkenness.

By his own admission, Sherman doubted at first a commander who was ignorant of books of strategy and history. He was soon reassured by the discovery that Grant's common sense supplied his lack of learning. Plenty of generals had books; but common sense won because it was so uncommon in the Civil War.

Fighting is the simplest thing in the world, whether with fists or with armies or with fleets. Instinct is the

true strategist. Grant's art of war was simplicity itself:
"Find out where your enemy is. Get at him as soon
as you can. Strike at him as hard as you can, and keep
moving on."

That is it: Grant kept moving on, sometimes, alas,
through slaughter, costly blunders, bloody mistakes.
Everywhere his watchwords were the same: "I propose to fight it out on this line if it takes all summer."
He kept going ahead on the principle that the sooner
the terrible business was finished the less bloodshed
there would be.

A shudder of horror ran through the Nation at the
frightful bills he sent back from Shiloh, Vicksburg and
the Wilderness. He was called a butcher. His rusty
private's blouse, his careless slouch and his sluggish
carriage lent him an air of roughness at first glance.
And the grim, changeless expression of his face as,
cigar in mouth, he silently looked on at slaughter, gave
an impression of indifference. Yet he quit the shelter
of his headquarters at Shiloh and slept in the mud and
rain to get out of sight and sound of the wounded and
dying.

Those of his staff who once found him flung face
downward on his camp bed in speechless agony knew
that this man behind his front of iron was not tough-
fibered after all. There was a feminine fineness in his
relations with Sherman and Sheridan, who formed with
him the trinity of success in the war. Never a shadow
of jealousy or distrust fell between them.

Such greatness as Grant had lay not so much in his
intellect as in his nature, not so much in his thoughts
as in his instincts. After sternly demanding the unconditional surrender of Fort Donaldson, and after its
fifteen thousand troops had laid down their arms at his

feet, "he left the officers of his own army," the Confederate commander of the fort tells us, "and followed
me, with that modest manner peculiar to himself, into
the shadow, and there tendered me his purse. . . .
He was afraid the light would witness that act of generosity and sought to hide it from the world." The
two foemen had been classmates at West Point, and
only eight years had passed since the victor had been
rescued from want in New York by this vanquished
general in gray, Simon Bolivar Buckner.

No conqueror ever was higher-souled than Grant at
Appomattox. Sad and depressed, as he tells us, at the
downfall of a valiant foe, he met Lee as if that foeman
in war were a neighbor in trouble. Shrinking from his
triumph, he had to be twice recalled by the Confederate
chieftain to the subject of their meeting, the naming of
his terms of peace.

These were as simple as they were unprecedented.
The soldiers of the South were hungry; they should be
fed. They were going home and would need their
horses for the spring plowing; they should take them.
Lee's hand moved toward his sword for the purpose
of surrendering it. Without a word Grant stopped
him by a silent wave of his own hand. The guns outside began to roar over the victory. The victor silenced
them, as he had hushed the cheers over the Confederates at Vicksburg. The great war was won; but the
noble conqueror turned away from Richmond without
entering the fallen capital.

III

GRANT IN THE WHITE HOUSE

(1869) March 4, Grant inaugurated President, aged forty-six.
September, "Black Friday" in Wall Street.—(1872) The "Ala-
bama" claims settled by arbitration. Grant re-elected. The
Credit Mobilier scandal exposed.—(1873) Sept. 19, great panic in
Wall Street.—(1874) April, Grant vetoed Inflation Bill. Decem-
ber, Resumption Act passed.—(1876) February, "Whisky Ring"
exposed. March, Belknap, Secretary of War, impeached.—(1877)
March 4, Grant retired from the Presidency.

WITH the passing of Lincoln, Grant towered above not
only all the other generals of the Civil War, but also
above the statesmen of that day, above even the great
political parties themselves. A man without a party,
he stood wholly for the Union. A magnanimous victor, aloof from the bitter passions of the men who had
only talked while others fought, he alone stood for the
reunion of North and South. It was less his fault than
the fault of our political system that he gave up to
party what was meant for all. There was no place for
him to serve, as there never is a place for any American to serve our Government in peace, except as a partisan and a politician.

When he became President, it was Grant's misfortune to know no one except his associates in the war.
The self-respecting among these kept away from him.
But the self-seekers and the camp followers crowded
about a man who never forgot and who never distrusted
a friend, not even when he came bearing a Greek gift,
and Senator Charles Sumner spoke scornfully of the
administration as a "gift enterprise."

The modest President and the conceited senator, who
plunged into a bitter feud, never were sympathetic.
When Grant heard some one say with surprise that

Sumner did not believe the Bible, he quietly remarked, "Well, he didn't write it."

Another little brood that preyed upon Grant's kindly disposition was composed of a few of his relatives and Mrs. Grant's. For them he laid himself open to a charge of nepotism, which was exaggerated but which no other President had incurred.

Grant's first act, in making up his Cabinet, was characteristic. Never having held a council of war or consulted any one in the army, he did not consult the Republican leaders. His Secretary of the Treasury, A. T. Stewart, the New York merchant, could not serve because the law debarred an importer from that office. His Secretary of the Navy was to fame unknown outside his city of Philadelphia. It took the mails three weeks to find in his obscurity an Attorney-General that the President appointed without knowing where the man lived. In selecting a Chief Justice, he pursued the same hit-or-miss plan and had to send in a third name before the Senate would give its assent.

Two of the seven places in the Cabinet were given to Galena, the President's little home town, the Secretaryship of State falling to Congressman Elihu B. Washburn and the Secretaryship of War to John A. Rawlins. There were sound personal reasons for the selection of Gen. Rawlins, who had been Grant's vigilant watchdog in the army, standing between him and the bottle and between his too trusting nature and false friends. These latter needed now more than ever to be warded off, and the untimely death of this frank and loyal friend early in the administration left a place which remained sadly vacant.

The many scandals of the administration were mostly traceable to the betrayal of Grant's childlike confidence in unworthy friends. "Black Friday" in Wall Street cast its shadow on his family circle itself. A brother-in-law had inveigled the guileless President into the net of Jim Fiske and Jay Gould, who attempted to corner gold on the strength of the inside information which they had wormed out of him. As quickly as Grant discovered the trick, he smashed the corner.

The "Whisky Ring" involved the President's private secretary. A member of the Cabinet was impeached for squalid transactions, but by accepting his resignation Grant let him dodge conviction.

The Civil War was followed by the most corrupt period in our political life. Rascally politicians noisily distracted the people from real evils with sham battles against the "rebel brigadier." The "bloody shirt" was made to cover a multitude of sins while patriots went in loudly for "the old flag and an appropriation."

Although Grant himself was above just suspicion, the next highest official, Vice-President Colfax, was driven into retirement under a cloud, and the third highest, the Speaker of the House, James G. Blaine, was accused of bartering his influence for private gain.

Reconstruction remained for ten years after the war a prolific source of political demoralization. Lincoln's plan having been torn up in the savage strife between Congress and Johnson, the Southern States were converted into rotten boroughs for political adventurers from the North and for the white riff-raff of the South. Out of the first batch of twelve Southern senators, ten were Northern "carpet baggers," who had rushed South to exploit the negro vote, and an even half of the congressmen were squatters from the North.

A liberal section of distinguished Republicans revolted against Grant's election to a second term, but they were mostly leaders without followers. The popular revolt did not come until the panic of 1873 had plunged the country into six years of hard times, and a tidal wave in the election of 1874 swept the Democrats into control of the House.

Great occasions aroused Grant to independent action in peace as in war. In vetoing a currency inflation bill, in calling for the resumption of specie payments and in the peaceable settlement of the "Alabama" claims against Great Britain—the first great international arbitration—he measured up to the expectations of the people, who never lost faith in the soundness of the man because he had failed as a politician. First in war, he did not prove himself first in peace; but deep down beneath the bitterness of parties and factions, Grant remained always, through good report and bad, first in the hearts of his countrymen.

IV

SLINGS AND ARROWS

(1877-9) Grant's tour of the world.—(1880) June, defeated for nomination for third term. Entered the firm of Grant & Ward, bankers, in New York.—(1884) Failure of Grant & Ward. Grant began to write his "Personal Memoirs." Afflicted with cancer of the throat.—(1885) March 4, The rank of General revived for him. July 23, died, aged sixty-three.

THE last scene of all that ends the strange, eventful history of Grant was the strangest . . . and most pathetic.

When a cry of Cæsarism was raised in Grant's second term, there appeared a little book, "The Coming Crown," which amusingly portrayed "the imperial family." Somehow the simple soldier President did not fit well into the picture as "Emperor Ulysses I." But the "Crown Prince Frederick," "Prince Jesse," and the other "Imperial Highnesses" were better suited to their absurd parts in this burlesque court at the White House.

The only member of the Presidential family who won much popular favor was Nellie Grant. Being a spirited, unconventional girl, Nellie was sent away from her throng of courtiers to give her time to mature in Europe. And she came home engaged to Algernon Sartoris, an Englishman whom she met on shipboard. The match was not at all to the liking of her fond father. After he had given her away in a brilliant White House wedding, he was found lying on his bed, his face buried in a pillow, a prey to grief.

When Grant left the White House, freed from public care for the first time in fifteen years, his uppermost wish was to visit this daughter in England, where he was surprised by the public welcome that greeted his arrival. He was "puzzled to find himself a personage," said James Russell Lowell. But his political friends were quick to see in his triumphs abroad a chance to restore their own prestige at home, and they urged him on until he had completed a tour of the world, which remains, perhaps, unequaled in brilliance. As he went his way from London to Tokio, emperors and kings honored him, marshals paraded their troops before him, statesmen consulted him. He bore himself amid all the splendid pageantry as simply as if he were an onlooking bystander.

Coming home after a three years' absence, he weakly yielded to the politicians, who were using his name in a desperate adventure to regain power for the "Stalwart" faction of the Republican party. But the wise, unwritten law against a third term was vindicated in his defeat in the Republican convention of 1880.

The simple truth is Grant was in need of employment.   After counting over his money after his long, costly trip, he saw, as he wrote to a friend, that he would have "to live in Galena or on a farm," . . . if not in the White house!

Failing the White House, he was tempted by a "young Napoleon of finance" into the whirlpool of New York and to become a partner in a Wall Street bank.   Into that blind venture he put what little money he had and most of all . . . his name.

The great but modest soldier had always a weakness for mere rich men, who had succeeded where he failed. Established in a big house in New York, with the money rolling in upon him under the conjuring tricks of his partner, the hero of Appomattox actually felt flattered by the thought that at last he was a "success" and could meet millionaires on a level!

After dwelling three years in that fools' paradise he was rudely awakened from his dream of wealth by the "young Napoleon's" request that he go borrowing from William H. Vanderbilt to save the bank from crashing.   He was lame from a fall on an icy street when the truth was broken to him, but he limped into the Fifth Avenue palace of the multi-millionaire and came out with one hundred and fifty thousand dollars.

As he entered the bank, two days later, he was met with the crushing news that the firm of Grant and Ward had gone down in a shameful failure.   Hours afterward a clerk found the broken man still sitting at his desk in silent despair, his head dropped forward, his hands gripping the arms of his chair.

The trial of the partner and of another man involved in the big swindle, which ended in their conviction and imprisonment, opened Grant's eyes to what a dupe he had been.   "I have made it a rule of my life," he grieved, "to trust a man long after other people gave him up; but I don't see how I can ever trust any human being again."

Had not a stranger, grateful for "services ending April, 1865," come instantly to his rescue, Grant would have been reduced to actual want in New York again, as he had been thirty years before, when he landed in the city an ex-army officer in disgrace. William H. Vanderbilt took from him the little real estate that he owned, even his swords, even the trophies of his victories in war and of his triumphs abroad. These lat-ter were afterward given to the Government and are now treasured in the National Museum at Washington, a melancholy reminder of an extraordinary pawn.

Out of bad came good. Grant opens his "Personal Memoirs" with a frank admission that he consented to write that great narrative only because he was living on borrowed money when a publisher proposed the undertaking. As he pursued his theme, he was gratified to discover an unsuspected gift for unfolding a moving tale of his adventures and achievements in the field. He wrote on until he had finished a story as imposing in its directness and simplicity as his own nature. And the first sales of it brought his wife, when he was gone, more money than all the earnings of his lifetime.

One day, in the midst of his writing, as he was eating a peach, he felt a stabbing pain in his throat. A deadly cancer had him in its clutch. With grim heroism, he fought it until he had completed the two volumes of his "Memoirs," although he was reduced to the necessity of whispering his dictation in the ear of a stenographer. Finally he was left speechless and had to write out the closing chapters on a pad in his lap.

At the coming of summer, he was taken to a cottage

on Mt. McGregor in upper New York. There he silently welcomed, as he sat on the piazza, the visitors who came to see him, among them Gen. Simon Bolivar Buckner. To that classmate at West Point and foeman at Fort Donelson, Grant gave his last message to his countrymen, a message of rejoicing that his sufferings had united North and South in a common sympathy.

RUTHERFORD BIRCHARD HAYES

I

ANOTHER DARK HORSE

(1822) Oct. 4, birth of Rutherford Birchard Hayes at Delaware, Ohio.—
(1842) Graduated at Kenyon College, Ohio.—(1843-45) In Harvard Law School.—(1852) Married Lucy Ware Webb.—(1858-60)
City Solicitor of Cincinnati.—(1861) Major in Ohio Volunteers.—
(1862) Lieutenant-colonel; wounded in Battle of South Mountain.
—(1863) Colonel.—(1864) Brigadier-general.—(1865-67) Member of Congress.—(1867-71) Governor of Ohio.—(1876-77) Governor.—(1876) June 15, nominated for President by Republican
National Convention at Cincinnati.

RUTHERFORD BIRCHARD HAYES' nomination for President in 1876 over James G. Blaine, Roscoe Conkling
and Oliver P. Morton took the country by surprise
almost as much as the earlier nominations of Polk and
Pierce. Yet the defeat of the favorites in the race
was quite in keeping with custom.

All parties for a generation had shown a tendency
to prefer the less-known over the better-known candidates. Fremont, the first Republican nominee, had
almost no political record, Grant had none at all, and
Lincoln was nominated over Seward only because he
had the shorter record.

The convention system always tends toward what
James Parton described as "the exquisite economy of
Nature, which ever strives to get into each place the
smallest man that can fill it." It simply missed its
calculation in Lincoln. Hayes also proved to be rather
more of a man than the politicians expected him to be.

Hayes had a geographical advantage, and the map

is unduly important in our politics. All the Presidents that the Republicans elected between Grant and Harding inclusive were Ohioans by birth, excepting only Roosevelt. It is doubtful if he ever would have been nominated for the Presidency if death had not promoted him to it in the first place.

Another consideration favored Hayes. Just as the old Democratic party, when it was under domination of the South, used to nominate "Northern men with Southern principles," the Republican party, as it became the representative of the business interests, resorted to the strategy of nominating Western men with Eastern principles.

Hayes was a transplanted Connecticut Yankee, whose people migrated westward by way of Vermont. By the accident of birth he was an Ohioan, but in blood, in temperament and in thought he was wholly a New Englander, a straight-laced Puritan in character and a scholar in tastes.

Like Jackson before him, he was a posthumous child, having been born ten weeks after his father's death. A rich bachelor uncle, Sardis Birchard, became a father to the fatherless boy; sent him to college in Ohio and to the Harvard Law School, finally leaving him his house and fortune, two years before the nephew's nomination for President.

This is no story of a running fight with poverty and ignorance. None of the Presidents has trod a straighter, a narrower or a smoother path to the White House. The story teller is thrown into despair at the outset by the assurance of one of Hayes' college mates, Stanley Matthews, that "he never got caught in any scrapes; he never had any boyish foolishness; he never had any wild oats to sow."

The child was father of the man. Hayes' life is

bare of personal anecdotes and dramatic contrasts. A lawyer and public man in the border city of Cincinnati in the stirring days before the Civil War; an officer in the volunteer army throughout the long conflict, where he was wounded in battle and where he gallantly commanded a division under Sheridan; in Congress for two terms in the turmoil of reconstruction; thrice elected Governor of Ohio in close, exciting contests . . . yet this man moved so noiselessly through all those great scenes that he was looked upon as an almost unknown actor on the National stage when he made his entry as a nominee for President. For twenty years he had been playing his several parts and always playing them fairly well, but without becoming a star or catching the spotlight.

When Ohio entered him as her favorite son, so little account was taken of him that other candidates permitted the convention to go to his State, thus repeating the mistake of the unsuspecting politicians who let the convention of 1860 go to Lincoln's State. Here is another parallel: a majority of the delegates when they arrived in Cincinnati in 1876 were for Blaine, just as a majority went to Chicago favorable to Seward. And Blaine lost the nomination, precisely as Seward lost it at Chicago, by an adjournment over night. If the ballot had been taken, as it properly should have been, while the convention was aglow from the eloquence of Robert G. Ingersoll's tribute to the "Plumed Knight," the convention would have been swept off its feet for the "Man from Maine." How many men have lost the Presidential nomination by just such a narrow mischance!

When the balloting came the next day, Hayes remained fourth and fifth through four ballots. He was nominated on the seventh only when the field was forced to combine upon some one in order to beat Blaine, who had risen to within thirty votes of victory.

Amid all the confusion and intriguing, the convention followed the cold logic of the situation. The Republican party was sadly divided by factions and badly discredited by scandals. Hayes had no part in any of the quarrels and no responsibility for the corruption at Washington.

Floundering in hard times, the country was tired of the old war cries and was ready to turn to new questions. The first of these was the currency, which had been inflated and demoralized by the war, and Hayes had carried Ohio for governor in the fall before on a hard money platform. He was the logical candidate for President, perhaps the only Republican who had any chance to win at the polls.

II

THE ONLY DISPUTED ELECTION

(1876) Nov. 7, Tilden, the Democratic candidate, elected President on the face of the returns. Nov. 8, the Republicans claimed Hayes' election.—(1877) Jan. 30, the electoral commission appointed. Feb. 26, the Wormley's Hotel Bargain between Republicans and Southern Democrats. March 1, Hayes started for Washington. March 2, declared elected. March 5, inaugurated President, aged fifty-four.

OUR political system was put to three severe tests in the brief course of fifteen years, and happily it weathered them all. The first and greatest was the Civil War. The impeachment of Andrew Johnson was the second. The third was the angry controversy over the Presidential election of 1876.

The tidal wave which swept down the Republicans in the Congressional election of 1874 still was running so strongly in the campaign of 1876 that Hayes himself never was confident of his success. Nor was the country surprised to read in the headlines the morning after election that Tilden, the Democratic candidate, had won the race.

The Republican national headquarters in New York city shut up shop early election night and the Republican campaign managers went to bed, resigned to defeat. While those politicians slept, four members of an editorial staff in New York still scanned the returns and debated the headline to be written for the waiting presses of the *Times*, then a Republican paper. One of them was stoutly insisting that the election should not be given up as lost when a telegram came in from the Democratic headquarters asking for information as to the result. That symptom of uncertainty in the camp of the supposed victors decided the question.

While the presses of the *Times* were roaring that the election was in doubt, a member of the little editorial council rushed over to the Fifth Avenue Hotel to cheer up the Republican headquarters. As he entered the hotel, he was well met by William E. Chandler, who was just coming in from his home in New Hampshire. Together they succeeded in arousing the sleeping chairman, Zach Chandler of Michigan, who made the wires hum and threw the country into a mad uproar the next day with this claim: "Hayes and Wheeler have one hundred and eighty-five votes and are elected."

The brilliant headliner of the Chicago *Times*, a Democratic paper, thus recorded in flaming type the fluctuations in the feelings of the Democrats in the first three bewildering days after the election: Wednesday, "Glory to God in the Highest"; Thursday, "Lord, We Believe"; Friday, "Let Us Pray."

Tilden was elected on the face of the returns, with

two hundred and three electoral votes to one hundred and sixty-six for Hayes, and he had also a plurality of two hundred and fifty thousand in the popular vote. His election indeed rested on the same basis as Cleveland's in 1884 and Wilson's in 1916. But in 1876 the Republicans had not yet acquiesced in the suppression of the negro vote in the South. And if the negroes had not been "persuaded," by various means, from going to the polls, Tilden could not have been elected.

Both the Republicans and the Democrats claimed to have carried Louisiana, South Carolina and Florida, and from those States two sets of returns were sent to Washington. Who should decide between them? The Constitution provides merely that the president of the Senate shall, in the presence of the Senate and House, open the certificates, "and the votes shall then be counted."

But when there are two sets of votes, who shall say which shall be counted? "The president of the Senate," answered the Republicans, because the president of the Senate was a Republican. "The two Houses," said the Democrats, because one of the Houses was Democratic.

This, indeed, had been the way of doing it. But even if that practice had been followed, the problem would not have been solved. The Republican Senate and the Democratic House never would have agreed. The result would have been . . . two Presidents or no President at all, presumably with Grant holding on to the White House by main strength.

Compromise was necessary to save the Government from chaos and the country from another civil war. The bitter dispute was left to fifteen men, one-third of whom were senators and another third were representatives, equally divided between the parties. To guarantee a calm, judicial decision the remaining third were justices of the Supreme Court.

Nevertheless, the commission proceeded to decide every essential question in favor of Hayes by a strict party vote of eight to seven. Alas, the partisan zeal of that feverish hour burned just as fiercely beneath the gowns of the justices as under the frock coats of the legislators, and only two of the five men drawn from the court had Democratic antecedents.

The judgment of the commission was without force in law until adopted by the two opposing Houses, and some disappointed Democrats in the House balked at ratifying the decision against Tilden. But representatives of Hayes whispered to certain Southern Democrats in a secret conference at Wormley's Hotel in Washington that if they would let the Republicans have the Presidency, the Republican President would let them have their own State Governments. The bargain having been struck, it was kept. After a turbulent night session of the House, the result of the election was declared at four o'clock in the morning of March 2, 1877, just fifty-six hours before the inauguration.

For three months Hayes himself had been alternating from day to day between expectations of success and defeat. Even when he started for Washington on March 1, he was still so uncertain that he frankly told the people of Columbus in his parting speech that he might be back with them and in the governor's chair again in less than a week.

This President-elect had passed through an ordeal such as had tried none of his predecessors, and he passed through it with becoming self-restraint. It was a strange ordeal also for the country. The capacity for self-government is measured by the readiness of men and parties and interests to compromise, to sacrifice, even to abide a momentary evil for the sake of the longer good.   The American people had stood that acid test.

III

A NEW EPOCH

(1877) April, President Hayes withdrew federal troops from Southern State capitals. Banished alcoholic liquors from the White House. June and July, ordered out federal troops in the great railway strike.—(1878) Vetoed Silver bill, which was passed over his veto.—(1879) Specie payments resumed.—(1893) Jan. 17, death of Hayes, aged seventy.

"HE serves his party best who serves his country best." . . . With those watchwords Hayes sacrificed himself and his administration to reunite North and South, to cleanse the Civil Service and to regenerate the Republican party.   So quietly, so coldly, so undramatically did he go about all those great objects that he remained to the end of his term one of the most misunderstood, most underestimated Presidents, the Republican leaders hating him as an apostate and the Democrats despising him as a fraud.

He selected one of the most distinguished Cabinets in history.   But he did it without consulting party leaders or considering the claims of factions, and the offended Senate threatened and muttered for nearly a week before it confirmed the nominations.   To the disgust of "practical politicians" he "threw away" a high-class foreign mission on a man like James Russell Lowell, "a dashed literary feller," as Senator Simon Cameron said.   He enraged Roscoe Conkling by flinging the political machine of that imperious senator out of the federal offices in New York City.   He would also have made a start toward the removal of the civil service from politics and spoils-mongering had not both parties combined in Congress to thwart his every effort in that direction.

Hayes' boldest challenge to the Republican politicians was his abandonment of their twelve-year struggle to reconstruct the Southern States from Washington. Ever since Congress had seized from Lincoln's lifeless hand the control of reconstruction, the entire proceeding had been a tragic failure, creating an orgy of corruption and violence in the South and demoralizing the politics of the whole Union.

It was an attempt, so common in this country, to solve by mere political methods a problem that was not at all political. The fatuous politicians at Washington gave the ballot to the negro in the expectation of setting up Republican States in the South, but they did not give a cent of money with which to educate him to read the ballot and to see that it was counted. They gravely invested him with equal civil rights at law, but they left him economically unequal and a dependent on the whites. When he asked for "forty acres and a mule," they only laughed at him. Yet it was the one thing he needed first of all . . . and surely he had earned it by his "two hundred and fifty years of unrequited toil."

Inevitably the educated and propertied whites wrested the Government from the hands of an illiterate and penniless race in State after State. When Hayes came in, there were only two Republican State Governments remaining in the South, and he promptly withdrew the federal bayonets that were propping up those feeble survivors in South Carolina and Louisiana. Thereupon they collapsed in an hour, and their imported governors, hurriedly repacking their carpet bags, returned North by the next train.

Hayes had merely completed the reconstruction of the Southern States on Lincoln's plan. Unfortunately it was too late to make it the same healing measure that the great emancipator had designed it to be. For unlimited negro suffrage had been thrust into the Constitution, contrary to Lincoln's advice, with the evil result that a solid South continues to plague the Nation.

Hayes came to the Presidency in the depths of an industrial prostration, when wandering bands of tramps thronged the highways of the land, and soon the first great railway strike paralyzed transportation between the Atlantic and the Mississippi. In response to the popular cry for "more money," both parties in Congress were for repealing or modifying the resumption act and for inflating the currency with greenbacks or silver coinage. The President firmly resisted such a surrender. Had not his veto of the Silver Bill been overridden, he would have saved the country from taking the first step on the road that led it to the brink of free silver in 1896.

All that independence cost Hayes the support of the political time servers and the applause of the partisan press. These united in denouncing and ridiculing him as a renegade in politics and as a sniveling hypocrite in private life.

Both Mr. and Mrs. Hayes were more devotional in their religion than any other tenants of the White House. The day was regularly opened with all the household kneeling at morning prayers, and often the evenings were given over to the singing of the familiar old hymns.

The White House "went dry" for the first time under the Hayes', and the President was held up to contempt as a man too stingy to stand treat and too weak to resist a domineering wife. Senator Conkling's lips curled into a sneer as he portrayed the henpecked husband taking a furtive drink behind the door or secretly quenching his thirst with "loaded" oranges.

It was true that the White House chef, perhaps at the instigation of some of the bibulous Cabinet, relieved the arid situation at first by serving Roman punch in oranges at the State banquets, a refreshing course which Secretary Evarts hailed as the "life-saving station" in the long, formal dinners. When Mr. and Mrs. Hayes discovered the trick, they ordered the cook to turn the joke on the guests, by giving the ice a rummy flavor but without putting in a drop of rum. Whether the Presidential couple, smiling behind their napkins, or those who continued to smack their lips over this item in the menu were really fooled, history saith not.

Robert G. Ingersoll said that Hayes went in by one majority and came out unanimously. Nevertheless, the Republican party was so discredited in 1876 that it was unable to get an undisputed majority even of one. At the end of the Hayes administration it was strong enough to carry the country in 1880 and inaugurate a President with a clear title.

Hayes found the North and South divided and he left them more nearly reunited than they had been in a generation. He found the national currency paper and he left it gold and silver. He found the prosperity of the country at dead low tide and he left it at high tide.

It fell to Hayes to ring down the curtain on the epoch of the Civil War and to usher in another epoch. The voices of the past cried out against him; but in his complete retirement from politics he lived to hear the voices of the new time give a more favorable and a more just verdict on his administration.

JAMES ABRAM GARFIELD

I

THE LAST OF THE LOG CABIN PRESIDENTS

(1831) Nov. 19, James Abram Garfield born at Orange, Ohio—(1856) Graduated from Williams College.—(1858-61) President of Hiram College.—(1858) Married Lucretia Rudolph.—(1860) Member of Ohio Senate. Admitted to the bar.—(1861) Colonel in Ohio Volunteers.—(1862) Brigadier-general.—(1863) Major-general.—(1863-80) In Congress.—(1880) Elected to the Senate.

JAMES ABRAM GARFIELD was the latest, it is fairly safe to say the last, of the Presidents born and bred in log cabins. Notwithstanding that humble start, he was one of the half-dozen scholarly men who have sat in the Presidential chair.

Both the paternal Garfields and the maternal Ballous, the forbears of this Ohio President, were New Englanders and among the best types of Yankee yeomanry. His struggling, laborious youth and young manhood made Garfield also a representative of that greater New England which spread itself over the upper half of the Middle West.

When the boy was only two, his pioneer father died fighting a forest fire, leaving "four young saplings," as he called them, to the care of his wife, who had to carry on the frontier farm alone and face alone the problems of bringing up her two boys and two girls. With the help of her elder son in the field and of her elder daughter in the cabin, she raised the food for her little brood, and grew and wove and sewed the wool

197

that clothed them.   More than that, she was their teacher, too, cultivating their young minds and training up their characters.   Among all the widows' sons in the Presidency, none owed more to his mother than the son of Eliza Ballou Garfield; and none began earlier to pay his debt, nor kept on paying it more faithful and gratefully.

A big, strong, hardy boy, "Jim" Garfield had to work his way in the world from the age of ten or twelve.   Chopping wood at seventy-five cents a cord and his board; driving mules on the towpath of a canal or serving as deckhand on the boat itself at ten dollars a month and keep; haying, harvesting, carpentering and teaching school, he put himself through academies and through college.

He also won a wife along the way.   In a co-educational academy, which he attended, he met and wooed Lucretia Rudolph.   After his graduation at Williams College, he faithfully returned to claim his "Crete," and their marriage is the first—doubtless it will not be the last—romance of "co-eds" in the matrimonial story of the Presidency.

In his preparatory school, which afterward became Hiram College, Garfield was janitor at first, until it was discovered that he could teach the other pupils English literature just as well as he could tend the fires, draw the water, sweep the floors, wash the windows and ring the bell.   Poverty is a good grindstone for putting a sharp edge on the few who happen to have the tempered steel in them; but it sadly dulls the many.

Garfield's was a long, rough road to an education. But it insured him a keen thirst at the end, and when at last he arrived at Williams College back in his ancestral Massachusetts, a big, blonde-bearded man of twenty-five, he was ready to drink dry that fountain of learning. He used to say that his ideal of a college was a pine log, with Mark Hopkins (the president of Williams) sitting on one end of it and himself on the other.

If he had stayed in New England, Garfield would have been a professor or a preacher. He became both after returning home; but every man in Ohio is, or at least used to be, a politician also. He was principal of his old academy at Hiram and doing more or less lay preaching in the pulpit of the Christian or "Campbellite" church, when he was elected to the State Senate. He was still serving in those varied capacities when he led a regiment to the front at the outbreak of the Civil War.

With his lifelong habit of study, the green colonel went to war with a sword in one hand and a book on the military art in the other. Soon he knew something of the principles of his new job, and this enabled him to rise more rapidly than the other political colonels.

Before he smelled powder or came in sight of the enemy he was placed in command of a brigade and ordered to chase the Confederates out of the Kentucky mountains. At thirty he was the youngest brigadier in the army. After Shiloh he became chief of staff to Gen. Rosecrans, and for a bold expedition, which he led through the enemy's country after the battle of Chickamauga, he was made major-general.

Entering Congress at the end of 1863, he became in due time chief of staff to James G. Blaine, the Republican leader of the House. He proved himself a brilliant lieutenant in peace as in war; but he did not develop the qualities of independent leadership. He was too fair, too moderate a partisan and rather too amiable, too soft or too considerate to be able to play that part in those swashbuckling days at Washington. Nor did he have the strength to keep himself wholly clear of the shadow of suspicion that fell upon so many public men in a period when fine moral scruples were blunted in the rough combats of politics.

While he was a member of Congress and on a visit to New York, Lincoln was assassinated, and the event inspired one of Garfield's most memorable and eloquent speeches. The great city was dazed and trembling from the shock, when a meeting was held in Wall Street for the purpose of calming and steadying the people. Standing on the granite steps of the Sub-Treasury, where George Washington had taken the oath of office, the tall, broad-shouldered, yellow-haired, yellow-bearded congressman from Ohio lifted up the spirits of the angry and the despairing in the bewildered multitude that surged at his feet, by appealing to their faith in a great overruling power:

"Clouds and darkness are around Him; His pavilion is dark waters and thick clouds; justice and judgment are the habitation of His throne; mercy and truth shall go before His face! Fellow citizens, God reigns and the Government at Washington still lives!"

II

THE ONLY PRESIDENT TO SEE HIMSELF NOMINATED

(1880) June 7, James A. Garfield nominated for President by Republican Convention. November, elected President.

GARFIELD is the only President who was present at his own nomination. The Presidential lightning struck him as he sat in his seat in that most extraordinary and exciting National Convention which met at Chicago in 1880.

After many great wars in history, partisan bands have kept up the strife for years in the form of brigandage, asserting the right to "live off the country" that they had fought to save. In our unmilitary but very political country, those bands after the Civil War went into politics, instead of taking to the saddle and the highway. They thrived on the spoils of office and in legislative jobbery, clans or factions springing up in many Northern States to battle for the control of the patronage and the special favors of legislation.

Although the Hayes administration had marked the end of that epoch, the clansmen refused to disband, and they made their last stand in the Republican National Convention of 1880. All the "Stalwart" clans, believing with a St. Louis editor that there was "one more President in the bloody shirt," seized upon the great name of Grant. Under the banner of the "Hero of Appomattox," they rallied against the "Half Breeds," who followed "the Plumed Knight," James G. Blaine of Maine. It was a wonderful battle; but its true object on both sides was given away by delegate Flanagan of Texas, when he blurted out in open convention, "What are we here for, if not for the offices?"

The rival champions in that remarkable tournament at Chicago were Roscoe Conkling, chieftain of the "Stalwarts," and James A. Garfield of Ohio, the spokesman of the "Half Breeds," although he was restrained from directly supporting Blaine by the instructions of his State in favor of the nomination of John Sherman. A handsome fop, Conkling carefully studied the right moment to make his theatrical entry upon the stage the first day. As he advanced down the aisle, he drew applause by his "grandiloquent swell, his majestic supereminent, overpowering, turkey gobbler strut," which Blaine had held up to the laughter of Congress years before in a never-to-be-forgiven speech. The next day Garfield took his revenge by entering while Conkling was speaking, and the welcoming cheers drowned the voice of the indignant speaker. On the third day the two came to grips in a debate, and the Ohioan scored on the New Yorker.

While the crowd still was cheering the victor in that round, Conkling wrote on the margin of a newspaper and sent to Garfield a mocking suggestion that he was playing to the gallery in his own interest: "I congratulate you on being a dark horse!"

In truth Garfield could not rise in the convention without helping himself more than he helped his candidate, John Sherman, who never had a chance to win. As ballot after ballot was taken, it became plain that neither could the "immortal 306," who followed Grant, overcome the prejudice against a third term in the White House. And it was made equally plain that this "Old Guard" never would surrender to Blaine.

A new candidate was necessary if the convention was not to fall to pieces in factions. One solitary vote for Garfield on most of the ballots had continued to point the finger of destiny at him. Wisconsin pointed all her fingers in his direction, when her delegation broke to him on the thirty-fourth ballot.

Garfield rose, with pallid face and dry lips, to a point of order. Senator Hoar of Massachusetts, who was in the chair, rapped him down. In two more ballots, he was nominated by a combination of the Blaine and Sherman men.

In the midst of the uproar, the nominee sat limp and perspiring in his seat. "Get me out of here," he faintly whispered to his seatmate, Ex-Gov. Foster of Ohio. Foster pushed him through the clamorous crowd in the hall into a wilder crowd in the street. There he tumbled the agitated candidate into a public hack, the top of which was frantically torn away, before the driver could whip his horses out of the mass of yelling, curious people who never before had seen a man struck by Presidential lightning.

The Garfield campaign opened badly. The "Stalwarts" sulked in their tents, and the effort to "fire the Northern heart" with the old war cries against the South had been made difficult by President Hayes' policy of reconciliation.

The Democrats had been carrying the country at every election for six years, and the September election in Maine foreshadowed another victory for them in the national election in November. But the bankers—"Wall Street"—took alarm, because the Democrats had won in Maine by a coalition with the Greenbackers, and they aroused the business interests to take a hand in the campaign. Those powerful forces brought the "Stalwarts" and "Half Breeds" together and compelled Conkling, Grant and the disaffected leaders to go to the rescue of Garfield.

The office-holders also were warned of their peril of being turned out, and the assessments on them helped to swell the biggest campaign fund in history up to that time. Garfield himself anxiously inquired of the chief collector at Washington, "How are the departments doing?"

It was the first of our national campaigns in which money talked out loud. The tide was turned in the October election in Indiana, as Chester A. Arthur frankly chuckled, "by a great deal of——" here the Vice-President-elect paused, silently washing his hands in invisible soap, and then he ironically added, " . . . tracts and political documents."

A more worthy aid to victory was supplied by Gen.

Garfield. His managers introducing for the first time the "front porch" method of campaigning, shipped crowds to his simple village home at Mentor, near Cleveland, where his daily chats, graceful and tactful, delighted his listeners and won the admiration of the reading public.

III

THE ASSASSINATION OF GARFIELD

(1881) March 4, James A. Garfield inaugurated President, aged forty-nine. March 23, sent to the Senate the nominations of federal officers in New York City. May 16, the Senate confirmed the nominations. May 17, Senators Conkling and Platt resigned. July 2, Garfield shot by Charles J. Guiteau in the Baltimore & Potomac railway station at Washington. Sept. 6, removed to Elberon, N. J. Sept. 19, died, aged fifty.—(1882) June 30, Guiteau hanged.

JAMES A. GARFIELD fell a sacrifice to the spirit of faction and of the spoils system. Although this gentle, kindly man hardly was of the heroic stuff out of which martyrs are made, his blood became the seed of better things in our politics.

Rarely has a President taken up the burden of the office with a larger measure of good will from the people, regardless of party and of faction, than flowed out to Garfield as he stood on the steps of the Capitol in the sunshine of his inaugural day, the picture of robust American manhood in its prime. His first kiss, after kissing the Bible in the presence of a multitude of witnesses, was for the aged mother, who in a forest hut had started him on his way to the White House and who held a place of honor beside the schoolmate sweetheart, who had been his faithful companion all along the road.

" 'One thing thou lackest yet,' and that is a slight

ossification of the heart," John Hay had written to the President-elect. It was a fatal lack. Had his heart been harder, Garfield would have made his administration wholly his own, lifting it above factions, and he might have lived through a prosperous term. Instead, he remained his few months in the White House what he had been in Congress, a lieutenant of Blaine, whom he appointed to the Secretaryship of State—"with the love of a comradeship of eighteen years"—and who became at once the power behind the throne.

It was a saying of Emerson that "the President pays dear for his White House." Garfield quickly found it a purchase of repentance and doubtless longed for the seat in the Senate, to which he had been elected only a few months before his nomination for the Presidency.

The only President, until Harding, to step directly from the Capitol to the White House, he was without executive experience or tastes. His whole training had been to debate and compromise, not to act or decide on his sole responsibility.

A lover of poetry and of all things beautiful and a constant student of literature, he groaned under the rude jostling of a sordid mob of office-seekers (an assassin among them). A genial soul who hated to say no, he found himself saying yes when he should not. "My God!" he exclaimed in bitterness of spirit, "what is there in this place that a man should ever want to get into it?"

Garfield himself was rather indifferent to factions, liking to get along with all men. He appreciated Conklings' reluctant but timely support in the campaign and invited him out to Mentor in the Winter to talk over the New York patronage. He thought of inviting him into the Cabinet itself, until Blaine whispered no.

Less than three weeks after he took his seat, Garfield

told the senator that he was not yet ready to consider the question of filling the New York offices. Only forty-eight hours afterward, he filled them, nominating for the highest of those offices Blaine's best friend and Conkling's worst enemy in New York.

With Garfield's hand, Blaine had thrown down the gauntlet to the haughty chieftain of the "Stalwart" clan, and a duel of factions was on in blind fury. The administration succeeded in beating Conkling in the Senate, where he opposed the confirmation of the offensive nominee. But the senator and his colleague, Thomas C. Platt, resigned their seats and appealed to the New York legislature to re-elect them as a vindication of their course. That sensational act shifted the battle to Albany, where Vice-President Arthur joined the two resigned "Stalwarts" in a desperate, no-quarter struggle with the "Half Breeds."

When the conflict was bitterest and when the "Stalwarts" were losing at Albany, a disappointed place hunter at Washington, Charles J. Guiteau, conceived the mad idea of saving the situation with a pistol shot, and he posted himself at the railway station, where his victim was to take a train for Massachusetts. The President was going back to Williams College, the goal of his struggling youth, and lay his honors at the feet of his alma mater. At a dare from one of his sons that morning he had leaped over his bed in the White House, and he was still smiling, like a boy off for a vacation, as he entered the waiting room at the railway station, with Blaine at his side. In two flashes of a revolver he fell forward on the floor.

With a shout of triumph, the assassin proclaimed the wild motive of his deed: "I am a Stalwart! Arthur is now President!" It is unnecessary to say that the "Stalwarts" had no more knowledge of Guiteau's

purposes than the Confederates had of Booth's.   But
just as the conflict of sections had crazed the one, the
other had been crazed by the frenzied quarrels of the
factions over a division of spoils.

The country was not only shocked but humiliated to
see this genial, sunny-hearted President of the republic shot down, as Henry Watterson said, like a dog or
a czar.   Through more than eleven weeks, for seventy-
nine days, a whole people, made kin by a touch of
nature, anxiously watched by his bedside.   When, at
last, the long, unequal fight was lost, sympathetic hearts
followed the wasted body to its native soil by the shore
of Lake Erie.

After twenty years in our meagerly paid public service, Garfield had left his wife and children hardly better
off than his mother and her little family had been left
at the untimely death of his father.   A grateful people
eagerly welcomed the opportunity to pay tribute to his
memory by providing a fund for the good woman, who
was to continue to bear his name through nearly forty
years of widowhood and for the education of sons who
were to wear it worthily.

CHESTER ALAN ARTHUR

I

THE MAN WHO FOUND HIMSELF

(1830) Oct. 5, Chester Alan Arthur born at Fairfield, Vt.—(1848) Graduated at Union College.—(1853) A lawyer in New York City.—(1859) Married Ellen Lewis Herndon, daughter of a commander in the navy.—(1861-2) Quartermaster-general of New York State.—(1871-8) Collector of the Port of New York; removed by Hayes.—(1880) January, death of his wife. November, Arthur elected Vice-President.—(1881) Sept. 19, took the oath as President, aged fifty.

THE public anxiety for Garfield through his long battle with death was deepened by a general dread of the Vice-President succeeding to the Presidency. The people as a whole knew nothing of Chester Alan Arthur, except that he had been only lately removed from the collectorship of the port of New York as a machine politician and that he had been nominated for the Vice-Presidency as a henchman of Roscoe Conkling.

He had practiced law in New York City for a quarter of a century without winning distinction at the bar. Even in the upheaval of the Civil War, he remained in comparative obscurity as the quartermaster-general of the State.

After the war he rose to be the Republican boss of New York City, with his headquarters in the Customhouse. True to the type, he preferred to remain always the man behind the scenes, making few speeches and never becoming a candidate for an elective office, until his nomination for the second highest office in the land.

If Arthur had not been put out of the Customhouse he never would have got into the White House. When Garfield was nominated in the Chicago convention, the victorious "Half Breeds" offered the second place on the ticket to the disgruntled "Stalwarts," like a bone thrown to a growling dog. Arthur whispered to Conkling that he would like it, and his chief carelessly tossed it to him. The ex-collector wanted the nomination as a vindication for his removal by President Hayes.

After Arthur had been sitting in the Vice-President's chair only a little more than two weeks, he opened a big White House envelope one day and flushed as he glanced at the unexpected contents—the nomination of a hated "Half Breed" to the collectorship of the port of New York. With an excited gesture, he summoned Senators Conkling and Platt, and the three "Stalwarts" flamed up with rage at the challenge to them from the new administration. When the New York senators resigned their seats and appealed to the Legislature of their State to re-elect them as a protest against the administration, the spectacle of the Vice-President descending to that mêlée lent color to the already unfavorable impression of him in the public mind.

When in the midst of the fight that was going against the resigned senators, Garfield was shot, the American people revolted at the thought that Arthur and the "Stalwarts" should profit by the assassination. The public mind revolted also at the prospect of a political boss enthroned in the White House, with his motley following about him.

That popular picture of Arthur, as a city politician out of the pages of *Puck,* was distorted and untrue, simply because the background was omitted from it. The real, the native character of the man had been shaped in surroundings very different from those in which the

country found him when he first came under its attention. Born in Vermont to a Baptist minister, a man of
education and high principles, who had come over from
Ireland and who soon afterward settled in New York
State, Arthur had grown up in village parsonages,
where the living was plain and the thinking high.

The father belonged to that moral and intellectual
aristocracy of Abolitionists, who braved the contempt
of wealth and the persecution of the thoughtless for the
sake of an ideal. The son had received an education in
a rural college and had plodded his way to the bar by
teaching country schools. That was the good American mold in which the man had been cast in his form-
ative period. His political experience had been only
an incident of his environment in New York City.

When the great test came and he stood silently for
three months in the shadow of the high office, Arthur
found himself, and he left petty politics and factions
behind him as he entered the White House. The public was incredulous at first, but was convinced at last
that he honestly meant to be President of all the people.

Some of his old associates in machine politics were as
astonished at the change that had come over their
"Chet" as Falstaff and his cronies were when Prince
Hal became King Henry V. Not that the new President coldly repelled the claims of friendship. He simply put first his obligations to the whole country, though
it cost him dear in the regard of men like Grant and
Conkling, who set him down as an ingrate.

"Why, general, if you were still president of the
New York County Republican Committee, you would
be here right now asking for this very thing," protested
the head of that organization.

"As president of the New York County Republican
Committee," Arthur frankly admitted with a smile, "I

certainly would; but since I came here I have learned that Chester A. Arthur is one man and the President of the United States is another."

He looked as well as acted the President. The first city man in a line of rural or small town men, Arthur was the best dressed man to sit in the chair since Washington, and perhaps the handsomest, with a tall, graceful figure, the manners of the great world and a grave but easy courtesy.

Although he was a widower President, his sister, Mrs. McElroy, was a charming mistress of the White House, and under them the social life of the mansion took on a more sumptuous tone. His son and namesake was away at school much of the time, but his little daughter, Nellie Arthur, lit up the household with song and laughter.

Mrs. Arthur died only the year before her husband's unexpected rise to the Presidency, and her absence from his side was a haunting sorrow to Arthur. He had ordered that everything in her room in their New York house on Lexington Avenue, even to the needle in her unfinished sewing, should remain just as she had left it, and the loyal husband kept the room always as a shrine to her memory.

II

AN ERA OF REFORM

(1883) Jan. 16, Arthur signed the Civil Service Law.—(1884) Defeated for the Republican nomination by Blaine.—(1886) Nov. 18, died, aged fifty-six.

IT is one of the pranks of fate that Chester A. Arthur, whom President Hayes put out of the New York Customhouse as a spoilsman and a political boss, should find himself in the White House, only seven months

after Hayes left it, and conducting a reform administration. It was the mandate and lesson of Garfield's
assassination that we must get rid of factions and
spoils or the Government itself might next be struck
down, as its chief had been. Arthur saw that this was
the logic of the tragedy which had thrust him into the
Presidency and he did his best to clean house.

The new President ventured only once to play his
favorite game of politics, when he received such a corrective rap on the knuckles that he kept his hand out of
it thenceforth. The next year after coming to the
Presidency he interfered with the Republican nomination for Governor of New York and dictated the choice
of a candidate. He made a good selection; but the people were in such a state of sensitiveness that they buried
the administration nominee under an unprecedented
majority for the Democratic candidate, Grover Cleveland.

At the same time a national tidal wave submerged
the Republicans and swept them out of the control of
the House. They were sadder and wiser when the old
Congress reassembled for its closing short session.
With breathless haste they rushed through the Civil
Service Law, which Grant, Hayes and Arthur in turn
had been vainly recommending in their messages.

The evils of the spoils system, which Jackson had
inaugurated fifty years before and which had been fostered by all parties, had grown with the growth of the
Civil Service. Our politics had degenerated into a
scramble for offices, and the distribution of patronage
had become the principal business of Presidents, senators and representatives.

The parceling out of jobs weighed as heavily on his
successors as it weighed on Lincoln, when his troubled
look one day led an anxious person to ask him if some

disaster had befallen our army. "No," the President explained, "it is not the war that is bothering me; it is the appointment of a postmaster for Browntown, Ind."

The race for preferment excited an unnatural appetite for public office, and the getting of a job was regarded as an exhilarating sport. From policeman, fireman and letter carrier to chief clerkship and consulship, every place on the payroll of city, state or nation went by favor. Two endless processions were forever moving, one made up of those who had been turned out or turned down and the other of those who were struggling to get in.

Senators and representatives in Washington regularly made the morning rounds of the departments in quest of places for a hungry crowd of hangers-on, who dogged their footsteps night and day. A member no sooner lost his seat in Senate or House than his successor pushed out his predecessor's favorites and pushed in his own.

"My influence is dead," a poor scrubwoman in the Treasury wailed to Senator Hoar, when her backer in Congress died, leaving her face to face with the prospect of being replaced by some one with a live "influence." The system bred spoils-mongers instead of statesmen, and these delighted in quartering their strikers and workers on the Government, who remained at the beck and call of the senators and representatives in every fight at home and who were required to pay two per cent of their annual salaries to the campaign fund of the party in power.

The Civil Service Law, which was passed in Arthur's administration, took out of politics the departmental clerkship in Washington, but eighty-five per cent of the federal employees as a whole were left under the spoils system. Nevertheless, the difficult first step had been taken toward the present comprehensive system, when all but a few hundred of the hundreds of thousands of permanent places are open equally to self-respecting applicants, regardless of parties or politicians.

Arthur also was the useful instrument of carrying forward the reconciliation of the sections. He was the first President in his generation who made no reference in his annual messages to the South or to a Southern question. He was indeed almost the first President in fifty years who felt free to ignore the unhappy issues of sectionalism.

When he stepped into the White House, Arthur found his party rent by faction. He left it more nearly united than it had been before in twenty years and with at least a chance to win again in 1884. He might himself have been the Republican nominee in that year if he had not scrupulously refused to take an active part in promoting his candidacy for the nomination.

Declining to remove the collector of the Port of New York, whom Garfield had appointed against his protest, he even permitted that officeholder to leave his post and oppose him in the contest at the National Convention. No other President has done so little to obtain a second term.

It was fortunate, not only for the sake of the high example he set, but for his own sake also. Arthur's health was not equal to the strain of another administration and another term in the White House, where perhaps he lived not wisely but too well. In less than two years after leaving the Presidency, followed by the good will of all the people, he was dead of apoplexy.

GROVER CLEVELAND

I

FROM OBSCURITY TO THE WHITE HOUSE IN THREE YEARS

(1837) March 18, Stephen Grover Cleveland born at Caldwell, N. J. (1841) His family removed to New York State.—(1854) An office boy in a Buffalo law office.—(1859) Admitted to the bar.—(1863) Assistant district attorney of Erie County.—(1865) Defeated for district attorney.—(1870) Elected sheriff.—(1881) Elected mayor of Buffalo.—(1882) Elected governor.—(1884) Elected President.

No OTHER man has stepped so quickly from obscurity to the Presidency as Grover Cleveland. When Garfield stood on the steps of the Capitol to be inaugurated, he never had heard the name of this Buffalo attorney, who was to stand in the same place four years afterward.

At forty-five Cleveland remained unknown outside his county. Before he was forty-eight he was in the White House.

It was a swift rise. Yet this man was no feathered Mercury. Slow of mind, with a narrow range of reading and of intellectual interests, Cleveland was stolid in manner and without brilliant qualities. But he had a character as rugged and immovable as a mountain. It had been built up in rural parsonages, where his father, a Presbyterian minister, was required to rear a large family and set an example to the community on six hundred dollars a year.

At the early death of his father, Stephen Grover, who simplified his name by dropping the first part of it, had to leave school and shift for himself. First he clerked in a village store at fifty dollars a year; next he taught in an asylum for the blind, and finally swept out a law office in Buffalo at four dollars a week, until he had industriously swept a path for himself to the bar.

For more than a quarter of a century he plodded along in Buffalo, a quiet, laborious, trusted, but not distinguished lawyer. Unmarried and without family or a home, he took no part in the social life of his community, where a hundred other Buffalonians may have been better known to their fellow-townsmen.

He had been an assistant district-attorney of Erie County and also its sheriff. But the first that was ever heard of him outside his neighborhood were his sledge-hammer vetoes from the mayor's office only two years before his election to the Presidency. The whole State of New York stopped to listen to his resounding whacks and next the whole country took notice.

Being mayor of Buffalo never would have made Cleveland famous; but being an honest mayor of any city in the United States at that time, a Mayor who had the courage of his honesty, was a distinction unfortunately rare. Almost everywhere partisanship was blindfolding the people while municipal rings and gangs picked their pockets of franchises, contracts and privileges for predatory interests—railway, street car and gas companies, contractors, and the petty criminals of the underworld.

It chanced in that particular year that two "big men" were dividing the votes of the Democratic State Convention for governor, and the "little fellow," this "veto mayor," slipped in between them. The Republicans had put up a machine-made ticket, and Cleveland personified the issue. He did not have to make a cam-

paign speech; his vetoes spoke for him, and he was
elected by 192,000 plurality, the biggest in the records
of New York up to that time.

After voting on election day, he sat down in the certainty of victory and wrote a letter to his brother. It
is a letter which reveals a side of the man that he never
turned to the public, and that is always the real side of
any public man. "I am honest and sincere in my desire
to do well," he wrote; "but the question is whether I
know enough to accomplish what I desire. . . . If
mother were alive, I should feel much safer. I have
always thought that her prayers had much to do with
my success."

Cleveland's two years in the governorship at Albany
were only an enlargement of his few months in the
mayorality of Buffalo. His promotion to the Presidency followed naturally.

In vain Tammany Democrats objected to his nomination for President. To their objections in the Chicago Convention of 1884, Gen. Bragg of Wisconsin
shouted: "We love him for the enemies he has made."

The theatrical rise of this man was not a mere ca-
price, a blind stroke of luck. On the contrary, he was
nominated and elected President because he was the
logical, commonsense choice; because this unknown, unambitious lawyer of Buffalo had become in two swift
years, the most conspicuous embodiment of the things
that the times called for—independence in politics and
a higher standard of conduct in office.

The national campaign of 1884 sank to a new low
level of mudslinging, when a great people seemed reduced to a humiliating choice between common honesty
and common decency. Inscribing on their banners,
"Public Office is a Public Trust," the Democrats bom-
barded the public character of Blaine, the Republican

candidate, with his "Mulligan letters," in which that thrifty statesman had sadly mixed politics and business. The Republicans retorted by assailing the private character of Cleveland, who commanded his friends in Buffalo to "tell the truth." But just what the truth was never has been told—to the public at least. The bachelor candidate himself made no other profession than that since he had been governor, with a special obligation to the people, his "walk had been correct in every shadow."

The independent, or "Mugwump" vote, with a brilliant array of newspapers, went over to Cleveland, skimming the cream off the top of the Republican party in New York, Massachusetts and in certain other quarters. But the brilliant personality of Blaine, a "magnetic man," stemmed the tide. Probably he would have succeeded in turning it had he promptly corrected the spokesman of a delegation of ministers in New York City, an alliterative clergyman, who addressed him on the eve of the voting as the opponent of "rum, Romanism and rebellion." The Democrats had not a minute to lose, and they did not lose a minute in thrusting before voters of the Catholic faith the Sunday preceding the election that slur on their church.

Nevertheless the election still was so close that the Republicans did not give it up until the third day. Cleveland was President-elect by virtue of a plurality of less than twelve hundred in the nearly twelve hundred thousand votes cast in the State of New York.

II

THE DEMOCRATIC MOSES

(1885) March 4, Grover Cleveland inaugurated President, aged forty-seven.—(1886) March 1, sent his "innocuous desuetude" message to the Senate.—(1887) March, appointed the first Interstate Commerce Commission. December, sent his famous tariff message to Congress.—(1888) Defeated for re-election.

GROVER CLEVELAND was the Moses whom Destiny hid in the bulrushes that he might in good time lead the Democrats out of their twenty-four years of bondage to defeat. The times demanded a new deal, and this called for a new man.

When the President-elect arrived in Washington, it may well be that he could not unaided have found his way to the White House. Certainly he had never been in it. Some say he never had been in town before and another story has it that he had visited it once, but only for a few hours while he hurried through some legal business.

Nevertheless, the heavy figure of the almost unknown President-elect stalked into the unfamiliar Senate chamber with calm self-possession. Nor did he nervously fumble a manuscript and read his inaugural, as the custom is. The veteran statesmen, among whom he stood for the first time, should have been warned by the spectacle of this novice on the national stage striding out onto the eastern portico of the Capitol without a sheet of paper in his hand and coolly addressing in his high, penetrating voice the largest audience that had ever assembled for an inauguration.

As he took the oath he departed from the time-honored precedent of swearing on a new copy of the Scriptures, which the clerk of the Supreme Court always has in readiness for the occasion. He had brought his own, the old, faded Bible his mother gave him when he left his boyhood home. And on its fly leaf was the inscription her fond hand had written to Stephen Grover Cleveland.

Here was a man who was to make his own precedents, a man who was to care for nothing that had happened before he happened. The first President after the Civil War to have had no active part in that strife, he was without a political past, and his face was turned wholly to the future.

Three of his seven Cabinet members he took from the South, which had been barred for a quarter of a century. On the other hand, he appointed a negro to the best-paying office in the District of Columbia.

He struck dismay to the greedy hopes of the Democrats, after their long wandering in a wilderness without spoils, by announcing that he would let the Republican office-holders finish their terms, with the exception of those who had been guilty of "offensive partisanship." When the Republican Senate attempted to interfere with such removals as he did make, he objected to the revival of an old statute "after an existence of nearly twenty years of almost innocuous desuetude." That phrase was too much for the senators, and the act was repealed.

Although a strong partisan, who appointed none but Democrats, Cleveland's stiff-necked resistance to his party's clamor for a "clean sweep" did more to dull the abnormal appetite for public place than anything that had been done before in sixty years. When Samuel J. Tilden was asked if this new leader had backbone, the old sage of Greystone squeaked, "Backbone! He has so much of it, it makes him stick out in front!"

Never could any one in politics say no more ungraciously than Cleveland. His grudging, disdainful doling out of jobs robbed office-seeking of its joy, making it a slow, wearisome and humiliating business.

Although he was an utter stranger to the public men of the country, and the Democrats were without training in official positions, his little gray eyes were shrewd detectors of merit in the procession of applicants that passed before him, and he brought into the service of the Government a large company of able men. Not that all his appointees were wisely chosen. But a senator or representative who foisted upon him an unworthy constituent remained a marked man. "Well," he snarled through his nose to one such offender, who came again with a recommendation, "Well, do you want me to appoint another horse thief for you?"

The unresting industry of the President and his long hours, stretching far into the night, were the despair of his subordinates. He was the hardest worked man in Washington, and his attention to the details of his administration were more a fault than a virtue. "He would rather do something badly for himself," said Tilden, "than have somebody else do it well."

He did not prove to be a constructive statesman. He ventured upon no experiments in law giving, the only notable legislative measure of his term having been the establishment of the Interstate Commerce Commission, which he approved but did not initiate. The real service that Cleveland did was to set up a new standard for public life and party leadership. And the country never since has tolerated a descent to the old standard. His bold independence, his self-forgetting courage infected governors and mayors. His example acted like a tonic everywhere, toning up the politics of the nation. For the first time since he had been quick to recognize and acclaim the genius of Lincoln, James Russell Lowell, notwithstanding Cleveland recalled him from his post as minister to England, felt free to declare that "the Presidential chair has a man in it, and this means that every word he says is weighted with what he is."

At last, Cleveland deliberately sacrificed himself for the sake of plain speaking. The prospects of his re-election were bright. His native conservatism had made him a favorite in the great financial center of New York, and the all-powerful business interests of the country were satisfied with him. But on the eve of the election of 1888 he upset the entire situation by sending to Congress his sensational tariff message, opening with the now oft-quoted words: "It is a condition which confronts us, not a theory."

High customs duties were piling up in the bursting vaults of the Treasury a huge surplus of money that ought to have been in circulation, where it was badly needed, and Cleveland devoted his annual message wholly to an earnest appeal for a reduction in the tariff. Friends begged him to let the troublesome question alone until after he should be safely re-elected. He regarded this hoarding of money as perilous and, ignoring the effect of the message on his own fortunes, he challenged the great protected industries, which defeated him at the polls.

III

A BRIDE AND GROOM IN THE WHITE HOUSE

(1864) July 21, Frances Folsom born in Buffalo.—(1885) Graduated from Wells College.—(1886) June 2, married President Cleveland in the White House.—(1913) Feb. 10, married Professor Thomas J. Preston at Princeton, N. J.

As THE Democrats had lost power under a bachelor President, James Buchanan, they regained it after a quarter of a century under another bachelor President. That strange coincidence was brought to an end by Cleveland's marriage in the second year of his administration.

Rose Elizabeth Cleveland, a spinster sister, had faithfully held her place in the White House by the side of her bachelor brother. But Miss Cleveland's tastes were more literary than social. By her own confession, she relieved the boredom of at least one function by conjugating a Greek verb behind her company smile.

From the day Cleveland entered the Executive Mansion at Albany, gossip busily made matches for him with one after another of the eligible women who appeared at his receptions. A special favorite of those persistent rumors was the pretty widow of one of his old law partners, Oscar Folsom, whose home was one of the few homes in Buffalo where this unsocial person had been in the habit of visiting. It was not suspected that his own choice all along was the daughter rather than the mother.

When she was a little girl, Frances Folsom used to climb up in the lap of "Uncle Cleve," who became her guardian at her father's death and finally her betrothed. This change in her relationship to him took place so gradually that it was unseen even by the spying eyes of her sister students at Wells College. They envied her the beautiful flowers with which the thoughtful governor and President remembered special occasions in her school life. They did not dream that she was to have the distinction of being the first college-bred mistress of the White House.

Mrs. Folsom and her daughter were guests of the President and Miss Cleveland in their first month at the White House. Even the wiseacres of Washington did not guess that the beautiful young girl who was present at a reception—all in white—would in another year be the bride of her host.

Miss Folsom had graduated and was traveling in Europe when the country was set in a flutter by the announcement of her engagement. She returned home to meet such an ordeal as no other American girl of twenty-two ever has faced. Her name was on every tongue in America; her picture was in every paper, and the press boats crowded about her ship, from which she was smuggled aboard a revenue cutter to avoid the curious crowd at the New York dock. While she watched from behind the curtains of her hotel window the President reviewing a Memorial Day parade in the square below, the marching bands played love tunes.

There had been only one marriage of a President, and John Tyler was a widower, which took some of the romance out of the occasion. For the first time a President was to marry in the White House. As Miss Folsom's mother had given up her home and as her grandfather's house was in mourning for his recent death, like the affianced of a sovereign she went to her husband's home to be married.

The wedding in the Blue Room was extremely simple, the only guests being a few relatives of the bride and groom and the members of the Cabinet. After the cake had been cut in the state dining room, the bridal pair succeeded in stealing out the back door under cover of darkness to a waiting train in a switch yard. They had eluded the curious crowds gathered in front of the White House and at the station, but not the ubiquitous press, whose locomotive was under steam and in readiness to pursue them, with a train-

GROVER CLEVELAND AND HIS WHITE HOUSE BRIDE, FRANCES FOLSOM

load of reporters, to their honeymoon retreat in the Maryland mountains.

Although Cleveland never had known the comfort of a house of his own, he disliked the publicity of the White House and had bought a suburban dwelling in what was then a remote and inaccessible corner of the District of Columbia. No President ever has been quite so jealous of his privacy and none has suffered more from its invasion.

The continued attention of a vigilant press wherever the Presidential couple went was indignantly resented by the bridegroom, who hotly denounced the "ghoulish glee" with which his family affairs were discussed. More malicious, more cruel were the unprinted tales which were persistently circulated as long as he remained in public life. His relations as a husband and even his children were made the subjects of all manner of atrocious stories, invented by malignant opponents, which the prejudiced and the credulous spread in whispers over the country.

Such attacks were too low to be met and parried. A President hardly can protest that he is not a cruel husband or the begetter of children blighted at birth. Cleveland was obliged to endure the torture in silence— something worse than assassination, as he once cried out in a circle of friends.

Mrs. Cleveland is said on one occasion to have given a pathetic hint of what the strokes aimed at the President through her little ones meant to a mother. With childlike bashfulness, a daughter was holding back from the greetings of a small company at the White House, when Mrs. Cleveland said, "Speak up, dear, or the people will be told that you are deaf and dumb."

Mrs. Cleveland herself was spared. At first her

girlish charms, afterward her womanly dignity and her maternal devotion made this most youthful the most beloved mistress of the White House. Although she changed her name—the first widow of a President to remarry—as Mrs. Preston she continued none the less to hold her special place in the kindly interest of her countrymen.

BENJAMIN HARRISON

THE SECOND HARRISON

(1833) Aug. 20, Benjamin Harrison born at North Bend, Ohio.—
(1852) Graduated from Miami College, Ohio.—(1853) Married
Caroline Lavinia Scott.—(1854) Becomes a lawyer in Indianapolis.—(1860) Elected reporter of the Supreme Court of Indiana.—(1861-65) Colonel and brevetted brigadier-general in
the Civil War.—(1876) Defeated as Republican candidate for
governor.—(1881-87) In the United States Senate.—(1888) Elected
President.—(1889) March 4, inaugurated, aged fifty-five.—(1892)
Wife died. Defeated for re-election.—(1896) Married Mrs. Mary
Scott Lord Dimmick.—(1901) March 13, died, aged sixty-seven.

BENJAMIN HARRISON'S administration proved to be
only an intermission between the two acts of the Cleveland drama. History gives but a passing glance at the
one President whose predecessor became his successor, who had to give up the Presidential chair to the
man he took it from.

Although Harrison had more brains than Cleveland, Cleveland had a larger nature, and that is what
counts most in the leadership of men. Even the author
of "Ben Hur," Gen. Lew Wallace, who was his campaign biographer, could not make a romance of the
life of this Ben.

Notwithstanding Benjamin Harrison was the grandson of President William Henry Harrison, in whose
house he was born, his father was poor and the boy
was brought up plainly. His opponents, when he was
a candidate for governor of Indiana in 1876, nicknamed him "Kid-Glove Harrison" in contrast with
their own candidate, "Blue-Jeans Williams," and in his
campaign for the Presidency he was caricatured as a

little man almost lost to sight under "grandfather's hat." But there was nothing of the social aristocrat about the man who had the longest ancestral line of any of our Presidents.

Graduating from a small Ohio college, Harrison married at twenty the girl to whom he engaged himself at eighteen, and they went to housekeeping in a little three-room cottage in Indianapolis. He was not admitted to the bar until after his marriage, and the first money he ever made was as a court crier at two dollars and a half a day. Later on he helped out his lean practice with his salary as clerk of the Supreme Court of the State. Then came the Civil War, in which he served gallantly as a colonel and marched with Sherman to the sea. Afterward he rose to a high and prosperous rank in the practice of law.

As in a dozen other instances, the Presidency overtook and surprised Harrison while he was going away from it rather than toward it. 'Tis strange how often this highest prize has fallen to men who had been disappointed in their races for lesser prizes.

The only political office Harrison ever held before his election to the Presidency was a seat in the Senate. Defeated for re-election to that body in the year before he was elected President, he left Washington with no thought that he would soon return as President-elect, and he frankly described himself as "a dead duck."

The only candidate that the rank and file of Republicans wanted to nominate in 1888 was Blaine. But he was not well, and he refused to make a contest for the nomination. At last he cabled from Scotland, "Take Harrison." And the deadlocked convention indifferently took him.

Harrison was one of the best public speakers we have had in the Presidency. His finished little speeches, which he daily delivered to the crowds that were railroaded into Indianapolis by the party managers, were helpful to his candidacy.

Money waxed still more eloquent in that campaign. Cleveland's tariff message was answered by a record-breaking fund for the Republicans. "Fry the fat out of the protected industries" was the command of the chairman of the Republican National Committee, Senator Quay of Pennsylvania, and those industries were done to a turn.

The more notable events of the Harrison administration—the McKinley Tariff Act; the Silver Act, which more than doubled the purchase of that metal by the treasury; the Sherman Law on the subject of trusts; the Dependent Pension Act and the first Pan-American Congress—hardly belong in this little story, because none of them originated with the President himself. He did not rise to leadership, and Congress took the reins. All the while he sat in the White House in cold aloofness.

A lone little figure throughout his life, the Presidency isolated him still more completely from his fellows. "Now, I walk with God," his closest political confidant was chilled to hear him say election night. Without offering a chair to his callers at the White House, he sat tapping his desk, impatient for them to go. "Don't feel insulted by anything he may do or say," a friendly apologist warned a party of men and women that he was about to lead into the Presidential presence; "it is only his way."

A senator said that when Harrison addressed ten thousand men he captured them all, but if they met him separately and privately, every one of them would come away his opponent. "I have only two enemies in the world," Speaker Reed drawled. "Harrison has appointed one of them to office in my town and pardoned the other out of the penitentiary." When the sarcastic Speaker was urged to get on the Harrison "band wagon," he retorted: "You should say 'ice wagon.'"

With the cry of "God help the surplus!" the Republicans gave the country in Harrison's administration the first "billion-dollar Congress," the appropriations for the two-year term rising to that unprecedented total. To the popular protest, Speaker Reed replied, "This is a billion-dollar country." But the country did not feel rich enough to pay the higher tariff rates of the McKinley Act.

That law was passed only seven weeks before the Congressional elections in 1890. Of course, everyone who had anything to sell seized upon the excuse to mark up prices. The "shopping women" rose in their fury at the higher cost of living, and the voters overwhelmed the Republican majority in the House.

That was the forerunner of a still greater political overturn in the Presidential election in 1892, when Harrison went down under a sweeping victory for Cleveland. The loss of his wife befell him only ten days before he lost the Presidency. After a few years, a widowed niece of Mrs. Harrison succeeded to the place of her aunt and became the companion of the ex-President's complete retirement from political life.

GROVER CLEVELAND AGAIN

THE ONLY EX-PRESIDENT TO COME BACK

(1893) March 4, Grover Cleveland inaugurated a second time, aged fifty-five. May, a great panic began. July 1, Cleveland underwent a surgical operation for cancer. Aug. 7, Congress met. Oct. 30, the Silver Act repealed.—(1894) July 4, Cleveland sent troops to Chicago to intervene in railroad strike. Aug. 27, the Wilson-Gorman tariff became law without President's signature. —(1895) Feb. 7, Cleveland made arrangement with J. P. Morgan and others for protection of gold reserve. Dec. 17, sent in his Venezuela message.—(1896) March 12, England agreed to arbitrate Venezuelan claims.—(1908) June 24, Cleveland died, aged seventy-one.

GROVER CLEVELAND will be doubly remembered, if for no other reason, because his name and his name alone appears twice in the list of Presidents which so many school children have to memorize. Many describe him as the twenty-second and twenty-fourth President. Nevertheless he remained one and the same President in both of his terms.

He had no more than left the White House in defeat and settled down to the practice of law in New York City than it was seen that he was still almost as much the leader of the Democratic party as when he was in the Presidency. Yet this ex-President had no machine, and no organization. He did not even have friends in politics, that is to say, personal friends. Always standing on his dignity with the politicians, he unbent only in the companionship of intimates as far removed from the political field as Joseph Jefferson, the actor.

In the four years of his retirement, he seldom saw party leaders. Yet so strong was the reaction against the Republicans and so loud the call for him in 1892 that he returned to the White House.

> "Grover! Grover! four more years of Grover!
> Out they go, in we go; then we'll be in clover."

So ran the favorite song of that campaign. But a second term never has been a field of clover for any President. It was filled with thistles for Cleveland.

One of the periodical panics of the nineteenth century smote the country with a financial and industrial paralysis in 1893, only two months after the inauguration. As usual, the party in power caught all the blame, and day after day a leading Republican newspaper of New York shouted in gleeful headlines: "Another bank gone Democratic!"

As the first means of restoring confidence, Cleveland called a special session of Congress for the purpose of having it repeal the Silver Act of the Harrison administration. The next day he submitted himself to the surgeon's knife for the removal of a cancerous ulcer which had appeared in the roof of his mouth. His grave physical condition was concealed from the panicky mind of the public, and the operation was performed in the closest secrecy aboard a yacht as it steamed slowly up the East River, off New York. Not until many years had passed was it known that when Congress assembled he faced it with a rubber jaw.

Under the pressure of the President, the Silver Act was repealed, but only after a bitter struggle which left the Democratic party hopelessly split. The passage of a tariff bill divided the party still more. It was such a lobby-made, log-rolling measure that Cleveland refused to sign it, but let it become law without his signature. After that sorry exhibition of themselves, the Democrats went down in a well-merited defeat in the Congressional elections of 1894.

To complete the general demoralization, the railroads were tied up in the Middle West by a big strike under the leadership of Eugene V. Debs. With the aid of injunctions and troops, Cleveland kept the roads open. But his unprecedented use of the federal power served to deepen the popular feeling that he was more concerned for the interests of property than for the interests of the working people, whose wages were continually going down.

In the depth of our domestic troubles the President sent his famous Venezuelan message to Congress. In it he announced that the British Government had rejected all our appeals for the arbitration of a land dispute, which for years it had been pressing in South America, and he boldly proposed that we ourselves should decide the question and then proceed to enforce our decision in order to prevent an encroachment contrary to the Monroe Doctrine.

Stocks tumbled headlong in London and New York, and there was much wild talk on both sides of the Atlantic. The President confidently reassured his troubled private secretary, "Thurber, this does not mean war; it means arbitration." And that was the outcome of all the hubbub. Cleveland's outburst of plain speaking had the effect of awakening the English people, as never before, to the value of American friendship, and it opened a new era in the relations of the two Governments.

Cleveland's hardest, longest battle in his second

administration was for the gold standard. Almost alone he upheld it through four years, abandoned by most of the Democrats and unaided by the gold Republicans in Congress, who were afraid of "hurting the party" with the silver people.

Throughout those years of doubt and panic, the business world morbidly watched the fall of the gold reserve. The treasury was overflowing with silver all the while, and if the Government should be reduced to the necessity of using it to redeem the paper money and bonds and to pay its bills, as it had a lawful right to do, the currency and all credits would at once crash down on to a silver basis.

The Nation's money being then in the absolute control of private interests, Morgan, Belmont and the Rothschilds finally were called in to be the protectors of the reserve. The huge profit they wrung out of the Government in its desperation shocked the country, bringing censure and even suspicion upon the President, who trusted rather overmuch in the disinterested patriotism of those kings of finance.

However that may be, for four years Cleveland's strong, resolute arms held the country from sliding down upon a silver basis. But for his lone, stubborn fight, the gold standard must have been lost before the campaign of 1896, when he gave the Republicans the issue on which they elected McKinley. He was too stout a partisan to enjoy such a left-handed indorsement by his opponents, and his estrangement from the Democrats under Bryan remained a heavy disappointment.

Although he left the White House a man without a party, men of all parties were compelled to respect him, not perhaps as a great but as a fearless President, as one of the strongest characters, one of the most masterful personalities that we have had in the Presidency. No one will question the truth of his remark, while he was in a painful struggle with the last enemy of all: "I have tried so hard to do right."

WILLIAM McKINLEY

I

THE MAN WHO WAITED HIS TURN

(1843) Jan. 29, William McKinley born at Niles, Ohio.—(1861-65) In the Civil War.—(1867) Became a lawyer in Canton, Ohio.—(1869-71) Prosecuting attorney of his county.—(1871) Married Ida Saxton.—(1877-91) Member of Congress.—(1892-96) Governor of Ohio.

WILLIAM McKINLEY challenged and disproved the old saying that the Presidency casts its shadow on no man but once and that the chance, if it be missed then, will never come again. Twice the Republican nomination seemed to be within McKinley's reach: in the National Convention of 1888 and 1892. Each time he put it away, content to wait his proper turn, when he did not have to shake the tree to bring down the ripened fruit of his patience.

The truth is not well enough understood that this greatest of political prizes is not to be won by unbashful wooing. In reality, our highest office oftener has sought the man. Seldom is it captured by those who seek it most; as for example, Clay, Webster, Cass, Douglas, Seward, Blaine, Sherman, Bryan.

The Presidency also has a pleasing way of recompensing adversity. A full half of the Presidents have received the White House as a consolation for their misfortune in missing lesser places.

McKinley was beaten for the speakership by Thomas B. Reed in 1889, and he left Washington as a defeated

236

(Copyright by Underwood & Underwood)

BENJAMIN HARRISON AND A SNAPSHOT PHOTOGRAPH OF
WILLIAM McKINLEY, ADDRESSING AN OPEN AIR MEETING

congressman in 1891, only six years before he returned as President-elect. Had he been speaker, and, instead of Reed, incurred the title of "Czar," or had he not been turned out of Congress . . . had he won those smaller honors, he well might never have won the highest honor. A disappointment manfully borne enlists the popular sympathy, and the author of the McKinley Bill entered the contest for the Presidential nomination in 1896 as one who had suffered martyrdom in the cause of the protective tariff.

That cause was to McKinley more than a mere partisan dogma. As the son of a small foundryman in Ohio, he was born to an "infant industry," and he was brought up on it. Not unlikely the destined apostle of protection carried the dinner-pail from which his hard-working parent ate his mid-day meal, seated on a heap of pig-iron at the flaming door of a blast furnace. When the boy's schooling was brought to an end by the "hard times" in the iron business, doubtless he heard the men in his father's trade charge all their troubles to the low tariff of 1857.

After teaching school a term or so, McKinley was called away from books to pass four years in the Civil War, that hard university which graduated the men who were to lead the Nation through four decades. Having gone into the army as a private in the regiment of another President-to-be—Rutherford B. Hayes—he came out at twenty-two a captain, with the brevet rank of major.

Becoming a lawyer at Canton, Ohio, again he found himself in the midst of industries in their struggling infancy. And for fourteen years he was the spokesman in Congress of that industrial district.

When he came to Canton the young major was a clean-cut, up-standing figure, genial in his nature but with a sober dignity. His readiness of speech, while on his feet, came from his practice of the art in the debating societies of his school days. His habits also had been properly formed in his boyhood, when he joined the Methodist Church at ten and grew up a youth who was as careful to keep his tongue as his collar clean.

All doors in the little town naturally swung open with a welcome to "such a nice young man," and a major to boot. Although he was yet poor when Ida Saxton, the banker's daughter, who had been to school in New York City and who had just come back from Europe, smiled yes to him while they were "taking a buggy ride," the banker father smiled, too, and made the young couple a wedding gift of one of the best houses in Canton. It was from the front porch of that honeymoon dwelling that McKinley made his campaign for the Presidency in 1896.

McKinley's is one of the best—and one of the most pathetic—love stories in the domestic records of the Presidency. With the birth of her second child, the wife was left an invalid. The death of both children within five years of her wedding day utterly overwhelmed her nervous organization, and her shattered health remained thenceforth the constant object of her husband's tender care.

Although he never could know from minute to minute when she would pass into a swoon, he made her his companion on his travels. Once when he hurried home from Congress, and the physicians had given up hope of saving her, his own ministrations and his prayers through a long night at her bedside recalled her to life.

The people of Columbus were eye-witnesses that while he was governor—after his defeat for Congress

—he never entered the State Capitol of a morning without turning to lift his hat in a smiling farewell to Mrs. McKinley in her hotel window across the street. By the same testimony, he sprang from his chair on the stroke of three every afternoon, no matter how weighty the business in hand nor how many might be in conference with him, and stepped to a window of the executive chamber, where he waved his handkerchief in greeting to the watching wife.

The same sentimental devotion continued in the White House, where the President was always quick to respond to every summons from Mrs. McKinley's apartments, carefully and cheerfully deciding perhaps a selection of ribbons while he kept the Cabinet or a crowd of senators waiting in his office. All this patience, kindness and unselfishness of the husband brought their reward to the political leader, playing a part in making McKinley one of the few Presidents who have borne the trials of that most trying office without losing their temper.

II

A GREAT REFERENDUM

(1896) June, McKinley nominated for President by the Republican National Convention at St. Louis. November, elected.

ALTHOUGH William McKinley was described by his opponents as "a statesman with his ear to the ground," he failed to hear the warning rumble of the mighty conflict of forces which was to shake the parties and the country to their foundations in the approaching campaign of 1896, the most exciting in our political history. Until that great battle between gold and silver was full upon him, McKinley looked forward to a one-sided contest on the tariff question and an easy victory for himself as "the advance agent of prosperity" and the herald of "the full dinner pail."

Protection had been his specialty, and naturally he preferred to prescribe his own favorite panacea for the ills of the country. On the subject of the gold standard, he was rather lukewarm, having started out in Congress as a free silver man and having voted afterward for all the compromise silver legislation.

Republican leaders generally and particularly those west of the Alleghenies dreaded to take a stand for gold in 1896. They had been timidly straddling the question for twenty years and throwing sops to the silver sentiment, and they shrank now from squarely facing the issue.

The Ohio State Convention nominated McKinley in March on a meaningless platform. On the eve of the St. Louis Convention in June, he drafted for the national platform a money plank which warily shunned the word gold. Even after the convention had cast this aside and nominated him for President on a flat declaration for the gold standard, he still clung to the tariff as the main issue.

"I am a tariff man, standing on a tariff platform," he said to his friends. "The money matter is unduly prominent. In thirty days you won't hear anything of it." In thirty days it was the only question that the people would talk about. Toward the end of August he reluctantly sidetracked protection and put gold first in his letter of acceptance.

The Democrats had come out for free silver, and Bryan was riding the high tide of his sensational campaign for Sixteen to One. Silver men and silver States had bolted the Republican ticket, and it had become startlingly plain that McKinley must win the votes of hundreds of thousands of Cleveland Democrats, who were for gold but who were also opposed to a high tariff.

At McKinley's back in the fight stood Marcus Alonzo Hanna of Ohio. That multi-millionaire had transferred his genius for organization from the iron, coal and shipping industry when Grover Cleveland challenged in 1887 the protection which his great business enjoyed, and he had jumped into politics with a determination to put an Ohio protectionist in Cleveland's place.

After making a losing fight for the nomination of John Sherman in 1888, Mark Hanna turned to McKinley. Together they made the well-matched team that was needed for a business campaign, like that of 1896.

The big railroads, banks, mines and manufacturing concerns had been for many years the ruling force in politics. They were the so-called "invisible government," controlling legislation and the courts by controlling the nominating machinery of both parties in State and Nation.

A prudent business in those days took care to have Democratic as well as Republican partners or directors, and these saw that their respective parties put up "safe" candidates on "safe" platforms. Having thus assured themselves that their interests would not lose, whichever side won, they contributed to the rival parties the money that enabled the politicians to conduct campaigns full of sound and fury, but signifying little.

In the disruption of the Democratic party, the larger wing at the Chicago Convention of 1896 slipped out of control of the "system," adopted a radical platform and proceeded to run wild. The "interests" saw themselves threatened for the first time with the loss of political power, and that prospect alarmed them more than Bryan's slogan of Sixteen to One.

At that critical juncture Hanna stepped to the front, incorporating McKinley's candidacy on business principles, capitalizing the fears of the business world and inducing it to underwrite the campaign with a staggering fund. The swift tide that ran against the Republicans in July was turned in September; but money did not do it. The men who gave the money did it. They took off their coats and plunged in to save the investment in Republican success, which Hanna had persuaded them to make, and their influence and example were worth more to him and McKinley than all their dollars.

With only one special interest behind him—the silver mine owners—Bryan was hauled to the voters. But Hanna hauled the voters to Canton by trainloads, delivering them f. o. b. at the candidate's lawn, where McKinley addressed the whole reading nation day after day without leaving his dooryard. At the same time millions and millions of campaign documents fell like snowflakes, covering the land with printed arguments and appeals.

Almost two million more voters came out on election day than had voted only four years before. Gold won and McKinley was elected in the greatest referendum that ever had been held.

III

A STRANGE FORTUNE

(1897) March 4, William McKinley inaugurated President, aged fifty-four.—(1898) Feb. 9, Spain's double-dealing revealed in the publication of a private letter from the Spanish minister. Feb. 15, the battleship Maine blown up in Havana harbor. April 21, war declared against Spain. July 7, Hawaii annexed. July 22, Spain sued for peace. Aug. 12, peace protocol signed. Aug. 14, city of Manila captured. Dec. 10, treaty of peace signed in Paris. Dec. 21, McKinley proclaimed a policy of "benevolent assimilation" in the Philippines.—(1899) Feb. 4, the Philippine War began. Feb. 6, treaty of peace ratified by the Senate. Sept. 6, Secretary Hay called on the Powers to agree to the "open door" in China.—(1900) Aug. 15, the Allied expedition to Pekin.

EVENTS make sport of the schemes of mice and men. McKinley entered the race for the Presidency on the tariff issue, was elected on the money issue . . . and the greatest problems that confronted him in the White House were the fate of a chain of islands off the coast of Asia, and the destiny of China!

Spain had been engaged for two years in a desolating struggle to hold in subjection the revolting island of Cuba, and two happenings pushed McKinley into the conflict in spite of himself. In a private letter, the Spanish minister at Washington scoffed at the President as a "politicastro"—in plain American, "a peanut politician"—and intimated that the fair promises which the Spaniards were giving him were only a trick to fool the administration and the American people. Within the week of that exposure, the battleship Maine was blown up in Havana harbor, with the loss of two hundred and sixty-six American lives.

After withstanding for nearly two months the popular outcry of "Remember the Maine," the President yielded, and war was declared. In ten days Dewey had smashed the enemy squadron in Manila Bay; in ten weeks, another squadron was sunk or captured off Santiago; in three months and a half, poor old Spain threw up the sponge.

Our navy proved itself efficient and quickly destroyed what small resistance the outmatched foe could hope to offer. Our little army of two hundred and seventy-five thousand men proved to be its own worst enemy, losing only three hundred and forty-five killed in action or dying of wounds, but sacrificing two thousand, five hundred and sixty-five lives to disease—pitiful victims, for the most part, of unsanitary camps here at home.

The small expeditionary force in Cuba easily whipped the armed foe in front of it, but was nearly compelled to retreat by invisible foes in its rear: plagues and hunger. Untrained and incompetent line and staff officers—politicians and "sons of somebody" —were largely responsible for the breakdown of camp hygiene, the medical service and the service of supply.

It took twice as long to make peace as to make war. The Philippines caused all the trouble. As we had not captured the islands in the war, many believed that we should let them alone. But McKinley decided to demand from Spain the surrender of the Philippines.

The members of the Cabinet were divided. Judge Day, the Secretary of State, who became the head of our peace commission, favored the annexation of nothing more than a naval base. At the end of a long discussion the Secretary asked why his motion was not put to a vote. "I was afraid it would be carried," the President replied with a smile.

McKinley's course was influenced by a fresh out break of rivalry among the European Powers for ports and islands and spheres of influence, particularly in the Far East, and the President was ambitious to open for the country a new era in its relation to the world

"The currents of destiny are flowing through the hearts of the American people," he confidently announced as he felt the public pulse on a Western tour.

A cry of imperialism was raised against this plunge into Asia. The "anti-imperialists" included some distinguished Republicans and virtually all the Democrats, and the treaty of peace was ratified at last with only one vote to spare in the Senate.

Without waiting for ratification, the President dispatched a military expedition to take over the Philippines, proclaiming to the revolting Filipinos the policy of "benevolent assimilation." The resulting war dragged its unpleasant length for two years before the inhabitants unwillingly bowed to their new master.

Not yet feeling the economic urge that drove crowded, over-industrialized Europe into the race for exploiting far-off lands, most Americans continued to be indifferent to commercial opportunities in the Philippines, and the archipelago remained a liability rather than an asset on the national ledger. Having had so much to do at home, in the development of resources infinitely richer than those of any foreign field, there was a tendency to leave the islands more and more to the Filipinos, and in 1935 we started them on the road to independence.

It was the strange fortune of a President whose entire public life had been wholly absorbed in domestic questions to plant the flag in the distant Philippines and to send it to the pink walls of the Forbidden City of China. In the march on Pekin, for the rescue of the foreign legations from the siege of the Boxers, or Chinese revolutionists, the United States joined other Powers for the first time in a military expedition. It is to the credit of the McKinley administration that it did what it could to curb the rapacity of the Japanese,

German and Russian governments and soldiery, which brought infamy upon a campaign that was undertaken in the fair name of humanity. "What I want," the President said, in explaining his position, "is the friendship of China when the trouble is over."

Under the high statesmanship of John Hay, the Secretary of State, the United States had already, before the Boxer rebellion, laid a restraining hand upon the nations that were looting Chinese territory and had drawn from them pledges to keep an "open door" to the trade of all nations in the ports they were seizing at the point of the gun. The "open door" continued to be the aim of our course in the East. Had it been possible for us to follow it and induce others to follow it until the giant of the Orient awakened from his long slumber and shook off his foreign despoilers, an emancipated China would have been the imposing monument of William McKinley's Presidency.

IV

THE THIRD ASSASSINATION

(1901)   Sept. 5, McKinley's last speech at Buffalo.   Sept. 6, 4:07 P. M., shot by Leon F. Czolgosz.   Sept. 14, 2:15 A. M., died, aged fifty-eight.   Oct. 20, the assassin put to death in the electric chair.

AFTER his re-election by the largest plurality on record at that time, McKinley entered his second term with his party united behind him and with the good will even of his political opponents. No other President ever was spared so completely the bitter with the sweet of success as this most softly spoken, most ingratiating man.

McKinley quarreled with no one.   Although tears

of regret came into his eyes when Senator Hoar told him that he must break with him on his Philippine policy, he took the senator's hand and assured him: "I shall always love you, whatever you do." When he asked Senator Cullom whether he would get very angry if he overruled him in the appointment of a certain Illinois man, the senator had to confess: "Mr. President, I could not get mad at you if I tried." An indignant congressman, who stormed in upon him one day, said to his friends as he came out: "I don't know a blamed word he said, but it's all right, boys."

As time went on, McKinley had strengthened his Cabinet and his administration by going outside of politics and drafting into the public service, doubtless with the aid of Hanna's advice, a group of unusually able men. Hay, Root, Taft, and Knox were the more notable among those discoveries.

McKinley hoped to distinguish his second term by opening a new and brilliant era of expansion for American trade and shipping. To test public sentiment, he began a tour of the country a few weeks after his inauguration; but this was stopped at an early stage by the serious illness of Mrs. McKinley while they were in California.

Postponing all public plans, he returned across the continent with his wife and stayed by her side in the old home at Canton while she rested through the summer. When she was again well enough to travel, they went to Buffalo in September to attend the Pan-American Exposition, where he outlined in an address the new departure which he hoped to see the country make:

"Isolation is no longer possible or desirable," was the keynote of the speech which had been for months taking form in his mind. "Our capacity to produce has developed so enormously . . . that the problem of more markets requires our urgent and immediate attention. . . . Reciprocity is the natural outgrowth of our wonderful industrial delevolpment. . . . If, perchance, some of our tariffs are no longer needed . . . why should they not be employed to extend and promote our markets abroad?"

In that broad spirit of forward-looking statesman- ship, this champion of protection and of the home market delivered what was to be his farewell address. The next afternoon he revisited the exposition to hold a reception in its Temple of Music. He was urged to avoid the risk of exposing himself at close range to a great crowd. "Why should I?" he protested. "No one would wish to hurt me."

In that trusting spirit, the President smiled into the face of a young man, who approached him in the course of the long, closely packed procession, and he offered his hand in greeting. But the right hand of the young man was wrapped in a handkerchief, and out of that ambush he fired two pistol shots at the President.

Too late, the guard of Secret Service men, detec- tives and soldiers seized the assassin and threw him to the floor. Notwithstanding his foreign-sounding name —Leon F. Czolgosz—he proved to be a native-born citizen, like Booth and Guiteau. Like them also he was the tragic product of evil conditions. As Booth had been unbalanced by the sectional hatred of the Civil War and Guiteau by faction strife, Czolgosz had grown up in the bad social conditions of some of our big industrial centers, where he fell an easy prey to the wild doctrines of anarchy or nihilism.

The wounded President was caught and supported by anxious hands. The ruling passions of his life— kindness to all and his devotion to Mrs. McKinley—

triumphed over the pain he was suffering. "Don't let them hurt him," he begged as he saw his assailant struck by an excited man. In the next instant he whispered to his private secretary, "My wife—be careful, Cortelyou, how you tell her—oh, be careful."

An immediate operation in the Emergency Hospital of the Exposition was decided upon, and the patient repeated the Lord's Prayer as he passed under ether. When the surgeons had finished their work he was carried to the residence of his Buffalo host, John G. Milburn, where Mrs. McKinley bravely had received the terrible news.

For six days the President made such steady progress that the physicians felt warranted in announcing that he was out of danger. That night there came a turn for the worse, and the next day all hope was abandoned.

"It is God's way," the dying man said in perfect resignation. "His will, not ours, be done," and he murmured his favorite hymn, "Nearer, My God, to Thee." He could still raise his arms to enfold in one more embrace the wife who piteously insisted, "I want to go, too, I want to go, too." Out of his faith, he reassured her, "We are all going. We are all going."

A mighty chorus of "Nearer, My God, to Thee" arose from the altars of the Nation, as the body of McKinley was carried to the Capitol in Washington and thence to its resting place on a green hill at Canton. Mingled with the sorrow of the people was a feeling of humiliation that their country, the great republic, should have a blacker record of assassination than any despotism, that the simple, freely chosen chiefs of our democracy should be less safe in their lives than czars or sultans. For the third time in hardly more than third of a century, a President had been assassinated; three out of the seven Presidents elected in thirty-six years had been murdered, and these the gentlest.

THEODORE ROOSEVELT

I

THE STRENUOUS LIFE

(1858) Oct. 27, Theodore Roosevelt born in New York city.—(1880) Graduated from Harvard.—(1882-4) Member of New York legislature.—(1884-6) A ranchman at Medora, N. Dak.—(1886) Defeated for mayor of New York.—(1889-95) Member of National Civil Service Commission.—(1895-7) Member of New York Police Commission.—(1897-8) Assistant Secretary of the Navy.—(1898) Colonel of the Rough Riders in Cuba.—(1899-1900) Governor of New York.—(1900) Elected Vice-President.

THEODORE ROOSEVELT was, with Jackson, the most popular of our Presidents. With the exception of Lincoln's, his was the raciest, the most interesting character that we have had in the Presidency.

Yet he was born apart from the multitude whom he led. He might have lived and died a stranger to the masses of his countrymen but for one thing: He had not the health to enjoy the life of ease which opened to him at his birth.

Roosevelt had to fight for his very breath in his gasping, asthmatic childhood. He had to fight even to see until he was thirteen, when it was discovered that the awkward, stumbling boy was in need of eye-glasses. He had to fight to get into Harvard without the stimulating companionship and competition of schoolmates. His uncertain health had put him out of step with his fellows and, except for a few months, he never attended a public or private school. All the while he had to fight for the strength to hold his own among the hardier, rougher boys who, boylike, picked on the timid

251

weakling, and he built up his frail body and braced up his courage by constant exercise at home, in the fields and in the woods.

Finally he took a post-graduate course in physical culture in the wild West, where the "four-eyed tender-foot" had to fight the battle of his youth all over again in a strange world, with entirely different standards for measuring a man. As a ranchman out on the blizzard-swept plains of North Dakota, he had to make good by working as hard and by daring as much as the next fellow; keeping his saddle for forty hours at a stretch on a "round up," and showing himself on occasion quicker with his fists than some bar-room rowdy was with his guns. In the end, the frontier made over the raw material from Fifth Avenue into an American of the type of Washington, Jackson and Lincoln, all frontiersmen.

Having overcome the disadvantages of being born poor in health, Roosevelt next overcame the disadvantage of being born with a rich father. In the entire story of the Presidency there is in reality no better example of a "self-made" man.

After he had fought his way to a robust manhood, Roosevelt found that he could not be content to dawdle in a club window or be a mere looker-on in the world. Having contracted the fighting habit, he could not stop fighting, and he fought his way into politics and into the legislature.

The ward politicians did not want any "silk stocking" from the "Avenue," and the gilded youth of Murray Hill, "who never worked and never will," snickered at "Teddy" for mixing up with "the groom and the saloon keeper" at the district headquarters. But he retorted that if this was the governing class in New York, he wanted to belong to it. Still they kept on

(Copyright by Underwood & Underwood)

THEODORE ROOSEVELT AND WILLIAM H. TAFT, WITH A PHOTOGRAPH
OF THE SOUTH FRONT OF THE WHITE HOUSE.
(By the Clinedinst Studio, Washington)

laughing at him for twenty years, until one day they saw him laughing back at them from a window of the White House.

Roosevelt cut his eye teeth in political leadership in the corrupt, machine-run legislature of New York. He could not have chosen a more thorough school for instruction in the hidden, muddy springs of parties and politics. His experience at Albany put realism into his idealism and made the academic reformer over into the most intensely practical politician we have had in the Presidency. It also lightened his zeal with humor, his moral indignation with a saving tolerance, enabling him to enjoy and pass along "Tim" Campbell's moving appeal to him not to "let the Constitution stand between friends."

He decided at the outset to act in each office as if it it was to be the last that he ever would get, and for nearly fifteen years after he left the legislature, he could not have been elected to anything in the boss-ridden State of New York. For a long time he was "shelved" on the Civil Service Commission at Washington, until a reform mayor of New York appointed him on the four-headed Police Commission; but it was soon single-headed so far as the public could see, and that head was full of teeth for police grafters and law-breakers. At thirty-eight the most that he could ask of the Republican politicians, with any hope of getting it, was the assistant secretaryship of the navy.

McKinley was reluctant to let him have even that modest post, for fear that he might shake the tranquil atmosphere of his administration. The President's premonition was correct. The assistant secretary contrived to keep things so stirred up, in his clear-eyed anticipation of war with Spain, that the entire administration sighed with relief when at last he went off to lead his Rough Riders to the fighting front in the Spanish War.

In five months he was back from Cuba in the far more troublesome rôle of a popular hero. The New York machine was in such sore need of a good name to pull it through the pending election that it met him at the wharf and humbly laid at his feet the Republican nomination for governor. In the governorship, he realized the worst fears of Boss Platt that he harbored, as the Boss naïvely wrote him, "various altruistic ideas," and that he was "a little loose on the relations of capital and labor, on trusts and combinations and . . . the right of a man to run his own business in his own way."

The only thing to do with this wild engine was to turn the switch and shunt it on to the side track of the Vice-Presidency. Roosevelt loudly protested that he wanted to be re-elected governor. While Platt was trying to push him on to the national ticket, McKinley and Hanna just as earnestly tried to push him back on to Platt. The Republican National Convention of 1900 rose up and roared his nomination for Vice-President, flinging him, in spite of himself, upon the tide that led to fortune.

II

THE SQUARE DEAL

(1901) Sept. 14, Theodore Roosevelt took the oath as President, aged forty-two.—(1902) Oct. 15, settled the coal strike.—(1904) November, elected by a plurality of 2,545,515.—(1906) Railroad rate regulation. Meat Inspection Law. Pure Food Act.—(1908) Roosevelt opened first conference on national conservation of natural resources.

AT the cracking of a twig in the still depths of the Adirondack Mountains, Roosevelt turned to see a guide coming out of the woods with the unexpected news that McKinley's condition was worse. Although he hastened to Buffalo, the Vice-President did not arrive there until the President had been dead thirteen hours.

The new President requested all the members of the Cabinet to remain in office, and he pledged himself to continue unchanged the policies of his predecessor. He did not mean to be either a Tyler or a Johnson. Neither could he be a McKinley. He was Roosevelt, and his administration became his own.

The money magnates and the great corporations had financed Republican success in the gold and silver campaign of 1896, and for four years they had directed the policies of the party and the Government without question from anyone. Huge combinations, trusts and mergers were swiftly bringing into the control of a small group of men the banks, factories, mines, forests, railroads, the whole economic life of the country.

Theodore Roosevelt owed nothing to the men and interests that had been running the administration and Congress by long-distance telephone from New York. Nor had he any selfish, personal gain to make by challenging that powerful, invisible Government. The instant popularity that he won in the White House assured his election to the Presidency, if he would only keep quiet and not "disturb business."

But he foresaw the time when the people would reassert their sovereign ascendency and that they would wreck the Republican party if it stood in the way. To guard against its meeting that fate and to avert a radical uprising, he proceeded to unshackle his party.

A bare catalogue of the measures of Roosevelt's crowded administration, the first constructive administration since the Civil War, must suffice here: the smashing of the Northern Securities Company, which stopped the plans for all other railroad mergers; the new Interstate Commerce Act, which brought railroad rates under Government control; the Meat Inspection Act; the Pure Food Law; the establishment of the Department of Commerce, with power to investigate and report on the books and business of corporations; the rescue of lands, forests and water power from further encroachments by private interests and their conservation in the national interest.

Each act of legislation was pushed through a balky, reluctant Congress, against the desperate resistance of the lobby, by the pressure of a public opinion which was almost cruel in the force that Roosevelt could summon from it. With it he overwhelmed the coal barons of Pennsylvania, who lightly defied him when he called upon them to arbitrate a strike which was causing an anthracite fuel famine on the edge of the winter.

The exploiting interests could not alarm the country with the cry that this wealthiest man in the Presidential line until his time—wealthiest at birth and death, leaving an estate totaling $881,082—was the enemy of honest wealth and of private property. They spread instead, in ominous whispers, the story that he was going insane and finally that this careful athlete, who was always in training as if for a prize fight, was a drunkard. At the first appearing in print of this latter yarn, he jumped on it with a libel suit and killed it forever.

The people of both parties believed that Roosevelt was only trying to start a "square deal," as he declared. They liked his plain way of saying what he had to say and they seldom missed the point of anything he said.

He knew better than most of the Presidents what the

people themselves were saying, all kinds of people. The doors of the White House were wide open, and there never was any telling who might be there, where senators and Rough Riders, ambassadors and frontier "bad men," poets, journalists, prize fighters and explorers mingled. In the midst of them, the President bounded about in his overflowing energy, discussing men and nations, Senate, House and courts with a freedom that took away the breath of the cautious.

Roosevelt had both more callers and correspondents than any of the Presidents before him. It is estimated that he wrote one hundred and fifty thousand letters in his seven years and a half in the Presidency. He was also a great traveler, traveling fifty thousand miles and visiting every State in his first term. Wherever he went he was equally at home, with a knack of getting in close touch with the spirits of the crowd.

No other President has lived the life of America so completely. He was an Easterner in the East, a Westerner in the West, and he was, in fact, half Southerner, with two uncles in the Confederate navy and a mother who remained to her death an unreconstructed "rebel." "Take that man out of Texas," a Texan Democrat exclaimed. "He'll win every vote in the State. He campaigns next to the ground." When the election of 1904 came, he was elected by an immense popular plurality, three times larger than ever had been given to any candidate, the first Vice-President to receive the Presidency from the people after receiving it from the hand of death.

The statutes that were enacted in Roosevelt's administration were experiments, and most of them still are of doubtful effect. He was a greater preacher than lawgiver. With the Presidency for his pulpit, he held up

before the Nation and, indeed, the world, higher standards of moral duties, of social obligations, in business
as well as in politics, in the home as well as in public
life. Only the lesser half of his influence and his record will be found written on the parchments of Congress. The larger half he wrote on the conscience of
the country.

III

THE BIG STICK

(1903) Feb. 6, Roosevelt induced Great Britain and Germany to arbitrate with Venezuela. November, the Panama revolution.—
(1905) May 12, brought Russia and Japan to agree to discuss
peace. Aug. 29, the Peace of Portsmouth.—(1906) The Nobel
peace prize awarded to Roosevelt.

At the outset of the Roosevelt administration a fearful citizen begged the Rough Rider not to permit his
fighting spirit to plunge the country into an international war. "What!" the President exclaimed; "a
war, and I cooped up here in the White House?
Never!"

Many forgot the first half of the old motto that
Roosevelt made his own: "Speak softly and carry a
big stick." No man ever had a simpler faith in the
efficacy of first "talking it over," man fashion, with an
adversary, whether a senator or an ambassador.

The meddlesome Kaiser Wilhelm II was the earliest
to feel the "big stick" that he might see if it was only
stuffed with straw. Germany and a Tory government
of England were on the point of seizing territory as a
security for some claims against Venezuelan citizens
when Roosevelt succeeded in dissuading England from
such a step, but he failed to induce Germany to arbitrate the matter. Thereupon he told the German ambassador that unless the Berlin government consented

to arbitration in ten days, he would send Admiral
Dewey to stop the Germans from landing in Venezuela. The ambassador protesting that the kaiser
could not back down at so late a stage, Roosevelt replied that he was not arguing with him, but was simply
telling him what would happen.

After waiting a week without an answer from Berlin, he told the ambassador that he was going to cut
the limit to nine days and that unless Germany agreed
in forty-eight hours to arbitrate, Dewey would sail.
In thirty-six hours the ambassador came back with a
message announcing that Germany consented. Chuck-
ling behind a straight face, the President publicly
praised the kaiser to the skies as a devoted friend of
the great principle of arbitration.

Europe was as quick as America to see that there
was a strong man in the White House. Although as
intensely American as any President, Roosevelt was
also a man of the great world, who interested foreigners hardly less than he interested his own people, the
kaiser alone rivaling him in international celebrity. "I
saw two tremendous forces of nature while I was
gone," John Morley said on his return to England
from America. "One was Niagara Falls and the other
the President of the United States, and I am not sure
which is the more wonderful."

Germany replaced her ambassador at Washington
with an old personal friend of the President, and the
kaiser sent his brother, Prince Henry, to this country
on an errand of propaganda. Not to be outdone,
France dispatched a distinguished special embassy and
also chose for ambassador, Mr. Jusserand, who could
not only talk books with Roosevelt but who could also
qualify for the "Tennis Cabinet," which took the place
in this athletic administration of the "Kitchen Cabi-

net." England cast aside her trained diplomats to send to Washington James Bryce, the best-liked Englishman in America. Meanwhile, emperors and kings entered into personal correspondence with this republican magistrate as if he were an intimate of the royal circle.

In good time Roosevelt employed the influence of his unique position before the world to bring to an end the Russo-Japanese War. Shrewdly choosing the right moment to step in, he appealed to the two belligerents with a common sense and a simple directness that a friend would use in bringing together two quarreling neighbors. Afterward he steered the Peace Conference at Portsmouth against its will steadily toward a peace of reconciliation. An impatient Russian declared that his "steel wrist" hammered out a treaty that neither of the Powers wanted at that time and that "the terrible American President—Lo Strenuoso—was capable of locking the conferees into a room and starving them into submission."

Instead of starting a war, the "big stick" stopped the only great war that broke out in the period of its sway. Not a cloud appeared even momentarily on our own horizon in the seven years and a half of Roosevelt's administration. The special trophy of his Presidency was not a military medal but the Nobel prize, which was awarded to him in 1906 as the world's foremost peacemaker.

The one suspicion of a stain on the "big stick" was incurred in Roosevelt's dealings with Colombia over a right of way for an Isthmian canal through the State of Panama. A dictator of Colombia, after agreeing to cede us the canal strip for ten million dollars, broke his agreement in a desire to get more. Roosevelt was not to be stopped in constructing the canal, any more than a Union Pacific locomotive was stopped by the rope which the Indians drew across the track. After he had drafted a message to Congress, proposing the taking of the necessary land regardless of the government of Bogota, the State of Panama, which was anxious to have the canal constructed and was eager to gather in the ten million dollars for itself, seceded from Colombia under the protection of American warships . . . and the canal was dug. The United States has since confessed the irregularity of its procedure by indemnifying Colombia to the amount of twenty-five million dollars.

While the Roosevelts were its tenants, the White House was an example and the center of the simple family life of America . . . "not a second-rate palace," the President said, "but the home of a self-respecting American citizen."

A few months after graduating at Harvard, Roosevelt married Miss Alice Hathaway Lee of Boston, whom he had met in his college days. That bride of his youth passed from life as her daughter—Mrs. Alice Roosevelt Longworth—entered it. On the same day in the same house his mother died, and it was from the shadow of that double bereavement that he turned to a new life in the wild West.

Nearly three years afterward he sailed from New York, directly following an unsuccessful campaign for mayor, to marry a friend and neighbor of his childhood, Miss Edith Kermit Carow, who was sojourning in Europe. The wedding took place in London, and on the register of St. George's, Hanover Square, curious visitors may read the "marriage lines" of "Theodore Roosevelt, ranchman."

As the wife of the President, Mrs. Roosevelt was called upon to act as hostess to a larger number and variety of guests than any other mistress of the White House, and so generously was she endowed with tact that she was among the few in that trying position to have escaped criticism. When she went to live there with her family of six children, she found herself cooped up in "a five-room flat," most of the place being given over to offices. In her term the old mansion was transformed into a comfortable home, and the remodelled White House, altered without any sacrifice of its character, testifies to the good sense and good taste of both Mrs. Roosevelt and the President.

WILLIAM HOWARD TAFT

PRESIDENTS ARE BORN NOT MADE

(1857) Sept. 15, William Howard Taft born in Cincinnati.—(1878) Graduated at Yale.—(1880) Graduated at Cincinnati Law School. —(1881-3) Assistant prosecuting attorney.—(1885-7) Assistant county solicitor.—(1886) Married Helen Herron.—(1887-90) Judge of Superior Court.—(1890-2) Solicitor-General of United States.—(1892-1900) United States Circuit Judge.—(1900-04) Commissioner in and Governor of the Fhilippines.—(1904-8) Secretary of War.—(1909) Inaugurated President, aged fifty-one.— (1912) Defeated for re-election, with only eight electoral votes.— (1921) Chief Justice.—(1930) March 8, died, aged 72.

WHEN Taft and Roosevelt rode up Pennsylvania Avenue on March 4th, 1909, it was the first time since Jackson and Van Buren had passed that way side by side, more than seventy years before, that a retiring President would not have preferred another seat-mate and successor than the one whom the fortunes of politics had thrust upon him. Perhaps already even "dear Theodore" and "dear Will" were not wholly pleased with each other.

The Presidency is too big a gift for any man to make or for any man to accept. The giver humanly cannot help expecting more gratitude than the recipient humanly can acknowledge.

Roosevelt alone had selected his successor. He forced his enemies to accept him with the terrifying threat: "If you don't take Taft, you'll have to take me." And he had to set a watch on his own friends to keep them from stampeding the convention to him.

Naturally, everyone assumed that we were to have a Roosevelt administration by another name, and it was expected in the campaign that the ex-President would not go farther away from the White House than Oyster Bay.   Instead, he plunged into the depths of Africa.   He might as well, when he was a ranchman, have flung an Eastern guest on the back of a bucking broncho and abandoned him to his own resources. For Taft was an utter tenderfoot in politics.

The fate of William Howard Taft would be pathetic if he himself had not met it and borne it with a smile. He did not invite it, having had no taste for political life, and he was without the least desire for the Presidency when Roosevelt made him his heir.

He was abler, more upright, more independent than some far more successful Presidents.   But by bent and training he was a judge, and the White House is no place for a judge.   The only other President who had sat on a bench was—of all men—Andrew Jackson, and "Old Hickory" seems not to have acquired overmuch of the judicial temperament.

Executive force and the judicial mind are the positive and negative poles of the battery.   If a President stops to weigh the evidence, consult precedents and prepare an opinion, enterprises of great pith and moment are turned awry and lose the name of action.   In the crises that make or break his administration and his leadership he must decide on his instincts, his intuitions, and find his reasons afterward.

Taft passed all but two of the first twenty years of his manhood in courts, either as a law officer or as a judge.   He had no other wish than to spend his life in the same congenial atmosphere, as he took a train in Ohio on a certain day in the year 1899.   On that fateful train he fell in with Gen. Corbin of the army, until then a stranger to him, and the general returned to Washington with the enthusiastic conviction that he had discovered the right man to give a code of laws to the Philippine Islands.

Taft earnestly protested, when McKinley sent for him, that he wished to stay on the bench; but he was talked into going.   Four years afterward Roosevelt offered him a justiceship in the Supreme Court of the United States, the highest honor to which his heart ever had aspired.   But he put aside the temptation from a pure sense of duty to his "little brown brother."

As lawgiver and governor at Manila, he had won the confidence of his Oriental subjects, and rather than desert his post before his task was finished, he sacrificed the dearest ambition of his life.   In a year and a half Roosevelt had him in his Cabinet as Secretary of War—and soon had him in his eye for the Presidency.

Roosevelt had the weakness of his strength.   He thought he was strong enough to make a President. But real Presidents are born, not made.

The moment Roosevelt was gone, the standpatters, the reactionary forces emerged from their seven and a half years in the cyclone cellar.   The moment the political broncho felt the tenderfoot on its back, it bucked and threw Taft from the seat of leadership. The next thing the rank and file of Republicans knew, the party was slipping back into the old rut from which Roosevelt had jerked it when first he laid upon it his masterful hand.

The people refused to go back.   Eight months after Taft's inauguration, the election of 1909 sounded a clear warning of the disaster that overwhelmed the party in the congressional election of 1910 and which all but destroyed it in the Presidential election of 1912.

According to a story that was told of Taft, a curious stranger asked a gatekeeper at the Union Station in Washington where he would stand the best chance of seeing the President in the few spare hours that he had between trains. "Right where you are," was the reply. "He's always either taking a train or getting off of one."

Taft was the first President to draw the salary of seventy-five thousand dollars, as Grant had been the first to receive fifty thousand dollars after the increase from the original compensation of twenty-five thousand dollars. Congress had also adopted, two years before he came in, the custom of allowing twenty-five thousand dollars yearly for the traveling expenses of the President, and he became the great Presidential traveler, making a record of one hundred and fifty thousand miles in four years, as he went about the country appealing for a reversal of the verdict against his administration. In vain he strove to turn back the tide, which only sported with him.

After having elected him in 1908 by one million, two hundred thousand plurality, the people parted with Taft in 1912 more in sorrow than in anger . . . and most of them still are sorry. They did not question that he was a good President, but that is a secondary consideration. A President must be first of all a politician and a leader.

After having borne himself like a good loser for eight years, Taft was rewarded by President Harding with the highest official honor that ever has fallen to an ex-President and with a post far more coveted by him than the Presidency itself—the Chief Justiceship of the United States, which he enjoyed the nine remaining years of his life.

ANOTHER ROOSEVELT CHAPTER

THE BULL MOOSE

(1909) March 23, Roosevelt sailed for East Africa.—(1910) June 18, returned home.—(1912) February, "My hat is in the ring." June, defeated for Republican nomination. August, nominated by the Progressive party. Oct. 14, shot in Milwaukee.—(1913) Oct. 4, sailed for South America.—(1914) May 18, returned home.—(1917) June, his application for war service declined.—(1919) Jan. 6, died, aged sixty.

IF ever the name of Theodore Roosevelt shall cease to live in political history and legend, it will still shine forth from the metal tablets on the exhibition cases in the National Museum at Washington, where curious visitors in generations to come will pause to look in amazement at the great beasts which this Nimrod of the Presidential line slew in the jungles of Africa. Those cases should serve also to prove an alibi for Roosevelt from the charge that he was the slayer of the Republican elephant.

Contrary to the unreflecting opinion, the Republican party was already disrupted and defeated while Roosevelt was roaming the far-off wilds of East Africa, when his political revolution was completely overthrown by a counter revolution. As President he had made the party again somewhat like unto what it was in its youth, the great organ of liberalism and progress, giving it such a hold upon the people as it never had before. He returned to find it, as he believed, the party of standpatism and reaction, with a tidal wave of popular dissatisfaction flowing against it.

Nevertheless he went at once on a wearisome, hope-less tour of the country in an effort to save the party in the congressional elections of 1910, and he took the stump again in 1911, with the same barren result. The doom of the Taft administration in the Presidential election of 1912 already was sealed, when a group of Republican governors appealed to the ex-President to be the party candidate and to lead a forlorn hope. Even he would stand only a sporting chance to win the election, and he responded in sporting terms: "My hat is in the ring."

Although Roosevelt swept, by a majority of more than four hundred thousand, the eleven Republican States having popular primaries, Taft was renomi-nated with the aid of the delegates from the Demo-cratic States of the South and the "steam roller" of the Old Guard. That reversal of the popular verdict re-sulted in a bolt and the formation of the Progressive party. The National Convention of the new party was a medley of "good" millionaires from Wall Street, highbrows from academic groves, cowboys from the plains and a "lunatic fringe," all singing, "Onward, Christian Soldier," as they rallied around their insur-gent chief when he declared, "We stand at Armaged-don and we battle for the Lord."

This naturalist in politics supplied a symbol and nickname for his new party when he assured a reporter in the midst of his losing fight for the Republican nomi-nation: "I feel as strong as a bull moose." The "Bull Moose" indeed proved to be amazingly strong at the polls, where it carried six States and left only two to the elephant—Utah and Vermont—with the Democratic mule winning the Presidency in a walk.

While campaigning in the middle of October, Roose-velt was shot by a crazy man in Milwaukee. "He pinked me," he admitted to the anxious bystanders, but he insisted on continuing his ride to the hall where he was to speak. "I will deliver that speech or die," he persisted, and he spoke with the bullet hole in his chest undressed and bleeding.

The next year, this unresting ex-President outdid his African exploits by plunging into the tropic wilderness of Brazil. At fifty-five, he was less fitted for the hardships which he had successfully braved in the Dark Continent four years before, and he never again was to be the robust embodiment of that strenuous life which, for a generation, he had practiced as well as preached.

The life of the Progressive party was as short as its rise was sudden. Although its founder smilingly vowed in 1916, "I am still a Progressive," he gave his earnest if not enthusiastic support to Charles E. Hughes, the Republican nominee.

For two years before America entered the war, his pen—he was on the staff of magazines and newspapers—was continually goading the country out of its neutral position in the great struggle. After we got into the conflict, it continued to goad the country to go faster and farther.

Roosevelt was eager to lead another band of Rough Riders to the front, but President Wilson sustained the objection of the military advisers of the Government to any volunteer organizations. "I am the only one he has kept out of the war," the disappointed applicant retorted on the campaign slogan of the President.

He found proud consolation in the service in the field of all four of his sons. At the supreme sacrifice of the youngest, Quentin, who fell battling in the air, he turned a brave front to the public and gave no outward sign of the cruel hurt which the blow must have caused the heart of a father so fond. "Only those are fit to live who do not fear to die," was his message from the shadow of the loss of his baby boy.

Old foes hailed him as the hope of the Republican party in 1920. He smiled at the suggestion, though his intuition and his increasing ailments may already have warned him that he had fought his fight and finished his course. Both his parents were short-lived, and he had exceeded his natural prospect of life, when the final summons came to him as he slept in his home at Oyster Bay before the dawn of a January day in 1919.

The death of no other ex-President, of no other private citizen in any land has called out such a worldwide expression of regret. To Americans, it was like a death in the family. For twenty years "Teddy" had been passing in and out of their homes like a familiar, and touching their lives on every side. He had excited among them the same instinctive affections and the same furious resentments that are reserved for kith and kin. First and last, all had agreed and all had disagreed with him, and with equal violence, but remaining all the while immoderately proud of him as the very personification of themselves, of America. Even in his simple grave, he still bears mute testimony to the democracy and the real Americanism which were exemplified in the many-sided life of Theodore Roosevelt.

WOODROW WILSON

I

A PROFESSOR IN POLITICS

(1856) Dec. 28, Woodrow Wilson born at Staunton, Va.—(1879) Graduated at Princeton.—(1882) Graduated from Law School, University of Virginia.—(1882-3) Attorney in Atlanta, Ga.— (1883-5) Graduate-student at Johns Hopkins University.—(1885) Married Ellen Louise Axson of Savannah, Ga.—(1885-8) Associate professor at Bryn Mawr.—(1888-90) Professor at Wesleyan University in Connecticut.—(1890-1902) Professor at Princeton.— (1902-10) President of Princeton.—(1911-13) Governor of New Jersey.—(1913) March 4, inaugurated President, aged fifty-six.

THE Presidency is a looking-glass, in which we may see reflected the changes in the social conditions, thought, manners, tastes and in the dress of the country. With the rise of democracy, Jefferson was the first President with unpowdered hair. A succession of log-cabin Presidents, which opened with Jackson and closed with Garfield, marked the appearance and the disappearance of our frontier. The Civil War is registered in the very faces of the Presidential gallery, which were clean-shaven until the advent of Lincoln, the four soldier Presidents that came after him having been "bearded like the pard." Then came the era of the business man, with three chief magistrates wearing the unstatesmanlike mustache.

In the eighty years that we remained largely an agricultural country, all our Presidents, with a solitary exception, were farmers' sons. With the growth of our urban population, most of the Presidents were town born.

While a college diploma remained the privilege of a class, our democracy often preferred to follow uneducated or self-educated leaders. Now that higher education is in a process of democratization, all but three of the Presidents elected since Lincoln have been college graduates.

In this age of ours, when men are going to school to learn business and farming and all manner of vocations, it was natural that there should appear in the White House a man like Woodrow Wilson, who had learned politics in the classroom rather than in the wardroom. The eighth of our Virginia-born Presidents—in reality he was not a Virginian, but the son of an Ohio clergyman and of an English mother—was a student or teacher of the science, or rather the art, of governing for thirty years before he held a political office.

That fact was left out of their reckoning by the Democratic bosses of corrupt, machine-ruled New Jersey, when they summoned the president of Princeton University from the golf links one afternoon in the fall of 1910 to receive their nomination for governor. When this supposed novice in politics declared, as he floundered through what he had to own up was his first political speech, that if elected governor he would govern, the politicians nudged one another and laughed in their sleeves at the idea of a professor trying to run their machine. They laughed aloud when they saw him actually sit down in the governor's chair at Trenton and begin to play politics out of a book.

Of all things, it was a book which he himself had written in his youthful school days merely as a thesis for his Ph.D. at Johns Hopkins. The young graduate-student made the discovery that our Constitutions, State and national, created a vacuum, which the bosses had rushed in to fill. In Europe, the executive and

PRESIDENT AND EDITH BOLLING WILSON

the legislature are one and the same thing; here they are separate, with no one authorized to direct or lead the entire Government. Consequently the headless affair in Washington and in every State capital had fallen under an unauthorized, irresponsible bossism of one kind or another. Wherefore the author contended that a governor or President, as the only official known and responsible to all the people, should lead, not leaving the job to some hidden party machine or managing politician in the secret control of selfish private interests.

When at last the theorist had a chance to try out his theory on the New Jersey government, lo! it worked like a charm. Laboring together, Gov. Wilson and the legislature made over in two crowded years the election, corporation, public utility and labor laws of a most reactionary State.

Alas, popular leadership is neither a science nor an art that can be taught out of a book. It can be acquired only in fellowship with the people, and Woodrow Wilson had less contact with the life of the Nation than any of our Presidents.

Where other leaders of our democracy have appealed to the emotions, he was one of the least dramatic of our Presidents, with no anecdotes to popularize him, with no legends of his youth or myths about his political career to vitalize him to the general imagination. He owed his various successes at the polls to the cold logic of the political situation and little to his popularity. His academic aloofness from politics, at a time when politicians had fallen into disfavor, made him the available man for governor in 1910. As a candidate for nomination as President he ran a poor second to Champ Clark in the popular primaries of the Democratic party in 1912, when he was nominated at Baltimore only after forty-five ballots, and then only as a result of Bryan's overthrow of the steam roller. Finally he was elected by the division of the Republicans between Roosevelt and Taft, though he received a smaller vote than the Democrats had polled in three preceding elections.

It was the tragedy of Woodrow Wilson's nature that when the elements were mixed in him, magnetism was denied him, that loadstone which draws the hearts of men. The head was the powerhouse of his leadership.

II

FOUR CROWDED YEARS

(1913) The Underwood Tariff. The Tariff Commission established. (1914) The Federal Reserve Act. Federal Trade Commission established. Clayton Anti-trust Act. Aug. 6, Death of Mrs. Wilson.—(1915) The Coast Guard established. The Seamen's Act. Dec. 18, Marriage of the President and Mrs. Edith Bolling Galt.—(1916) Hours of Service Law for railroads. Farm Loan Law. Philippine Government Act. Child Labor Law. Adamson Eight-Hour Law. Re-election of Wilson.

AFTER Woodrow Wilson had been teaching in the classroom for a quarter of a century that the President ought to be more like a prime minister, "trying to co-operate with other human beings" than "a mere department . . . hailing Congress from some isolated island of authority," the opportunity came to him to put his theory in practice. When Congress met in extra session, a month after his inauguration, he walked in and delivered his message in person, reviving, after the lapse of more than a century, a custom which Jefferson had stopped only because he happened to have a poor voice and was an awkward speaker.

For more than a hundred years Presidents had been keeping away from the Capitol, except when they went there for an hour to sign the bills of an expiring Congress. The rest of the time they carried on a more or less secret diplomacy with the other half of the Government, a mile away, as if it were some rival power in Europe.

President Wilson adopted at the outset of his Presidency the attitude of a sort of member at large of both Houses, sauntering unheralded into the seldom-used President's room, which adjoins the Senate Chamber, and talking things over in the open. That common-sense, democratic plan of leadership resulted—while it lasted—in the best exhibition of quiet, smooth team work between the executive and legislative departments that we have ever had. There was neither a quarrel nor a deadlock throughout that pre-war period.

The President succeeded, not by arousing a personal loyalty to himself but by the force of his ideas. "I have had a majority on the floor, but," he admitted, "never a majority in the cloak room."

The quality of the product of that leadership may be open to question, but the quantity represents a bigger grist than the legislative mill has ground out in any other like space of time. Here are the outstanding items in the peace record of the Wilson administration: Tariff revision, the first income tax, the Federal Reserve Act, the Federal Trade Commission, the Clayton Trust law, thirty arbitration treaties, the Seaman's Act, the Farm Loan Law, the Repeal of Panama Tolls, the Shipping Act, the Child Labor Law, the Purchase of the Danish West Indies, and Federal Aid for Good Roads.

The Federal Reserve Law is concededly as great a piece of constructive legislation as any that has been enacted in this country. We were absolutely without a financial system, and the money of the Nation was in the irresponsible control of a few big banks in New York. A single private citizen exercised far more power over the national currency than the national Government itself.

President Cleveland hired J. Pierpont Morgan to be the protector of the helpless Treasury in 1895, and President Roosevelt turned to him to save the financial life of the country in the panic of 1907. All the while an absurd system or lack of system left the great business of the United States without enough currency whenever it was most needed and with too much of it when the need was least.

Every attempt to remedy that situation had failed, because private financial interests naturally wished to keep control of the money. The Aldrich Bill in the Taft administration, while systematizing our banking and currency, proposed to continue and give the sanction of law to that private domination, and Congress refused to pass it.

The Federal Reserve Act of the Wilson Administration reversed the Aldrich plan and gave the Nation, through the Government, the control of its own money. It is agreed now that, without the new system, our finances could not have weathered the gale of the World War.

Woodrow Wilson was the relentless driving force that pushed through the Federal Reserve Bill and the rest of the legislative program, and he incurred the implacable hostility of powerful interests. The only other President to challenge the supremacy of this element in our politics was Roosevelt, but the harder it fought him, the closer the people as a whole drew to him.

The electric spark was omitted from Wilson's composition, and this omission denied him a flowing communication with his fellows, a natural limitation which was set by his lack of physical vitality and confirmed by the life he led until he was suddenly thrust into the hurly-burly of politics. His isolation, his impersonal leadership chilled the emotions of the people, even when their minds approved his policies and admired his abilities. Nor did he have a Cabinet which could supply the lacking element of popularity.

His was a lonely figure in the White House. He came to the Presidency a stranger to public men, and no President can make new friends—real friends; he can only make sycophants. When his wife died, leaving him without a close companion in the midst of heavy cares, the hearts of the people warmed to him as at no other time, and they almost resented his remarriage, because it broke that tie of sympathy between them and him.

His re-election in 1916 was one of the big surprises of our Presidential elections. For many hours after the polls closed he appeared to have been badly beaten, and Hughes went to bed with all indications pointing to his election.

After all the great industrial States, which had decided elections in the past, except Ohio, had sent in reports of Republican victories, the tide was turned by the Far West, which had been almost forgotten in the reckoning, but where the conservative interests had less influence. At last the returns from remote hamlets in the Sierras gave California to the President by less than four thousand plurality. He had lost all but two of the Northern States east of the Missouri, and yet had won by carrying all but two of the States west of that river, where the women voters are supposed to have rallied to him, because "he kept us out of war."

III

MOMENTOUS DECISIONS

(1916) May, Germany promised the United States to observe international law on the seas.   June, Republican and Democratic Conventions declared for neutrality.   Oct. 26, President Wilson confessed at Cincinnati that "Neutrality is played out." Dec. 20,
asked the belligerents to discuss peace.—(1917) Jan. 22, proposed
that we should join in world league for peace if the belligerents
stopped fighting.   Feb. 3, broke off diplomatic relations with Germany on her renewal of ruthless submarining.   Feb. 26, asked Congress to authorize arming of our merchant ships, but Senate fili-
buster defeated him.   March 12, proceeded to arm them.   March
21, called Congress in extra session.   April 2, his war message.

As HE stood at the clerk's desk in the hall of the
House of Representatives on the evening of April
second, 1917, President Wilson was the central figure
in one of the great moments of world history.   Not
only his own people but mankind stopped to listen.

Wilson had been re-elected only five months before
because "he kept us out of war."   Alas, the war would
not keep out of the United States.

For two years and a half President and people
together had continued to draw back from the yawning inferno into which events were pushing them.   As
lately as June, 1916, both political parties in their
national conventions, agreed on one thing and one
thing only: Each squarely declared itself in favor of
neutrality.

Nevertheless Wilson himself publicly admitted a few
days before his re-election that "neutrality is played
out."   As the one remaining means of keeping us out
of war, he tried to stop the war in December and
again in January, by appealing to the belligerents to
make peace.   His voice was drowned in the roar of
the guns.

The conflict took on new fury with the resumption

of ruthless submarining, which Germany had modified the year before at our demand. President Wilson thereupon handed the German ambassador his passports, and next he proposed that we should arm our merchant ships. The filibustering Senate failing to give him that authority, he proceeded himself to arm them. But our shipping vanished from the sea, with its hidden terror, and our export trade was paralyzed. At last he called the newly elected Congress in extraordinary session to "receive a communication . . . concerning grave matters of national policy."

Did he mean war or something short of war? All afternoon of the meeting day, while Congress was organizing and getting ready to receive that history-making message, the country and nations beyond the sea waited in suspense.

No other President in the whole course of his service has had to take so many momentous decisions as Woodrow Wilson had to make in the solitude of his study at the White House in those anxious days before the assembling of Congress. He could not divide the burden of such a heavy responsibility; he had to bear it alone, and without a precedent to guide him.

The course seemed plain enough, once we had entered upon it. But first the President had to chart it by himself. Should we give a further trial to armed neutrality? Or should we, as in 1798, enter upon an independent naval warfare, against the submarine menace to our shipping? Or should we back the Allies with money and supplies, but leave them to do the fighting? Or should we join forces with them unreservedly, contrary to the historic policy of America to go it alone?

Those alternatives were in every mind in that bewildering period, and Wilson had to choose between them in framing the policy to be submitted to Congress. He made the bolder choice of going into full coöperation with the Entente Allies, pooling with them all our resources, our man power, our money power and our producing power, and of resorting for the first time in our history to compulsory universal military service.

The broad plan which he unfolded and which Congress quickly approved assured in advance the success of the great, unparalleled undertaking, and he pushed it through to victory with grim, unrelenting persistence. Americans generally assumed at the start, and the British Government agreed with them, that we should not have to send a large army to Europe, if indeed any at all. But, after the collapse of Russia, and when it became an imperative necessity for us to go at double-quick to the relief of the broken line in France, the foundation was so well laid that we rose to the unforeseen emergency, building up in a year and a half an army of four millions and sending two million soldiers across the Atlantic.

The brains of the country, all the talents were mobilized for the war, merchants and scientists, bankers and railroad men, labor leaders and clergymen, each being charged with the task for which his training fitted him. The chronic weaknesses of our war-making —patronage and favoritism—rarely were permitted to show their heads. Mistakes aplenty were made in meeting some of the new problems of warfare. But at least we did not repeat the mistakes of our past wars. For once our soldiers were not sent to the front under political generals and colonels and left dependent upon the supplies of political contractors. For the first time in our military history, politics was shut out of the army, by a resolve that President Wilson took and kept.

"It is a race between Wilson and Hindenburg," said Lloyd George, when the big German drive surprised the Entente and smashed through its front in the spring of 1918. We astonished ourselves and dumfounded the German general staff by the speed and efficiency with which this unmilitaristic Nation put an immense army into a field three thousand miles away.

IV

A WORLD TRAGEDY

(1917) Aug. 27, President Wilson replied to the Pope that there could be no peace with German autocracy.—(1918) Jan. 18, laid before Senate his Fourteen Points. Feb. 11, his Four Points. Oct. 5, Germany opened its appeals to him for peace. Oct. 14, replied that the German people must speak for themselves. Nov. 5, country rejected his appeal for election of Democratic Congress. Nov. 11, the Armistice. Dec. 4, President sailed for Paris.—(1919) Jan. 18, Peace Conference opened. Feb. 14, League Covenant completed. Feb. 15, President sailed home. March 13, arrived in France again. July 8, returned home. Sept. 3-28, on speaking tour. Oct. 2, paralyzed. Nov. 19, Peace Treaty failed in Senate.—(1924) Feb. 3, Death of Woodrow Wilson, aged 67.

IT fell to Woodrow Wilson not only to lead the country into the war, but it was also his fortune to be the spokesman of the Allied peoples, the master propagandist in a war of propaganda. Whether he stood before a joint session of Congress or amid the white headstones of Arlington Cemetery or by the tomb at Mt. Vernon, he had the civilized world for his audience, his words thundering and flashing above the roar of Armageddon, and making themselves heard in the entrenchments and the capitals of the enemy as well as of the Entente.

With the downfall of the Czar, that sinister partner in the Entente, and with America drawn into the war, the President idealized the conflict, in the light of those two events, which happened within three weeks of each other, as a struggle between the free peoples and autocratic government, a fight to make the world "safe for democracy," a war against war. That idealization simplified the issue to the popular imagination, making the war seem, at least, no longer a wrestle for power and trade, but a duel between democracy and autocracy, with the American President and the German kaiser typifying the contending hosts.

The Central Powers at first scorned, then distorted and finally suppressed the President's indictments of them. His messages and speeches were smuggled over the border by spies and airplanes. Enemy soldiers and peoples were forbidden, under the penalty of treason, to pick them up; but they passed from hand to hand, from mouth to mouth in secret circulation, and sometimes were hidden under hearthstones in the cottages of the peasantry, who treasured them as a new gospel of deliverance from war.

The Presidency of the United States was carried to the summit of world influence, becoming the lofty tribunal from which the moral judgments of humanity were pronounced. No European premier could speak with the dynamic force of the elected chief of America, whose speeches were accepted as the impartial verdict of a great jury of a hundred million detached and disinterested pople, the largest body of public opinion anywhere. "It is the voice of posterity," exclaimed a French statesman, at the reception of the President's war message, which was read in the schools and posted on the dead walls of France. Avenues, streets, squares and bridges of ancient cities were renamed for Wilson, and men toiled up Mt. Blanc, with the stars and stripes in their hands, to bestow his name on an Alpine peak.

It was neither Woodrow Wilson nor yet the Presi·

dent of the United States who had the power so to fuse the peoples in a fraternity of faith and unify the Allied front at home and abroad. The man and the magistrate had become the tongue of the silent masses of war-stricken Europe, on both sides of No Man's Land, articulating their mute longing for emancipation from militarism and imperialism. A mighty force had laid hold upon him, making him its mouthpiece, its amplifier, and giving his words such a dominion over the minds of multitudes as the words of none other ever had wielded.

Finally it fell to this republican chief to pronounce the doom of the autocracies which he had challenged. The German and Austrian emperors themselves made him the arbiter of their fate, when their governments came to him as suitors for peace and offered to surrender on the basis of his Fourteen Points. The reply, which was flashed back from the White House, that the peoples of Germany and Austria must speak for themselves before the President would refer to the Allies the request for an armistice, was the death sentence of kaiserism, and down went thrones that had stood an age.

Even in the midst of those negotiations by wireless across the Atlantic, the unmaker of emperors and kings was himself unmade, when the country rejected his appeal for an indorsement of his leadership, in the return of a Democratic Congress at the election of 1918, and when the voters by a million majority placed the President's opponents in control of both Houses. The Government thus was deadlocked between the parties in one of the great crises of history, and the peace of the world straightway became ensnarled in one of the fiercest of partisan conflicts.

Other governments were saved from that plight,

first by postponing elections until after the war (something we could not do under the rigid provisions of a written constitution), and secondly by a parliamentary system of rule, under which the executive (the Cabinet) must resign when it loses its majority in the legislative body.

The American executive, on the contrary, cannot relinquish his constitutional responsibilities to Congress. It remained the Democratic President's sworn duty to negotiate the treaty of peace, and it was equally the sworn duty of the Republican Senate to decide whether it should give its "advice and consent" to the ratification of the treaty. That division of authority resulted in a world tragedy.

Since he was sponsor of the terms of peace that the Allies and Germany had agreed to, the President felt it to be his duty to go in person to the Conference at Paris, notwithstanding the virtually unbroken tradition that a President must never leave the country. On his arrival in Europe he was hailed as the apostle of a new order by the masses in France, Italy and England and by the liberated peoples of the fallen empires. But the disciples of the old order, the ruling classes, well knew that his own country was not united behind him, and they challenged him to a long combat behind the locked doors of the Big Four in Paris, where he was left to grapple almost single-handed with the forces that have kept Europe a cockpit since history began. To save the League of Nations, which he regarded as the larger, more permanent principle at stake, he felt himself forced to yield step by step on questions of reparations and military frontiers and to the demands for a settlement that promised to divide the world again, as in 1914, between the armed camps of rival alliances.

After having been away from home seven months, except for a hurried winter trip to Washington at the adjournment of Congress, the President returned to find that his compromises at Paris had weakened him among his supporters, and that his long absence had strengthened his opponents. In an effort to rally the people to his side, he went on a trans-continental speaking tour, contrary to the earnest advice of his physician, and in disregard of the warning of nature that he had received in France, where at one time he broke under the strain of his lonely battle.

When he had struggled for more than three weeks against a mingled indifference and opposition to the League of Nations, he was compelled by physical exhaustion to return to Washington, where a cerebral hemorrhage, on the fourth day afterward, resulted in the permanent paralysis of his left side. With his fall, the losing fight for the League of Nations went on leaderless until the final failure of the Treaty of Versailles in the Senate.

After weeks of silence and then many months in a wheel chair, the pathetic figure of the stricken President, with drawn face and labored step, reappeared again at the Capitol on the occasion of the inauguration of his successor on March 4, 1921. Finding his body weaker than his will, reluctantly he abandoned, only at the last moment, his plan to take part in the ceremony. "The Senate fell down on me," he said, with grim humor, "but I am not going to let it see me fall down." Driving to his newly chosen home only a mile or so from the White House, he became the first retiring President to take up a residence in Washington, which remained the shrine of his loyal followers until his increasing invalidism found release in death, on Sunday, February 3, 1924.

Time alone can write the last line of this extraordinary chapter in the story of our Presidents. Events so stupendous can be fully and fairly viewed only at a distance. The years, not the hours, hold the answer to the familiar question of what the verdict of history will be on Woodrow Wilson.

*

* *

*

In the last year and five months of the Wilson administration the country was left with but the pale shadow of a President, as it had been once before for more than eleven weeks while Garfield lingered mortally wounded by an assassin's bullet. Only the few in the closely guarded secrets of the sick room knew how long President Wilson was incapacitated within the meaning of the Constitution, which provides that in case of the "inability" of the President "to discharge the powers and duties" of his office "the same shall devolve on the Vice President." At first his hand was guided in signing documents and Mrs. Wilson gave out assent to necessary actions, which included a veto of the Volstead Prohibition Act and even a recasting of the Cabinet. The annual message in December, 1919, was written by trusted members of the administration. When Republican Senators insisted upon investigating the competence of the Chief Executive, Senator Fall of New Mexico, although an implacable opponent, returned from his extraordinary errand to the bedside of the invalid with the report that he found him mentally clear. Still the question remains of how and by whom shall a President's "inability" be determined, and an answer to it may be imperatively demanded in some time to come.

WARREN GAMALIEL HARDING

I

THE SIXTH OHIOAN

(1865) Nov. 2, Warren Gamaliel Harding born in town of Corsica, Ohio.—(1884) Became editor of the Marion *Star*.—(1891) Married Mrs. Florence Kling de Wolfe.— (1900-4) Member Ohio Senate.—(1904-6) Lieutenant-governor.—(1910) Defeated for governor.—(1915-21) In United States Senate.

"MAIN STREET is moving into the White House," a bystander in Washington remarked, with a curl of the upper lip, at the inauguration of Warren G. Harding. Instead of resenting that supercilious classification, Mr. and Mrs. Harding made a boast of it, and admitted that they were "just folks."

With a strange uniformity, all but two of our Presidents (Roosevelt and Taft) had been, like Harding, country bred or small town folks. Only three or four others among them ever had made their homes in big cities.

Harding's election maintained another tendency toward uniformity in the Presidential line. When he faltered on the question of becoming a candidate, his sponsor, Henry M. Daugherty, argued with him: "Ohio has always had a candidate. If she doesn't have one this time, the rest of the Union will think we have seceded." And he became the sixth President to be elected from Ohio—the seventh to have been born in that lucky State. He was also the fourth Ohioan to die in office.

With Virginia supplying five other Presidents—eight were born of that fecund mother of Presidents—about forty per cent of all our chief magistrates in 140 years of the presidency had been chosen from two states. More than half had been either Ohioans or Virginians by birth. Five were residents of New York; three of Massachusetts; three of Tennessee; two of Illinois. Louisiana, New Hampshire, Indiana, Pennsylvania and New Jersey each contributed one, and the remaining thirty-seven states supplied not one of thirty Chief Magistrates. Not a President came out of the vast country beyond the Mississippi until 1929, when the honor leaped across plains and mountains to the Pacific Coast.

Fortune was equally partial in its distribution of this capital prize among the occupations of the American people. All but half a dozen of our first thirty Presidents were bred to the law. But that long time monopoly did not fare well in the twentieth century, with not a practicing lawyer in the presidency in the first two decades of the century. Theodore Roosevelt attended a law school but never entered the profession. Wilson abandoned it in his young mannood. Taft passed most of his life in courts, but he was at the bar only four years.

With four-fifths of thirty Presidents drawn from such a minor fraction of the population as the legal profession and two others from a still smaller fraction, the military profession, the farmers, the dirt farmers in what was long a predominantly agricultural country were represented by Washington alone—the only one among them to live by farming. The millions of followers of manual trades had but a solitary representative in Johnson, the tailor. The numerous teaching

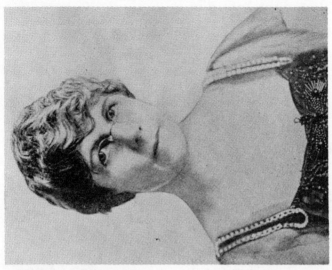

(*Copyright by Underwood & Underwood*)

PRESIDENT AND FLORENCE KLING HARDING

profession had but one President—Wilson. The writers are entitled to claim Theodore Roosevelt, as writing was his only private gainful occupation.

Harding was not only the first editor in the White House but he was also the first President to be drawn from the great business life of the country. As a publisher and printer and director in various enterprises of his home town, his success as a business man was substantially evidenced by an estate that inventoried, at his death, not far from three-quarters of a million, all built up by his own abilities and exertions in a small community. He was the wealthiest President, except Theodore Roosevelt, until Hoover's term.

Starting at scratch in the race of life, the son of a country doctor, Harding was a ten-year-old rustic when his father transferred his practice to the larger field of Marion and when he himself rode into that town astride a mule, to behold with wondering eyes the community of four thousand with which he was to grow up, prospering in its increasing prosperity. After attending one of the many little academies that Ohio used to flatter with the name of college, he left school at sixteen and served both as reporter and printer in his apprenticeship to his life-calling of editor and publisher of the Marion *Star*. He was fortunate and happy in an unusually close business and political partnership with a wife more high-spirited and perhaps more ambitious than he, and to whom he brought lasting consolation for the unhappiness of an imprudent girlhood marriage which, like Mrs. Jackson's, had ended in divorce.

Once he had assured himself of a good income from his private vocation, Harding turned to the favorite avocation of Ohioans, and entered politics by way of

the State Senate, from which he stepped into the lieu-
tenant-governorship.   The next step on the political
ladder he missed, when he was defeated as the Republican candidate for governor in 1910.   But, as we have
seen happen so often in these glimpses of our Presidents, he was quickly rewarded with a higher honor
for having borne well the failure to win a lesser
one.

It is likely to help a man in politics to give people a
chance to be sorry for him.   We crave the privilege of
pitying the great, as with Lincoln, or of smiling at
them and calling them by a nickname, as with Roosevelt.   It was the calamitous misfortune of Wilson that
he did not, probably could not let us do either with him,
and he himself used to confess his helpless longing to
be hailed as "Woody."   Men were so sorry for "Warren," when his candidacy for governor was submerged
by the Democratic tidal wave of 1910, that they hastened to make up for it by sending him to the United
States Senate in 1914 and to the White House in 1920.
A good loser is a winner.

II

A BOLD STROKE

(1921) March 4, inaugurated President, aged fifty-five. Nov. 11,
    burial of the Unknown Soldier.   Nov. 12, opening of the Wash-
    ington Arms Conference.—(1922) Feb. 6, Conference finished its
    labors.

THERE are three classes of entrants in the Presidential
sweepstake: (1) nation-wide candidates, (2) favorite sons, and (3) dark horses.   It was merely as the
favorite son of Ohio that Senator Harding entered
the Republican National Convention of 1920.   He
had qualified for even that classification by a narrow

margin in the popular primary of his State, where the national candidacy of Gen. Leonard Wood had pressed him closely in the polling.

In his modest misgivings as to his fitness for the Presidency, Harding had been literally pushed into the fight by his friends in Ohio and in the Senate, where his kindly gifts had made him a social favorite. His chief pusher, Harry M. Daugherty, was also a true prophet when he foretold in the presence of a newspaper reporter at New York in February what happened at Chicago in June: "At the proper time, after the Republican National Convention meets, some fifteen men, bleary-eyed with the loss of sleep and perspiring profusely with the excessive heat, will sit down in seclusion around a big table. I will be with them and will present the name of Senator Harding to them, and before they get through they will put him over." So it fell out, even to the heat.

Probably that convention was as perspirative as any ever held on the prairie in good corn weather. When the spiritless contest between the three leading candidates—Wood, Lowden and Johnson—had been becalmed on a glassy sea twenty-four hours; when there was hardly an unwilted shirt left in the thousand suitcases of the delegates, and when they faced the prospect of sweltering a second week in Chicago hotels, at an expense of twenty dollars and twenty-five dollars a day for a room, the interests behind Harding, which had patiently bided their time, started the cry among the impatient delegates: "Let's nominate Harding and go home!" Just in time for them to catch the Saturday night trains homeward, they compromised on the Ohioan. By the way, it was the first time that all the principal candidates were themselves on the scene, contrary to an old taboo that had been defied and smashed by Roosevelt in 1912, when he took charge in person of his fight against Taft.

An overwhelming Republican victory was plainly predestined at the outset of the campaign, which the candidate conducted from his "front porch" at Marion, supplemented by a few speaking tours. But an unprecedented majority of seven millions in the election outran the expectations of the most sanguine and was nearly three times greater than the record majority for Roosevelt in 1904.

Having only to move a mile from his senatorial to his Presidential residence, the President-elect was hailed by the Washingtonians at his inauguration as a fellow townsman. The one shadow on the scene was cast by the faltering figure of his predecessor, broken by the heavy burden he had borne through eight most trying years.

It is the custom for the President, as well as the President-elect; as they ride side by side to the Capitol (the former seated in the place of honor on the right), to acknowledge the cheers of the crowded Avenue, because he still is, for a few minutes more, the representative of the Nation. But as they return, he sits on the left and no longer takes to himself any share in the public homage, since he is once more only a private citizen.

When Harding saw the painful exertion that it cost Wilson to lift his hat in response to the cheering along the route from the White House, it was characteristic of his considerate nature that he should have ceased to raise his own. In that supreme moment of his life he seemed to forget himself in his solicitude for his wounded foe.

Back to "normalcy," as he phrased it, was the keynote of the new President's inaugural. His efforts to steer his administration by that course often were baffled by a world in the throes of "abnormalcy" following the war. The platform on which he was elected and his campaign speeches committed him to some substitute for the League of Nations, and he described it as an "association." Between opposition in his party at home to any international political co-operation, and reluctance abroad to give up the League in hand for an association in the bush, he and Secretary Hughes were unable to mature the project or develop an effective policy.

Nevertheless it was a timely and brilliant stroke in foreign policy that gave the Harding administration what seems now to be its surest title to a place in history. The Conference for the Limitation of Armament, which the President convened at Washington in 1921, was initiated, it is true, by a popular demand, which the Senate voiced, for stopping the naval competition that had sprung up between the United States and Japan. But it was the administration that wisely broadened the scope of the plan to include an effort to limit the even more dangerous political and economic rivalries in the East.

The Conference succeeded at a time when all other international conferences were failing, because it was opened with a concrete proposition so bold and yet so simple that public opinion could grasp it, and once it grasped the idea it held on to it until it was adopted. Secretary Hughes' proposal, which startled the world by its directness, was this: As the United States, Great Britain and Japan each had a naval building program that was laying heavy burdens on the people and accentuating rivalry among them, they should agree to retain the relative standing on the sea they then had, which was expressed as a ratio of five-five-three respectively, instead of continuing a futile armament race.

That meant the scrapping of hundreds of thousands of dollars' worth of unfinished ships, mostly by this Government, but also the saving of hundreds of thousands more in finishing the ships. It meant, in addition, the acceptance by England, for the first time in centuries, of an equal on the sea.

The Conference stopped the naval race for a few years, and it ended the Anglo-Japanese Alliance which was confusing Anglo-American relations. It substituted for that military compact a peace compact, signed by the four naval powers—America, Britain, France and Japan—for mediation in all disputes. Finally it made a covenant among all the nine powers present—America, Britain, France, Italy, Belgium, Holland, Portugal, Japan and China—to respect the integrity of China. But this became only another scrap of paper in 1930, with the Japanese advance against the Chinese.

As a fitting and dramatic prologue, the ceremonial of the burial of the Unknown Dead, symbolizing the sacrifice in the World War, took place the day before the Conference met, with the delegates of the nine participating governments and the military chiefs of the Allied Armies in attendance at the National Cemetery at Arlington. Harding's graceful figure, on that most memorable day of his Presidency, was ready for the sculptor, and his deeply stirred emotions left no room for doubt of his passionate earnestness in convoking the nations for the promotion of peace.

III

A FATAL TOUR

(1923) June 20, President Harding started on tour of the West and Alaska. July 8, arrived in Alaska. July 26, landed at Vancouver, B. C. July 27, engagements canceled on account of illness. July 29, arrived at Palace Hotel in San Francisco. Aug. 2, died, aged fifty-seven.

THE first senator to become President, Harding was the second man to step directly from either wing of the Capitol into the White House, Garfield having been the only other to have made the transition without a break. Notwithstanding that would seem to be the natural order of promotion, there is a rooted prejudice in the public mind against choosing for the Presidency a man who has been long and continuously in Washington. Hence all our Presidents, in the forty years between Garfield and Harding, were drawn either from governorships, the Cabinet or from unofficial life.

With a senator in the White House who had been the special choice of the senators, it was assumed that there would be an unusual display of team-work by the President and Congress. But a team is nothing without a driver, and no one had received a mandate to drive. The campaign pledge to "end executive autocracy," such as the party platform arraigned Wilson for having exercised, would have tied even stronger, rougher hands than Harding's, and Congress itself developed no unified leadership.

The very bigness of the Republican victory in 1920 was a misfortune for the victors. Necessarily a seven million majority had to be made up of such a variety of moods and opinions as to confuse its meaning and to leave the administration without a clear chart for its course.

Harding had promised in the campaign to be guided by the "best minds," but he found to his bewilderment that "as many men, so many minds." He was naturally more of a conciliator than a leader, but the divisions that rended his party in 1910-12 reappeared with its return to power and refused to be reconciled even by his conciliatory spirit. The huge Republican majorities in the two Houses of Congress fell apart into factions and "blocs," which resulted in a sharp political reaction in the election of 1922 that all but wiped out the wide Republican margin in each House.

The President himself was more spared from bitter personal hostility than any President in recent times, except McKinley. He had the wisdom—and the courage it required—to choose three or four exceptionally strong, independent characters for his Cabinet, which diverted public attention from less worthy selections.

For the purpose of rendering to the people an account of his stewardship and of personally investigating the confused conditions of Alaska, the President entered upon an extended tour in the summer of 1923. Mrs. Harding, who accompanied him, had been seriously ill in the winter, and his anxiety for her had weighed heavily upon him. She in turn was not without a wifely concern for his physical condition, which had grown sluggish in the conventional restraints of the Presidency.

Unfortunately his good nature left him unprotected against the mistaken hospitality of thoughtless enthusiasts on his long, hot trip, and against the selfish demands upon his strength by local boosters. He was worn out and a very sick man on his return from Alaska, where he was the first of our chief executives to visit the wide spaces of that territory. He persisted, notwithstanding, in going through exhausting programs at Vancouver (where he was the first President to call on our next-door neighbors, the Canadians), and also at Seattle and finally in making the long journey to San Francisco.   There at last he succumbed to rebellious nature and reluctantly canceled his plan to go home by way of the Panama Canal and Porto Rico.

Two Presidents having broken down in four years under the strain of a Presidential tour, the attention of the public was sharply drawn to the abuses and dangers attending the custom.   Washington himself had introduced it, and Congress, in recent years, had given it the sanction of law by appropriating twenty-five thousand dollars a year for the President's traveling expenses, in addition to his seventy-five thousand dollars salary.

To be sure, it took less time and energy to go by special train from the Atlantic to the Pacific in Harding's day than it required for the first President to go by coach over wretched roads from New York to Portsmouth, N. H., in 1789.   But the people themselves, in their mistaken democracy, have made it far harder for a President to travel in recent decades.   The bustling and pulling and hauling of him, the heedless requisitions and clamorous pressure upon him, by committees and crowds alike, all out for a holiday at the expense of their distinguished victim, are beyond the physical endurance of anyone but an athlete in training.

Yet the people now have less reason than their fathers had for insisting that the President should leave his real post of duty at Washington to "show himself to the country."   With the aid of the motion picture, radio and television, a far greater multitude have seen and heard the latest President than saw or heard President Taft in all his one hundred and fifty thousand miles of going up and down the land.

It seemed as if the Nation had received a much needed lesson cheaply, when the attending physicians issued a hopeful bulletin from the bedside of President Harding at the Palace Hotel in San Francisco. To the relief of sympathetic and anxious millions, apparently he had won the battle, after struggling four days against an attack of pneumonia. He had indeed made the hard grade; but the effort had left him utterly exhausted.

In the early evening, while his devoted wife was reading to him a favorable press review of his administration, she thought she saw him falling asleep, and she paused. "That's good; go on," he urged her in drowsy tones. Before she could resume, he was dead, "without a word or a groan," the doctors attributing the sudden end to a stroke of apoplexy or the rupture of a blood vessel in the brain.

The good news of the afternoon left the country wholly unprepared for the shock of the bad news that was tolled by the bells in the night. As the funeral train made its long journey from coast to coast, to the Capitol and on to the last resting place at Marion, the people united in public tributes of respect to the memory of a President, the first in more than seventy years, to die a natural death while in office. They were still more deeply touched by a feeling of personal sorrow for the loss of a friend.

CALVIN COOLIDGE

I

NEW ENGLAND'S WINDFALL

(1872) July 4, Calvin Coolidge born at Plymouth, Vermont.—(1895) Graduated at Amherst College.—(1897) Admitted to the Massachusetts bar.—(1899-1900) In City Council of Northampton, Mass.—(1900-01) City solicitor.—(1905) Married Miss Grace Goodhue of Burlington, Vt.—(1907-08) In Massachusetts House of Representatives.—(1910-11) Mayor of Northampton.—(1912-15) In State Senate (President, 1914-15).—(1916-18) Lieutenant-governor.—(1919-20) Governor.

NEW ENGLAND had not seen one of her own sons in the White House for more than two-thirds of a century, when the prize for which Daniel Webster and James G. Blaine had vainly struggled half a life-time and which was summarily denied George F. Edmunds and Thomas B. Reed, dropped as a windfall at the unexpectant feet of Calvin Coolidge between two August days of 1923.

From the death scene at San Francisco, the country turned upon its new President, at the opposite side of the continent, a puzzled but hopeful gaze, in an effort to see what it had drawn in the lottery of fate. It beheld a strange personality, somewhat the strangest to take its place in the line in many a year; not at all Presidential in its outlines, as Harding's was, but unique within and without; racy of the soil from which it sprang and with the tang and twang of the Yankee.

Not only was this the first New Englander in the Presidency since Franklin Pierce; here also was the first President since Garfield literally to have sprung from the soil, to have been born and brought up on a farm; the second farmer's son since Lincoln. After having cleared out the British redcoats in the Revolution, a Massachusetts Coolidge had cleared that farm in the Vermont wilderness. Four generations of Coolidges had wrung a meagre living from its reluctant fields atop the Green Mountains before Calvin mowed it in vacation time while, by methods known only to New England thrift, it was being made to pay his way through academy and college, aided by the village store.

In those days of his youth he was John Calvin, having been named for his father; but, like Stephen Grover Cleveland and Thomas Woodrow Wilson, he dropped his first name when he went out into the world, thereby increasing his chances for the Presidency. For have not more than two-thirds of our Presidents had each but a single Christian name? In fifty years had not every candidate with two given names lost the Presidential race, whenever matched against a man who was not thus weighted down at his christening?

Not far away from the little farm that raised a President is the birthplace of Stephen A. Douglas, who may or may not have said that Vermont was a good place to hail from and that he had hailed from there at the first chance. However that may be, so many Vermonters in the course of a century have emulated the "Little Giant" in going West that the State has fallen from the sixteenth to the forty-fifth rank in population. The town of Plymouth itself, like many of its sister hill towns of New England, has dwindled away a full half since the Fourth of July, 1872, when there was born to it the first President to have for his birthday the natal day of the republic.

For those who stay behind on the niggard acres of

PRESIDENT AND GRACE GOODHUE COOLIDGE

New England's upland farms, the inexorable conditions of survival are toil and thrift. Nor are there better teachers than these of simple living and straight thinking, provided only that the pupil has the hardihood to endure such stern instruction. It is an unequalled training school in the patient self-control and the quiet self-reliance that mark the character of the latest but not, by any means, the first President to graduate from it.

A strong father, whose qualities of leadership had enabled him to run the annual town meeting and which gave him a seat in the House and Senate of his State, had to take the place of the mother, who died when Calvin was twelve; and the motherless child was reared in the Puritan fear of soft indulgences.

"I remember," the grown-up boy once said in a newspaper interview, "asking father one day for a cent to buy a stick of hoarhound candy. He refused my request and explained gravely that it looked as if the Democrats were going to carry the national election that fall and that it behooved prudent people to be exceedingly careful. But when Garfield had won and father was assured of the safety of the country for another four years, he gave me the cent out of the jar where he and mother put any spare coins." And the interviewer was pointed to the cherished jar on the mantlepiece at the home of the Coolidges in Northampton.

"I never made any rules for Calvin to follow," the father once said. "If there are rules," he explained shrewdly, "it gives a boy a chance to break them. I told him to do his work well, and he always did. That was what my father taught me, and that was what his father taught him." And he added, "It always seemed to me that Calvin could get more sap out of a maple tree than any of the other boys around here."

As the twig was bent on that mountain farm, the tree still was inclined when it was transplanted at college, in a Northampton law office and in the field of Massachusetts politics. The son remained as frugal of words and emotions as his father had been of cents in the household savings bank.

"I went in more for educating my mind than my legs," he had said of his college days. Nevertheless, his class seems to have divined the native wit of its noiseless member when it selected him to deliver the humorous oration on Class Day. But his classmates fell down badly when they balloted on the question of which of them would go farthest in life; only one among them guessed right.

The lawyer, in whose Northampton office the lean, auburn-haired graduate of Amherst College "read law," was surprised one day to learn from a newspaper that his student had been awarded the prize in a national competition among college seniors for the best essay on the causes of the War of Independence.

"Have you written your father about this?" the lawyer asked.

"No; thought I wouldn't bother him," the winner replied and then relapsed into his accustomed stillness.

"I have generally been able," he said, "to make enough noise to get what I wanted." Somehow the young man contrived to make enough noise to get what he wanted in the formation of a life partnership. The sound foundation of his career was completed by his marriage to an opposite in spontaneity and vivacity, but who yet had her partner's freedom from pretensions and his independence of the superfluities that load so many people down. One-half of a two-family house on a modest side street of Northampton, at a monthly rental of thirty-three dollars, sufficed them till they moved into the White House—and they got along without a car.

As the bystanders watched this shyly silent man, without any of the usual tricks of the game, win success after success at the polls, they gave up the conundrum in despair and called it "Coolidge Luck." But the Vermont hills do not breed a dependence on luck.

Moreover, hardly another President has had to make his way, as he made his, from the very bottom rung of the political ladder. Harding was able to skip everything below the State Senate. Roosevelt began as an assemblyman; Cleveland as a sheriff. Wilson started in almost at the top of elective offices, as governor; Harrison as a United States senator; Arthur as Vice-President. Taft never knew what it was to run for office, until he ran for the Presidency itself. Coolidge, on the contrary, took every rung in the ladder from common councilman to governor.

Thus he learned politics and acquired experience in government from the ground up; all the way from ringing door-bells in a neighborhood canvass, to manœuvering the forces of public opinion in State and Nation. As he looked back over that path by which he had come to the Presidency, he sat down in the White House and wrote a Northampton shoemaker, who had helped him at the outset: "If it were not for you, I should not be here."

As the puzzled politicians watched Calvin Coolidge, disregarding all the rules of their craft, step from office to office, they asked one another, over and over again, "How does he do it?" Perhaps he himself came as near as anyone to hinting the answer, when he replied to a man who inquired if it was true that he had never been defeated at the polls but once and then for the school committee: "No; but I've always been prepared to be."

II

THE HOMELIEST INAUGURATION

(1919) Sept. 9, the Boston Police Strike. November, Calvin Coolidge re-elected governor of Massachusetts.—(1920) June, nominated for Vice-President by the Republicans. November, elected.— (1921) March 4, inaugurated Vice-President.—(1923) Aug. 3, sworn in by his father as President, aged fifty-one.

WHEN it was supposed that Calvin Coolidge had mounted the political ladder as high as he was likely to go and would have to come down, the Boston police strike in 1919 raised a question that drew the attention of all the country to the governor of Massachusetts and to his answer to that question: "There is no right to strike against the public safety by anybody, anywhere, any time." What Governor Coolidge did and did not do in the police strike still may be a subject of dispute; but no one questions that what he said about it made him President.

Following his triumphant re-election to the governorship, on the heels of the strike, his friends entered him for the Republican nomination for President the next year. But in the slang of the psycho-analyists, New England had developed, in her long exclusion from the White House, an inferiority complex, and she did not take the chances of her candidate seriously. When even Massachusetts faltered in his support, and her distinguished senior senator, Henry Cabot Lodge, came out for another, Governor Coolidge suddenly withdrew his name, which was nevertheless presented to the convention by a divided delegation from his State.

The only campaigning in his interest took the form of a book of his speeches, entitled "Have Faith in Massachusetts," which a few friends widely distributed at an expense of some fifty thousand dollars. As this was read all over the country, its homely axioms sank into many minds and stayed there:

"We need more of the office desk and less of the show window in politics." . . . "Let men in office substitute the midnight oil for the limelight." . . . "Duty is not collective; it is personal." . . . "Men do not make laws; they do but discover them." . . . "Expect to be called a standpatter, but don't be a standpatter. Expect to be called a demagogue, but don't be a damagogue. Don't hesitate to be as revolutionary as science. Don't hesitate to be as reactionary as the multiplication table." . . . "The people who elect a man to get what he can for his district, will probably find that they have elected a man who will get what he can for himself."

Although the Massachusetts governor remained in the back of many a head in the convention, he was left out of the combinations that resulted in a nomination for President and also out of the plans that were made for the selection of a nominee for Vice-President. As the choice of the inner circle for this latter place was about to be perfunctorily ratified by an exhausted convention, the mention of the name of Calvin Coolidge by a lone voice from Oregon, over in a far corner of the hall, acted like a lighted match tossed into a heap of fireworks. The galleries were the first to ignite, but the delegates themselves soon were aflame in an all-enveloping conflagration, and there was a wild stampede to Coolidge, who was nominated by an overwhelming vote.

With his election, the inescapable oblivion attaching to his office shut down upon Vice-President Coolidge, until the news of the serious illness of the President surprised him in the midst of a vacation on his native farm in Vermont, and turned the spotlight upon him. Miles from the railroad and the telegraph, he was even beyond the call of the telephone, when men in motor cars raced in the night up the side of the Green Mountains to awaken him with the unexpected announcement that he had been promoted to the Presidency while he slept.

Quickly a wire was strung into the farmhouse that until then had sternly disdained such a modern convenience, and the Vice-President was put in communication with the Attorney-General in San Francisco and the Secretary of State in Washington. On their advice, he took the oath of his new office at once, his father, as notary public, administering it between two and three o'clock, in the light of a kerosene lamp on the sitting-room table. With grim self-repression, the notary performed the solemn function normally reserved for the Chief Justice of the United States. As calmly as he had given his boy his chores to do, he swore his son to execute the office of President, and to preserve, protect and defend the Constitution. Nor could the seductive prospect of reflected glory beguile the spartan father from his duties at home to see Calvin take up his duties at Washington.

After that homeliest of inaugurations, and when the sun was yet hardly above the mountain tops, the new President started for the capital. As he was leaving, he turned aside from the functionaries and press correspondents, who had torn through the night to reach him, and visited alone the grave of his mother, to draw from her cherished memory, no doubt, an inspiration for his guidance in the high tasks that had fallen to him.

The sixth Vice-President to be elevated to the Presidency by the death of a President, he was the first whose accession did not portend an overturn in the policies of his predecessor. When Harrison was succeeded by Tyler, Taylor by Fillmore, Lincoln by Johnson, Garfield by Arthur, and McKinley by Roosevelt, the transfer of power in each instance amounted to a political revolution, because each of those Presidents and Vice-Presidents belonged to opposing factions or schools of political philosophy. Harding and Coolidge, on the contrary, though far apart in manner and temperament, were both identified with the same conservative group in the Republican party.

For the first time, moreover, President Harding had included the Vice-President in his Cabinet and made him a member of his official family. Such a relationship would have been irksome if not impossible in most instances, as the custom has been for party conventions to select an ill-matched team, with the studied purpose of balancing the ticket between conflicting elements. Calvin Coolidge had only to change places at the council table when he sat down in the Presidential chair and faced the heavy responsibilities of the highest post to which an American can be called.

III

A YANKEE SPHYNX

(1923) August 4, Calvin Coolidge opened presidential headquarters at a Washington hotel. — August 13, Occupied the White House. — (1924) Feb. 18, Resignation of Sec. Denby. — March 28, Resignation of Atty. Gen. Daugherty. — June 12, Coolidge nominated for President by Republicans at Cleveland. — July 7, Death of Calvin Coolidge, Jr. — Nov. 4, Coolidge Elected. — (1925) March 4, Inaugurated. — (1926) Jan. 27, Senate consented to World Court. — March 19, Death of Col. John C. Coolidge, the President's father.

CALVIN COOLIDGE'S sudden promotion to the presidency caught the political leaders in the midst of an open debate as to whom they should put in his place on the ticket with Harding the next year. Many of the elder statesmen still frankly went on in the easy assumption that he would be only an *ad interim* President, merely filling out the term of his deceased predecessor, and they cast their eyes about for a successor to him.

Nothing could have been more natural than for the "big noises" of politics, our stereotyped statesmen, to have lost their reckoning in the presence of the wry, shy surface of this accidental tenant of the White House. He himself has explained his "complex": "When I was a youngster, if I heard that there was a stranger in my mother's kitchen, it was a sore trial for me to go in and speak to him. Early in life, I made up my mind that this was something I must fight." And he fought it all the way up to the presidency!

Still there was the precedent which debarred from a presidential term of their own the Vice Presidents whose feet had been thrust into dead men's shoes. Roosevelt alone had broken the rule, and this latest President by succession was no Rough Rider hero but a stranger both to the leaders and to the people. It was said that he never had passed a night in a sleeping car until after his nomination for Vice President, so little had he traveled beyond the borders of New England.

And there was the ancient superstition that the folks out in the wide open spaces would not warm up to a New Englander in national politics. That ghost was laid at the first test. The people were as ready to welcome this New England act on the political stage as they had been to welcome rustic New England dramas on the theatrical stage. "That old kerosene lamp is just as good as a log cabin," a senator shrewdly reckoned, as he hastened to crowd upon the Coolidge bandwagon.

Calvin Coolidge became over night a legendary character, an idealized composite of all the traits and virtues of his race. Pilgrims in automobiles by the hundreds and thousands from the forty-eight states made a mecca of the mountain hamlet of four or five houses in Vermont, where a President was born in the back room of a cross roads store and was sworn in by his own father. With his parental pride hidden like a guilty thing in his Puritan consciousness, the father, until his death, received his visitors with a native dignity, opened an album for their autographs and let them sit in the chair where his son sat as he signed the oath . . . with an old penholder that had served the frugal family some fifty years!

Traffic police became a necessity at Plymouth Notch the next summer, when Calvin returned for his vacation in the midst of the campaign of 1924. The daily word and camera pictures of the President in such a background so took the public fancy that his baffled opponents railed at him for "posing" and "playing politics" and raged at the "Coolidge myth," though he was doing only what he had done in the more than twenty summers since he went out into the world.

Fortune often has befriended President Coolidge's party. That capricious goddess never came to its aid more opportunely than when she opened to him the door of the White House. Not at all in anger but altogether in sorrow, the country had been losing its hope in President Harding, whose easy-going ways were resulting in rough going for his party. But when, in the winter following his death, investigations by the Senate uncovered scandals that eventuated in the criminal indictment of two of his cabinet appointees and the forced resignation of another, public opinion refused to hold his successor responsible.

All round the world it was the cold gray dawn of the morning after the disillusionment of victory in a war which both sides equally lost, as they lose in every war. Mankind had grown wary of experiment and weary of adventure. The nations were sick with fear of Bolshevism, on the one hand, and of bankruptcy, on the other. In their terror and bewilderment, they wanted only to stop awhile and sit tight. And here in the White House, by act of Providence, was a Heaven-sent quiet man, as set as his own Green Mountains; no mere standpatter, but the first convinced, instinctive, stand-without-hitching conservative in the twenty years since McKinley.

Excursions in idealisms and crusades for democracy, accompanied by financial inflation and followed by deflation, had left the people intent only on getting a living. They heard gladly the new gospel that "the business of America is business," as it fell from the thin, taut lips of a President who practiced what he preached, with no golfing, riding, tennis playing or any softer indulgence to interrupt the day's work.

It was a time for budgeting and retrenchment. Tax reduction and economy had become as blessed words as Mesopotamia, and who could get more mileage out of a dollar than a Vermonter?

A third of the big national debt was owed to us, in turn, by our associate nations in the war. When the new President was asked, at the outset, if the rumor was true that he was in favor of canceling those borrowings by the Allies, he answered the question, after the fashion of his canny folk, by asking another: "They hired the money, didn't they?"

A new political factor took the politicians by surprise and went to the assistance of a President who held the record of only one defeat in nineteen elections. The radiophone made the Democrats the laughing stock in 5,000,000 homes that listened in on more than two weeks of faction and sectarian snarling at the Democratic National Convention in Madison Square Garden, New York. On the other hand, the President's Yankee metallic tones made a "perfect radio voice," and he "came over the air" so well that everybody "got him."

The Democrats having made a farce of their campaign at the start, the needed melodrama was contributed by the candidacy of the elder Senator LaFollette of Wisconsin, with the attendant danger of the three-cornered election being thrown into a House of Representatives where no party had a majority. As the alternative to that chaos, the President swept every state in the North, with the solitary exception of Wisconsin, and broke into the old solid South itself. With the sweet of that triumph was mingled the bitter of a great domestic sorrow, earlier in the year, in the death of his younger son and namesake, and he faced both dispensations with the same impenetrable mask.

The President and the political leaders remained all the while at arm's length. Within a month before his almost unanimous nomination, Congress overrode his veto of the Soldiers' Bonus Bill and flouted his objections to an increase of pay for postal employees and to the insertion in the Immigration Bill of a gratuitous clause excluding Japanese immigrants. A few weeks after his signal endorsement at the polls, the Senate made bold to deny him the traditional privilege of a President to choose his own cabinet advisers, rejecting his nominee for Attorney General.

He was unable to prevent the revolt of the western wing of his party against the eastern, on the question of legislation that would compensate agriculture for the advantages that manufactures derive from a high protective tariff. In due time, the popular primaries also tended to reflect the same spirit of independence, in retiring senators who had relied on their support of the President to pull them through.

Apparently President Coolidge's popularity was too personal to be transferred or shared. The country seems to have accepted him less as a leader than because he stood alone; less for his measures than for himself: — a shrewd, honest, hard-working, capable administrator; an executive who minded his own business and indulged in no lost motions for the sake of pretending to do what he could not, to be what he was not; a President who wore his honors quietly, simply, and with the dignity of a man boldly self-reliant, yet knowing his limitations and humbly keeping within them; who went his own way, unafraid to be himself.

IV

"I DO NOT CHOOSE TO RUN"

(1927) August 2, Coolidge's Puzzling Renunciation, sprung upon the
    Country from Rapid City, South Dakota.—(1933) January 5,
    Died at Northampton, Massachusetts, aged 60 years and six
    months. January 7, Buried at Plymouth, Vermont.

NOTHING in Calvin Coolidge's presidency was wiser
than his leaving it . . . with the laconic announcement, "I do not choose to run for President in 1928."
The personification of prudence and frugality, he
found himself by a prank of fortune taken for a joy
ride on the wildest of American booms. Himself an
exemplar of the simple life, it was his ironical fate to
preside over a national orgy of extravagant living.

"Keep cool with Coolidge" had been the slogan of
his victorious campaign in 1924. In two years more
the country was running its highest recorded temperature of feverish speculation in stocks and bonds, in
land and building. A boiling Wall Street market took
its name from a President who never had turned his
hand over to make money. Sometimes, alas, it also
took its cue from him when he and his Secretary of
the Treasury, Andrew W. Mellon, fed the roaring
flames with optimistic assurances. Those official pro-
nouncements solemnly were echoed by certain professors, who learnedly argued that we were in a "new
era," with the blue sky no longer the limit, and the
prices of stocks and bonds soared into the illimitable
stratosphere.

Meanwhile we were pouring out a flood of exports
on the world and preventing our foreign customers
from paying for them by maintaining a high tariff wall
against imports. Nor could they well remit in gold since
we already had drained into our coffers forty per cent

of all that token metal. There was nothing left for us to do but to lend our buyers abroad the money with which to pay us. Exporting capital as well as commodities, we sent our go-getting young men up and down the earth to gather in foreign securities, national, municipal and industrial, which were peddled out to American investors by high pressure "bond salesmen," whose name became legion.

That fool's paradise of prosperity made the President's re-election sure, when he astonished and puzzled the country with his declination of it in 1927, on the fourth anniversary of his accession to office. He was, at the time, spending the summer in the Black Hills of South Dakota. Until Theodore Roosevelt's term a president had taken his yearly vacation much like any citizen, leaving the cares and pomp of Washington behind him, and we heard nothing of "Summer White Houses." In contrast with the plainness of his private life, Coolidge kept up the presidential state wherever he went. He took with him on his vacations the largest retinue that ever had attended a chief magistrate on such an occasion, including a company of marines and a carload of press correspondents and photographers. To the amazement of these he handed them his great renunciation in a single sentence, written by his own hand on a sheet of paper.

The meaning of "I do not choose" became the riddle of the nation. Only those versed in the idioms of northern New England sensed the finality it expressed. For it was as Vermont as maple syrup. When a Vermonter says "I dew not chewse" to do a thing, there's an end on't; he is as set as his Green Mountains. But even the President's own political manager, who had not been taken into his confidence, contended that the country was left none the less free to choose him again.

A clamorous "draft Coolidge" movement persisted until the Republican National Convention of 1928 reluctantly called the roll for the nomination of another man.

Coolidge's self-elimination continued to puzzle the country after his retirement, but he never vouchsafed a postscript to his original announcement. When the "Coolidge Market" and "Coolidge Prosperity" collapsed within the year of his leaving the White House, some credulous folk were sure that he had been sufficiently weather-wise to foresee the crash and had got out betimes. But he had sounded no warning of the brewing storm in his last message to Congress in December, 1928, which was a song of praise for the prosperity that still abounded.

A quoted remark by him in private conversation to the effect that "ten years is a long time to be President" suggests that his decision may have been influenced by a shrewd reflection that two terms had been too much for the temper of every re-elected President, from Washington to Wilson, and too much for the public temper also. His own re-election would have given him the longest tenure of any tenant of the White House and would have stretched the tradition against a third term.

Still that consideration would not account for the complete retirement from politics in which this lifelong politician shut himself the moment he walked away from the Hoover inauguration to the train which was waiting to carry him back to Northampton. Is it not more likely that he looked within himself and perceived the waning of a never robust vitality, which was in fact destined to cut short his life before the end of another presidential term?

He went back to his half of the old two-family

house, but he was so irked by the gaze of public curiosity that he retreated from its little porch on the street. Ultimately he sought the seclusion afforded by another house, set in nine acres of ground sloping down to the Connecticut River. He went back to his old law office, but not to resume the practice of a profession which he always had treated with indifference. Rarely could he be persuaded to make a public appearance. In the forlorn hope campaign of his party in 1932, he limited his activities to the writing of an article, the delivery of a speech in New York and to a brief radio talk. He complained that he was having difficulty in breathing.

Almost exhausted by the labor of preparing his thirty minute address for the New York meeting, he vowed to the veteran journalist, Henry L. Stoddard, that he would never again go through the "agony of making a speech." Following the overwhelming defeat of the Republicans and the sweeping victory of Roosevelt and the New Deal, he sighed that the "new fangled things so popular now" admonished him that we were "in a new era to which I do not belong."

When he first returned to Northampton, he seems not to have intended to stay there but to look for some remunerative employment elsewhere. Among the opportunities presented to him, none passed the test of his scruples against the involvement of his name and prestige with any business having governmental or political relations. "I don't want the Senate investigating me," he drawled. He accepted a membership in the directorate of a life insurance company and the chairmanship of a board that was organized for the study of the transportation problem.

Like three other ex-Presidents, Van Buren, Grant and Theodore Roosevelt, he wrote an autobiography.

A newspaper syndicate engaged him in 1930 to write daily a two hundred word comment, for which it paid him about as many thousands of dollars a year. Although this alone gave him the largest income that ever had been received by an ex-President, he refused to continue the series a second year.

Returning summers to his native Plymouth Notch, he built an addition to his father's little cottage. In his ever failing health, his mind grew increasingly morbid. But only those close to him were at all prepared for the news that surprised his countrymen on January 5, 1933, when, in his sixty-first year, he dropped dead in his Northampton home, "The Beeches."

His death befell in the depths of the depression, for which the country had taken savage vengeance on the Republican party in the preceding November. The woods were full of scapegoats, loaded down with the sins of a nation that was looking back with bitter remorse and recrimination to the excesses committed in the period of Coolidge's presidency. But he himself escaped the day of wrath. He had made no pretension to controlling events. In fact, he had been chosen with an implicit mandate to let business alone, to give it a free rein. Although the people were in a violent reaction from his political and social philosophy, they were not estranged from him. They had continued to chuckle over the latest in an endless chain of anecdotes about this quaint member of the big American family.

On a stormy, wintry day, the cross-roads hamlet in the mountains of Vermont which had the unique distinction of having seen both the birth and inauguration of a President saw also his burial in a steep, rocky slope where, he had said, "My dead lie, pillowed on the loving breast of our everlasting hills."

HERBERT CLARK HOOVER

I

A NEW ROAD TO THE WHITE HOUSE

(1874) August 10, Herbert Clark Hoover born at West Branch, Iowa.—(1895) Graduated at Stanford University.—(1897) Mining engineer in Australia.—(1899) Married Lou Henry of Monterey, California, and went to China.—(1902–17) Headquarters in London.—(1909) Published "Principles of Mining."— (1912) In collaboration with Mrs. Hoover, published translation from the Latin of Agricola's "De Re Metallica."—(1914) August-September, shipping home American tourists stranded by the World War.—(1914-17) Chairman of American Commission for Relief of Belgium.—(1917-19) Food Administrator of United States.—(1919) Chairman Supreme Economic Conference at Paris.—(1920) Chairman European Relief Council.

PLEASE let it be said once again that we may trace in the lives of our presidents the outlines of the ever changing life of our country. For one more example, take a certain young mining engineer, whose professional training and natural gifts would have been absorbed by his own land if only he had started out a few years earlier. But mining had become rather a settled business with us and the frontier of American adventure had passed overseas, to Africa, to the Antipodes and to Asia by the time Herbert Clark Hoover graduated with the first class at Stanford University in 1895.

That is why, in the generation when American trade and enterprise expanded world-wide, a president-to-be made his first appearance on the front page of the newspapers of his native country under a foreign

PRESIDENT AND MRS. HOOVER

date line. It was a cable dispatch from London, at the outbreak of the World War, that introduced the name of H. C. Hoover to his own people. Although it had long been known to his craft the earth round, the press of the United States searched its "morgues" in vain for an "obit" or a picture of the man who had gone to the rescue of frantic American vacationists in Europe, suddenly caught by the tidal wave of armed conflict at the peak of the tourist season of 1914, when he was entrusted by the American Ambassador in England with the job of gathering up, financing and shipping home thousands of stranded compatriots.

The story of this thirtieth president registers still other changes in the history of the nation. After the presidency had been for one hundred and forty years the exclusive possession of men born on the old colonial seaboard or within the bounds of three among the states carved out of colonial territory—Vermont, Kentucky and Ohio—the time had more than come for the honor to pass farther westward. And it crossed the Mississippi River to choose an Iowan by birth, a Californian by adoption.

This first native son of the great prairie in the presidential line was also the first of the Quaker faith. His predecessors, moreover, had been of British ancestry, with the exception of two who were of Holland descent. Hoover was the first president to spring from the great stream of German migration to Pennsylvania—the "Pennsylvania Dutch"—with a name that was traced back ultimately to a Huber from Switzerland.

'Twas a tall, lean-figured but round-faced 17-year-old boy who knocked at the door of Stanford University in California just as it was opening for its first term. A son of the blacksmith in an Iowan village and of a strong mother whose spirit often moved her to eloquence in the Friends Meeting House, he was orphaned in early boyhood and had grown up in the family of an uncle in Oregon. As he emerged from the self repression of the gray Quaker colonies where he had passed his life, he was a bashful, almost tongue-tied lad, with about three hundred dollars behind him in all the world and with four years of college tuition and expenses ahead of him. To meet these, he served as office boy to a professor, worked a newspaper and laundry route, ran a lecture and concert course—with young William Jennings Bryan among his lecturers—and he went off to the mountains in summers with mining and geological expeditions.

He lost much time, he lamented afterward, "just to make a living;" but he was also making the beginning of a life that else might not have turned out so well. If he could not be of the fraternity elite at college, he did join in the overthrow of their domination of student politics, and he slowly built up friendships that were loyally to follow him round the globe on his unique course from Palo Alto to the White House—with a "co-ed" from Stanford ever by his side.

Graduating in the depth of the business depression that followed the panic of 1893, he pocketed his diploma for the time being and went to work in a Nevada mine with the pick and shovel of a common laborer. As quickly as he could stake himself with savings from his daily wage of two dollars and a half, he took a more congenial job, but without pay, in the office of a San Francisco mining engineer, who was not long in seeing that the youngster was worth fifty dollars a month. When the engineer received a request from Australia, where there was a gold rush and a British company wished to install American machinery and methods, he picked Hoover for the work and gave him a chance that was better than anything this country was likely to offer so young a man in that chosen specialty.

Straightway the twenty three year old engineer uncovered in himself executive gifts which brought· him a call to China. Arranging by cable from opposite sides of the world a marriage with Miss Lou Henry of Monterey, California, whom he first met in a geologist's laboratory at Stanford, they were married between sailings and entered upon a twenty year journey, which took them to China, to Ceylon, Burma, the Malay Peninsula, Russia, Siberia and to Africa. From being a shrewd consulting physician of sick mines, Hoover became a prosperous director, promoter and financier of mining properties, with a home in London from 1902 to 1917, mostly at Red House, with its walled garden. But he had also for a time a country residence on the Thames with the more prophetic name of White House!

With a chain of offices that encircled the globe, from London to Melbourne, Shanghai and San Francisco to New York, this first millionaire in the presidency was accounted several times a millionaire at forty, when the World War brought his career to an end in a week and opened another to his organizing genius. As he saw military lines and naval blockades cutting off his far-scattered mines from their markets and the whole structure of his widespread international enterprises seemed about to crash, he wrote to one of his American partners, "I suppose we're all broke." While he was picking up the pieces—and shipping stranded American tourists home—the call came to him to organize the feeding of millions of Belgians, entrapped between the gray hosts of invading Germans, who were trampling their fields, and the Allied fleet, which closed their ports against food from abroad.

Really rich chances awaited him from the war's demands for the zinc and lead of his mines; but he flung the reins of his great business to his staff and gave himself wholly to saving a nation from starvation. In the seven years to come, as Chairman of the Belgian Relief until America herself entered the war, then as Food Administrator in the United States and finally as Chief of the Supreme Economic Council of the Allies, billions of dollars passed through his hands; but he received not a cent in compensation for his services, which left him, at the end, "the weary Titan," in the words of a colleague at Paris, John Maynard Keynes, the English economist.

When, upon our entry into the war, Mr. Hoover was summoned by President Wilson to the head of the Food Administration he had been away an even twenty years. But he had been back in every year save one, and his two sons already had returned to go to school in California. He was no expatriate, and home had remained all the while where his heart was, round about the campus at Stanford. Alien skies had not alienated even the accent of his native prairie.

As Food Administrator, it was his duty to feed the American army in France and to assure the Allied Armies of their full share of food from our great store. With money appropriated by Congress, he kept market prices high enough to induce the farmers to raise more; but he must also coax our civilian population to eat less. Without the authority of a line of law and relying wholly on winning the voluntary cooperation of the public, he succeeded in rationing the most extravagant and wasteful nation in the world, which loyally obeyed his traffic-like signals for meat less and wheatless days, when a hundred million people were inspired by his leadership with a sporting pride in Hooverizing.

II

AN ENGINEER IN POLITICS

(1921-28) Herbert Hoover Secretary of Commerce.—(1928) June 14, nominated for President by the Republicans at Kansas City. June 28, Governor Smith nominated by Democrats at Houston. Nov. 6, Hoover elected.—(1928-29) Nov. 19 to Jan. 6, On good will tour of Latin America.—(1929) March 4, Inaugurated, aged 54. March 26, First break in Wall Street. April 15, Special session of Congress. May 28, Law Enforcement Commission appointed. Oct. 5, President and Premier MacDonald conferred at Rapidan Camp on Naval Limitation. Oct. 29, The great Wall Street crash.

MEN on horseback had galloped into the White House out of all the wars until the World War. The American who emerged with the greatest popular prestige from that colossal combat of the machines of modern warfare was a noncombatant who never had worn an epaulette or carried a gun. He had, instead, fed the victims of the conflict in Belgium, then the allied armies in France and, at last, the defeated enemy in Germany.

Nor had Herbert Hoover—who somewhere dropped the middle name of Clark—ever voted in a national election, and his fame was a potential asset for either political party. As a member of the Wilson administration, who had seconded the unsuccessful appeal of his chief for the election of a Democratic Congress in 1918 and indorsed the President's stand at Paris for the League of Nations, he was the logical nominee for the Democrats in 1920, until he aligned himself with the Republicans early in that year. And he received a scattering vote on the roll call in the convention of each party.

The professionals gave a cool welcome to the selection of such an outsider for even the non-political post of Secretary of Commerce in the Harding Cabinet in 1921. But he won the grudging tolerance of many of them by his helpful counsel to committees of Congress and by his efficiency in greatly enlarging the usefulness of his department to the domestic and export business of the country. Still the old stagers in Republican politics were reluctant to admit the truth that he was their only available man when President Coolidge surprised the nation—including apparently even Mrs. Coolidge—with the announcement that he did not "choose to run" again in 1928.

The nomination of such a newcomer in politics would have been unthinkable in the first century of our national history, when all our presidents, with the exception of Taylor and Grant, had served life-long apprenticeships. Excepting those two soldiers, they had all sat in Congress, and most of them had seen service in the executive department also. But that was our political era which closed with the completion of reconstruction.

Thereafter politics grew less and less fertile in the production of men, and the parties found it increasingly desirable to import their presidential candidates from more productive fields than the routine of office holding. Two-thirds of the nine presidents from Cleveland to Hoover inclusive never sat in Congress, and a third never had held a post of any kind under the federal government. But they all were politically minded and had been active in the ranks of their parties, excepting only Taft and Hoover, who never had occupied an elective office before they were elected to the highest. And those exceptions seem to prove the rule that a president should have an inborn taste or aptitude for the art of governing, which is politics.

With his nomination in 1928, Mr. Hoover's political career was launched in a stormy sea. Unhappy prejudices strange to a national campaign were stirred to bitter dregs by the appearance of a new type on the presidential stage in the candidacy of the Democratic nominee, Governor Alfred E. Smith of New York, an offspring of the great nineteenth century immigration, a sachem of Tammany Hall and a communicant of the Catholic Church, at whose ancient altar two Chief Justices of the United States and a general of the army but no president had worshipped.

The temper of the contest was heated still further by the introduction of prohibition as an issue between the parties for the first time since members of both had united to place the eighteenth amendment in the Constitution in 1920. With Governor Smith boldly declaring for repeal, Mr. Hoover as emphatically took his stand in favor of continuing what he termed a great experiment, "noble in motive."

The tariff, "Coolidge prosperity" and a promise of farm relief enabled the Republicans to close their ranks generally. The Democratic lines crumpled under the impact of the resistance to innovations posed by Governor Smith's candidacy and campaign, and even the solid south went to pieces, from Virginia to Texas.

Prosperity was the trump card of the Republicans, and they played it to the limit. There were many disinterested persons who entertained the belief that a great and new kind of social revolution actually was in peaceable progress, redistributing and diffusing the wealth of the nation as never before and promising to make real at last the boast that this is a commonwealth.

Hoover himself visualized the approach of the day when poverty would be no more. Discarding as out-of-date McKinley's slogan of "a full dinner pail," he substituted the "full garage," with a "chicken in every pot." Statistics of automobiles, radios, electric washing machines and our abundance of all manner of things rolled off his tongue like water running away from a fountain as he asserted that those material blessings had been made possible only by Republican policies under Harding and Coolidge.

Immediately after the election, a President-elect with a longer experience than any other in the foreign field started on a good will tour of South America, which occupied more than half of the interval before his inauguration. He no sooner took office than he resolutely set about to remove the most serious cause of resentment toward us among our neighbors by adopting a policy which looked to the withdrawal of American military intervention in certain republics of the Caribbean. He also concerted with Premier Mac-Donald of England, as they sat side by side on a log at the President's fishing camp on the Rapidan River in Virginia, the London Naval Conference, which resulted in a brief accord among the principal naval powers of the world for a limitation of armament. With Japan engaging in an imperialistic adventure in Manchuria, he enunciated the "Hoover Doctrine," which served notice that the United States would not recognize any transfer of territory or property in violation of the Kellogg pact, whereby the nations had renounced the employment of armed forces as an instrument of policy.

At home, the President appointed a Farm Board, composed of able men, to wrestle with the problem of fulfilling the platform promise to restore agriculture to an equality with tariff-protected industry. He also selected a distinguished commission to study the means of enforcing the prohibitory and other laws. Its eleven members made eleven reports on the subject of prohibition, and the President himself, in his message to Congress, added a twelfth, in which he stood his ground in favor of the eighteenth amendment. But the amendment was foredoomed in a poll taken by the Literary Digest, which reflected an irresistible swing in public opinion to the side of repeal.

Mr. Hoover made a harder job of the presidency than any man since Cleveland had plodded at it. Taking no real vacation in four years, he hardly lifted his eyes from his desk to greet callers, and while they tarried his unresting hand drew geometrical designs on a writing pad. For exercise he indulged in no golf or other game but met a chosen group punctually at seven each morning for a round of medicine ball on the White House lawn. Toward the country he turned a humorless countenance, and if the people cannot laugh with a President they will not weep with him.

The administration had got off to an unfortunate start when a special session of Congress, which was convoked in the month after the inauguration, plunged into the longest tariff wrangle on record. The storm of criticism always raised by a general revision of the customs schedules was increased by the exposure before a Senate investigating committee of the lobbying that was going on in the framing of the pending Smoot-Hawley bill. The crowning misfortune of the administration came in the collapse of the "Coolidge market" in Wall Street, under an avalanche of more than sixteen million shares of stock that were dumped on the exchange one black October day in 1929.

III

A RUGGED INDIVIDUALIST

(1929) Oct. 29, the great Wall Street crash. Nov. 19-27, President
Hoover's series of White House Conferences on the depression.—
(1930) Great drought in the Southwest. Nov. 4, Republican re-
verses in election.—(1931) June 20, Hoover Moratorium proposed. July 6, finally accepted by France. Sept. 21, England went
off gold. Oct. 6, President asked bankers to organize National
Credit Institute. Dec. 8, Recommended to Congress Reconstruction Finance Corporation.—(1932) April 22, Senate investigation
of banking began. May 29, Bonus army entered Washington.
June 16, Hoover renominated. July 28, Bonus army camp
broken up. Nov. 8, Roosevelt elected. Nov. 12, Hoover invited
President-elect to conference on war debts.

THE country as a whole confidently had awaited a
President with Mr. Hoover's genius for efficiency and
administration, the first great business man in the
White House. Students of government may have been
less confident but they were none the less interested to
see an engineering mind, little trained in politics, applied to the art of governing and to the strategy of
popular leadership. For the duties of the presidency
are perhaps two-thirds political and only one-third
administrative in character.

Unluckily for that experiment, the problem was
made abnormally difficult for Mr. Hoover by a reaction in business which, as always, brought a correspond-
ing reaction in politics. Had he not been President,
he would have been the first man in America whom
the President would have summoned to the rescue in
such an emergency. But being President himself, he
needed to be a politician as well as an engineer.

He and his party having invited and received a
mandate to maintain prosperity, they found themselves in the awkward plight of having to administer
adversity. Naturally they were reluctant and slow to

see or admit the mere existence of such a thing, and they whistled the assurance that "prosperity is just around the corner" until the phrase became a byword. In fairness it should be recorded that few if any foresaw the stress to which the federal government would be subjected in the course of the downward spiral of business and employment. All other administrations had left the country unaided to ride out like storms in the past. In the hard times that began in 1873, President Grant did nothing. In a similar situation, following the panic of 1893, President Cleveland did no more than maintain the gold reserve in the Treasury.

Hoover was the first President to intervene in a depression, and he had no examples for his guidance. In the swift progress of organization, our businesses had been tied together across lines of trade, across state lines and even national frontiers until all the boundaries that once divided them, like the water-tight compartments of a ship, had been abolished. No unit could save itself alone. All units must sink or swim together. The one man in a position to see the problem as a whole and to make himself heard by all was the President of the United States.

In the month after the Wall Street crash, President Hoover began to put forth his leadership in White House conferences with financial, industrial, commercial and labor leaders. His counsels in favor of maintaining production and pay rolls may have served to cushion the fall. Certainly the decline escaped such violent disturbances as the Pullman Strike of 1894 and the Railroad Strike of 1877, which lowered the public morale in two former depressions.

A stalwart believer in what he termed "rugged individualism," the President was slow to advance beyond a moral to a political and governmental intervention in the crisis. As a sign of his confidence that the gale soon would blow over, he proposed in December, 1929, and Congress enacted a reduction in the income tax for a year. He balked at the appropriation of public money for the aid of distressed farmers in a widespread drought in 1930 and, instead, he led a successful Red Cross campaign for raising a $10,000,000 relief fund. When, at length, he did compromise with Congress, he insisted that the legislation should be limited to authorizing loans, rather than gifts, for seed and fodder, but not for human food. In his annual message of twelve thousand words in 1930, the principal measure he proposed for meeting the depression was a modest increase in public works. He restricted his action in behalf of the unemployed to the appointment of a committee to stimulate voluntary contributions for their relief.

The President's first radical political remedy for our ills was aimed at saving Europe from a threatened collapse in the early summer of 1931. There had been some welcome signs that the depression was arrested or slackening when the closing of an Austrian bank sent a shock through the European continent. Germany had been propping up Austria with loans and England had been propping up Germany by the same means. The Vienna failure started a run on gold, which menaced the gold standard generally and the whole world structure of finance, whose central faith was expressed in the common saying "as sound as the Bank of England."

The President was persuaded by European advisers that to save that ancient faith in the Bank of England and to save the gold standard it was imperatively necessary for him to take the lead in arranging a moratorium for one year on the war debts owed to us, and on all other intergovernmental obligations, including German reparations. Putting in two hundred long distance telephone calls for leading senators and representatives, he satisfied himself that Congress would consent to such a debt holiday, and he communicated the proposal to foreign governments. The Hoover Moratorium was welcomed and applauded everywhere except in France, which objected and negotiated for more than two weeks before accepting it, and in the interval the psychological effect of it was dissipated.

Within three months England went off gold. Whether as a consequence or merely as a coincidence, the depression was halted in that country at once but plunged to lower depths in this country through a year and a half more. The dollar was left virtually alone in a world of devalued currencies and the dearest of all the great monies. A long raid started on the American store of gold, drawing it away to Europe in some critical periods at the rate of twenty-five million dollars a day and also draining it and our paper currency into the strong boxes of hoarders at home.

The President met that latest crisis by resorting again to nonpolitical action and called upon the stronger banks to organize a credit fund for the protection of the weaker banks against the panic. When Congress met in December, 1931, he went beyond all precedents in our history and proposed that the government itself should go to the rescue with its own money and credit. His recommendation was expanded by the legislative branch in the prompt passage of the bill for the creation of the Reconstruction Finance Corporation, familiarly known as the R.F.C. He submitted still other proposals mainly aimed at checking the growth of a Treasury deficit, which was to reach an accumulated total of four billions at the end of the closing fiscal year of his administration.

Mr. Hoover's program was developed too late. For his party had lost control of the House of Representatives in the mid-term election of 1930, and the Senate remained Republican in name only, with the insurgents of that party as much opposed as the Democrats to the administration. The presidential campaign was only a few months away, and both parties were jockeying for positions in the race.

As the business of the country sank to new low levels, the people watched with dismay the squabbling and floundering of a divided and leaderless government at Washington. Public faith was shattered by the exposure before a Senate committee of devious methods employed by the heads of New York's two largest banks. Iowa farmers took to the open road in a strike against the marketing of crops at ruinous prices. An age of barter was returning in vast stretches of the agricultural regions. A "Bonus Expeditionary Force" of World War veterans, marching on Washington, presented a tactical problem that was muffed, and the breaking up of its camp within sight of the Capitol resulted in more than forty casualties, with three of them fatal.

In a desperate campaign for re-election, the President disregarded the example set by all his predecessors, with the warning exception of Taft, and went out from the White House to battle against the tide of dissatisfaction that had been gathering momentum for two years. His effort to galvanize the prosperity issue of 1928 was mocked when he prophesied that under a Democratic tariff "the grass will grow in the streets of a hundred cities" and "weeds will overrun the fields of millions of farms." Striving on to the end, he halted his homeward bound train at a Nevada station the night before election and spoke into the microphone his last appeal against a verdict that was sealed almost at the outset of the depression.

With the election of Roosevelt, Hoover did not relax his arduous labors. While hastening back to Washington from his California home he sent to his winning opponent an invitation to a conference at the White House, in the hope that they might co-operate in settling the question of the foreign war debt. The long gap between administrations, which a pending constitutional amendment would shorten in the future, could not be bridged by two men who were still more widely divided.

The outgoing President lavished no smiles on the inauguration of his successor. A "wearied Titan" again, he departed for New York at the end of a scene obviously painful to him and retired within a hotel apartment from the March hurricane of events which signalized the change of administrations at Washington. After resting a few days, he went on to Palo Alto, where he occupied himself with the World War Museum he had founded, until in due time he advanced to an attack on the New Deal from his home on a hilltop above the campus of his Alma Mater, whence he had started in youth on a voyage of life unique in the story of our presidents.

FRANKLIN DELANO ROOSEVELT

I

ANOTHER ROOSEVELT

(1882) January 30, Franklin Delano Roosevelt born at Hyde Park, New York.—(1896) Entered Groton School.—(1904) Graduated at Harvard.—(1904-07) Columbia Law School.—(1905) Married Eleanor Roosevelt.—(1907) Admitted to New York Bar.—(1910 and 1912) Elected and re-elected to the State Senate.—(1913-20) Assistant Secretary of the Navy.—(1920) Democratic candidate for vice President.

WHILE Theodore Roosevelt in 1911 was fighting "like a bull moose," to recapture the Republican machine, which had reverted to the standpatters after he left the presidency, the country first heard of another Roosevelt who was battling with the Democratic machine in the New York Legislature. This twenty-eight year old state senator, Franklin Delano, appeared to be running true to the Rooseveltan form, but many were surprised to find him on the other side of the party fence. Indeed a younger Theodore Roosevelt in after years characterized him as a political maverick who did not bear the Republican brand of the family. The family was in fact distinctively Democratic until President Theodore's father went Republican in the era of the Civil War, forsaking the political faith of his own father, whose other son, Robert Barnwell Roosevelt, remained for forty years a wheel horse in the Democratic party.

Moreover Franklin D. sprang from the Hudson

PRESIDENT AND MRS. ROOSEVELT

River tribe of Roosevelts, which had been separated from T. R.'s Oyster Bay tribe for five generations, and the two were only fifth cousins. They were more nearly related by marriage than by blood. For T. R. was the uncle of F. D.'s wife Eleanor, orphaned daughter of his only brother, Elliott. He had left the White House to give her away at the altar, where his own daughter (afterward Alice Roosevelt Longworth) was maid of honor. Notwithstanding the difference in their political antecedents, the strenuous President was the hero of the bridegroom, who had the year before bolted the absurd Democratic ticket of 1904 and cast his first ballot for his Republican cousin.

The New York papers reported the wedding under the headline, "Roosevelt-Roosevelt," and T. R. remarked after the ceremony, "It is a good thing to keep the name in the family." He could hardly have dreamed that between them they would also keep the presidency in the family. For at that time, only two names had been repeated in the list of Presidents— Adams and Harrison. One other family had returned to the White House, when Zachary Taylor, a kinsman of Madison, became its tenant. So stood the batting average of heredity in the greatest of our national games.

Franklin Delano Roosevelt is a blend of some of the oldest blood of both New York and New England, with no fewer than eleven Mayflower ancestors. Born to James Roosevelt and his second wife, Sara Delano, his birthplace at Hyde Park was the farm from which he went to the White House, the only President to have remained under the roof where he was born. It is suggestive of the migratory habits of this land of the covered wagon that but four among Franklin Roosevelt's thirty predecessors still dwelt in their native

towns at the time of their election to the presidency :—
the two Adamses of Quincy, Massachusetts, Van Buren
of Kinderhook, New York, and Taft of Cincinnati.

To the farm at Hyde Park, the great-grandfather
of Franklin had retreated some seventy miles up the
Hudson from the advance of New York City upon
the rural quiet of his country seat at Harlem; but the
great grandson resented any reference to the ancestral
acres as an "estate." He was jealous of the distinction of having been "born and raised" on a farm, to
him a real dirt farm, and proud of his knowledge of
horses and cattle, fields, forests and birds.

Within that domain he passed a boyhood sheltered
from the world by a zealous father, who was fifty-four
at his birth, and as the only child of a bride mother at
27. Tutored in the seclusion of a home of ease and
plenty, though not of great wealth according to the
standards of New York, he grew up without schoolmates and with few eligible playmates in a countryside
where his parents dwelt in the manner of what the
English term a "county family." Young cousins
abounded in the great metropolis down at the mouth
of the river, but he rarely saw the city except when
he was taken there to embark on a voyage across the
Atlantic. He had been to Europe eight times but
never to school when, at fourteen, he was conducted
by his father to Groton School in Massachusetts.
From Groton, where the boys were carefully chosen
from his own set, he passed on to the "gold coast"
at Cambridge and the select clubs of Harvard University. On his merits, he won the editorship of the
college daily newspaper, The Crimson, and that highest prize of undergraduate scholarship, a Phi Beta
Kappa key.

It was a strange bringing-up for a popular leader.

Cousin T.R. had the versatility to be both an aristocrat and a democrat, and he remained always at home
in the little world where he was born, even while it
laughed at his forays into the larger, ruder world.
F.D., on the contrary, being country-bred, was reared
apart from his native caste, and few of his associations
and friendships derived from it. Harvard manifested
more interest in Alfred Emmanuel Smith, when that
alumnus of Fulton Fish Market ran for President,
than it displayed four years afterward in the candidacy
of Roosevelt '04.

It was while he was in the Columbia Law School
that Franklin D. married. After a few years of law
practice, he was nominated for the State Senate by
the Democrats of Dutchess County, but merely for
the purpose of filling out their ticket with a respectable
name in a district they had last carried in the year
their twenty-eight year old nominee was born. His
Democratic allegiance had been confirmed by the laying on of hands in his early youth, when his father
took him to the White House to see Cleveland. Notwithstanding Grover ran for President three times, he
always affected a disdain for the office, and he sighed
as he patted the head of the lad in a sailor suit, "My
little man, I am going to make a strange wish for you
and it is that you may never be President of the
United States."

The young candidate for the Senate took in earnest
the apparently empty compliment of his nomination,
and the Republican politicians at Poughkeepsie laughed
at the sight of him clattering up and down the roads in
a hired automobile. As folks came out to see the yet
strange sight of a motor car campaign, Franklin stood
up in the seat and roundly denounced bosses and bossism. To the equal surprise of the Democrats and the

Republicans, he won the election handsomely, and his winning issue was put to the test at the first fall of the gavel in the Senate Chamber at Albany.

Election of United States senators by the people had not yet come, and the first business of the Democratic Legislature was to choose a senator. In accordance with an old New York custom, the choice really rested with the boss of the majority party, and Boss Murphy of Tammany Hall sent in the name of a henchman. Up sprang the new anti-boss Senator from Dutchess County, and his tall, spare figure became the storm center of a revolt of twenty-one Democratic members, who held the Legislature in a deadlock for ten weeks, when the Tammany chieftain had to withdraw his man.

Senator Roosevelt ran for a second term, or rather he lay in bed with typhoid fever while his Republican district re-elected him by a largely increased majority. He hardly had resumed his seat at Albany when he was appointed Assistant Secretary of the Navy in the incoming Wilson administration. The post appealed to him as a student of naval history and as a collector of pictures and models of ships—he was an inveterate collector of stamps. He liked the office also because it had been held by T.R., and it became a family heirloom, with T. R. Jr. succeeding F. D., after which came the turn of a cousin, Theodore Douglas Robinson, and next of Henry Latrobe Roosevelt. F.D.'s term was the most active of all, as it included World War I.

Going to the Democratic National Convention at San Francisco in 1920 to battle for the policies of Woodrow Wilson, including the League of Nations, the Assistant Secretary of the Navy was surprised by his nomination for vice President. He must have been less surprised by his defeat at the polls, after a gallant but desperate campaign on the stump.

In the Legislature, in the Assistant Secretaryship of the Navy and in his vice Presidential candidacy, F.D. had been following in the footsteps of T.R. Now it looked as if he had lost the trail for good and all under a Republican landslide.

II

THE MAN WHO WAS BORN AT 39

(1921) August, Franklin D. Roosevelt stricken by infantile paralysis.— (1924) June, Christened Alfred E. Smith the "Happy Warrior" in nominating speech at Democratic National Convention in New York. October, His first visit to Warm Springs, Georgia.— (1928) June, Again placed Governor Smith in nomination at Houston Convention. October, nominated for governor.—(1929-33) Governor of New York.—(1932) July 1, Nominated for President. November 8, Elected.

LIKE the first Roosevelt in the presidency, the second steeled his will power and strengthened the fibres of his character in a battle for health. We have seen how often the highest honor in American public life has been won by those who were handicapped in the race. None among them was so cruelly disadvantaged as that born favorite of fortune, Franklin D. Roosevelt, to whom wealth and position, education and preferment had come as a gift until, in a night, he was stricken helpless by an attack of infantile paralysis.

It was in 1921 and he was 39, a superb example of robust manhood. After a day of vigorous exertion in sailing, swimming and in beating out a brush fire, he went to bed in his summer cottage on Campobello Island, just across the Canadian boundary in the Bay of Fundy. He awoke the next morning ill and lame, and in three days the muscles of his legs had lost the power to control the knees. He was never again to stand unaided. The pity in the eyes of all who looked down upon the apparently hopeless wreckage of him was like a challenge, and his soul rose up to meet it . . . "I'll beat this thing!"

That was the beginning of a spiritual rebirth. The man was born again at 39, unable to stand alone but triumphant over fear. "If infantile paralysis couldn't kill him, the presidency won't," said his wife ten years later, and the memory of that conquest no doubt became the counselor of his courage in every moral and political exigency.

The infection swiftly had come and gone, leaving him with mind and body unaffected, except his long legs, which were sixty pounds of dead weight. Only in the buoyancy of water could he free himself from that burden, and he found at Warm Springs, Georgia, a pool which nature herself heats to a temperature suitable the year round for the one form of exercise he could take. He had continued—mostly in a wheel chair—his law practice in New York, along with the vice presidency of a bonding insurance company. His knees could be locked though held rigid and unbending, only with the aid of heavy iron braces, until they were replaced by an aluminum frame. Nevertheless he relearned how to drive an automobile and even to ride a horse.

The handsome figure that had stood forth in the San Francisco convention in 1920 reappeared on crutches at the next national convention at Madison Square Garden, New York, in 1924. He had then seconded the name of Governor Alfred E. Smith of New York for the presidential nomination. Now, four years afterward, he was the manager of the Governor's candidacy, and he gripped the speaker's desk for support as he christened him the "Happy Warrior" in his nominating speech. In another four years, he spoke again for his friend, and the national convention at Houston in 1928 accepted his choice.

Over the long-distance telephone from Syracuse to Warm Springs he was dissuaded by the nominee for President from his resolve to go on uninterruptedly with the job of building up the remaining muscles of his legs, and he was nominated for Governor of New York as an aid to the national ticket. Despite the Hoover avalanche that year, he was elected, and he displayed in the governorship a capacity for administration and for working with a Legislature that was under the control of the opposition party. He also disclosed a gift for interesting the people in their government, as he talked with them over the radio or from his car, and in his campaign for re-election he simplified the question of hydro-electric power down to the waffling iron of the housewife. When the votes were counted in 1930, he stood forth before the country as the first Democrat in almost half a century to carry up-state New York, and his more than 700,000 plurality in the whole state broke an all-time record for governor.

Thrice since the Civil War, the Democrats had chosen governors of New York to carry the standard of the party in the nation—Tilden, Cleveland and Smith. They turned now to Governor Roosevelt.

The "Happy Warrior," although he had announced that he himself was not a candidate, grew unhappy at the prospect of his sponsor in three conventions receiving the nomination. Sharply denouncing as demagogic a reference by Roosevelt to "the forgotten man," ex-Governor Smith entered the race against him, for the purpose, as he said of "putting a chock under the wheels of the bandwagon!" Several divergent elements joined him in a movement to "Stop Roosevelt," which included most of the delegates from New York, who were under the domination of Tammany. But they could not coalesce in a united opposition, and they succeeded in stopping him only until the fourth ballot in the Chicago convention of 1932.

*

* *

*

President Wilson, remarking the ever increasing burdens of the presidency, foretold the coming of a day when we should have to choose our Presidents from among athletes only. He himself soon was to lend emphasis to the warning by breaking down under the load, and it was speedily emphasized again by the death of Harding. There is statistical evidence that the office is now taking ten years off the lives of its incumbents in comparison with the men who presided over the simpler government of what still was mainly an agricultural nation until the Civil War. The vital statistics of the fifteen Presidents before 1860 give us an average President who was fifty-eight at his inauguration, lived fourteen years after he left the White House and died at seventy-four. From among the fifteen next in the line, we have an average President who was fifty-one at his inauguration, survived his term only seven years and died at sixty-four. Those whose lives were cut short by assassination are not included in the computation of the average years of survival in retirement and the average age at death.

*

* *

*

A "whispering campaign" obviously was invited now by the nomination of the only cripple ever proposed by a major party for the most arduous post in the nation, really in the world. That attack was parried at the start by Governor Roosevelt taking to the air for the first time in the history of presidential candidates. Flying from Albany to Chicago, he was the first nominee to deliver before the convention which nominated him his speech of acceptance . . . to the tune of "Happy Days Are Here Again." The doubt of his physical qualifications was still further allayed by his sailing at the wheel up the New England coast with a crew of youngsters. The question was entirely removed from the realm of debate as he went on his stumping tours, which carried him from Boston to San Francisco. Instead of taking with him on his campaigning the customary doctor of medicine, he was accompanied by doctors of philosophy, who busily assisted him with researches and suggestions, and a press reporter nicknamed them the "Brains Trust."

His speeches were dismissed by his opponents and sometimes by his own followers as mere vote-catching promises. Yet he really had no need to electioneer; his election was a foregone conclusion. He did need, if his administration was to be constructive, to prevent the verdict of the country from being merely a negative expression of discontent and a desire for change. He sought a specific mandate for what he called a "New Deal," and his speeches, re-read in the glaring light of his first year in office, were seen to have been careful and sometimes even tedious specifications of many of the measures he was so soon to press through Congress.

While a candidate for President, Roosevelt the Governor had to sit in judgment on the powerful

Democratic machine in his own state, which he had defied at the beginning of his political career twenty years before. He already had removed from office the Tammany sheriff of New York County. In the midst of his campaign, he had to hold hearings on charges against the popular, twice-elected Tammany Mayor of New York City, which were abruptly terminated by Mayor Walker choosing discretion as the better part of valor and resigning his place.

The election was the most sudden and complete reversal in our political records. The 6,300,000 majority for Hoover in 1928 was turned into a majority of 7,000,000 for Roosevelt in 1932. Where the Democrats had lost all but eight states in 1928, they carried all but six only four years afterward, with more seats in Senate and House than ever before had been held by any party. Although they had won four presidential contests since the Civil War, they found themselves for the first time in those seventy years on top instead of under a real landslide.

III

HISTORY MADE IN TWENTY MINUTES

(1933) Feb. 15, Attempted assassination of President-elect Roosevelt by Zangara at Miami. March 4, Inaugurated 31st President, aged 51.

WHEN the history of the great depression shall be written, a highly significant chapter may be missing. Historians in after times hardly will appreciate the thrill of delighted surprise which swept through the American people at the discovery of the kind of President Franklin Delano Roosevelt showed himself to be in the first forty-eight hours of his term. Only two and a half weeks before his inauguration, he gave a measure of his character while under an assassin's fire in Florida. He kept his head and, in his solicitude for Mayor Cermak of Chicago, who was mortally wounded by a bullet aimed at the President-elect, he coolly ignored the peril to himself. Some dramatist in a time to come may find a play under the title, "If Zangara Had Not Missed." The constitution then did not contain its present provision for meeting the contingency of a man dying in the interval between his election to the presidency and the inauguration.

Roosevelt never had been put to the test of exercising independent power until he was clothed with it on the steps of the Capitol at the gravest of all inaugurations save Lincoln's in 1861. He had served only as a subordinate in the Wilson administration, and it had been necessary in his governorship of New York to adapt himself to an opposition legislature. In such roles he proved himself a tactful and ingratiating gentleman and won the doubtful fame of a facile politician, adept in the art of carrying water on both shoulders. His polite but persistent shying off from co-operation with the retiring President, when summoned into White House conferences, was regarded as proof of an incapacity for decision and responsibility by those who overlooked the fact that he held an emphatic mandate not to accept but to change the Hoover policies. Even the good humor his countenance beamed was distrusted as the outward sign of a shallow optimism, and cynical Washington greeted him as a "boy scout with an india-rubber smile."

Warned by some cheerful caller, as the story is told, that if he failed he would be the last Democratic President, Roosevelt assented and went further, with the prediction that if he failed he would be the last President of the United States. That dread eventuality haunted many minds in the grimly hushed multitude out under a gray sky at the last fourth of March inauguration; for the twentieth amendment, already ratified, fixed January 20 as the inaugural date thenceforth.

With thirteen million unemployed, twenty million on public doles and as many million more not making a living on their farms, the people were panicky from the sensation of sinking for three years and fearful that the bottom had dropped out from under their feet. Leadership had been destroyed in business as well as in politics. Stark exposures of an electric power magnate and of New York bankers were shattering to what confidence remained in things as they were.

After ten thousand banks had failed in ten years, the survivors began in February to close their doors against runs on their gold and its paper tokens. At last, the unbelievable happened: the great banks of New York and Massachusetts, with all banks throughout the land, shut down. The severe deflation of all values possibly had not left a solvent fiduciary institution in the country, if forced to dump its assets on a glutted market, and the crash of one big life insurance company well might have had a disastrous effect.

While on his way to the Capitol, the President-elect paused at the altar of St. John's Church to seek a strength beyond his own. The presence of his mother at the inauguration afforded him a filial satisfaction denied to all but two of his predecessors, Garfield and McKinley. Mrs. James Roosevelt was eighth among the mothers of Presidents to be spared until the inaugurations of their sons, but she was the first to have voted for the election of a son to the presidency. In contrast with those eight surviving mothers, only four fathers of our chief magistrates lived to see their sons attain the goal fondly set for a multitude of American boys while yet in their cradles.

One more note in passing: This was the installation of the thirty-first, not the thirty-second President. The medal struck for the occasion so designated Roosevelt, and that may be accepted as an official correction of an absurd mistake in arithmetic which arose from counting Cleveland as two Presidents merely because his two terms were separated.

The President-elect, leaning heavily on the arm of a son still taller than himself, walked with labored step down the ramp provided to smooth the way for him and out on to the inaugural platform, where two other men with Dutch names had stood in the past, and he rested his left hand on an ancient family Bible, printed in the language of his Dutch ancestors. After he had been sworn by Chief Justice Hughes, he returned to the long neglected form explicitly prescribed in the constitution and himself spoke the impressively simple sentence, "I, Franklin Delano Roosevelt, do solemnly swear that I will faithfully execute the office of President of the United States and will to the best of my ability preserve, protect and defend the constitution of the United States."

As those words and the inaugural address that followed went winging their way through the air to every corner of the land, a continent was brought within the bounds of the Greek ideal of a democratic state, where all the citizens should be in hearing of a speaker's voice. Out from millions of radio boxes, in homes and stores and shops, there sounded a bold challenge to the drooping faith of a people in themselves and their government.

The nation never had undergone such a quick emo-

tional change in any other hour of its history as it
experienced between one and two o'clock of that inauguration day. Not even in war had the people ever
responded so unanimously and unreservedly as they
responded to the proffer of leadership which came to
them that unforgettable noontime. They had been
trying to run away from the depression until their
retreat had degenerated into a rout, and they had
fallen apart into jealous and suspicious factions along
partisan, sectional and class lines. While they listened to the unmistakable accents of the old American
spirit, their lost unity was restored; they got their
country back. In twenty minutes they faced about
for a confident advance against the battalions of misfortune. The mood of the depression was broken.

In his inaugural the President announced that the
money changers had fled from the high seats of the
temple and that the rulers of business had abdicated.
Those normally powerful citizens assented or acquiesced as he resolutely grasped the dangling reins of a
leaderless nation. He promised action, and he gave it
with a speed that took the breath of a people who
had seen their government helplessly divided and
stalled. Even while the parading bands in the inaugural procession were playing "Anchors Aweigh,"
in compliment to a one-time Assistant Secretary of
the Navy, he was issuing orders from the reviewing
stand for full steam ahead. For the first time a Cabinet was nominated, confirmed, sworn and called into
session on inauguration day. The next day, notwithstanding it was Sunday, the President took charge of
the closed banks and summoned an extra session of
the new Congress, which met on Thursday and passed
an emergency banking bill before adjourning for the
night.

At the end of an amazing week, the new man in the White House went on the air with a "golden voice" and revealed an engaging radio personality, seeming to drop in like a neighbor to talk over the problems of the nation directly and plainly with each of twenty million listening households. The speech instructor in Teachers' College at Columbia rated him the best radio speaker in the world. A flood of fourteen thousand telegrams in a fortnight gave a measure of the resurgence of popular interest in government. The clerks required to handle an unexampled volume of communications by mail and wire, which poured in at the rate of one hundred and fifty thousand pieces a month, overcrowded the executive offices, and additional quarters had to be annexed across the street in the War Department. A daily average of four hundred letters under Harding and Coolidge and six hundred under Hoover shot up to thirty-eight hundred in the opening year of Roosevelt's term, and three hundred thousand telegrams greeted him on his first birthday in the presidency.

Mrs. Roosevelt inaugurated a new deal in her sphere of activity, and her incoming mail, which quickly grew to twenty-five hundred letters a week, was equal in volume to that received by Presidents themselves in the past. The public was not sure what to think of her breaking out of the traditional harem-like seclusion in which the mistresses of the White House had been confined, with their minds always veiled and their lips sealed. She went her way nevertheless, with the strenuousness of Uncle Theodore . . . holding press conferences with women writers, going to and fro, unguarded, by train and plane or at the wheel of her roadster . . . descending into coal mines, climbing up on dams, lecturing, writing, broadcasting.

The problem of keeping physically fit had pressed increasingly upon Presidents. T. R. rode horseback, played tennis, boxed and led parties on long tramps. Taft, Wilson and Harding were golfers. Coolidge took his daily walks. Hoover had his medicine ball. Here was a President who would have to propel himself along the corridor connecting the White House with the executive building in a wheel chair, from which he was lifted, or with his own powerful and agile arms vaulted into the chair at his desk, rarely to leave it in the course of the day's work, not even for luncheon, which was brought to him on a tray. Some friends provided his one means of exercise by making a gift to the White House of a swimming pool, which was constructed in the covered passage-way leading from the mansion to the offices.

Almost for the first time since the exuberant days of another Roosevelt, laughter rang out unrestrained in the White House, and guests were told to follow the direction of the loudest laugh if they wished to find the President himself. Spontaneous simplicity and informality took the starch out of the place. Newspaper correspondents spread abroad enthusiastic reports of the changed atmosphere as they came away from free and easy press conferences where they heard themselves and high dignitaries of the government called by their first names.

*

* *

*

The White House that welcomed its third Democratic tenant in half a century had undergone many changes since its threshold was crossed by the first. When Cleveland took up his residence within its historic walls, it still was lighted by gas; but electric lights and bells were installed in the next or Harrison administration. By a wise remodeling of the interior under Theodore Roosevelt, when the offices were removed to a new wing, and by the elevation of its roof in Coolidge's term, the old structure was expanded into a four story house of sixty-eight rooms, fourteen baths (instead of the two in Cleveland's day) and ten lavatories.

Yet, subtract from that imposing total the four public parlors, the state dining room, where one hundred and forty guests may be seated, and all the quarters occupied by attendants and servants and storage and there remains for the President's private use only a fifteen room dwelling: ten bedrooms, three living rooms, a breakfast room and, of course, the kitchen, from which he himself must provide the food for what Taft called the two finest boarding houses in Washington, one for the white and the other for the colored help of the White House.

The staff grew with the house, from one secretary, five clerical assistants and five domestics in the Cleveland era to four secretaries and about one hundred and fifty employees under Hoover, including twenty military aides and sixty-odd police and secret service men. The President's purse also was enlarged meanwhile. Where Cleveland, with a salary of fifty thousand dollars, had to pay the wages of the servants, the cost of his tours and official dinners, his doctors' bills and supply his own carriage and team, his successor, fifty years afterwards, received a salary of seventy-five thousand dollars and twenty-five thousand more for travel and public entertainment, with all his help, his doctors, even his dentistry paid by the government, which also provides eleven automobiles and the chauffeurs to drive them. But Hoover did have to feed twenty-two servants. It cost the Treasury in all more than half a million a year to pay the President and his staff and for the upkeep of the White House.

IV

THE NEW DEAL

"Opinion in the United States," the late James Bryce truly observed, "is so sure of its strength that it does not hesitate to let the President exceed his constitutional powers in critical times." The world was despairing of democracy and resorting to dictatorships when the unexpected audacity, resourcefulness and smiling confidence of President Roosevelt in attacking the gravest crisis since the Civil War rallied the American people to his side. With his trolley on the feed wire of popular support, the amazing man in the White House, like a magician pulling white rabbits out of a hat, shot up to the Capitol bill after bill as fast as they could be prepared by relays of advisers, whom he called in from all quarters, and by his Brain Trust of young college professors, that twentieth century model of the Kitchen Cabinet in the low-brow days of the Republic. Those measures were almost as swiftly enacted by a so-called "rubber-stamp" Congress, which invested him with more authority than ever was entrusted to any of his predecessors.

At the extra session of 1933 and the regular session of 1934, billions of dollars were appropriated in lump sums to be spent or lent by the President on relief and work for the unemployed, to save homes and farms from foreclosure, and states, cities, towns, banks and businesses from bankruptcy. Into his hands was surrendered the control of the currency, with permission to print billions of new money, and he took the country off the old gold standard and gathered into the Treasury all the gold in banks and pockets, at a profit of two billions for the government from his devaluation of the gold content of the dollar about forty percent. Sweeping authority also was conferred on him to regulate industry, commerce and agriculture, and to remake the tariff in trading agreements with other nations. Catching the tempo of the White House, conventions hastily assembled in thirty-seven states and rushed through the repeal of national prohibition on December 5th, 1933. Almost as swiftly a corps of intelligent young detectives in the Department of Justice, under the President's orders and with the aid of new laws, were capturing or exterminating the kidnapers and gangs of murderers and robbers, who had been terrorizing the country with defiant impunity as they freely operated across state lines in automobiles and airplanes.

With the disarming manner of a flexible leadership, the President frankly admitted that much of his emergency legislation was experimental. "If we cannot do it one way, we will do it another," he assured his millions of listeners on the air, who deserted the movies to tune in on his fireside talks. "I have no expectation of making a hit every time I come to bat." "Theodore Roosevelt once said to me, 'If I can be right seventy-five percent of the time, I shall come up to the fullest measure of my hopes.'"

In such a whirlwind of action there were mistakes and failures. The President's appeal by telegraph (May 16, 1933) to the princes, potentates and presidents of the other fifty-four nations of the earth to renounce armaments for offensive warfare fell on deaf ears in the capitals of the military powers. Attempting to rescue the foredoomed London Economic

Conference, he summoned to the White House premiers and other high representatives of foreign governments; but he himself was to break up that futile
assemblage with a telegraphic rebuke (July 3, 1933)
which he sent from a naval vessel as he was returning
to Washington from his sea-side cottage on Campobello Island. Nor was he able to obtain from debtor
governments any new terms on their war debt that
he cared to lay before Congress, and all of them,
excepting only Finland, stopped paying us anything
on account of the eleven billions owing to us. At
home, he failed to effect important permanent results
under acts which gave him almost a free hand to
slash the routine expenditures of the government and
reorganize its departments and bureaus.

As the emergency legislation went into operation,
administrations and bureaus multiplied at Washington
beyond counting and were familiarly known by the
initials of their long names. The capital city was
afloat on what Alfred E. Smith called an alphabet
soup. The most renowned were the A.A.A. (Agricultural Adjustment Administration) and the N.R.A.
(National Recovery Administration). Those two
agencies were set up respectively in response to the
appeals of the farmers and captains of industry to aid
them to combine in extricating themselves from the
demoralization of the depression.

While representatives of distressed industries were
crowded into Washington in the sweltering summer
of 1933 to negotiate codes of fair wages and hours
and trade practices which should abolish child labor,
the sweatshop and cut-throat competition and recognize the right of workers to organize for collective
bargaining with employers, the President decided to
take a short cut to those objectives. Going on the

air (July 24) he launched a crusade for hastening re-
employment by calling upon all employers, big and
little, factories, corner stores and barber shops alike,
to come under a temporary blanket code. Blue eagles
on posters in tens of thousands of shop windows signi-
fied compliance with the presidential request and also
conveyed an implicit invitation to boycott all who
failed to display that symbol of the N.R.A. Foremost among the recalcitrants was Henry Ford, who
quietly defied the thunderbolts in the talons of the
symbolical eagle.

After the emotional fervor of that mid-summer
campaign, there came a chilling frost of disappointment and reaction in the fall. But ultimately most of
the business of the country, with eighteen million
workers, was brought under six hundred codes, which
set up standards that in many respects did good service
in the emergency and may have left lasting benefits.

The depression really had started on its way out
in the first springtime of the Roosevelt Administration
when confidence was restored in leadership, in government and in the banks, which were strengthened against
failure and panic by the elimination of unsound insti-
tutions, the suspension of gold payments and by an
insurance of deposits. As recovery proceeded, it
gained in speed until it degenerated into a characteristic American boom, which collapsed on July 20.
Thenceforth the pace was soberer and sometimes tedi-
ously slow; but the country did not again slip back to
the low level of the winter of 1932-3. Farmers found
themselves better off than they had been in several
years. The epidemic of farm and home foreclosures
and business failures had been overcome. The downward spiral of deflation had been arrested.

Even with several millions re-employed, a huge total

of unemployed remained a stubborn and discouraging problem. The Administration combated it with jobs for the idle under the Civil Works Administration and the Public Works Administration in the winter of 1933-4, followed by the Emergency Relief Administration in 1934 and the Works Progress Administration in 1935. The cost of that warfare on idleness and poverty swelled the public debt to staggering proportions, but the national credit was unshaken and the Treasury was able to borrow at a reduced rate of interest on bonds which went to a premium as soon as issued.

As the economic storm subsided, critics ventured up on deck and denounced the captain as a dictator, whose New Deal was regimenting the lives of the American people and slowing down a natural, almost world-wide improvement. As Lincoln had been censured for prolonging the Civil War by insisting on removing the cause of it with the abolition of slavery, Roosevelt likewise was blamed for delaying recovery by his insistence on taking measures against certain excesses, which he regarded as largely responsible for the unparalleled severity of the depression in the United States.

Mr. Roosevelt was quoted at one time as privately predicting that he would be the conservative candidate in 1936. But the conservatives refused to be drawn toward him in the middle of the road, and thereafter he veered more toward the opposite side in an effort to keep the Progressives from getting out of hand. Throughout 1934 the Republican party remained helplessly prostrate and unable to give effective expression to the mounting opposition. The state and congressional elections in November of that year resulted in the greatest victory ever won by an administration in mid term.

The President did not press the advantage of his added prestige when the new Congress came in with its increased Democratic majorities. On the contrary, he gave it a looser rein than he held over the former Congress. His Brain Trust and a succession of advisers faded out of the picture. The driving force of his leadership slackened, and he met with defeat in the Senate, at the outset of the session, on the old question of America joining the World Court. Going in person to plead for his veto of the Veterans' Bonus, his objections were overruled by the House the moment his back was turned, and he was barely sustained in the Senate. Twice he put his strength to the test in the House on the most extreme clause in a bill for bringing electric utilities under federal authority and was overwhelmingly defeated in each instance. His more forcible opponents throughout the session were not on the Republican but on the Democratic side.

The President suffered his most serious reverse in neither the Senate nor the House but in a little chamber between, where the New Deal came to judgment at the bar of the Supreme Court on the question of its constitutionality. The gold legislation, on which the monetary policy of the administration rested, barely squeaked through a divided Court in February, 1935. But the N.R.A. was ruled out by a unanimous decision, on May 27, which Chief Justice Hughes handed down in an opinion whose sweeping implications cast a dark shadow of doubt on the validity of the A.A.A. and other key measures of the "Roosevelt Revolution." At a press conference, running to the unprecedented length of an hour and a quarter, the President prophesied that if the national government should be rendered powerless to deal with what had become national economic and social problems and relegated to "horse and buggy days," when there were no such problems, the country would have to decide in the next five or ten years the biggest issue it ever had faced.

The upset of the N.R.A., without one of the nine justices of the Supreme Court dissenting, emboldened opponents and doubters of the Roosevelt leadership. While Congress talked and balked at wearisome length and the editorial pages of the newspaper press grew more unanimously hostile, the President refrained from the radio, and the once intimate partnership between him and the country suffered a loss in understanding and sympathy. At a special election in a Rhode Island Congress district, a Democratic majority of twenty-one thousand in November, 1934, was turned into a Republican majority of fourteen thousand in August, 1935, due in part to the agitation in textile centers against the processing tax on cotton, which the A.A.A. was paying out in bounties to the planters. A "whispering campaign," such as once was fomented against the first President Roosevelt, spread abroad now similar stories and from similar sources of the insanity of the second Roosevelt.

After Congress had been cutting capers throughout a hot summer, with the President alternately relaxing and jerking the bridle, it repented in haste and gave him the substance of his ambitious program, including several postscripts suddenly added by the White House or by the legislators themselves. Following the exciting session, he announced that his basic program was substantially completed, and he assured the panting business world of a "breathing spell."

Some of the immense mass of legislation will set up, subject to the judgment of the Supreme Court, new landmarks on the course of American political, economic and social progress. The objects of the New

Deal, as they were embodied in law in the first two and a half years of the Roosevelt Administration, may be summarized here only in bare outlines.

*

* *

*

AGRICULTURE—To restore farming to an equality with protected industry and make the tariff equally effective for its products, farmers may enter into agreements with the Agricultural Adjustment Administration to adjust the major crops to fit demand and receive in return benefit payments out of taxes collected from processors of those crops; Federal loans on farms and certain farm products to save the former from foreclosure and the latter from being dumped on a glutted market.

ALCOHOL—Federal regulation of interstate traffic in spirituous liquors.

ARMY and NAVY—The former more closely coordinated with the militia of the states and the latter to be built up to treaty strength.

AUTOMOBILES—Buses and trucks placed under Interstate Commerce Commission.

BANKING—Federal Reserve System reorganized, with larger control of credit by the government, with investment business divorced from banking, and deposit insurance for all qualified banks.

COMMUNICATIONS—The radio, telegraph and telephone under Federal Communications Commission.

COAL—Principles of N.R.A. Code re-enacted in special law.

CRIME—Operations of kidnapers, murderers and robbers across state lines made a federal offense.

GOLD and SILVER—Gold coinage stopped; gold clauses in public and private obligations cancelled; dollar devalued slightly more than 40 per cent in relation

to gold; all gold taken over by the Treasury and na-
tionalized; policy declared to be the building up of a
silver reserve in the Treasury until it is one-fourth
the value of the gold stock.

HOMES—Loans to save them from foreclosure.

HOUSING—Guarantee, in part, of private lending
for building or repairs.

LABOR—Wagner Act to secure workers in organizing independently of employers for collective
bargaining through representatives of their own choosing.

NEUTRALITY—The President to place an embargo on shipment of arms, munitions or implements
of war destined for any nation at war before March 1,
1936; a permanent license system for munition workers
and shippers, and the President is authorized to warn
citizens off ships under the flag of a belligerent.

SECURITIES—Issuance of securities for interstate sale and the stock markets placed under Securities
and Exchange Commission.

SOCIAL SECURITY—To encourage the more
general adoption by the states of a social security system, they are offered federal aid for the assistance of
the needy above the age of 65, of the needy blind, of
dependent children; for health service for mothers and
children; for vocational training of the disabled;
federal taxes on pay rolls in all states, which will be
refunded 90 per cent to employers in those states which
set up an unemployment insurance system conformable
to the standards of the act; a federal old age annuity
system, beginning in 1942, with a fund contributed by
employers and employees, with specified exceptions; a
separate system of retirement pay for railroad employees.

TARIFF—The President empowered in foreign
trade agreements to raise or lower customs duties 50
per cent.

TAXES—Increased on great incomes and estates;

also a graduated corporation tax; new taxes on gifts, capital stock, excess profits and on inter-corporation dividends.

TENNESSEE VALLEY — Development of its water power to serve as "a yardstick" for measuring costs and prices of power corporations; incidental development of the Valley as a social and industrial experiment station.

UNEMPLOYMENT—Total appropriations for 1933–6 of about $9,000,000,000 for co-operation with states and municipalities in relief and work relief and in Public Works, with the federal government undertaking to provide work for all able bodied, leaving the unemployables to the care of local government; Civilian Conservation Corps increased to 600,000 youths; resettlement of low income families; aid for idle and indigent young people to stay in schools and colleges.

UTILITIES—Interstate transmission of light and power and the financing of the industry placed under federal authority, with the holding company system limited.

V

ROOSEVELT REVOLUTION

(1936) November, Roosevelt re-elected in biggest sweep of a century. (1937) Sit down strikes. Feb. 6, Country shocked by "Court Packing" Plan.—(1938) Failure of the "Purge."—(1937-40) Reversals by the Supreme Court sustained New Deal.

A SIGN at the New Hampshire entrance of a bridge to Maine, after the election of 1936, warned the traveler, "You are now leaving the United States." The point of the jest was that Maine and Vermont alone had withstood the flood tide of Roosevelt victories which rolled over 46 of the 48 states. It was the most nearly unanimous choice of a president since the unopposed re-election of James Monroe in 1820, when the two party system briefly had disappeared. That system was functioning in 1936, but the parties had changed sides.

The Democrats found themselves cast in the unaccustomed role of advocates of a vigorous central government, while the Republicans awkwardly were playing the unfamiliar part of opposing that centralization of power which they had championed from the birth of their party. In backing the New Deal, the Democrats had become as Federalist as Alexander Hamilton; and in upholding States' Rights, the Republicans had become the disciples of Thomas Jefferson.

While the Sage of Monticello contended that a government which governed least was best for this then simple, agricultural country, he confessed a fear that his political system would be unsuited to a more complex society. Shortly after our urban population outgrew the rural, the Democratic party broke the will of its founding father and revolted against its last Jeffersonian leader, President Grover Cleveland.

With his New Freedom, President Woodrow

Wilson continued to lead the Democrats away from their ancient faith in laissez faire, a "let alone" policy. That revolution was carried still further by Franklin D. Roosevelt's New Deal.

With the enfranchisement and the education of the many everywhere under representative government, naturally they demanded a fuller share of the benefits that mostly had been going to the privileged few. So long as the Democrats had clung to their historic position as defenders of States' Rights, which are neither food nor drink, they could not compete with Republican promises of "a full dinner pail" and "a chicken in every pot." The New Deal gave them, at last, a bread and butter appeal, and straightway they became the majority party under the Roosevelt leadership.

Unlike Monroe, Roosevelt did not take advantage of his overwhelming vote of confidence to usher in another "Era of Good Feelings." On the contrary, his second administration was stormier than the first. It opened with "sit down strikes" against employers who still were resisting the recognition of organized labor and its legal right to collective bargaining, which the New Deal had provided in the Wagner Labor Relations Act.

"I see," said Roosevelt in his second inaugural, "one third of a nation ill housed, ill clad and ill nourished." In his first administration he had attacked those inequalities, which were a reproach to the richest country on earth. Adverse decisions by the Supreme Court had implied a threat to rule out as unconstitutional the major measures of the New Deal.

His sweeping victory at the polls was strong drink for the President, and it went to his head. With only an hour's warning to the Congressional leaders who would have to carry on his fight at the Capitol, he made a frontal assault on the Court. The country was shocked and his own party divided by his request for authority to appoint new justices to offset the justices who were still serving on the Court after having reached the age of seventy years. Unlike all but two other Presidents who had served a full term, Roosevelt still had no appointees of his own in the Court, where there had been no vacancy in four years.

His argument that the advanced ages of the anti New Deal justices were responsible for their conservative attitude was too thin to disguise his real purpose to "pack the Court." Oliver Wendell Holmes had not retired until he was ninety-one, and he was a hero of the New Dealers. The most progressive sitting member, Justice Brandeis, was eighty-one.

In a furious wrangle, all but twenty of the seventy-five Democratic senators fell away from their party leader in the White House. The President's Dutch was up, and he marked out certain of his opponents for defeat in the congressional election of 1938. This was stigmatized by his critics as a "purge," which linked it with the blood purges by the dictators, Stalin and Hitler. Again, he failed, and the reason for his failure provides an interesting lesson in American politics.

With all the immense growth of centralized power, which began in the Civil War, the party organizations remained still as strictly divided as ever by state lines. There never had been any semblance of a national machine. Even Roosevelt's appointees to federal offices in the states did not owe their jobs to him but to local organizations or leaders that had recommended their appointments. He could not rally them to his banner against their senators and representatives. A president of the United States and commander in chief of the army and navy had not a county chairman nor a precinct captain at his command.

The American ship of state has as many bulkheads as there are states. These safeguard it against capture by an ambitious dictator, against a coup d'etat or a putsch. In the heyday of the bosses, the dictatorship of the Platts, Quays, Coxes, Murphys, Hagues, Huey Longs or Crumps was limited to their respective states. Not one of them could swing a vote on the other side of a state line.

The ultimate dependence of a president is on public opinion. With its force behind him, he is the most powerful man in the land, sometimes in the entire free world. Without it, he is as helpless as Wilson was in his crusade for the League of Nations and Roosevelt in his fight for the Court plan.

After losing the battle, Roosevelt nevertheless won the campaign, and the New Deal was saved from judicial veto. Under the guidance of Chief Justice Hughes, the Court followed the "illiction returns," in the words of Mr. Dooley, and overruled itself. A retirement act for Supreme Court Justices having been passed by Congress, three of the "nine old men" availed themselves of its provisions and retired from the bench. Two others died, and Roosevelt had five vacancies to fill in his second term.

With the re-interpretation of a few words in the Constitution, a peaceable revolution was accomplished. Thus the American system of government was justified of the boast that it provides the means of orderly change to meet changing conditions, that it can be made the effective alternative to violent revolutions.

VI

THIRD TERM TABOO BROKEN

(1940) June-July, Wendell Willkie nominated by Republicans and Democrats nominated Roosevelt for third term. August-September, Roosevelt rushed munitions to aid of England and exchanged fifty American destroyers for bases in British possessions. September 16, signed first peace-time draft. November, Roosevelt's third election. —(1941) January 6, proclaimed Four Freedoms. March 10, signed Lend-Lease Act. July 7, U.S. forces in Iceland. August 14, Atlantic Charter.

A FEW weeks before Roosevelt's first inauguration in the spring of 1933, Adolf Hitler elbowed and pushed his way up from a beer cellar to the head of the German government. A onetime anarchist, Benito Mussolini already had overthrown the constitutional government of Italy. Japan lay under the spurred heels of military adventurers, who had gained power by assassination and terror.

Those three witches out of Macbeth were concocting in their bubbling cauldrons more toil and trouble than this planet ever had known. Like the American President, the dictators were products of the Great Depression. Unlike the New Deal, which put the jobless to work building river dams and school houses and gathered idle youths from the streets into a Civilian Conservation Corps, not into military camps, Hitler, Mussolini and the Japanese swashbucklers set their unemployed to building the biggest war machines in history. They were blatant enemies of individual liberty and despisers of the "decadent democracies."

In accepting his second nomination in 1936 Roosevelt announced that America had a "rendezvous with destiny." How grim it was to be he could not have foreseen, but in his "quarantine speech" the next year he met the challenge of government by coercion to government by consent. In the end, he was to be the champion of the free state in a battle to the death with the police state.

The opponents of the New Deal contend that it failed to solve the ugly problem of unemployment in a land of plenty. For prosperity never was fully restored until war orders started all the factory chimneys to smoking. Also the question was left unanswered of whether the American economic system was capable of the self discipline necessary to cure itself of the habit of running to the two extremes of boom and bust.

The New Dealers, on the other hand, contend that the Roosevelt policies aided America to escape the dictatorships that war and depression spawned throughout much of the world; that the corrective measures of the New Deal won at least a respite for capitalism from the major surgery it underwent in communist Russia, fascist Italy, nazi Germany, socialist England and Scandinavia. They point to France, which adopted few or no remedies, and the collapse of its morale under the first blow of war.

The advocates of the New Deal insist also that it restored the faith of the American people and other peoples in free government; that it rescued from despair a supposedly "lost generation" of apparently unwanted young people, who were to become the pride of their country as they battled their way to victory in the hardest of all wars.

When the choice of a successor to Roosevelt had to be made in 1940, the goosestepping soldiery of Hitler and Mussolini were overrunning Europe. France was falling. The British were retreating from Dunkirk and whistling to keep up their courage "There will always be an England." Winston Churchill was trumpeting the call to battle on the beaches and in the hedgerows of the island.

Only the searcher of his heart could know the feelings of Roosevelt as he stood on the banks of the American Rubicon which no president in one hundred and fifty years had crossed in defiance of the unwritten law against a third term. Sidestepping the question of his candidacy, he told those who raised it in his press conferences to put on a dunce's cap and go stand in a corner. Really, he didn't have to seek a third term. His nomination was a necessity to the Democrats, who had no one to replace him. For his overshadowing stature or his ego or both had not been favorable to the growth of presidential timber in his vicinity.

The Republicans were in much the same plight. Their barren opposition to the New Deal and their isolationist record in Congress had not developed a leader to fit the emergency. They turned to a dark horse, Wendell Willkie, and entrusted the Republican standard into the hands of a lifelong Democrat, who came to the national convention without a pledged or instructed delegation behind him.

While the Republicans were nominating a Democrat for president, Roosevelt placed two Republicans in charge of departments which would be most important in event of war. His new secretary of war, Henry Stimson, had served in two Republican cabinets and been Hoover's secretary of state. For secretary of the navy, he chose Frank Knox, the Republican nominee for vice president four years before.

Willkie repudiated the isolationism of the Republicans in Congress and advocated the foreign policy the administration was pursuing. He even cooperated with the President by refraining from making an issue of the fifty destroyers which had been sent to the relief of beleaguered England in exchange for permission to build American bases on British islands in the Atlantic.

It was not publicly known at the time that Roosevelt also had rushed a million rifles and a thousand cannon to Britain when Churchill was admitting out of the corner of his mouth that his people had hardly anything except bottles to throw at an invader. Nor did Willkie question the first peace-time draft in our history, which was to violate campaign tactics by marching young men into training camps while their parents were marching to the polls.

All that cooperation across party lines seemed to take the fight out of Roosevelt. Some of those closest to him feared that he didn't much care how the election went, and they took thought of ways to arouse his interest. When the President and Willkie closed in on each other toward the end of the contest, both yielded to the temptation of promising to keep the country out of a war, in which it already was pretty well involved.

The tradition against a third term, that supposedly holy of holies, quickly disappeared as a talking point on the stump. Notwithstanding the Republican Old Guard sat on its hands, Willkie made a good run against the "Champ," as he called the President, who did not win in a walk. The Republicans carried ten states, instead of the two in their column four years before, increased their total vote from 16,000,000 to 22,000,000 and pulled Roosevelt's plurality down from nearly 11,000,000 in 1936 to less than 5,000,000.

After the election, the President sent his friendly enemy to England as an embodiment of American unity. He gave Willkie credentials also for a tour of his "One World." The late Republican candidate returned the compliment by rebuking "the psychopathic hatred" of "That Man in the White House," whose name was unspeakable in counting rooms and clubs.

In his message to Congress after the election, the

President proclaimed the Four Freedoms, which added freedom from want and fear to the ancient freedom of speech and religion. The first major measure of the third term was a daring act of creative statesmanship, Lend-Lease, which provided aid for the nations that were engaged in a war of resistance to the aggressions of the Axis Powers. With their industries under bombardment, they could not survive without the product of our industries, which were beyond the range of enemy bombs. But they did not have the dollars with which to pay for those indispensable purchases.

Lend-Lease made America "the arsenal of democracy," as Roosevelt phrased it. It opened the flood gates of our production for Britain, Russia and China. It poured out $50,000,000,000 worth of ships, planes, tanks, guns, ammunition, food and all things needful. Even Stalin, no flatterer of this "capitalistic, imperialistic" country, said the war could not have been won without Lend-Lease.

With the United States navy convoying a gulf stream of supplies across the Atlantic under orders to shoot at sight of a German submarine, every last step was taken "short of war." It was a well kept secret for years that the President had authorized a race with Hitler for the making of the first atom bomb. Professor Albert Einstein had interested him in the experiment as early as the fall of 1939.

Roosevelt also had begun laying the foundations of peace before the United States entered the war, when he met Prime Minister Churchill at sea in August 1941. When the declaration they made in the Atlantic Charter that every people had a right to a government of their own choosing was causing trouble in India and elsewhere in Britain's far flung dominion, Churchill protested that the Charter applied only in lands captured from the Axis. But Roosevelt insisted that it was meant for all peoples, and it became the cornerstone of newly risen nations within the British Empire.

While Hitler's hordes were seizing the European coasts of the Atlantic, the Japanese were grabbing the Asiatic shore of the Pacific. Unless those aggressors were halted, the western hemisphere would be reduced to an island in an enslaved world, with American trade and travel subject to the terms of the dictators. Caught between conquering forces in Europe and Asia, Roosevelt had to look two ways at once as the ship of state skirted the red maelstrom of war.

VII

LEADING THE WORLD FROM A WHEEL CHAIR

(1941) December 7, Japanese planes attacked Pearl Harbor.—(1942) January 1, United Nations launched at the White House.—November 7, American army landed in North Africa.—(1943) January, Roosevelt and Churchill in conference at Casablanca.—(1944) February, Roosevelt ill and in retirement.—June 6, American army landed in Normandy.—November, Roosevelt elected fourth time.

PEARL HARBOR was a disaster for the American fleet in the Pacific. But it spelled catastrophe for the Japanese Empire. "The day that will live in infamy," as President Roosevelt termed it in his war message, dawned upon a United States angrily disunited and heatedly disputing whether this country could keep out of a conflagration which was making the globe a ball of fire. Only a month earlier the majority of Republicans combined with a minority of the Democrats in the House of Representatives and came within one vote of letting "the boys go home" from the training camps, which would have stripped the army of most of its trained men.

By nightfall of that unforgettable Sunday, December 7, 1941, the American people were unified in all their might by a surprise attack from the air on the naval base at Honolulu while a pretended peace mission from Japan was in conference at Washington with Cordell Hull, the Secretary of State. The commanders at Pearl Harbor were picked on as scapegoats for the sins of their superiors in Washington, who also were caught off guard. Our government having drawn a dead line on Japanese aggression in Asia, the President and his advisers were dreading an act of defiance from the farther shore of the Pacific. They were uneasily aware that the country could not be united behind a war to save Singapore for the British and Indonesia for the Dutch Empire. It never entered their imagination that the masters of Japan would be so stupid as to bring the war to us on our side of the ocean and invade American soil in Hawaii.

Prime Minister Churchill hastened over from England on the first of the several occasions when he was to be a guest at the White House. Thenceforth he was in constant communication with Roosevelt and, by his own calculation, he sent the President 950 messages in the course of the war. The two leaders were together on the bleak Christmas Day of 1941, when the Allies were being pushed around all over the map. They joined in launching the United Nations on New Year's Day of 1942.

The tragedy of his old chief, Woodrow Wilson, haunted the memory of Roosevelt all through the war. It caused him to tread warily, sometimes timidly in his approach to postwar problems. It made cowards of a generation of public men, who were afraid or ashamed of being caught with high aims. Idealist and idealism had become terms of opprobrium.

Pearl Harbor set a new landmark, fixed a turning point in American history. With Japanese planes bombing us in the west while German submarines were prowling so close to our eastern shore that the bright lights of Broadway had to be dimmed, our fancied isolation went glimmering through the dream of things that were. The oceans had ceased to be our defensive moats and became our menace.

Moreover, Britannia no longer was ruling the wave and guarding the peace of the seas. With England's cities and factories under aerial bombardment, her finances strained to the breaking point by two world wars and her empire falling apart, the supremacy she had exercised throughout the nineteenth century was at an end. The reins of leadership fell to the unwilling and unready hands of America, as the richest, most productive of nations, indeed the only solvent great power.

A President of the United States led the world from a wheelchair through the greatest crisis of modern civilization. Roosevelt became the personification of the hopes of all free peoples. His jauntily tipped cigarette was their beacon light of confidence.

He gave the most successful conduct of a war this unprepared, unmilitary nation ever had known. More fortunate than Lincoln, he was so well advised in his choice of commanders on land and sea and in the air that almost none had to be replaced when tested by battle.

While he gave generals and admirals a free hand in their respestive theaters of a global war, the commander in chief had to decide problems of major strategy when the Allies or his own staffs disagreed. It was his decision that the war in Europe should come first and the war in the Pacific second. His was the responsibility of determining where and when to take the terrible risks of invasions overseas, thousands of miles from our base.

His gamble on the North African expedition, which he reluctantly made, resulted in removing Italy from the Axis and freeing the Mediterranean. A still more daring play was the landing on the Normandy beaches, which he had been in favor of making earlier. That direct attack on Hitler's fortress of Europe led to the downfall of the German dictator in less than a year. Roosevelt's greatest gamble of all was in staking $2,000,000,000 on the chance of winning the race with Germany for the atom bomb, without letting Congress or most of his Cabinet into the secret of the "Manhattan Project."

When the President submitted to Congress, at the outset, his two-year plan for the production of 185,000 airplanes, 120,000 tanks, 55,000 anti-aircraft guns and 18,000,000 tons of shipping, it was pooh-poohed as tall talk. With the scientific brains of the country, the captains of industry and labor leaders mobilized in overcrowded Washington, most of his quotas were exceeded. The greatest army and navy of all time were organized, with more than 12,000,000 men and women in uniform.

In fighting the depression and the war, the Roosevelt administration spent more money than had been spent by all previous administrations together. The wonder is that when the Republicans captured Congress in 1946, with the promise to "open every session with a prayer and close it with a probe," no scandal was uncovered in any of the executive departments or in the hastily organized civil agencies at Washington.

In the first wartime presidential election in eighty years, the war did not become in 1944 the political football it was in the campaign of 1864, nor foreign policy the partisan issue it was in the First World War. At the request of Roosevelt's opponent, Governor Thomas E. Dewey, the administration took into its confidence the governor's adviser on international problems, John Foster Dulles. That eventuated in the first bi-partisan foreign policy in an often unhappy experience of this country.

With Dewey's acceptance also of the major objectives of the New Deal, he centered his campaign mostly on his contention that younger men, with fresher energies, were needed to replace an administration, which he said, and said truly, had grown old and tired in twelve years of power. Roosevelt did show signs of the wear and tear of three terms, filled with the crises of a depression and a war. There was doubt among his friends if he could endure the strain of a fourth term. He had suffered a severe illness in the early spring of that election year, when his vanishing into the seclusion of Bernard Baruch's South Carolina estate gave rise to rumors that he was in various hospitals, with convincing details regarding the surgery he was reported to be undergoing.

Although he campaigned with a show of his old-time gaiety and with his old-time punch, he rarely stood on his feet but remained seated in an automobile while speaking at great outdoor rallies. Rashly, he insisted on touring New York City under a downpour of chilling rain.

The electorate had got in the Roosevelt habit. A multitude of voters never had cast a ballot for any other presidential candidate. In a light poll, due to many service men not taking the trouble to vote, the President's lead was reduced to a plurality of 3,600,000 and he lost twelve states to Dewey. The country again had decided that it was best not to swap horses while crossing a stream.

VIII

HE GAVE HIS LIFE FOR PEACE

(1943) January, Roosevelt and Churchill at Casablanca.—November, Conference of Big Three at Teheran.—(1945) February, Big Three met at Yalta.—March 2, Roosevelt's last address to Congress.—March 7, American troops cross the Rhine.—April 1, opening of Battle of Okinawa, Japan's last stand.—April 12, American army crossed the Elbe in Germany and death of Roosevelt, aged 63 years, 10 weeks and two days.

WHERE Cousin Theodore shocked the traditionalists by being the first president to leave the bounds of the United States, when he stepped across the line from the Canal Zone into the Republic of Panama, the people could never know in what strange land Franklin D. would pop up forty years later. A voluntary censorship by the press and radio hid his whereabouts behind a curtain of silence. The existence of a retreat, "green walled by the hills of Maryland," which he called Shangrila, was not known to the public until after his death. Never were more secrets kept by so many Americans, a people normally not given to reticence.

In his travels of nearly 300,000 miles to confer with other chiefs of state and to inspect military camps, Franklin D. sailed the seas and rode the air from Canada to the Argentine, from Alaska and Hawaii to Persia. The first hint of his approach was the appearance of an advanced detail of secret service men. They called Falla "the informer," because that famous dog insisted on being taken for a walk at every stop of a presidential train trip, and the sight of him was a plain tip off that his master was aboard. Until an elevator was installed in the president's plane, "The Sacred

Cow," the provision of a ramp at an airport plainly heralded the coming of the world's only V.I.P.—very important person—who could not walk up or down a flight of steps.

The country never knew that the President was not in the White House until the announcement of his attendance on a meeting of the Big Three at Teheran or Yalta. Those conferences dramatized the solidarity of the Grand Alliance, but their diplomatic value was to be called into question. Doubts were to be raised whether any Big Three could be big enough to decide among themselves the destinies of the human race.

Roosevelt was an incurable optimist and romanticist in foreign affairs. In the wide sweep of his imagination, he knew all the questions. It is not so certain that his impulsive, on-the-spot answers to them always were sufficiently considered and realistic. In reducing, as those meetings did, the relations of government to terms of personality, he may have relied overmuch on the power of his charm to soothe the savage breast of the Russian bear and to tame the British lion.

Roosevelt was to stand on his feet for the last time when he took the oath at his fourth inauguration, a ceremony which he shifted from its accustomed place on the steps of the Capitol to the beautiful south portico of the White House. On his return from Yalta and his last meeting with Stalin and Churchill, his intimates testify to the shock they suffered at the sight of his gray, haggard face, his shrunken figure and his fading voice. In making his report to Congress of that last effort to hold Russia and the west together in peace as they had been in war, he referred publicly for the first time to his infirmity. He apologized for remaining in his wheel chair rather than bear the weight of ten pounds of leg braces.

He was a burnt out volcano when he went for his last vacation at the "Little White House" on the side of Pine Mountain at Warm Springs in his "other state" of Georgia. It was more than twenty years since first he had delighted to exercise his legs in the warmth of those waters. It was nearly seventeen years since reluctantly he had given up that treatment and yielded to Al Smith's appeal that he run for Governor of New York.

The help he had received at Warm Springs led him to do what he could to aid other sufferers like himself, who lacked his financial means. In his second term, he organized the National Foundation for Infantile Paralysis. A suggestion over the radio started the yearly March of Dimes to the White House, which overwhelmed the mail clerks in the executive offices with a torrent of 2,680,000 dimes that first year. The annual campaign for contributions centers on Roosevelt's birthday, January 30, and the gifts to the Foundation in 1948 alone, three years after his death, amounted to more than $18,000,000.

The making of life-long friendships was not among the gifts of this man who made friends with the multitude. He had no cronies from his Groton and Harvard student days. To Wendell Willkie, he had sighed what a lonely place the presidency was, with virtually every caller who enters its office door coming not to give but to get something. The few whose selfless devotion he trusted were official associates, and most of them broke under their loyal effort to keep pace with "the boss." Louis McHenry Howe, Marvin McIntyre, Miss LeHand were gone from his secretariat. The latest of his favorites to go, General Watson, had died at sea on the way back from Yalta. Nor was he again to see Harry Hopkins, whom the physicians had ordered to leave the home-coming ship from Yalta for a rest in Morocco.

The death of Sara Delano Roosevelt meant more to her son than a like loss means to most men of his age. For this only child of hers had lived until he was near three score under the roof of a loving but imperious mother, whose patrician mind disapproved of the strange bedfellows politics had made for him. Like another president, Madison, he never knew any other than the parental home. And Dolly Madison and Eleanor Roosevelt, the two most spirited wives of presidents, each dwelt for thirty-five years as a guest in the house of a mother-in-law.

When Roosevelt himself died at Warm Springs of a cerebral hemorrhage, the end of the terrible war was in sight. He had seen American armies cross the Rhine and advance toward a junction with the Russians on the Elbe in the heart of Germany. He had watched our forces in the Pacific emerge from the humiliating helplessness of the first six months after Pearl Harbor to break the Japanese offensive at Midway, begin its own advance at Guadalcanal, raise again the stars and stripes over the Philippines and become the master of the vastest of oceans, with the Japanese naval and merchant fleets wiped out. It was not given him to know that Japan was fighting with such fanatical desperation on the island of Okinawa because she was aware that it was her last chance to save the homeland. It was to be her last battle.

In going to Yalta, he had staked his life on winning the confidence and cooperation of Russia in the building of the peace. Whether, living, he could have averted the cold war is like the unanswerable question which still we are asking about the death of Lincoln in another victorious April and on the eve of another era of reconstruction.

An estate appraised at $1,943,888, which realized more than $200,000 from the sale of his stamp collection, ranks Roosevelt with Hoover as the only millionaires in the presidency up to their day. He had given to the government his birthplace and life-long home at Hyde Park, with a library which friends had built to house the papers of his eventful period. In the first years following his death he was the subject of more books than any other American ever had been in a like time.

Many university professors of history were asked by Professor Schlesinger of Harvard to anticipate the verdict of posterity on Franklin Delano Roosevelt. Lincoln came out first in the poll, Washington second, Roosevelt third, Wilson fourth, Jefferson fifth and Jackson sixth. Theodore Roosevelt was first in the secondary division, Cleveland second, John Adams third and Polk fourth. Under the classification of average presidents, were John Quincy Adams, Monroe, Hayes, Madison, Van Buren, Taft, Arthur, McKinley, Johnson, Hoover, and Benjamin Harrison in that order. Tyler, Coolidge, Fillmore, Taylor, Buchanan and Pierce were ranked below average. W. H. Harrison and Garfield were omitted because of the brevity of their terms. Grant and Harding were put down as failures.

A more distant view of the presidents is taken by the electors who choose Americans worthy of monumental busts or memorial tablets in the Hall of Fame on University Heights in the Bronx in New York. Only those who have been dead at least twenty-five years are eligible for consideration. Up to and including the election of 1945 these ten presidents had qualified for ad-

mission to that Valhalla: Washington, the two Adamses, Jefferson, Madison, Monroe, Jackson, Lincoln,
Grant, Cleveland. No doubt Theodore Roosevelt and
Wilson would have been included in that company but
for the time limit, as in due course Franklin D. Roosevelt also surely will join those immortals.

Photographs of grieving faces, often with tears on
them, that lined the way from Warm Springs to the
grave in the rose garden at Hyde Park are documents
for future historians. They will bear witness that this
wealthy aristocrat, with the most sheltered life of any
president, until his own suffering made him kin to all
in any way disadvantaged, was first in the hearts of the
burden bearers of society, whose load he had done
what he could to ease.

HARRY S. TRUMAN

I

LEAST AMBITIOUS PRESIDENT

(1884) May 8, Harry S. Truman born at Lamar, Missouri.—(1917)
Left parental farm at 33 for World War I.—(1919) Married at
35. Opened store in Kansas City.—(1921) Store failed.—(1922)
Elected to County Board.—(1924) Defeated.—(1926-34) On
County Board.—(1935) U.S. Senator at 50.—(1941) Chairman of
Truman Committee at 57.—(1944) Elected Vice President.—(1945)
April 12, President at 60.

No ONE as unambitious as Harry S. Truman ever had
found his feet on the top rung of the ladder of ambition. He was fifty-seven before he rose to national attention, as Chairman of the Truman Committee in the
Senate, and at 60 he was in the White House. He had
not wanted the vice presidency in 1944, when southern
reactionaries and northern city politicians forced the
Democratic nomination upon him in order to get rid
of Vice President Wallace. He had wanted still less to
be president when the death of Roosevelt thrust upon
him that capital prize in the lottery of politics.

In the White House, he felt like a cat in a strange
garret. He admitted so loudly that he was not cut out
for the place that party leaders went to work on him
to stop his talking about it until they had time to build
up a man to succeed him. He didn't want to run for
election to a term of his own but wanted only to get
out of what he called "a big white jail" as soon as he
could under the Constitution.

When, in 1948, he was chosen president in his own

right, he was the first man since Zachary Taylor in 1848 to be elected to the presidency from below the parallel of 39, 43 north latitude—that is to say the Mason and Dixon Line. He was a southerner by ancestry, birth and residence. His ninety-two-year-old mother, the ninth mother to see a son elevated to the highest station in the land, still liked to pose as an "unreconstructed rebel." Teasingly, Harry called her "the old rebel." But when, as President, he received an honorary degree from a Texas college, he struck out of the citation a grotesque reference to a yarn about her having refused to sleep in the Lincoln bed while a guest at the White House, and her daughter said it wasn't so.

This Missourian also was the second president, Hoover having been the first, chosen from that two-thirds of American soil lying between the Mississippi River and the Pacific Ocean. He was of the pioneer breed, his people having followed the frontier from Maryland and Virginia to Kentucky and on to Jackson County, Missouri, where and when the west was at its wildest. Jackson County was a base for the "border ruffians," as they were called by the northerners, who themselves were armed with Sharp's rifles to enact on the stage of "bleeding Kansas" the prologue of the Civil War. After that war, Jesse James, the train robber, remained the best known and not the least popular son of the County until it could boast a president of the United States.

Truman was not a native of Jackson County but was born at Lamar, Missouri, the temporary residence of his parents. When the spotlight of fame was turned on the village, it took some research to identify the presidential birthplace. He had been named Harry for an uncle and that was destined to be the first diminutive among the given names of the chief magistrates. A middle initial was bestowed on the baby, but a middle name was omitted, in order that the S might impartially stand for both his grandparents, Anderson Shippe Truman and Solomon Young.

Truman's was a slow climb up the steeps of fame. Although Kansas City was the booming metropolis of Jackson County, it did not lure him from his father's farm until he was thirty-three. His mother boasted he could milk with both hands, plow the straightest row of corn in the County and sow a wheat field without leaving a bare spot. No president before him had as clear a claim to the title of dirt farmer. Had it not been for World War I, his sober wishes might never have strayed from that sequestered vale of life and he might have kept the even tenor of his way until he died to fame and fortune unknown. By the way, no other war had to wait so long as twenty-seven years to get its first veteran into the presidency.

Having been unable to enter West Point because of a defective eye sight—he put on spectacles at nine—Truman pursued his native military bent as a diligent member of the National Guard and as a student of the campaigns of his heroes, the Confederate generals. With his battery incorporated in the army, he went to the front in France. As captain he stood the battle test and was mustered out with the rank of major. He won also the life-long affection of his comrades. "He had great fortitude and courage," a member of his company has testified, "and he was one of the fastest calculators of artillery data in the whole division."

Like the doughboy in the hit song of the day, there was no keeping Captain Harry down on the farm after he had seen gay Paree. In partnership with one of his sergeants, he opened a men's furnishing goods store in

Keystone View Co.

HARRY S. TRUMAN

Kansas City. At thirty-five, he felt for the first time that he was in a position to marry. His bride was Elizabeth Virginia Wallace, always known as "Bess," "the only girl I ever went with," said the bridegroom.

The Kansas City store was caught by a postwar deflation with goods bought at inflation prices, and it failed. But Truman refused to go into bankruptcy, and the creditors were paid one hundred cents on the dollar, though it took years of tight pinching to clear up the debt.

Another president of the name of Abraham Lincoln also was a failure in his only business venture as a village storekeeper in New Salem. Like him, Truman turned to politics, and a war comrade in France took him to see an uncle, Boss Tom Pendergast. Not the least of the evils of bossism is its control of the opportunity of young men to enter politics. Pendergast happened to be in need of a commodity of good names for his show window, and he could use a clean young fellow from the sticks to help him fasten his Kansas City dictatorship on the entire county. He put Truman on his slate and elected him to the County Board.

By the testimony of his beneficiary, Pendergast never asked him to do a dishonest thing. A most zealous searching of the record failed to uncover the least trace of any wrong doing by Truman in the spending of many millions for the construction of highways and of a new court house. He himself said that the only money he ever "stole" was from the surplus he had saved in the building of the court house. Instead of turning it back into the treasury, he used it to pay for a statue of Andrew Jackson, for whom the county was named.

At fifty, Truman still was paying off the debts of his store and living with his wife's mother in Independence. He needed a more remunerative post, and he asked

Pendergast to make him county tax collector. That juicy plum had been promised to someone else, and he was bowled over with the offer of a United States senatorship by the Boss, who was now bringing the Democratic state machine under his control.

When he was up for election to a second term in 1940, Truman's patron had been in prison for a failure to include some of his boodle in his income tax return. A mob of his henchmen also were behind bars for election frauds, and the Kansas City machine was a wreck. But the Senator said he would not desert a sinking ship, and he barely squeezed in between two anti-machine candidates. When the Boss died, his one-time protégé flew out to the funeral, which was honored by the attendance of the Vice President of the United States.

After an undistinguished but not an unuseful service in the Senate, Truman rose one day in 1941 and proposed a watch dog committee on the expenditure of the big war appropriations. That Truman Committee was something quite new in the way of congressional investigations. It did not follow the familiar pattern of prosecutor, judge and jury in the atmosphere of a criminal court. On the contrary, it made itself a helpful critic and counsellor of the departments. Somehow its Republican members were restrained from their natural thirst for the blood of a Democratic administration, and all its thirty-one reports were unanimous.

Truman went to the National Convention of 1944 to place another man in nomination for vice president. But the boys who run with the city machines had a fellow feeling for him and the southerners regarded him as one of themselves. By that anti-Wallace combination, he was put over, against his protests, as Roosevelt's running mate. He wanted to stay in the Senate where he had won the respect and liking of a body which had received him with the suspicion that he was only the stooge of an unsavory boss.

The success of the Truman Committee had lifted him atop a tide that was sweeping him on to an undreamed of fortune. In less than three months after his inauguration, the Vice President received by telephone a summons to the White House. On his arrival there, the yet unreleased news of the death of Franklin D. Roosevelt was broken to him. Characteristically, he asked Mrs. Roosevelt, "What can I do to help you?" As characteristically, she replied, "Is there any way we can help you?" The next day he returned to the Capitol as President. In unfeigned humility, he said to a group of friendly reporters, "Last night the whole weight of the moon and the stars fell on me. I've got the most awful responsibility a man ever had. If you fellows ever pray, pray for me."

II

ON A ROLLER COASTER

(1945) April 12, Truman took the oath as President. May 7, Germany surrendered. June, Truman addressed San Francisco Conference. July 16, test explosion of atom bomb in New Mexico desert. July 17, attended meeting of Big Three at Potsdam. August 6, first use of atom bomb on Hiroshima. August 9, second atom bomb dropped on Nagasaki. August 14, Truman announced surrender of Japan.—(1946) September, Wallace out of Cabinet. November, Republicans captured Congress.—(1947) March 1, Truman proposed aid for Greece and announced "Truman Doctrine," of containment of Russia, beginning of Cold War. June 5, "Marshall Plan" for European recovery announced by the Secretary at Harvard.—(1948) Feb. 2, Truman's Civil Rights Message. July, Truman nominated and called extra session.

TRUMAN was the seventh vice president to be thrust into the presidency by the hand of death. Neither he nor any of the six before him would have been chosen for the higher office in the first place. None of them, except Theodore Roosevelt, was of presidential caliber, and the members of the Old Guard thought they were laying him away on the shelf when they nominated him for vice president against his strenuous protests.

Vice presidents have had the misfortune to accede to the presidency in crises of one kind or another which confronted them with weighty problems they were ill prepared to meet. Truman's accession occurred at the most critical time of any of those abrupt transitions of power. Although victory was near in the European theater of World War II, victory in the Pacific seemingly was yet far off, at the end of a long, bloody road to Tokyo. All the questions of peace and reconstruction for a world in chaos were awaiting American leadership, under a new, untried president with no experience in foreign affairs.

In that bewildering situation, the American people gave fresh proofs of their capacity for self discipline, for self government, by rallying, regardless of party lines, to the support of a strange, little known chieftain. They gave him such a whole-hearted welcome as no accidental president ever had received. He had great occasions to meet at once, and he met them without discredit—addressing the San Francisco Conference for the organization of the United Nations, attending the Potsdam Meeting of the Big Three for a first attempt at a postwar settlement, announcing the unheralded advent of the "Atomic Age" with the dropping of atom bombs on two Japanese cities, which speedily was followed by his breaking to the world the news of the surrender of Japan.

He recalled the only ex-president to public service, and employed his experience by sending him on arduous missions to study the food situation in Europe. Hoover also became chairman of a commission which made the most thorough survey of the machinery of the executive departments and submitted blueprints for a complete reorganization.

After the dazzling glamor of Roosevelt, Truman did not look presidential, and he disdained to act the part. He was cast in the mould of the folks that Lincoln said the Lord must like or he would not have made so many of them. His type was less familiar to the people on the Atlantic seaboard, but if you traveled anywhere between the Mississippi and the Pacific, you would see hardly a crowd without someone in it to remind you of Harry Truman.

His lack of pretension and his native modesty instantly won the good will of the public, and the gravity of affairs aided to give him a long political honeymoon. His refusal to put on magisterial airs was a credit mark for him in public opinion. But his forgetfulness that he was president sometimes got him into trouble. In his casual "off the cuff" remarks, he still thought it was only Harry Truman speaking, until he saw the reporters rushing from him to the telephone or read the big newspaper headlines the next morning. At other times, he fell into a Jackson County use of words which shocked the ear of the nation.

Generally, the country was as forbearing toward the first musician in the White House, who played the piano well, as the frontier audience was requested to be by the legendary sign in the dance hall, "Don't shoot the pianist; he is doing the best he can." His daughter, Margaret, an only child, also was musical and ventured to sing on the concert stage.

Even the Roosevelt magic had been unequal to keeping the peace among the strange bedfellows that the depression and the war had crowded into the Democratic party. Before the passing of "Mr. Big," they had begun to kick one another out on the floor. The party continued to fall apart under the new leader, and the country turned to the Republicans in the election of 1946, when it gave them the control of both Houses of Congress for the first time in sixteen years.

The national unity in a bi-partisan foreign policy withstood the strain of a government divided between the Capitol and the White House. A Democratic President and a Republican Congress agreed on the policy of "containment" for Russia. A deadline was drawn on Russian expansion by the "Truman Doctrine," when American aid was provided for a weak government in Greece against a Communist insurrection. Next came the ambitious Marshall Plan for strengthening all free nations against communism by pouring out billions of American dollars for their economic recovery.

That was the beginning of what came to be called the "Cold War," which eventuated in the North Atlantic Pact. This was the first peacetime military alliance with Europe since George Washington had made the cornerstone of our foreign policy the isolationism of his Farewell Address. Yet, from earliest colonial times down to World War II, this country never had succeeded in isolating itself from any conflicts which threatened an unfriendly control of the opposite coast of the ocean.

In the swift procession of events, the popularity of President Truman had violent ups and downs on the roller coaster of public opinion polls. It sank to the bottom of the chart when he approved in advance a speech by Henry A. Wallace, his Secretary of Commerce, without understanding that it ran counter to the Russian policy of his Secretary of State, General George C. Marshall. As a result of that blunder, he had to dismiss Wallace from the Cabinet. This caused the disaffection of many northern progressives. It was followed the next year by the revolt of southern conservatism against the President's Civil Rights Message, which proposed federal legislation for removal of discriminations against negroes.

Jesters changed an ancient maxim to say, "To err is Truman." Luckily for the President, the Republican Congress also was running up errors on its score card. It had mistaken the mood of the country for weariness with the New Deal and with a readiness to go back again to the normalcy of the pre-depression era. The dominant faction, particularly in the House, assumed that the presidential election of 1948 already was "in the bag," and such had been the rule when a party won a mid-term congressional election. A Democratic Senator, indeed, proposed that Truman should anticipate the inevitable by resigning in a way that would bring in a Republican president at once and thus spare the country a two-year interregnum in a perilous time.

With the parties changing sides on the historic question of federal power and State Rights, the Democratic solid south became the ally of the Republicans in Congress, voting to override Truman's vetoes and to reject his recommendations. At the Democratic National Convention, the leaders tried to bridge with a weasel-worded plank in the platform the yawning chasm between the northern and southern wings of the party. But the question was carried to the floor in an amendment that placed the party squarely behind the Civil Rights Message. The amendment swept the convention, while some delegates from the south walked out.

The Democrats thus were split three ways as they faced the campaign of 1948. A Progressive party was organized and put a ticket in the field, with Wallace at the head of it. Another ticket was nominated by southern bolters, to whom a North Carolina headline writer gave a name that stuck—Dixiecrats.

No president whose party had lost a mid-term Congressional election ever had been reelected. Sometimes a party had saved itself by turning to a new leader. Democratic city machines in the north and the southerners agreed on drafting General Eisenhower to replace Truman, but the General refused to let his good name become a pawn in such a political game.

It was a surly convention that reluctantly nominated the President. But he brought it to its feet by stepping on the rostrum at 2 A.M. and making a fighting speech. He announced that he would call Congress back to Washington in a mid-summer session and challenge the Republicans to prove their sincerity by enacting into law the fair promises they had made in their platform. The session stalled, and that gave Truman his issue against "the do nothing 80th Congress," which he rated the worst since the reconstruction Congress that came within one vote of removing President Johnson on impeachment.

III

BIGGEST ELECTION UPSET

TRUMAN'S victory in 1948 was the biggest upset in the record of the forty-one presidential elections that had gone before. It dumbfounded the prophets who had agreed in predicting a walkover for Dewey. In his overconfidence, the Republican candidate did not meet the President's issue of a "do nothing Congress," but put on a "do nothing" campaign. He did not care to weight himself down with responsibility for the congressional record of his party, but played safe and tried to glide into the White House on smooth platitudes. His avoidance of questions which had divided the Republicans ever since Theodore Roosevelt challenged the standpatters, raised doubts of whether he could cope with the Old Guard if elected.

By contrast, the country saw Truman in there punching at every "whistle stop" of his train, which carried him 31,000 miles for the delivery of 351 speeches, translated from the script of his "ghost writers" into the Missouri vernacular. Although at sixty-four he was the oldest candidate for president since Buchanan in 1856, his was the hardest campaigning ever waged.

As he went his way, to and fro across the continent, the Democratic leaders who came aboard his car had difficulty in keeping a straight face when he told them he was going to win. The press men with him looked at one another in puzzlement day after day and wondered whether he was fooling himself or only trying to fool them. Meanwhile he kept his eyes on the audiences and refreshed his confidence in the sympathy he read in their faces. The Republicans reassured themselves that he drew bigger crowds than Dewey only because of the curiosity to see a real live president.

Newspaper and radio commentators were all but unanimous in foretelling a bad defeat for Truman. The election of Dewey was reduced to an arithmetical certainty by the public opinion polls, which had built up a superstitious faith in their uncanny accuracy. One of them announced in September that it would not bother any further with a foregone conclusion.

Most of Truman's own Cabinet gave up the fight before it began. They held aloof from his campaign and didn't open their pocketbooks. High officials in Washington boxed up their house furnishings and sent them home, while expectant Republican office holders were in the real estate market for the residences the Democrats were planning to vacate.

Those who sat up with the amazing returns never will forget that election night. There had been several close contests before. Tilden in 1876 and Hughes in 1916 went to bed winners only to lose the prize seemingly in their grasp. But 1948 was not a close election.

The Truman trend was uninterrupted throughout the night and clear across the continent. Yet, the figures were unbelievable because so unexpected. The Democratic headquarters in a New York hotel remained almost as deserted as the proverbial sinking ship. In another hotel close by, the Dewey rendezvous was crowded and all set for the first Republican jubilation in sixteen long years. A balcony was in readiness for the appearance of the victor. A special detail of secret service men was waiting at the hotel and all set to spring to the protection of the president elect, while the real holder of that title was asleep more than a thousand miles away in a Missouri hideout.

Truman was too dead tired from his campaigning to listen to its results as they came over the radio. Afterward, he gave an imitation of the familiar voice of a well-known broadcaster saying at 11 o'clock that although Truman was a million votes ahead, later returns from the rural districts would wipe out that margin. When he was waked up at 4 A.M. by a secret service man and told that he would better tune in, he heard the same voice explaining that although Truman was leading by two million, it did not mean his election but that the contest would be thrown into the House of Representatives.

The oracles had overestimated the weakness of Truman and underestimated the weakness of the Republican party. Truly, it was about as difficult a choice as ever had been presented to the electorate, which yawned with indifference and stayed home by the millions.

The strength of the Wallace progressive ticket also was overestimated. It started as high as ten million, fell to five million and dwindled away to a little more than one million at the polls. As the Communists moved in and all but took possession of this third party, Democratic progressives moved out. Since nearly half of Wallace's total in the whole country came from New York, where he ran on the ticket of the American Labor party, he had the satisfaction of keeping the Empire State out of Truman's column.

Governor Thurmond of South Carolina, the candidate of the Dixiecrats, made a slightly better showing than Wallace. He won the electors of South Carolina, Alabama, Mississippi and Louisiana, where the Democratic organizations bolted Truman. It was the first time since LaFollette in 1924 that a third party had broken into the electoral college. While the Dixiecrats failed to defeat the election of Truman, they succeeded beyond their wishes in disrupting what was left of the Solid South and hastening the end of the one party monopoly in the states comprising that bloc.

The prognosticators also left out of their calculations a curious but persistent factor. When, if ever, has a representative of the great dark-eyed majority of humanity won a presidential election? Was it not written in the book of fate that Truman's blue eyes would give him a decisive advantage over Dewey's black eyes?

An ancient political superstition also was upset in that upsetting election. The American voters long had the doubtful repute of being band-wagon chasers. In his "American Commonwealth," James Bryce characterized it as the "fatalism of the multitude." He argued that in a country where the majority rules, people are inclined to believe that the majority must be right and to line up in a campaign on the side that appears to have the largest numbers.

There also had been a contrasting belief that popular sympathy was with Cinderella. In Truman's plucky, single-handed, up-hill campaign, "the game little guy" became the subject of common remark. Few of the twenty-four million voting for him could have had any idea that he would win. The outcome raised the question of whether the appeal of the under dog to the emotions is not stronger than the lure of the bandwagon.

Finally, the spirit of Roosevelt was an imponderable that could not be calculated in the mathematics of the poll takers. The man who had carried four elections from a wheel chair won a fifth from his grave. It subtracts nothing from Truman's rightful credit to point out that his campaign increasingly was aimed at the elements which his predecessor had been marshalling on the Democratic side since 1932—organized labor, the farmers and the minority racial groups. He aroused them from despair or persuaded them from outright hostility, some of them at the eleventh hour, and brought them to the polls in sufficient numbers to turn the tide.

The victorious Truman could afford to smile at what he called "Wednesday morning Democrats," who had been invisible in his campaign. Some of them opened their check books for the first time that morning and raised $600,000 in contributions to the successful party. The President had another laugh at the expense of the Republicans in the 80th Congress who made an unprecedently liberal appropriation for an inauguration which they expected was to mark their triumphant return from exile. This enabled the Democratic victor to give himself the most elaborate induction ever staged in Washington.

Although the Democrats had recaptured both Houses of the 81st Congress, the southerners joined the northerners only to organize those bodies and give themselves, under the seniority rule, most of the committee chairmanships. After that, from time to time, as their conservatism was challenged, they rejoined the Republicans in the same coalition that had dominated the 80th Congress.

The Truman administration was assured of a place in history by the bi-partisan foreign policy, ably sponsored on the Republican side by Senator Vandenberg of Michigan. The Truman Doctrine for the containment of Russian expansion, the Marshall Plan for European recovery, the military alliance of America with western Europe in the Atlantic Pact are all historic measures. To these the President added in his inaugural address the outline of a global policy of co-operation to raise the living standards of backward peoples everywhere, by the development of their often rich natural resources, with the aid of American loans and American technology.

*
* *
*

Congress was kind to the re-elected President personally. It was even generous in raising to $100,000 a year the presidential salary, which had been $25,000 until Grant's second term, then $50,000 until Taft, after which it had remained at $75,000. That pay had been cut about one half when it was brought under the income tax in the term of Hoover, who said that he had hardly enough left for cigarette money, after taxes and official expenses. No smoker himself, Truman had reckoned that his take home pay was about $80 a week. To relieve the drain on a president's finances, Congress increased the expense account of the office from $40,000 yearly to $90,000, and that is tax free.

Notwithstanding Truman was the first president successfully to appeal from an advance notice of eviction served in a mid-term congressional election, and receive a new four-year lease to the White House, he dared not return to it because of its rickety condition. Instead, he moved across Pennsylvania Avenue to Blair House and informed Congress that it was in for a reconstruction bill of several million dollars. Engineers and architects had agreed in recommending that nothing less than an entire new, fire proof building should be erected, but within the old historic walls. These would remain unchanged, a cherished heirloom of all Americans.

DWIGHT DAVID EISENHOWER

I

THE DEMOCRATIC GENERAL

(1890) Dwight David Eisenhower born at Denison, Texas.—(1915) Graduated from West Point.—(1915–40) Followed military career.—(1942) Commanded invasion of North Africa.—(1944) Commanded invasion of Europe.—(1945) Accepted surrender of Germany.—(1948) Became president of Columbia University.—(1950) Was appointed Supreme Commander of the NATO forces in Europe.

DWIGHT DAVID EISENHOWER was catapulted into the White House from the battlefields of Europe. During the first fifty years of his life no thought of entering the realm of statesmanship seemed to cross his mind. As the United States began to build up its military forces in 1940, following the outbreak of World War II in Europe, he did set for himself what he thought was a high goal. He wanted to command an armored regiment. Though he was not to achieve that particular ambition, he soon found himself commanding the international forces that invaded Europe from the coast of Normandy and destroyed Adolf Hitler's empire.

From the moment that Eisenhower returned to the United States a celebrated war hero, he was a potential President. At that time any mention of politics was an unwelcome encroachment on his wholly military role. In 1945 President Truman had indicated to the General at Potsdam that he would be willing to help him (Eisenhower) win the Presidency in 1948. But Ike, as he was familiarly known to the country as well as to his intimate friends, did not even nibble at the bait. From his pinnacle of victory in a world-wide contest even the Presidency had the appearance of being an anticlimax.

When the Eisenhower-for-President movement became a serious embarrassment to his continued military career in 1948, Ike took drastic measures. He wrote a letter to Leonard V. Finder, New Hampshire publisher, declaring, "I am not available for and could not accept nomination to high political office." In effect he said that, having spent his life in the country's military forces, he did not think he had the special qualities "for the most important office in the world." Going further, he expressed the conviction that "the necessary and wise subordination of the military to civil power will be best sustained, and our people will have greater confidence that it is so sustained, when life-long professional soldiers, in the absence of some obvious and overriding reason, abstain from seeking high political office. . . ."

But Eisenhower had caught the public fancy. Politics continued to trail him, like an unwelcome shadow, until he embraced it and embarked upon an entirely new career.

The future General-President had been born in Denison, Texas, on October 14, 1890, the third of seven sons. His parents, David J. and Ida Elizabeth (Stover) Eisenhower, moved to Abilene, Kansas, while Dwight was still a baby. There he grew to manhood. The Eisenhowers were poor, but poverty did not weight them down. Dwight grew up in an environment which laid great emphasis on duty to God, the Christian virtues, the value of hard work, and the desirability of taking advantage of one's opportunities.

Dwight became fully aware of the family's limited

DWIGHT DAVID EISENHOWER

resources when he reached college age, but that did not discourage him. For a year he worked in a creamery from 6:00 P.M. to 6:00 A.M. and sent part of his earnings to his brother Edgar to pay his tuition at law school. Dwight himself was thinking of studying engineering, but a friend urged him to seek admission to the United States Naval Academy. He took the competitive examinations for both the naval and military academies, passed both, and was appointed to the Army's famous officer training school at West Point.

Cadet Eisenhower was graduated from the Military Academy, with a high rank in his class, in 1915. He had demonstrated capacity for sustained effort, an unusual ability to get along with his fellow students, and a casual manner that was to astonish many of his associates after he became a famous General. Assigned to an Army post in Texas as a lieutenant of infantry, he met Marie Geneva (Mamie) Doud, and within a year they were married.

When the United States began expanding its military forces in frantic haste just before its entry into World War I, Eisenhower became a captain in charge of training officers and later the commander of a tank training school. The war ended in November, 1918, just before he was scheduled to leave for the fighting front in Europe.

Home for Captain Eisenhower and his bride was wherever he might be sent, and in the period between the wars he served in many Army camps within the States and abroad. In 1921 the young couple suffered the severest blow of their lives when their three-year-old son died of scarlet fever. A year later a second son, John, was born to them, and he was to follow his father in a military career.

After a tour of duty in the Panama Canal Zone,

where he was in charge of an infantry battalion, Eisenhower was chosen to accompany General Douglas MacArthur to the Philippines as an adviser. Japan's attack on Manchuria in 1931 had put the Philippines in jeopardy. One of the chief tasks of General MacArthur and Major Eisenhower was to draw up a plan for defense of the islands. Eisenhower remained at this post until Europe's much hated dictators, Adolf Hitler in Germany and Joseph Stalin of the Soviet Union, divided Poland in 1939 and thus brought on World War II. Then he returned to the United States and worked day and night to build up its neglected military forces. After Japan's assault on Pearl Harbor took the United States into the war, Ike was assigned to the War Plans Division of the War Department despite his yearning for a troop command. There he outlined the strategy for the war in the Pacific and later worked out a plan for joint Allied operations in Europe. This work was done so well that, notwithstanding his own recommendation of another, he was assigned to command the assault on Hitler's European fortress.

Eisenhower's rise was meteoric because he constantly threw all his energy into his job. In addition he had the happy faculty of grasping quickly the basic facts of a military situation and thus of cutting to the heart of complex problems. In working out his first plan for recouping American fortunes in the Pacific, for example, he correctly saw that it would be a long time before American reinforcements could go to the Philippines; he therefore insisted that a base be established in Australia and that communications be kept open at all cost so that the peoples of Asia would not lose faith in America.

General Eisenhower had one other profound conviction—that, as the war had brought many nations into a common cause, it was absolutely necessary for them to work smoothly together. "I am almost fanatic," he wrote to a friend, "in my belief that only as we pull together, each of us in the job given him, are we going to defend and sustain the priceless things for which we are fighting." His great ability to weld many disparate elements into a unified fighting force made him the ideal commander for the Allied assaults on the Axis powers.

The first major move in which the United States participated, under Eisenhower's command, was the invasion of North Africa. With the Germans routed from that continent, the victorious Allied forces took Sicily and soon brought a collapse to the Axis' strength in Italy. Meanwhile Eisenhower had been transferred to England as Supreme Commander, Allied Expeditionary Forces, in charge of the momentous assault to be launched against Hitler's seemingly impregnable defenses across the English Channel.

This was a colossal undertaking, which was made the more difficult by Prime Minister Churchill's preference for striking at Germany through the "soft underbelly" of the Balkans. On June 6, 1944, the hard-working, tough-minded general from Abilene led half a million men, with 15,000 aircraft and 6,000 ships, in a successful invasion of Normandy. Less than a year later Hitler's power had collapsed, and the worst war in history was near an end.

After accepting the unconditional surrender of the Nazi high command, Eisenhower dreamed of an easy retirement in a peaceful world. But the refusal of the Soviet Union to cooperate in any acceptable settlement soon made it evident that nothing more had been won than a termination of hostilities. Instead of going fishing, Eisenhower became Chief of Staff of the Army for a little more than two years. His chief tasks were to inject some order into the country's frantic demobilization and to work unceasingly for unification of the armed services.

In 1948 Eisenhower put his uniform aside and became president of Columbia University in New York because he felt there was an urgent need for keener appreciation among civilians of the momentous issues confronting the world. Soviet Russia was rapidly extending its subversive conquests in Europe as well as in Asia. North Korea, under Soviet tutelage and guidance, attacked South Korea and precipitated the United States and other members of the United Nations into a war against aggression. After the fall of Czechoslovakia, nine European nations, the United States, Canada, and Iceland entered into a defensive alliance known as the North Atlantic Treaty Organization (later enlarged to fifteen countries). Each ally pledged itself to regard an attack on one of them as an attack on all.

Eisenhower was everywhere recognized as the logical man to build up the new joint defense system, and he responded immediately to President Truman's call. As he flew to Paris to take up this assignment, the whole free world was immersed in gloom because the forces of aggression which had been unleashed in Korea, with the aid of the Soviet Union and Communist China, appeared to be winning over the "police action" which had been launched by the United Nations and the United States.

While inspecting and organizing troops under the new NATO banner, Eisenhower preached the doctrine of European unity and solidarity in the Atlantic community. He became for Europe a symbol of American good faith in this new venture into a common defense policy. Though he left NATO while it was still in its initial growth period, he laid the groundwork for the most successful regional defense system of modern times.

II

GENERAL IN POLITICS

(1951) Urged to run for President.—(1952) Nominated for President by Republican Party and elected. Visited Korea.—(1953) Offered atoms-for-peace plan.—(1955) Attended Summit Meeting at Geneva.—(1954) Offered plan to save Indochina and create SEATO.—(1955) Asked Congress for authority to defend Formosa.—(1955–57) Stopped British-French-Israeli war against Egypt and enunciated doctrine for protection of Near East.— (1953–58) Shapes new defense policy.

THE redrafted General had scarcely settled down to his task in Paris before American politicians began a hegira to that city to urge that he become a candidate for the Presidency. As he had never been identified with either political party, these appeals came to him from eminent Democrats as well as Republicans. Indeed, a Gallup Poll indicated that he was the favorite candidate in both parties, with 40 per cent of the Democrats naming him and 30 per cent of the Republicans. A draft-Eisenhower movement among the Republicans opposed to the candidacy of Senator Robert A. Taft got under way in September, 1951, but it could claim no support from the General at that time. Taft had been campaigning diligently for some months.

Eisenhower acknowledged his Republican voting record and convictions in January, 1952, after a visit from Senator Henry Cabot Lodge, Jr., and at the same time indicated that he would not seek the nomination. This was a sufficient signal for his supporters to drive ahead with their plans, and the New Hampshire and

Minnesota primaries convinced him that, if released from his NATO assignment, he should return home and make a vigorous race. He returned in June, retired from the Army after thirty-seven years of service, and plunged into a hot political contest with Senator Taft.

At the Republican National Convention in Chicago a bitter fight broke out over the right of the contested delegations to vote before they had been seated. The victory of the Eisenhower forces in this contest and in the fight over the actual seating of the delegates forecast his victory for the nomination on the first ballot. In a dramatic post-nomination meeting with Taft, the widely respected "Mr. Republican" swallowed his resentment sufficiently to pledge the General his support. Once more Ike's skill as a conciliator had been demonstrated.

A stiff contest was assured when the Democratic party nominated Governor Adlai E. Stevenson of Illinois. A polished speaker, Mr. Stevenson gave a surge of strength to the Democratic cause. But he could not match General Eisenhower's standing with the rank and file of voters or overcome the strong feeling that, after twenty years of Democratic rule, it was "time for a change." At times Stevenson tried to rival Eisenhower in promising "change," but this brought him into collision with the Truman Administration, whose support was vital to him.

Eisenhower also had his share of embarrassments. Senator Joseph R. McCarthy of Wisconsin and a few other right-wing extremists who were exploiting the Communist issue were anathema to the General, but he felt that he could not denounce them without splitting the Republican party. As the campaign warmed up, there was also a question as to whether his running mate, Senator Richard M. Nixon of California, would be forced off the ticket. Nixon came under fire because a group of Californians had supplied him with an $18,235 expense fund to finance his extra travel, clerical help, postage, and so forth. After concluding that Nixon's political integrity had not been compromised, Eisenhower stood by him through a severe political storm which abated only after the Republicans disclosed that Stevenson had used a similar expense fund as Governor of Illinois.

President Truman's conduct of the Korean War became the hottest issue, and Eisenhower announced that, if elected, he would go to Korea in an effort to bring the war to "an early and honorable end." This struck a responsive chord, and voters swarmed into the polls to give Ike the largest vote (33,936,234 to 27,314,992 for Stevenson) ever received by a presidential candidate up to that time.

The President-elect kept his pledge by flying off to Korea secretly before his inauguration. He returned determined to increase pressure on the Chinese and North Koreans until they would agree to an armistice. The new Secretary of State, John Foster Dulles, let the Chinese know that, if no accord were reached and the Chinese continued to fight, the United States would attack the Manchurian bases where the aggressor forces had been free from pursuit. An armistice was concluded in July, 1953.

Foreign policy was destined to be the dominant interest of the Eisenhower years. The threat of Communist conquest still hung heavily over the world. Under the Truman Administration, bipartisan efforts had created the Marshall Plan to aid the economic recovery of Western Europe and the North Atlantic Treaty Organization to counteract aggression. The basic Eisenhower policy was to extend and strengthen the cooperative ventures of the free world against the rise of Communist power.

Along with this effort to tighten up the defenses of the free world went a persistent drive to improve relations between the United States and the Soviet Union. The U.S.S.R.'s notorious dictator, Joseph Stalin, died soon after Eisenhower attained power. The new President seized upon the occasion to emphasize the perils of the arms race and the so-called cold war and to urge the new Soviet leadership "to help turn the tide of history." If the Soviet Union would demonstrate its sincerity and peaceful purpose, he said, the United States would "ask its people to join with all nations in devoting a substantial percentage of the savings achieved by disarmament to a fund for world aid and reconstruction."

On December 8, 1953, in a dramatic address to the United Nations General Assembly, Eisenhower unveiled his atoms-for-peace plan—one of the most hopeful cooperative ventures ever undertaken by the U.N. Pointing to the horrors of atomic war for all participants, he pleaded with responsible statesmen "to take this weapon out of the hands of the soldiers" and put it "into the hands of those who will know how to strip its military casing and adapt it to the arts of peace." Several years of patient negotiations were necessary to induce the Soviet Union to match the United States' and Britain's gift of fissionable materials to the world atomic pool thus created for peaceful purposes, but the undertaking finally became a reality.

The peace moves of Eisenhower's first term came to a climax at the summit meeting in Geneva in 1955. Demands for such a gathering had arisen simultaneously in many lands. It was Eisenhower who insisted that it be an open meeting devoted to broad discussion of major causes of friction between the East and West and not a secret session from which deals of the Yalta type might be expected to emerge. The aim, he said, was to create a new atmosphere that would be conducive to further negotiations.

The high-light of the conference was President Eisenhower's "open skies" proposal in which he offered to give the Soviet Union a complete blueprint of United States military establishments and to permit unlimited aerial reconnaissance in return for similar favors from the U.S.S.R. This generous offer was hailed throughout the free world, but Soviet Premier Nikolai A. Bulganin and Nikita S. Khrushchev, the Communist party boss, failed to match it on behalf of the Soviet Union. The only definite action of the conference was to instruct the foreign ministers of the four conferring powers—Britain and France in addition to the United States and the U.S.S.R.—to continue working in accord with the general principles there laid down for European security, the reunification of Germany, arms limitation, and freer cultural contacts. When the West attempted to follow through on these objectives at a subsequent Foreign Ministers' conference also at Geneva, it encountered a stone wall of resistance.

The Administration succeeded, however, in eliminating some of the lesser irritants that were threatening to disrupt an uncertain peace. The threat of a Communist seizure of power in Iran as an aftermath of the British-Iranian oil dispute was averted by a combination of patience and firmness. The explosive Trieste dispute between Italy and Yugoslavia was finally settled by means of a compromise that proved mutually acceptable. A peace treaty for Austria was finally attained after 379 meetings on that subject with Soviet officials. Stern measures were planned through the Organization of American States to prevent the addition of Guatemala to the Communist camp, but a revolution in that little country rendered the proposed intervention unnecessary.

Though the Eisenhower Administration failed to convert its allies across the Atlantic to the proposed European Defense Community, it did help to bring West Germany into the North Atlantic Alliance and the Western European Union. The defense system of the free countries of Europe was thus notably strengthened, and West Germany's new military power was linked with that of free Europe as a safeguard against possible future aggression from that quarter.

The United States was near the brink of war several times during the first Eisenhower term. The closest call probably came in Indochina where France was fighting Communist guerrillas. The United States sent enormous quantities of arms and supplies to help the French but stopped short of participating in the actual fighting. When Dienbienphu came under heavy siege, the French pleaded for an American air strike at the Communists. Fearful that the loss of Indochina would mean a Communist sweep through Southeast Asia, Eisenhower and Dulles tried to organize a united defense movement. The President promised to go to Congress with a request for broad military action in Indochina if such intervention were requested by the Indochinese authorities, if the French gave assurance of complete independence for the three Indochinese states, if the United Nations would indicate an interest in the problem, and if the British and some free Asian countries would join in the movement. The French and British rejected this proposal at first, but finally agreed to accept it if no armistice could be obtained from Communist China in the negotiations then going on in Geneva. The upshot of the Geneva negotiations was a division of Vietnam between the Communist and non-Communist factions. This was a bitter disappointment for the President, but he found some satisfaction in having saved South Vietnam from Communist control. With American aid, that torn segment of a country was to become an anchor of freedom in strife-bedeviled Asia.

Out of this experience also came the Southeast Asia Treaty Organization—SEATO—a somewhat weaker version of the North Atlantic Alliance. This agreement binds Britain, France, the Philippines, Australia, New Zealand, Thailand, Pakistan, and the United States to a mutual defense policy and to protection of the Indochinese states. Along with the treaty went the Pacific Charter pledging the SEATO powers to the promotion of independence for "all countries whose peoples desire it and are able to undertake its responsibilities."

Formosa was another close call. Determined to prevent this large island, which the United States had wrested from Japan in World War II, from falling into the hands of the Chinese Communists, Eisenhower negotiated a mutual defense treaty with Chiang Kai-shek. Chiang had been in control of Formosa since his expulsion from the Chinese mainland by the Communist régime. The treaty was carefully safeguarded, however, to prevent Chiang from drawing the United States into any war designed to reestablish himself on the mainland.

The Communist government at Peiping repeatedly threatened to capture Formosa by military force. In late 1954 Red China launched a series of attacks on Quemoy and other offshore islands (steppingstones to Formosa) held by Chiang's forces. President Eisenhower promptly went to Congress with a bold request for authority to use United States armed forces, if necessary, to repel any assault against Formosa or the Pescadore Islands. Both houses of Congress gave almost unanimous approval.

As Red China continued her fulminations, a storm blew up over charges that the United States was risking war to defend the Quemoy and Matsu islands, which had always been regarded as part of China. The President had made it clear, however, that the United States would not defend these islands unless a thrust against them could be unmistakably recognized as part of an attack against Formosa. Chiang sought assurances that the offshore islands which he held would be defended in any event, but Eisenhower and Dulles flatly refused to make any such commitment. Peiping and some American politicians continued to fume over the arrangement, but the policy served its purpose of preventing an attack on Formosa that would certainly have begun a war.

The so-called Eisenhower Doctrine that was applied in Formosa and elsewhere means simply that the United States regards some areas as being so vital to the security of the free world that it would fight, if necessary, to save them from Communist domination. In such cases, Eisenhower and Dulles believe, the safest course is to let the world know the American intention so that no potential aggressor will start a conquest under the mistaken notion that he can get away with it.

The policy is based on the conviction that World War I, the war in Korea, and possibly World War II would not have been begun if the aggressive governments behind them had known in advance that they would be confronted by the military might of the United States. Eisenhower and Dulles concluded that the risk of war could be substantially diminished by informing the troublemakers in no uncertain terms that aggression in areas vital to free-world security would not be tolerated. The policy was much distorted and abused because of an indiscreet magazine article purporting to explain it; nevertheless, it made United States diplomacy a more potent influence on the side of peace than it had ever been before.

The application of the Eisenhower Doctrine to the Near East evolved out of a very complex situation. The efforts of Gamal Abdel Nasser, President of Egypt, to play Moscow off against Washington caused the United States to cancel its offer of aid in the construction of the proposed Aswan High Dam on the Nile River. Nasser retaliated by seizing the Suez Canal, Europe's most vital life line, which was then under international control. The United States sought to restrain British and French excitement over the seizure as well as to ease their economic problems resulting from the loss of shipping through the canal. At the same time American influence was used in numerous conferences to work out a satisfactory compromise to assure continued international control of the waterway.

When Israel, Britain, and France invaded Egypt— in part because of Nasser's intransigence over the canal and in part to retaliate for border raids into Israel— the United States stood firmly against this resort to force. Through the United Nations a truce was arranged, and the President used his influence to force the withdrawal of British, French, and Israeli troops. The Soviet Union threatened the invading powers. The situation was further complicated by the fact that Soviet troops were brutally suppressing the revolt in Hungary against Communist rule. The aberration of the British and French left the United Nations especially weak in dealing with the Hungarian revolt and put severe strains on the North Atlantic Alliance.

British and French anger against the United States flared for a time, but the NATO alliance weathered the storm and was buttressed by a heads-of-state conference attended by President Eisenhower at Paris in 1957. As soon as the crisis within the West had passed and the 1956 election in the United States was over, Eisenhower moved to strengthen the defenses of the Near East through increased economic cooperation and military assistance. The President also asked Congress to authorize the use of United States armed forces, if necessary, to protect the "territorial integrity and political independence" of the nations of the Near East, if they should request such aid against overt Communist aggression.

Congress fretted and fumed over the request for a couple of months and then finally passed the Eisenhower resolution through both houses by large majorities. The result was not, of course, to liquidate the problems of the Near East but to add a persuasive reason why Moscow should not push her adventuring in that troubled part of the world too far.

Throughout the Eisenhower years defense policy was a subject of lively controversy both in regard to the size of the defense budget and to the organization of the military establishment. As in other matters, the President's tendency was to follow a middle course, with a military budget of roughly $35 billion a year. This was a decline from the military spending during the Korean War but nearly three times the sum of the pre-Korean outlays.

In an effort to maintain an adequate defense without straining the nation's economy, the Administration laid increasing emphasis on nuclear weapons, long-range bombers and, later, missiles. Its reasoning was that the best hope of avoiding war lay in being able to retaliate against any possible attack with such devastating force that no potential enemy would dare to start a war.

Critics of this policy assert that it left the United States unprepared to meet possible limited assaults, the so-called brush fires, and that the nation became dependent upon a weapon that it would never dare to use. In the absence of any effective agreement to prevent the military use of thermonuclear power, however, the United States had to be prepared in this field to ensure its survival. All other aspects of defense policy were necessarily subordinate to this overriding fact.

In 1957 the whole world was startled by the launching of the Soviet Union's first sputniks, thus demonstrating that the Russians were ahead of the United States in the development of long-range ballistic missiles. The confidence of Americans in their defense system was shaken in some degree, and American prestige abroad sustained a blow. In part these psychological losses were overcome by the launching of the American earth satellites early in 1958. But the Russian achievement ushered in a new era in defense and in the exploration of outer space.

President Eisenhower responded by naming a new scientific adviser, Dr. James R. Killian, by stepping up the missile programs, by recommending increased emphasis on scientific education, and by the creation of a civilian agency to explore outer space. Here again his critics insisted that his actions were tame and inadequate in the face of a great potential menace. Certainly the President's proposals were more modest than those advanced by some of his advisers and by some members of Congress.

III

DOMESTIC POLICIES

(1954) Tested anti-depression tools. Launched new farm policy.—
(1953–55) Controversy over TVA and Dixon-Yates. Plagued by
McCarthyism.

THE Eisenhower years brought the first real test of
the country's anti-depression measures. After the great
depression of the thirties, Congress had enacted numerous statutes designed to prevent any repetition of that
experience. But President Roosevelt had not succeeded
in restoring a high level of economic activity until
World War II brought new demands upon the economy. When the war was over, the pent-up demands for
civilian goods of all kinds had kept economic activity
at a high level for several years. Then the war in Korea
had brought a new spurt of buying and plant expansion along with excessive inflation. So the anti-depression measures sponsored by two Democratic Administrations remained largely untested until the recession
of 1954.

Eisenhower's first year in office, 1953, was the most
prosperous the country had experienced up to that time.
When production fell and unemployment mounted in
the latter part of 1953 and in 1954, there was much
speculation as to whether a Republican Administration
would use the Democrats' stabilizing tools. But the
issue was not long in doubt. The President steadfastly
refused to adopt the "slam-bang" emergency program
urged by many critics, but initiated numerous remedial
actions aimed at specific weak spots in the economy.

Originally the Administration had intended to bal-
ance the federal budget before advocating tax relief,
but the recession changed its view. Its tax measures

plus reductions previously voted to take effect in 1954 brought the total tax cut to $7,400,000,000—the largest dollar tax relief ever granted in any year. Substantial sums thus flowed into consumption channels instead of into the Treasury. At the same time additional credit was pumped into the banks by the Federal Reserve System. Some industries were given special assistance, and grants-in-aid to the states were accelerated.

Along with these stimulants went psychological encouragement for business and industry to resume full-scale activity. The Government's judicious use of the anti-depression tools undoubtedly helped to bring a turn in the economic indices. The recession proved to be both mild and brief, and it was followed by several years of high-level economic activity, except in the field of agriculture.

In 1958 the Administration again found it necessary to combat an economic recession—in some measure a result of tightened restrictions designed to curb inflation. The President and the Democratic Congress found a good deal of common ground in working out recovery measures, but both moved slowly because of the continued danger of inflationary pressures.

Farmers were in trouble under both Truman and Eisenhower in part because of the large surpluses which had been built up during the postwar years. Congress had encouraged the production of basic commodities by continuing in effect the high, rigid price supports adopted in wartime when maximum production was essential. The Eisenhower Administration left the price supports in effect while it worked out a new program, as the President had promised to do in his campaign speeches, and then won from Congress authority to reduce the amount of its commodity loans to farmers from 90 per cent of parity to 75 per cent.

When this policy failed to relieve the squeeze on the farmer resulting from lower prices for his produce and higher prices for goods he had to buy, the Administration sponsored a "soil bank" law under which farmers were compensated for leaving some of their acres idle and for shifting other crop land to grass and trees. The effect was to supplement lowered farm income and encourage some conservation of soil, but no one regarded it as a final answer to the farm problem.

In his second term the President and Secretary of Agriculture Ezra Taft Benson sought further authority to lower price supports, with the object of restoring to the farmer a larger measure of control over his own operations. This was stoutly resisted by the Democratic Congress. Agricultural policy thus remained one of the sharpest issues between the two parties.

One other economic policy that provoked repeated controversy was Eisenhower's sponsorship of freer foreign trade. At first the opposition came largely from congressional leaders of the Republican party. Only a determined rally by the Democrats in the House saved the Republican President's bill for extension of the Reciprocal Trade Agreements Act and the further lowering of duties. As industrialization of the South proceeded, however, opposition among the Democrats increased, and the country witnessed the curious spectacle of a Republican President contending for lower duties against stiff opposition from many Democratic as well as Republican members of Congress.

Eisenhower's major retreat while he was in the White House, an exercise to which he was not accustomed, came in the hot battle over the Tennessee Valley and the Dixon-Yates contract. The President made the political error of questioning the policy under which the Federal Government subsidizes the electric power bills of everyone living in the Tennessee Valley. Beyond this, he challenged the TVA monopoly by an indirect method which brought down upon his head the indignation of all the public-power advocates. The result was a veritable Donnybrook Fair.

The squabble began with the request of TVA for funds to build a $100,000,000 steam plant to serve the Memphis area. Eisenhower noted that nearly $2,000,000,000 in federal funds had already been invested in the Tennessee Valley projects, mostly for power, and asked how a further draft on tax funds to provide more cheap power could be justified. The result, he said, would be further to enhance the Tennessee Valley's power to lure industries away from other areas not so favored at public expense. Why, he asked Governor Frank Clement of Tennessee, did not Memphis build its own power plant? This, he was told, would be impossible.

The President then instructed the Atomic Energy Commission to enter into a contract with Edgar H. Dixon, president of the Middle South Utilities, and Eugene A. Yates, of the Southern Company, for power to be supplied through the TVA system. The Dixon-Yates combine was to build its new plant near Memphis. Theoretically, it would be supplying power to the AEC, but actually the AEC would take its power from the TVA system at Paducah, Kentucky, and the Dixon-Yates power flowing into the TVA system would be sold to Memphis.

This awkward arrangement was brought into further disrepute by the fact that Adolphe H. Wenzell, a vice president of the First Boston Corporation on loan to the Budget Bureau, advised the Government on the contract, and First Boston later became finance agent for the Dixon-Yates group. Politicians seized upon this alleged conflict of interest and tried for months to inflate the controversy into a scandal. Finally, Memphis decided to build its own plant after all, to avoid having to take power from the Dixon-Yates interests. The President said he was delighted, and canceled the Dixon-Yates contract. Though he had originally suggested the Memphis plant, he was aware that the Memphis plant offered him an easy retreat out of the quagmire into which he had detoured from his original pursuit of a sound basic policy regarding TVA.

Ike's sharpest disillusionment came from the conduct of the Republican extremists who had been swept into office along with him. The General had supposed that, once he was elected, these men would show some degree of party solidarity. Eisenhower had given them nominal support during the campaign to avoid a party split. Instead of reciprocating, the super-patriots continued their campaigns to exterminate alleged Communists and traitors from the executive branch of the Government as fanatically and as ruthlessly as they had done under President Truman.

The President attempted to take the problems of loyalty and subversion out of the hands of the redbaiters by tightening security regulations and assuming responsibility for whatever housecleaning was necessary in the executive branch. At the same time he set up new safeguards to protect the rights of government employees who might be wrongfully accused. But every moderate move seemed to drive the fanatics to greater extremes.

By reason of the Republican victory, Senator Joseph R. McCarthy had become chairman of the Senate's Permanent Subcommittee on Investigations. He used that position to intimidate and badger officials of the International Information Administration and many other agencies. His intervention led to the banning of three hundred books from the libraries maintained by the United States in other lands on the ground that they contained Communist propaganda. The resulting furor was humiliating for the United States throughout the world and led to a stern denunciation of "book burning" by the President.

Broadening his bid for power, McCarthy denounced the President's foreign policy as being one of "whining, whimpering appeasement." Then McCarthy's attempt to browbeat General Ralph W. Zwicker because he refused to give testimony forbidden by a presidential order led to the notorious Army-McCarthy hearings. Secretary of the Army Robert T. Stevens first stood by General Zwicker and then negotiated with McCarthy an abject "surrender" which irritated the President as much as it did the country. Stevens was not asked to resign at that time, however, because the effect would have been further to magnify the prestige of the ruthless Senator from Wisconsin.

Throughout these trying times the President refused to be drawn into a personal fight with the Senator. Though he emphatically dissociated himself from what McCarthy was doing, praised General Zwicker, and promised to aid any executive employee in demanding fair treatment of congressional committees, he remained aloof from McCarthy's many efforts to lure him into a personal name-calling contest.

For this Eisenhower was much criticized, but his patience was finally rewarded. During the course of the hearing McCarthy urged federal employees to supply him with information in violation of the law if necessary. That was a step too far. His support in the Senate began to crumble, and the famous Watkins Committee hearings led to his censure and the collapse of his power. By allowing the Senator to destroy himself, Eisenhower maintained the dignity of the Presidency and avoided the split in the Republican party that his foes had been gleefully anticipating.

With the liquidation of McCarthyism, the Administration could properly have inaugurated far-reaching reforms in its security system. Instead, it was content with relatively minor changes. It had extended security screening to all government employees, whether or not they held "sensitive" jobs, and it had clung to that policy long after any need for it had passed. As the security checks against federal workers already on the job were completed, however, abuses were minimized and pressure for change in the system largely subsided.

IV

CONCILIATOR PRESIDENT

Questions of leadership.— Relations with Congress.— White House organization.—(1955) Suffered heart attack.—(1956) Eisenhower renominated and reelected.—(1958) Entered inability agreement with Nixon.—(1957) Sent troops to Little Rock to quell race riots.— Suffers decline in popularity.

THROUGH much of his tenure in the White House the quality of Eisenhower's leadership was under challenge. The President insisted on using his own methods of dealing with people rather than the methods used by Franklin Roosevelt, Harry Truman, or any other of his predecessors. Before his election some of his critics had expressed fear that his military background might encourage him to use dictatorial techniques in the White House. But the loudest cries against him, after he took office, were to the effect that he did not fight with all the resources at his command for the policies that he recommended to Congress.

Actually, Eisenhower was vigorous in his dealings with Congress. Every year he sent a large legislative program to Capitol Hill and worked hard for its enactment. His method, however, was to cultivate the good will of Congressmen, to discuss legislative problems with them, and to seek an executive-legislative partnership instead of using patronage as a club or resorting to threats, bribes, or intimidation.

Early in his first term the President invited every one of the 531 members of Congress to lunch or dinner at the White House in relatively small groups. His object was to get acquainted with them and to win their confidence. He made a practice of meeting weekly with the Republican leaders of the Senate and House, and occasionally held bipartisan conferences at the White House when especially momentous issues were under discussion. His special messages to Congress are numerous. In addition, the President organized a strong legislative liaison under General Wilton B. Persons. His corps of White House "bill pushers" worked as systematically and conscientiously as any similar group has ever done.

What Eisenhower refused to do was to adopt an imperious tone in his dealings with Congress. Having a profound respect for democratic procedures, he believed that he had no right to coerce Congress into doing what it was unwilling to do of its own choice. He would argue, conduct briefings, cultivate good will, keep his "bill pushers" busy, and appeal to public opinion for the support of his measures. But he would not stoop to the offering of a judgeship to swing a recalcitrant Senator behind a favored bill.

Of course, the Eisenhower method made it relatively easy for members of Congress to vote against his measures. The President made it clear in his later years that opposition to his program would cost Republican members of Congress his support at the polls, but this did not prevent many of them from voting against his projects. His refusal to crack the whip greatly perturbed many believers in the so-called strong executive theory of managing the presidential office. Yet the Eisenhower "batting average" is fairly good. When all the circumstances are considered, it may prove more impressive than the records of various predecessors who resorted to political coercion.

In appraising this record it is necessary to remember that after 1954 Eisenhower had a Democratic Congress to deal with. Certainly he could not have bossed or pressured a Congress under the opposition party. His one hope of making progress toward the goal he sought was to work in some degree of harmony with the legislative leaders. Another basic fact to remember is that, being a Johnny-come-lately in politics, Eisenhower never occupied a commanding position among the politicians, not even among those of his own party. In these circumstances he had good reason to look upon cooperation as the better part of valor.

In contrast to his relations with Congress, Eisenhower's organization of his White House aides did acquire a strong military cast. In effect he set up a general staff, with former Governor Sherman Adams, the Assistant to the President, functioning as a White House chief of staff. The staff made a practice of meeting regularly to plan its work, including general supervision of the administrative agencies, liaison with Congress, and relations with the press, radio, and television. In the economic field the President looks to his Council of Economic Advisers in addition to the Secretaries of the Treasury and Commerce. In the vital area of foreign relations and defense policy basic deci-

sions come out of the National Security Council consist-
ing of the President, the Vice President, the Secretaries
of State, Treasury, and Defense, the Director of the
Office of Defense Mobilization, and others at the President's pleasure.

Even Eisenhower's Cabinet evolved into a systematic
advisory body with a secretariat.   Previously the Cabinet had operated rather haphazardly.   Under Eisenhower its meetings came to follow an agenda carefully
prepared in advance, with the spadework being done by
a sub-Cabinet group in cooperation with the secretariat.
The sub-Cabinet group was also given the responsibility
of following up each decision taken to make certain
that it was properly carried out.

With this highly organized staff, including units and
agencies too numerous to mention here, the President
can draw upon expert advice in many fields on short
notice.   Difficult problems of a routine nature are
thoroughly threshed out by the experts before they go
to the President for final decision.   While Eisenhower
is clearly and unmistakably the directing force, he is
not a one-man show.   He works as the captain of a
team and makes each member of the team primarily responsible for the conduct of the department, unit, or
agency under his direction.   Eisenhower completed the
transformation of the Presidency into an institution.

A new phase of the Eisenhower Administration began in September, 1955, when the President suffered a
heart attack.   Both the domestic and international
horizons were suddenly clouded.   Stock prices took a
nosedive; hopes for the achievement of international
peace fell several notches; and the world fairly re-
sounded with prayers for his recovery.

Actually, the President's illness caused no national
emergency.   His smooth-working organization con-

tinued to function within the bounds of policy already
established. The period of his convalescence was relatively short, and his recovery appeared to be complete.
Full details of the President's illness and his physical
condition were reported to the country, in sharp contrast to the concealment of many presidential illnesses
in the past.

For some months there was widespread speculation
as to whether the President would seek a second term.
In February, 1956, however, his doctors reported that,
from a medical standpoint, he should be able to spend
"another five to ten years in rigorous activity." A few
weeks later the President announced to a radio-tele-
vision audience estimated at 75,000,000 persons that
he had no doubt that he could perform "as well as I
ever have all of the important duties of the Presidency"
and that therefore he would continue to serve if the
people should elect him once more.

This decision seemed to be shaken when the President underwent an operation on June 9, 1956, to remove an intestinal obstruction, but his quick recovery
made it possible for him to stand on his previous decision. The Republican party renominated him by wild
acclamation at its national convention in San Francisco.
The President demonstrated his recovery by delivering
a vigorous acceptance address to the convention on
August 22nd.

The 1956 campaign was a not too exciting repeat of
1952, for the Democratic party again nominated Adlai
Stevenson. To be sure, many of the issues had changed.
It was the Democrats who shouted in every hamlet,
"It's time for a change." The Republicans, too, had
new rallying cries. Prosperity and such peace as the
world could boast of redounded to their credit. Yet
the basic issue remained the men who headed the re-

spective party tickets, and once more Eisenhower's great personal popularity carried him to victory. His avalanche of 35,581,003 votes gave him 41 states and 457 electoral votes to 7 states and 74 electoral votes for Stevenson.

At San Francisco, Eisenhower had proclaimed the Republican party to be the "party of the future," but the voters did not see it that way. His victory was largely personal, with the Democrats winning majorities in both houses of Congress. His second term began in January, 1957, therefore, under a severe handicap. Yet the President and Congress found areas of agreement in many fields. Eisenhower has probably been the least partisan President to occupy the White House in the present century, and his attitude has been matched in large measure by that of Senate Majority Leader Lyndon Johnson.

Eisenhower's illnesses in 1955 and 1956 and a slight stroke in 1957 brought extraordinary concern about executive leadership during such emergencies. The Constitution provides that in case of inability on the part of the President to discharge the powers and duties of his office "the same shall devolve on the Vice President." No Vice President has ever been asked to sit in temporarily for an ailing President, however, because the Constitution does not make it absolutely clear that the President could regain his powers on his recovery. After his first illness, Eisenhower sponsored an amendment to the Constitution to remedy this defect, but Congress disagreed as to the details, and nothing came of it.

In 1958, therefore, Eisenhower entered into an agreement with Vice President Nixon that the latter would temporarily exercise the powers and duties of the Presidency in case of a presidential illness. The ar-

rangement would remain in effect only at the discretion
of the President and would not require the Vice President
dent to take the presidential oath. It was generally
hailed as an admirable attempt to carry out what the
Founding Fathers intended.

Eisenhower's policy of eliminating racial discrimination
tion from all governmental activity came to a climax
during his second term. Previously he had wiped out
the last vestiges of a color line in the military establishment
ment and in veterans' hospitals. His Committee on
Government Contracts went a long way toward creating
ing equal job opportunities for Negroes in corporations
doing work for the Government. The President also
supplied steady pressure to break down racial dividing
lines in restaurants, theaters, and other places of recreation
tion in the nation's Capital and elsewhere.

By 1957 moderation in racial policies was sufficiently
established for Congress to pass a civil rights bill for
the first time since Reconstruction days. This measure
was stripped of some provisions the Administration
favored, but it set up a Civil Rights Commission and
created a new position of Assistant Attorney General
for civil rights. The bill also buttressed minority voting
ing rights by providing that the Attorney General
could go into court and seek an injunction against any
person intimidating or threatening to intimidate another
other for the purpose of interfering with his right to
vote.

Shortly after this measure was enacted, however,
the South was suddenly incensed by the dispatch of
federal troops to Little Rock, Arkansas, to quell
violence over the admittance of nine Negro children to
a formerly all-white high school. Under the Supreme
Court's ruling that racial segregation in the public
schools is unconstitutional, Little Rock authorities had

worked out a plan for gradual integration of the races in the schools. The Federal District Court ordered the plan to be put into effect, but Governor Orval E. Faubus, saying that he feared violence, summoned the National Guard and excluded the nine Negro children assigned to the Central High School.

Eisenhower at first tried to meet this defiance of the federal courts by persuasion. After a conference with Faubus, the President expressed confidence that the governor would maintain order and respect for the law of the land. When Faubus failed to act, the President warned that he would take whatever action might become necessary to prevent obstruction of the machinery of justice.

The federal court in Little Rock ordered the governor to cease interfering with integration of the schools, and the National Guard troops were withdrawn. Violence then ensued when the Negro children attempted to enter the school. A presidential proclamation failed to halt the rioting, and federal troops were sent in to restore order. Eisenhower explained his course to the nation by saying, "Mob rule cannot be allowed to override the decisions of the courts."

The resort to military force, which brought embittered outcries from all parts of the South, was a painful experience for a President who had tried diligently to work out better racial relations by persuasion. But when confronted by open defiance of federal authority, Eisenhower was as firm in upholding the supremacy of federal law as Lincoln had been in 1861.

Little Rock brought a sharp decline of Eisenhower's popularity in the South, and Soviet Russia's spectacular gains in rocketry and the recession of 1958 further undercut his standing with the country. The President continued, however, to follow a moderate course, seemingly unperturbed by his critics. At no time did he prove to be a spectacular President. His chief claim to a place of special distinction among our Chief Executives lies in his unusual ability to read the temper of the country, his responsiveness to public opinion, his restraint in the use of power, his general adherence to high moral standards in government, and his persistent drive for a more secure world peace.

PRESIDENTIAL NOMINATIONS

Party and Place	No. of Ballots	Candidates	First Ballot	Last
		1832		
Democrat . . . . Baltimore		Andrew Jackson, Tenn. . . .	Unan.	
National Republican Baltimore		Henry Clay, Ky.	Unan.	
		1836		
Democrat . . . . Baltimore		Martin Van Buren, N. Y. . . .	Unan.	
		1840		
Whig . . . . . Baltimore	2	Wm. Henry Harrison, Ohio . . Henry Clay, Ky.	94 103	148 90
Democrat . . . . Baltimore		Martin Van Buren, N. Y. . . .	Unan.	
		1844		
Democrat . . . . Baltimore	9	James K. Polk, Tenn. . . . . Martin Van Buren, N. Y. . . . Lewis Cass, Mich. . . . . . Scattering	 146 83 37	Unan.
Whig . . . . Baltimore		Henry Clay, Ky.	Unan.	
		1848		
Whig . . . . . Philadelphia	4	Zachary Taylor, La. . . . . . Henry Clay, Ky. . . . . . . Winfield Scott, N. J. . . . . Daniel Webster, Mass. . . . . Scattering	111 97 43 22 6	171 32 63 14
Democrat . . . . Baltimore	4	Lewis Cass, Mich. . . . . . James Buchanan, Pa. . . . . Levi Woodbury, N. H. . . . . Scattering	125 55 53 18	170 33 38 4
		1852		
Democrat . . . . Baltimore	49	Franklin Pierce, N. H. . . . . Lewis Cass, Mich. . . . . . James Buchanan, Pa. . . . . Scattering	 116 93 47	282 4
Whig . . . . . Baltimore	53	Winfield Scott, N. J. . . . . Millard Fillmore, N. Y. . . . Daniel Webster, Mass. . . .	131 133 29	159 112 21

PRESIDENTIAL NOMINATIONS (*Continued*)

PARTY AND PLACE	No. of BAL-LOTS	CANDIDATES	FIRST BALLOT	LAST
		1856		
Democrat	17	James Buchanan, Pa.	135	296
Cincinnati		Franklin Pierce, N. H.	122	
		Scattering	38	
Republican . . .		John C. Fremont, Calif. . . .	359	
Philadelphia		John McLean, Ohio	196	
		Scattering	3	
		1860		
Republican . . .	3	Abraham Lincoln, Ill.	102	231
Chicago		W. H. Seward, N. Y.	173	180
		Simon Cameron, Pa..	50	
		S. P. Chase, Ohio	49	24
		Edward Bates, Mo.	48	22
		Scattering	36	7
Democrat	57	Stephen A. Douglas, Ill. . . .	145	151
Charleston		R. M. T. Hunter, Va.	42	
		James Guthrie, Ky.	35	65
		Scattering	30	35
		Adjourned without nominating.		
Northern Democrat	2	Stephen A. Douglas, Ill. . . .	173	181
Baltimore		Scattering	15	12
Southern Democrat		J. C. Breckinridge, Ky.. . . .	Unan.	
Baltimore				
Union	2	John Bell, Tenn.	68	138
Baltimore		Samuel Houston, Tex.	57	68
		J. J. Crittenden, Ky.	28	8
		Edward Everett, Mass.. . . .	25	9
		John McLean, Ohio	22	
		W. A. Graham, N. C.	22	18
		Scattering	18	10
		1864		
Republican . . .		Abraham Lincoln, Ill.	Unan.	
Baltimore				
Democrat		George B. McClellan, N. J. . .	202	
Chicago		Horatio Seymour, N. Y. . . .	28	
		1868		
Republican . . .		Ulysses S. Grant, Ill.	Unan.	
Chicago				
Democrat	22	Horatio Seymour, N. Y. . . .		317
New York		G. H. Pendleton, Ohio . . .	105	
		Andrew Johnson, Tenn. . . .	65	
		W. S. Hancock, Pa.	33	

· PRESIDENTIAL NOMINATIONS (*Continued*)

Party and Place	No. of Bal-lots	Candidates	First Ballot	Last
		S. E. Church, N. Y.	33	
		Scattering	70	
		1872		
Republican . . .		Ulysses S. Grant, Ill.	Unan.	
Philadelphia				
Liberal Republican .	6	Horace Greeley, N. Y.	147	482
Cincinnati		C. F. Adams, Mass.	203	187
		Lyman Trumbull, Ill.	110	
		B. G. Brown, Mo.	95	
		David Davis, Ill.	92	
		A. G. Curtin, Pa.	62	
		Scattering	2	57
Democrat		Horace Greeley, N. Y.	686	
Baltimore		Scattering	46	
		1876		
Republican . . .	7	R. B. Hayes, Ohio	61	384
Cincinnati		J. G. Blaine, Me.	285	351
		O. P. Morton, Ind.	125	
		B. H. Bristow, Ky.	113	
		Roscoe Conkling, N. Y. . . .	99	
		J. F. Hartranft, Pa.	58	
		Scattering	14	21
Democrat	2	S. J. Tilden, N. Y.	417	535
St. Louis		T. A. Hendricks, Ind.	140	60
		W. S. Hancock, Pa.	56	59
		Scattering	51	90
		1880		
Republican . . .	36	J. A. Garfield, Ohio		399
Chicago		Ulysses S. Grant, Ill.	304	306
		J. G. Blaine, Me.	284	42
		John Sherman, Ohio	98	
		Scattering	74	8
Democrat	2	W. S. Hancock, Pa.	171	705
Cincinnati		T. F. Bayard, Del.	153	
		A. G. Thurman, Ohio . . .	69	
		S. J. Field, Calif.	65	
		W. R. Morrison, Ill.	62	
		T. A. Hendricks, Ind.	50	
		Scattering	76	34

PRESIDENTIAL NOMINATIONS (*Continued*)

Party and Place	No. of Ballots	Candidates	First Ballot	Last
		1884		
Democrat	2	Grover Cleveland, N. Y. . . .	392	684
Chicago		T. F. Bayard, Del.	168	81
		A. G. Thurman, Ohio	88	
		S. J. Randall, Pa.	78	
		J. E. McDonald, Ind.	56	
		Scattering	36	54
Republican . . .	4	J. G. Blaine, Me.	334	541
Chicago		C. A. Arthur, N. Y.	278	207
		G. F. Edmunds, Vt.	93	
		J. A. Logan, Ill.	63	
		Scattering	49	65
		1888		
			80	544
Republican . . .	8	Benjamin Harrison, Ind. . . .	299	118
Chicago		John Sherman, Ohio	111	
		W. Q. Gresham, Ind.	99	
		C. M. Depew, N. Y.	84	100
		R. A. Alger, Mich.	72	
		W. B. Allison, Ia.	155	68
		Scattering	Unan.	
Democrat		Grover Cleveland, N. Y. . . .		
St. Louis				
		1892		
Democrat		Grover Cleveland, N. Y. . . .	617	
Chicago		D. B. Hill, N. Y.	114	
		Horace Boies, Ia.	103	
		Scattering	75	
Republican . . .		Benjamin Harrison, Ind. . . .	535	
Minneapolis		J. G. Blaine, Me.	182	
		Wm. McKinley, Ohio	182	
		Scattering	5	
Populist		J. B. Weaver, Ia.	995	
Omaha		J. H. Kyle, S. D.	265	
		Scattering	3	
		1896		
Republican . . .		Wm. McKinley, Ohio	661	
St. Louis		T. B. Reed, Me.	84	
		M. S. Quay, Pa.	61	
		L. P. Morton, N. Y.	58	
		Scattering	40	

PRESIDENTIAL NOMINATIONS (*Continued*)

PARTY AND PLACE	No. OF BAL- LOTS	CANDIDATES	FIRST BALLOT	LAST
Democrat . . .	5	W. J. Bryan, Neb.	119	500
Chicago		R. P. Bland, Mo.	235	106
		R. E. Pattison, Pa.	95	95
		Horace Boies, Ia.	85	
		J. C. S. Blackburn, Ky. . . .	83	
		J. R. McLean, Ohio	54	
		Scattering	81	67
Populist		W. J. Bryan, Neb.	1042	
St. Louis		S. F. Norton, Ill.	321	
		Scattering	12	
		1900		
Republican . . .		Wm. McKinley, Ohio	Unan.	
Philadelphia				
Democrat		W. J. Bryan, Neb.	Unan.	
Kansas City				
		1904		
Republican . . .		Theodore Roosevelt, N. Y. . .	Unan.	
Chicago				
Democrat		A. B. Parker, N. Y.	689	
St. Louis		W. R. Hearst, N. Y.	181	
		F. M. Cockrell, Mo.	42	
		Richard Olney, Mass.	38	
		Scattering	57	
		1908		
Republican . . .		W. H. Taft, Ohio	702	
Chicago		P. C. Knox, Pa.	68	
		C. E. Hughes, N. Y.	67	
		J. G. Cannon, Ill.	58	
		C. W. Fairbanks, Ind.	40	
		R. M. LaFollette, Wis. . . .	25	
		Scattering	19	
Democrat		W. J. Bryan, Neb.	888	
Denver		George Gray, Del.	59	
		J. A. Johnson, Minn. . . .	46	
		1912		
Democrat	46	Woodrow Wilson, N. J.	324	990
Baltimore		Champ Clark, Mo.	440	84
		Judson Harmon, Ohio . . .	148	

PRESIDENTIAL NOMINATIONS (*Continued*)

Party and Place	No. of Bal- lots	Candidates	First Ballot	Last
Republican . . . Chicago		O. W. Underwood, Ala..	117	
		Scattering	56	12
		W. H. Taft, Ohio	561	
		Theodore Roosevelt, N. Y. . .	107	
		R. M. LaFollette, Wis.	41	
		A. B. Cummins, Ia.	17	
		C. E. Hughes, N. Y..	2	
		Not voting	350	
Progressive . . . Chicago		Theodore Roosevelt, N. Y. . .	Unan.	
		1916		
Democrat . . . . St. Louis		Woodrow Wilson, N. J..	Unan.	
Republican . . Chicago	3	C. E. Hughes, N. Y..	253	949
		J. W. Weeks, Mass.	105	
		Elihu Root, N. Y.	103	
		A. B. Cummins, Ia.	85	
		T. E. Burton, Ohio	77	
		C. W. Fairbanks, Ind.	74	
		L. Y. Sherman, Ill.	66	
		Theodore Roosevelt, N. Y. . .	65	
		P. C. Knox, Pa.	36	
		Henry Ford, Mich.	32	
		R. M. LaFollette, Wis.	25	
		Scattering	62	36
		1920		
Republican . . . Chicago	10	W. G. Harding, Ohio . . .	65	692
		Leonard Wood, Mass. . . .	287	156
		F. O. Lowden, Ill.	211	
		Hiram Johnson, Calif.	133	80
		W. C. Sproul, Pa.	82	
		N. M. Butler, N. Y..	69	
		Calvin Coolidge, Mass.. . . .	34	
		R. M. LaFollette, Wis.	24	
		Scattering	73	49
Democrat . . . . San Francisco	44	J. M. Cox, Ohio	134	732
		W. G. McAdoo, N. Y.	266	267
		A. M. Palmer, Pa.	256	
		A. E. Smith, N. Y.	109	
		E. I. Edwards, N. J..	42	
		T. R. Marshall, Ind..	35	

PRESIDENTIAL NOMINATIONS (*Continued*)

PARTY AND PLACE	No. OF BAL-LOTS	CANDIDATES	FIRST BALLOT	LAST
		J. W. Davis, W. Va.	32	52
		Carter Glass, Va.	26	
		Homer Cummings, Conn. . .	25	
		Scattering	87	37
		1924		
Republican . . .		Calvin Coolidge, Mass. . . .	1065	
Cleveland		R. M. LaFollette, Wis. . . .	34	
		Hiram Johnson, Calif. . . .	10	
Democrat . . .	103	J. W. Davis, W. Va.	31	839
New York		W. G. McAdoo, Calif. . . .	431	
		A. E. Smith, N. Y.	241	
		J. M. Cox, Ohio	59	
		Pat Harrison, Miss.	43	
		O. W. Underwood, Ala. . . .	42	102
		G. S. Silzer, N. J.	38	
		Scattering		147
		1928		
Republican . . .		Herbert Hoover, Calif. . . .	837	
Kansas City		Calvin Coolidge, Mass. . . .	17	
		Charles Curtis, Kansas . . .	64	
		G. D. Goff, W. Va.	18	
		F. O. Lowden, Ill.	74	
		G. W. Norris, Neb.	24	
		J. E. Watson, Ind.	45	
		Scattering	5	
Democrat . . .		A. E. Smith, New York . . .	849	
Houston		W. F. George, Ga.	52	
		Cordell Hull, Tenn.	51	
		J. H. Jones, Tex.	43	
		J. A. Reed, Mo.	52	
		Scattering	52	
		1932		
Republican . . .		Herbert Hoover, Calif. . . .	1126	
Chicago		Scattering	28	
Democratic . . .	4	F. D. Roosevelt, New York . .	666	945
Chicago . . .		H. F. Byrd, Va.	25	
		J. N. Garner, Tex.	90	
		W. H. Murray, Ok.	23	
		J. A. Reed, Mo.	24	
		A. C. Ritchie, Md.	21	3
		A. E. Smith, New York . . .	201	190
		M. A. Traylor, Ill.	42	
		George White, Ohio	52	3
		Scattering	8	6

PRESIDENTIAL NOMINATIONS (*Continued*)

Party and Place	No. of Bal-lots	Candidates	First Ballot	Last
		1936		
Republican . . . Cleveland		Alf M. Landon, Kansas . . .		Unan.
Democratic . . . Philadelphia		F. D. Roosevelt, N. Y. . . .		Unan.
		1940		
Republican . . . Philadelphia	6	T. E. Dewey, N. Y.	360	4
		R. A. Taft, Ohio	129	316
		Wendell Willkie, N. Y. . . .	108	655
		A. H. Vandenberg, Mich. . .	76	2
		A. H. James, Pa.	74	1
		J. W. Martin, Mass.	44	
		H. McNider, Ia.	34	1
		F. E. Gannett, N. Y. . . .	34	1
		Styles Bridges, N. H. . . .	28	
Democratic . . . Chicago	1	F. D. Roosevelt, N. Y. . . .	946	
		J. N. Garner, Tex.	61	
		J. A. Farley, N. Y.	72	
		1944		
Republican . . . Chicago	1	T. E. Dewey, N. Y.		Unan.
Democratic . . . Chicago	1	F. D. Roosevelt, N. Y. . . .	1086	
		H. F. Byrd, Va.	89	
		1948		
Republican . . . Philadelphia	3	T. E. Dewey, N. Y.	434	Unan.
		R. A. Taft, Ohio	224	
		H. Stassen, Minn.	157	
		Earl Warren, Calif.	59	
		A. H. Vandenberg, Mich. . .	62	
		D. H. Green, Ill.	56	
		A. E. Driscoll, N. J.	35	
		R. E. Baldwin, Conn. . . .	19	
		J. W. Martin, Mass.	16	
		C. Reece, Tenn.	15	
		D. MacArthur, Wis.	11	
Democratic . . . Philadelphia	1	H. S. Truman, Mo.	947½	
		R. B. Russell, Ga.	263	

PRESIDENTIAL NOMINATIONS (*Concluded*)

PARTY AND PLACE	No. of BAL- LOTS	CANDIDATES	FIRST BALLOT	LAST
		1952		
Republican	1	D. D. Eisenhower, N. Y. . . .	845	
Chicago		R. A. Taft, Ohio	280	
		Earl Warren, Calif.	77	
		D. MacArthur, Wisc.	4	
Democratic	3	Estes Kefauver, Tenn.	340	275½
Chicago		A. E. Stevenson, Ill.	273	617½
		R. B. Russell, Ga.	268	261
		A. Harriman, N. Y.	123½	—
		R. S. Kerr, Okla.	65	
		A. W. Barkley, Ky.	48½	67½
		Paul Dever, Mass.	37½	½
		H. H. Humphrey, Minn. . . .	26	
		J. W. Fulbright, Ark.	22	—
		J. E. Murray, Mont.	12	—
		H. S. Truman, Mo.	6	—
		Oscar Ewing, N. Y.	4	3
		Paul Douglas, Ill.	3	3
		W. O. Douglas, Wash.	½	—
		1956		
Republican		D. D. Eisenhower, Pa		Unan.
San Francisco				
Democratic		A. E. Stevenson, Ill.	905½	
Chicago		A. Harriman, N. Y.	210	
		Lyndon Johnson, Tex.	80	
		S. Symington, Mo.	45½	
		A. B. Chandler, Ky.	36½	
		J. C. Davis, Ga.	33	
		J. S. Battle, Va.	32½	
		G. Timmerman, S. C.	23½	
		F. J. Lausche, Ohio	5½	

As the framers of the Constitution planned to leave to the electoral college the free choice of Presidents, the system of national nominating conventions was not inaugurated until 1832.

PRESIDENTIAL ELECTIONS

Year	Party	Candidates	Residence	Popular Vote	Plurality	Electoral Vote
1788		George Washington . .	Va.			132
		John Adams	Mass.			77
		Scattering				26
1792		George Washington . .	Va.			132
		John Adams	Mass.			77
		George Clinton . . .	N. Y.			50
		Scattering				4
1796	F.	John Adams	Mass.			71
	D.	Thomas Jefferson . .	Va.			68
	F.	Thomas Pinckney . .	S. C.			59
	D.	Aaron Burr	N. Y.			30
	D.	Samuel Adams . . .	Mass.			15
	F.	Oliver Ellsworth . . .	Conn.			11
		Scattering				22
1800	D.	Thomas Jefferson . .	Va.			73
	D.	Aaron Burr.	N. Y.			73
	F.	John Adams	Mass.			65
	F.	Charles C. Pinckney .	S. C.			64
	F.	John Jay	N. Y.			1
1804	D.	Thomas Jefferson . .	Va.			162
	F.	Charles C. Pinckney .	S. C.			14
1808	D.	James Madison . . .	Va.			122
	F.	Charles C. Pinckney .	S. C.			47
	D.	George Clinton . . .	N. Y.			6
1812	D.	James Madison . . .	Va.			128
	Ind. D.	De Witt Clinton . . .	N. Y.			89
1816	D.	James Monroe . . .	Va.			188
	F.	Rufus King	N. Y.			34
1820	D.	James Monroe . . .	Va.			231
		John Quincy Adams . .	Mass.			1

F. Federalist; D. Democrat.

PRESIDENTIAL ELECTIONS (*Continued*)

Year	Party	Candidates	Resi-dence	Popular Vote	Plurality	Electo-ral Vote
1824		Andrew Jackson . . .	Tenn.			99
		John Quincy Adams . .	Mass.			84
		William H. Crawford .	Ga.			41
		Henry Clay	Ky.			37
1828	D.	Andrew Jackson . . .	Tenn.	647,276	139,212	178
	N. R.	John Quincy Adams .	Mass.	508,064		83
1832	D.	Andrew Jackson . . .	Tenn.	687,502	57,313	219
	N. R.	Henry Clay	Ky.	530,189		49
	Ind.	John Floyd	Ga.			11
	A. M.	William Wirt	Md.			7
1836	D.	Martin Van Buren . .	N. Y.	762,978	26,728	170
	W.	Wm. Henry Harrison .	Ohio			73
	W.	Hugh L. White . . .	Tenn.	736,250		26
	W.	Daniel Webster . . .	Mass.			14
	W.	Willie P. Mangum . .	N. C.			11
1840	W.	Wm. Henry Harrison .	Ohio	1,275,016	145,914	234
	D.	Martin Van Buren . .	N. Y.	1,129,102		60
1844	D.	James K. Polk . . .	Tenn.	1,337,243	38,181	170
	W.	Henry Clay	Ky.	1,299,062		105
	L.	John G. Birney . . .	N. Y.	62,300		
1848	W.	Zachary Taylor . . .	La.	1,360,099	139,555	163
	D.	Lewis Cass	Mich.	1,220,544		127
	F. S.	Martin Van Buren . .	N. Y.	291,263		
1852	D.	Franklin Pierce . . .	N. H.	1,601,474	214,694	254
	W.	Winfield Scott	N. J.	1,386,580		42
	F. S.	John P. Hale	N. H.	156,667		
1856	D.	James Buchanan . . .	Pa.	1,838,169	496,905	174
	R.	John C. Fremont . . .	Calif.	1,341,264		114
	Am. & W.	Millard Fillmore . . .	N. Y.	874,534		8

N. R. National Republican.
A. M. Ant. Masonic.
W. Whig.
L. Liberty Party.

F. S. Free Soil Party.
R. Republican.
Am. American or "Know nothing."

PRESIDENTIAL ELECTIONS (*Continued*)

Year	Party	Candidates	Residence	Popular Vote	Plurality	Electoral Vote
1860	R.	Abraham Lincoln . .	Ill.	1,866,452	491,295	180
	D.	Stephen A. Douglas . .	Ill.	1,376,957		12
	D.	John C. Breckinridge .	Ky.	849,781		72
	Un.	John Bell	Tenn.	588,879		39
1864	R.	Abraham Lincoln . .	Ill.	2,216,037	411,428	212
	D.	George B. McClellan .	N. J.	1,802,237		21
1868	R.	Ulysses S. Grant . . .	Ill.	3,015,071	305,456	214
	D.	Horatio Seymour . . .	N. Y.	2,709,615		80
1872	R.	Ulysses S. Grant . . .	Ill.	3,597,132	763,007	286
	L. R. & D.	Horace Greeley . . .	N. Y.	2,834,125		63
	Reg. D.	Charles O'Connor . .	N. Y.	29,489		
	Temp.	James Black	Pa.	5,608		
1876	R.	Rutherford B. Hayes .	Ohio	4,033,768		185
	D.	Samuel J. Tilden . . .	N. Y.	4,285,992	252,224	184
	GbK.	Peter Cooper	N. Y.	81,737		
	Pro.	Green Clay Smith . .	Ky.	9,522		
1880	R.	James A. Garfield . .	Ohio	4,449,053	7,018	214
	D.	Winfield S. Hancock .	Pa.	4,442,035		155
	GbK.	James B. Weaver . .	Ia.	307,306		
	Pro.	Neal Dow	Me.	10,305		
1884	D.	Grover Cleveland . .	N. Y.	4,911,017	62,683	219
	R.	James G. Blaine . . .	Me.	4,848,334		182
	Pro.	John P. St. John . . .	Ks.	151,809		
	GbK.	Benjamin F. Butler . .	Mass.	133,825		
1888	R.	Benjamin Harrison . .	Ind.	5,440,216		233
	D.	Grover Cleveland . .	N. Y.	5,538,233	98,017	168
	Pro.	Clinton B. Fisk . . .	N. J.	249,907		
	U. Lab.	Alson J. Streeter . . .	Ill.	148,105		
1892	D.	Grover Cleveland . .	N. Y.	5,556,918	380,810	277
	R.	Benjamin Harrison . .	Ind.	5,176,108		145
	Pop.	James B. Weaver . .	Ia.	1,041,028		22

Un. Constitutional Union.   Temp. Temperance.   U. Lab. Union Labor.
L. R. Liberal Republican.   GbK. Greenbacker.   Pop. People's or Populist Party.
Reg. D. Regular Democrat.   Pro. Prohibitionist.

PRESIDENTIAL ELECTIONS (*Continued*)

Year	Party	Candidates	Residence	Popular Vote	Plurality	Electoral Vote
	Pro.	John Bidwell	Calif.	264,135		
	Soc. L.	Simon Wing	Mass.	21,164		
1896	R.	William McKinley . .	Ohio	7,104,779	601,854	271
	D. Pop.	William J. Bryan . .	Neb.	6,502,925		176
	N. Dem.	John M. Palmer . . .	Ill.	133,148		
	Pro.	Joshua Levering . . .	Md.	132,007		
	Soc. L.	Charles H. Matchett .	N. Y.	36,274		
1900	R.	William McKinley . .	Ohio	7,207,923	849,870	292
	D. Pop.	William J. Bryan . . .	Neb.	6,358,138		155
	Pro.	John G. Woolley . . .	Ill.	208,914		
	Soc. Dem.	Eugene V. Debs . . .	Ind.	87,814		
	M.R. Pop.	Wharton Barker . . .	Pa.	50,373		
	Soc. L.	Joseph F. Malloney . .	Mass.	39,739		
1904	R.	Theodore Roosevelt .	N. Y.	7,623,486	2,545,515	336
	D.	Alton B. Parker . . .	N. Y.	5,077,911		140
	Soc.	Eugene V. Debs . . .	Ind.	402,283		
	Pro.	Silas C. Swallow . . .	Pa.	258,536		
	Pop.	Thomas E. Watson . .	Ga.	117,183		
	Soc. L.	Charles H. Corrigan .	N. Y.	31,249		
1908	R.	William H. Taft . . .	Ohio	7,678,908	1,269,804	321
	D.	William J. Bryan . .	Neb.	6,409,104		162
	Soc.	Eugene V. Debs . . .	Ind.	420,793		
	Pro.	Eugene W. Chafin . .	Ill.	253,840		
	Ind. L.	Thomas L. Hisgen . .	Mass.	82,872		
	Pop.	Thomas E. Watson . .	Ga.	29,100		
	Soc. L.	Augustus Gillhaus . .	N. Y.	13,825		
1912	D.	Woodrow Wilson . . .	N. J.	6,293,019	2,173,512	435
	P.	Theodore Roosevelt .	N. Y.	4,119,507		88
	R.	William H. Taft . . .	Ohio	3,484,956		8
	Soc.	Eugene V. Debs . . .	Ind.	901,873		
	Pro.	Eugene W. Chafin . .	Ill.	207,928		
	Soc. L.	A. E. Reimer	Mass.	29,259		

Soc. L. Socialist Labor.
N. Dem. National or Gold Democrat.
Soc. Dem. Social Democrat.
M. R. Pop. Middle of Road Populists.

Soc. Socialist.
Ind. L. Independence League.
P. Progressive.

PRESIDENTIAL ELECTIONS (*Continued*)

YEAR	PARTY	CANDIDATES	RESI-DENCE	POPULAR VOTE	PLURALITY	ELECTO-RAL VOTE
1916	D.	Woodrow Wilson . .	N. J.	9,129,269	581,941	277
	R.	Charles E. Hughes .	N. Y.	8,547,328		254
	Soc.	Allan J. Benson . .	N. Y.	590,579		
	Pro.	J. F. Hanly . . .	Ind.	221,329		
	Soc. L.	A. E. Reimer . . .	Mass.	14,180		
1920	R.	Warren G. Harding	Ohio	16,152,200	7,004,847	404
	D.	James M. Cox. . .	Ohio	9,147,353		127
	Soc.	Eugene V. Debs . .	Ind.	919,799		
	Pro.	Aaron S. Watkins .	Ohio	189,408		
	F. L.	P. F. Christensen . .	Utah	26,541		
1924	R.	Calvin Coolidge . .	Mass.	15,721,464	7,339,019	382
	D.	John W. Davis . .	W. Va.	8,382,445		136
	Ind.	Robert M. LaFollette.	Wis.	4,801,258		13
	W'k'rs	Wm. Z. Foster . .	Ill.	37,277		
	Soc. L.	Frank T. Johns . .	Ore.	29,110		
	Am.	Gilbert O. Nations .	D. C.	16,044		
1928	R.	Herbert Hoover . .	Calif.	21,392,190	6,375,747	444
	D.	Alfred E. Smith . .	N. Y.	15,016,443		87
	Soc.	Norman Thomas . .	N. Y.	267,420		
	W'k'rs.	Wm. Z. Foster . .	Ill.	48,770		
	Soc. L.	Verne L. Reynolds .	N. Y.	21,603		
1932	D.	Franklin D. Roosevelt	N. Y.	22,821,857	7,060,016	472
	R.	Herbert Hoover . .	Calif.	15,761,841		59
	Soc.	Norman Thomas . .	N. Y.	884,781		
	Com'n'st	Wm. Z. Foster . .	Ill.	102,991		
	Pro.	Wm. D. Upshaw . .	Ga.	81,869		
	Lib.	Wm. H. Harvey . .	Ark.	53,425		
	Soc. L.	Verne L. Reynolds .	N. Y.	33,276		
		Scattering		76,482		

F. L. Farmer-Labor.   W'k'rs. Workers' Party.   Am. American Party.

Each elector cast his vote for two men, and the man receiving the highest total was President, and the next highest candidate became Vice President until that method was changed by constitutional amendment in 1804.

There was at the outset no popular vote for President in most states, where the choice of electors was made by the Legislatures.

Although the Democratic Party styled itself Republican until 1828, it is here designated Democratic from the beginning, in order to avoid confusion with the later Republican party.

PRESIDENTIAL ELECTIONS (*Concluded*)

Year	Party	Candidates	Resi-dence	Popular Vote	Plurality	Electo-ral Vote
1936	D.	Franklin D. Roosevelt .	N. Y.	27,571,612	10,889,699	523
	R.	Alt M. Landon . . .	Kans.	16,681,913		8
	Union	William Lemke . . .	N. D.	891,858		
	Soc.	Norman Thomas . .	N. Y.	187,512		
	Com.	Earl Browder . . .	N. Y.	80,181		
1940	D.	Franklin D. Roosevelt .	N. Y.	27,241,939	4,914,663	449
	R.	Wendell Willkie . .	N. Y.	22,327,276		82
	Soc.	Norman Thomas . .	N. Y.	116,798		
	Com.	Earl Browder . . .	N. Y.	48,789		
	Pro.	Roger Babson.........	Mass.	56,600		
1944	D.	Franklin D. Roosevelt .	N. Y.	25,602,505	3,596,227	432
	R.	T. E. Dewey . . .	N. Y.	22,006,278		99
	Soc.	Norman Thomas . .	N. Y.	74,757		
	Pro.	Claude A. Watson . .	Calif.	72,396		
	Soc. L.	Edward A. Teichert .	Pa.	44,674		
1948	D.	Harry S. Truman . .	Mo.	24,045,052	2,148,125	304
	R.	T. E. Dewey . . .	N. Y.	21,896,927		189
	S.R.	J. Strom Thurmond .	S. C.	1,168,687		38
	P.	Henry A. Wallace . .	N. Y.	1,137,957		
	Soc.	Norman Thomas . .	N. Y.	95,908		
	Pro.	Claude A. Watson . .	Calif.	95,075		
1952	R.	Dwight D. Eisenhower .	N. Y.	33,936,234	6,621,242	442
	D.	Adlai E. Stevenson . .	Ill.	27,314,992		89
	P.	Vincent Hallinan . . .	Calif.	140,023		
	Pro.	Stuart Hamblen . . .	Calif.	72,949		
	Soc. L.	Eric Hass	N. Y.	29,333		
	S.	Darlington Hoopes . .	Pa.	20,203		
1956	R.	Dwight D. Eisenhower .	N. Y.	35,581,003	9,549,681	457
	D.	Adlai E. Stevenson . .	Ill.	26,031,322		74*
	Pro.	Enoch A. Holtwick . .	Ill.	41,937		
	Soc. L.	Eric Hass	N. Y.	41,510		
	Soc. W.	Farrell Dobbs	N. Y.	5,198		
	S.	Darlington Hoopes . .	Pa.	846		

S.R. States' Rights
* Alabama's 11th electoral vote was cast for Walter B. Jones of Alabama.

PRESIDENTS' BIRTHS AND DEATHS

Name	Birthplace	Born	Died	Age	Burial Place
Washington .	Near Fredericksburg, Va.	Feb. 22, 1732	Dec. 14, 1799	67	Mt. Vernon, Va.
Adams. . .	Braintree (Quincy), Mass.	Oct. 30, 1735	July 4, 1826	90	Quincy, Mass.
Jefferson . .	Shadwell, Va. . . .	April 13, 1743	July 4, 1826	83	Monticello, Va.
Madison . .	Port Conway, Va. . .	March 16, 1751	June 28, 1836	85	Montpellier, Va.
Monroe . .	Westmoreland Co., Va..	April 28, 1758	July 4, 1831	73	Richmond, Va.
J. Q. Adams .	Braintree (Quincy), Mass.	July 11, 1767	Feb. 23, 1848	80	Quincy, Mass.
Jackson . .		March 15, 1767	June 8, 1845	78	Hermitage, Ten.
Van Buren. .	Kinderhook, N. Y. . .	Dec. 5, 1782	July 24, 1862	79	Kinderh'k, N.Y.
W. H. Harrison	Berkeley, Va. . . .	Feb. 9, 1773	April 4, 1841	68	North Bend, O.
Tyler . . .	Greenway, Va. . . .	March 29, 1790	Jan. 18, 1862	71	Richmond, Va.
Polk . . .	Little Sugar Creek, N. C.	Nov. 2, 1795	June 15, 1849	53	Nashville, Ten.
Taylor . . .	Orange Co., Va.. . .	Nov. 24, 1784	July 9, 1850	65	Louisville, Ky.
Fillmore .	Summer Hill, N. Y. .	Jan. 7, 1800	March 8, 1874	74	Buffalo, N. Y.
Pierce . . .	Hillsboro, N. H. . .	Nov. 23, 1804	Oct. 8, 1869	64	Concord, N. H.
Buchanan . .	Franklin Co., Pa. . .	April 23, 1791	June 1, 1868	77	Wheatland, Pa.
Lincoln . .	Near Hodgenville, Ky..	Feb. 12, 1809	April 15, 1865	56	Springfield, Ill.
Johnson . .	Raleigh, N. C. . . .	Dec. 29, 1808	July 31, 1875	66	Greeneville, Ten.
Grant . . .	Point Pleasant, Ohio .	April 27, 1822	July 23, 1885	63	New York
Hayes . . .	Delaware, Ohio . . .	Oct. 4, 1822	Jan. 17, 1893	70	Fremont, Ohio
Garfield . .	Orange, Ohio . . .	Nov. 19, 1831	Sept. 19, 1881	49	Cleveland, Ohio
Arthur . . .	Fairfield, Vt.. . . .	Oct. 5, 1830	Nov. 18, 1886	56	Albany, N. Y.
Cleveland . .	Caldwell, N. J. . .	March 18, 1837	June 24, 1908	71	Princeton, N. J.
B. Harrison .	North Bend, Ohio . .	Aug. 20, 1833	March 13, 1901	67	Ind'polis, Ind.
McKinley . .	Niles, Ohio	Jan. 29, 1843	Sept. 14, 1901	58	Canton, Ohio
T. Roosevelt .	New York	Oct. 27, 1858	Jan. 6, 1919	60	Oyster B., N.Y.
Taft . . .	Cincinnati, Ohio. . .	Sept. 15, 1857	March 8, 1930	72	Arlington, Va.
Wilson . . .	Staunton, Va. . . .	Dec. 28, 1856	Feb. 3, 1924	67	Washington
Harding . .	Corsica, Ohio . . .	Nov. 2, 1865	Aug. 2, 1923	57	Marion, Ohio
Coolidge . .	Plymouth, Vt. . . .	July 4, 1872	Jan. 5, 1933	60	Plymouth, Vt.
Hoover. . .	West Branch, Ia. . .	Aug. 10, 1874			
F.D. Roosevelt	Hyde Park, N. Y. . .	Jan. 30, 1882	April 12, 1945	63	HydePark, N.Y.
H. S. Truman.	Lamar, Mo.. . . .	May 8, 1884			
Eisenhower . .	Denison, Tex.	Oct. 14, 1890			

Whether Jackson was born on the North Carolina or the South Carolina side of the line is in dispute.

Monroe and Arthur died in New York; J. Q. Adams, W. H. Harrison, Taylor, and Lincoln in Washington; Johnson in Carter County, Tennessee; Grant at Mt. McGregor, New York; Garfield at Elberon, New Jersey; McKinley at Buffalo; Taft at Washington; Harding at San Francisco; Coolidge at Northampton, Mass. F. D. Roosevelt died in Warm Springs, Ga. The others died where they were buried.

PRESIDENTS' RESIDENCE AND TRAINING

Name	Education	Calling	Previous Offices	Age at Inauguration	Term
Washington Mt. Vernon,Va.	Com. School	Farmer	Soldier, Legis., Cong., Lt. Gen., Const'l Conv'n	57	1789–97
Adams Quincy, Mass.	Harvard	Lawyer	Legis., Cong., Dip., V. P.	61	1797–01
Jefferson Monticello, Va.	Wm.and Mary	Farmer	Legis., Cong., Gov., Dip., V. P.	57	1801–9
Madison Montpelier, Va.	Princeton	Farmer	Legis., Const'l Conv'n, Cong., Sec. State	57	1809–17
Monroe Oak Hill, Va.	Wm.and Mary	Farmer	Rev. Army, Legis., House, Sen., Gov., Dip., Sec. State and War	58	1817–25
J. Q. Adams Quincy, Mass.	Harvard	Lawyer	Dip., Legis., Sen., Sec. State	57	1825–9
Jackson The Hermitage, Tenn.	Com. School	Lawyer Store- keeper Farmer	Rev. Army, House, Sen., Judge, Major Gen., Gov.	61	1829–37
Van Buren Kinderhook, N. Y.	Com. School	Lawyer	Surrogate, Legis., Att'y Gen., N. Y., Sen., Gov., Sec. State, Dip., V. P.	54	1837–41
Harrison North Bend, O.	Hampden-Sidney	Farmer	Cong., Gov., Maj. Gen., Legis., Sen., Dip.	68	1841
Tyler Williamsburg, Va.	Wm.and Mary	Lawyer	Legis., Army of 1812, House, Gov., Sen., V. P.	51	1841–5
Polk Nashville,Tenn.	Univ. N. C.	Lawyer	Legis., Gov., Spkr H. R.	49	1845–9
Taylor Baton Rouge, La.	Com. School	Soldier	Maj. Gen.	64	1849–50
Fillmore Buffalo, N. Y.	Com. School	Lawyer	Legis., House, Comptroller, N. Y., V. P.	50	1850–3
Pierce Concord, N. H.	Bowdoin	Lawyer	Legis., House, Sen., Maj. Gen. Mex. War	48	1853–7
Buchanan Lancaster, Pa.	Dickinson	Lawyer	In War of 1812, Leg., House, Dip., Sen., Sec. State	65	1857–61
Lincoln Springfield, Ill.	Com. School	Lawyer	Soldier, Legis., Cong.	52	1861–5
Johnson Greenville, Tenn.	No School	Tailor	Ald., Mayor, Legis., House, Sen., Gov., V. P.	56	1865–9
Grant Galena, Ill.	West Point	Soldier	U. S. Army, Sec. War	46	1869–77
Hayes Fremont, O.	Kenyon	Lawyer	City Atty., Brig. Gen., House, Gov.	54	1877–81

PRESIDENTS' RESIDENCE AND TRAINING (*Concluded*)

NAME	EDUCATION	CALLING	PREVIOUS OFFICES	AGE AT INAUGURATION	TERM
Garfield Mentor, O.	Williams	Lawyer	Legis., Maj. Gen., House, Sen. elect	49	1881
Arthur New York	Union	Lawyer	Q. M. Gen., N. Y. Militia, Coll. Customs, V. P.	50	1881–5
Cleveland Buffalo, N. Y.	Com. School	Lawyer	Asst. Co. Atty., Sheriff, Mayor, Gov.	47	1885–9 1893–7
B. Harrison Indianapolis, Ind.	Miami	Lawyer	Court Reporter, Brig. Gen., Sen.	55	1889–93
McKinley Canton, O.	Com. School	Lawyer	Maj., Co. Atty., House, Gov.	54	1897–01
T. Roosevelt Oyster Bay, N. Y.	Harvard	Writer	Legis., C. S. Comsnr., Pol. Comsnr., Asst. Sec. Navy, Col., Gov., V. P.	42	1901–9
Taft Cincinnati, O.	Yale	Lawyer	Asst. Co. Atty., Asst. City Atty., U. S. Solicitor Gen., Judge, Gov., Sec. War	51	1909–13
Wilson Princeton, N. J.	Princeton	Educator	Gov.	56	1913–21
Harding Marion, O.	Com. School	Editor	Legis., Lt. Gov., Sen.	55	1921–23
Coolidge Northampton, Mass.	Amherst	Lawyer	City Council, City Atty., Court Clerk, Legis., Mayor, Lt. Gov., Gov., V. P.	51	1923–29
Hoover Palo Alto, Calif.	Stanford	Engineer	Sec. Commerce	55	1929–33
F. D. Roosevelt Hyde Park, N. Y.	Harvard	Lawyer	Legis., Asst. Sec. Navy, Gov.	51	1933–45
Truman Independence, Mo.	High School	Farmer	County Board, Sen., Vice President	64	1945–53
Eisenhower Gettysburg, Pa.	West Point	Soldier	Gen., U. S. Army; Pres. Columbia U.	62	1953–

First employments of Presidents: Washington, land surveyor; John Adams, Arthur, Cleveland and McKinley, teachers; Jackson, saddler's apprentice; Polk, clerk in a store; Fillmore, wool carder; Lincoln, farm hand; Garfield, mule driver on a canal; Harding, newspaper reporter.

PRESIDENTS' FAMILIES

Names	Parents	Father's Occupation	Wives	Sons	Daughters
Washington	Augustine . . . Mary Ball . .	Farmer . .	Mrs. Martha Dandridge Custis		
Adams	John . . . . . Susanna Boylston	Farmer . .	Abigail Smith	3	2
Jefferson	Peter . . . . . Jane Randolph	Farmer . .	Mrs. Martha Wayles Skelton	1	5
Madison	James. . . . . Nelly Conway	Farmer . .	Mrs. Dorothy Payne Todd		
Monroe	Spence . . . . Eliza Jones	Farmer . .	Elizabeth Kortright . . .		2
J. Q. Adams	John . . . . . Abigail Smith	Lawyer . .	Louise C. Johnson . . .	3	1
Jackson	Andrew . . . . Sarah Hutchinson	Farmer . .	Mrs. Rachel Donaldson Robards		
Van Buren	Abraham . . . . Mary Hoes	Farmer Inn-keeper	Hannah Hoes	4	
Harrison	Benjamin . . . Elizabeth Bassett	Farmer . .	Anna Symmes	6	4
Tyler	John . . . . . Mary Armistead	Lawyer . .	Letitia Christian	3	4
			Julia Gardiner	5	2
Polk	Samuel . . . Jane Knox	Farmer . .	Sarah Childress		
Taylor	Richard . . . . Sarah Strother	Farmer . .	Margaret Smith	1	5
Fillmore	Nathaniel . . . Phoebe Millard	Farmer . .	Abigail Powers	1	1
			Mrs. Caroline Carmichael McIntosh		
Pierce	Benjamin . . . Anna Kendrick	Farmer . .	Jane M. Appleton	3	
Buchanan	James. . . . . Elizabeth Speer	Store-keeper	Bachelor		
Lincoln	Thomas . . . Nancy Hanks	Farmer . .	Mary Todd	4	
Johnson	Jacob . . . . . Mary Macdonough	Sexton . .	Eliza McCardle	3	1
Grant	Jesse . . . . . Hannah Simpson	Tanner . .	Julia Dent	3	1
Hayes	Rutherford . . . Sophia Birchard	Store-keeper	Lucy Webb	7	1
Garfield	Abram . . . Eliza Ballou . .	Farmer . .	Lucretia Rudolph	4	1
Arthur	William . . . . Malvina Stone	Clergyman .	Ellen L. Herndon	2	1
Cleveland	Richard Falley . . Anna Neal	Clergyman .	Frances Folsom	2	3

449

PRESIDENTS' FAMILIES (*Concluded*)

Names	Parents	Father's Occupation	Wives	Sons	Daughters
B. Harrison .	John Scott . . . ElizabethP.Irwin	Farmer . .	Caroline Scott . . . . Mrs. Mary Lord Dimmick .	1	1 1
McKinley . .	William . . . . Nancy C. Allison	Charcoal Mfr.	Ida Saxton		3
T. Roosevelt .	Theodore . . . Martha Bullock	Philanthropist	Alice H. Lee . . . . . Edith K. Carow	4	1 1
Taft . . .	Alphonso . . . Louise M. Torrey	Lawyer . .	Helen Herron	2	1
Wilson . . .	Joseph R. . . . Jessie Woodrow	Clergyman .	Ellen L. Axson . . . . Mrs. Edith Bolling Galt .		3
Harding . .	George T. . . . Phoebe Dickinson	Physician .	Mrs. Florence Kling De Wolfe		
Coolidge . .	John C. . . . Victoria J. Moor	Farmer . . Store-keeper	Grace Goodhue	2	
Hoover . .	Jesse Clark . . . Hulda R. Minthorn	Blacksmith .	Lou Henry	2	
F.D.Roosevelt	James . . . Sara Delano	Director . .	Eleanor Roosevelt . . .	4	1
Truman . .	John A. . . . . Martha E. Young	Farmer . .	Elizabeth Virginia Wallace .		1
Eisenhower .	David J. . . . . Ida E. Stover	Storekeeper . and mechanic	Mamie Geneva Doud . . .	2	

PRESIDENTIAL SUCCESSION

In event of the "death, resignation or inability of the President," the presidency passes to the Vice President, and if there be no Vice President to the Speaker of the House, and if there be no Speaker to the President pro tem of the Senate and if there be no President pro tem of the Senate to the ranking member of the Cabinet, who is a natural born citizen and 35 years of age.

INDEX

Adams, Abigail, marriage to John Adams, 14; cleverest of Presidents' wives, 15; only woman to be wife of one President and mother of another, 15; her hard work on her farm in the Revolution, 15; first American woman at the Court of St. James's, 16; first mistress of the White House, and her amusing description of the place, 18; reconciled her husband and Jefferson, 19; her death, 19

Adams, Charles Francis, who inspired fear in Lafayette of an Adams dynasty, ix

Adams, President John, his slighting reference to Washington, 10; his plain antecedents, 14; his marriage to Abigail Smith, 14; defended British soldiers in Boston Massacre, 15; his motive for proposing Washington as commander-in-chief, 15; his diplomatic mission in the Revolution, 15, 16; his presentation to George III, 16; Vice-President under Washington, 17; kept Washington's Cabinet on becoming President, 17; his galling rôle under Hamilton's leadership, 17; his approval of Alien and Sedition Acts, 17; his preparation for war with France and the peace, 18; first President to reside in Washington, 18; reconciled by his wife to Jefferson, 19; died with Jefferson's name on his lips, 19;

on committee with Jefferson and Franklin to draft the Declaration, 22

Adams, President John Quincy, at 10 accompanied his father to Europe, 16; secretary of legation at 14, 46; watching the battle of Bunker Hill, 46; his lifelong diary, 48; crossing the ocean four times in boyhood, 48; at Harvard, 48; minister at The Hague, 48; marriage to Louise Catherine Johnson, 48; first American minister at Berlin, 49; elected to the Senate and his resignation, 49; bitter feud with the Federalists, 49; minister to Russia and minister to England, 49; Secretary of State under Monroe, 50; elected President, 51; denounced by Jackson and Randolph, 51; criticized by Ezekiel Webster, 52; personal appearance and habits, 52–53; defeated, 53; elected to Congress, 54; his long battle for the right of petition, 54–56; his death in the Capitol, 56; his indignation over honorary degree conferred by Harvard on Jackson, 69

Adams, Mrs. Louise Catherine, marriage to John Quincy Adams, 48

Adams, Sherman, 424

Anderson, Major Robert, his order received from Secretary Floyd, 131

Arthur, President Chester A., in the campaign of 1880, 203; his revolt against Garfield, 206; public dread of his succession to Garfield, 208; his antecedents, 208-10; his administration, 210; his defeat for nomination; his death, 214

Arthur, Mrs. Ellen Herndon, wife of Chester A. Arthur; her death, 211

Atom bomb, Roosevelt interested in experiment by Einstein, 370; his greatest gamble, 374; first successful test in New Mexico, 387-8; first bomb dropped on Hiroshima and second on Nagasaki, 387-8

"Barn Burners," The, a New York political faction, 107

Bennett, James Gordon, his campaign scandal against President Buchanan, 125

Benson, Ezra Taft, 418

Benton, Thomas H., altercation with Andrew Jackson, 60; champion of Jackson in the Senate, 67

Blaine, James G., accused of bartering official influence, 180; how he lost the Presidential nomination in 1876, 188; his candidacy in 1880, 201, 202; his domination of Garfield's administration, 205, 206; his campaign for President and defeat in 1884, 217, 218; how he nominated Harrison in 1888, 228

Booth, John Wilkes, his assassination of Lincoln; his death, 157, 158

Boston Massacre, the British soldiers in it defended by John Adams, 15

Bradbury, James W., coached Franklin Pierce for the Presidency, 120

Braddock, Gen. Edward, the

prayers at his burial read by George Washington, 5

Bragg, Gen. Edward S., "We love him for the enemies he has made," 217

Brougham, Lord, his tribute to Washington, 13

Brown, John, at Harper's Ferry, 128

Bryan, William J., his campaign for Presidency in 1896, 239-42; his part in the nomination of Wilson, 274

Bryce, James, British ambassador at Washington, 260

Buchanan, President James, anecdote of him and Jackson, 64, 65; expelled from college but readmitted, 124; his only love romance, 125; his niece acted as mistress of the White House and her monument to his memory, 126; his long official service, 126; his most tragic administration, 127-31

Buckner, Gen. Simon B., at West Point with Grant, 172; lending money to Grant, 172, 173; their meeting at Fort Donelson, 176, 177; his last visit to Grant, 185

Bulganin, Nikolai A., 409

"Bull Moose," The, 268

Burr, Aaron, his trial, viii; introduced Madison to Mrs. Dolly Todd Payne, 35

Butler, Benjamin F., selected for Secretary of State in Wade's Cabinet at impeachment of Johnson, 168

Byron, Lord, his tribute to Washington, 13

Calhoun, John C., in Monroe's Cabinet, 44; exponent of southern nullification, 68; exulting over rejection of Van Buren's nomination as minister to England, 76; in Tyler's Cabinet, 92, 93

California, the American flag raised over it by Gen. Frémont, 101; admitted as a free state, 108

Cameron, Simon, called Lowell "a dashed literary feller," 193

Campbell, Timothy J., "Don't let the Constitution stand between friends," 253

Cass, Lewis, defeated for President by Taylor, 107

Chandler, William E., his part in disputed election of Hayes, 190

Chandler, Zach, his part in disputed election of Hayes, 190

Charlotte, Queen, her reception of Abigail Adams, 16

Chase, Salmon P., presided over the trial of President Johnson, 168

China, the march on Pekin and America's declaration for "the open door," 245, 246; at the Washington Conference, 293, 294

Churchill, Winston, 403; trumpeting call to save England, 367; Atlantic Charter, 370; rushing to White House after Pearl Harbor, 371

Civil Service Reform, its adoption, 212, 213

Clark, Champ, his defeat by Wilson, 273, 274

Clay, Henry, leader of the war party in 1812, 37; aided election of John Quincy Adams and became his Secretary of State, 51; denounced by Jackson and Randolph, 51; anecdote of him and Van Buren, 77; quarreling with Harrison, 87; quarrel with Tyler, 92; nominated for President but defeated in 1844, 98, 99; his dislike of President Taylor, 106; "I would rather be right than President," 106; sponsored the Fugitive Slave Act, 114

Cleveland, Miss Rose Elizabeth, mistress of the White House in the beginning of Cleveland's term, 223

Cleveland, Mrs. Frances Folsom, first college-bred mistress of the White House; her marriage to Grover Cleveland; her popularity, 223–26

Cleveland, President Grover, his election as governor, 212; his antecedents, change of name and sudden rise, 215–17; his campaign for President and election, 217, 218; his inauguration, 219, 220; his battle with office-seekers, 220; "offensive partisanship," 220; "innocuous desuetude," 220; establishment of Interstate Commerce Commission, 221; Lowell's tribute to Cleveland, 221, 222; his tariff message and defeat in 1888, 222; his marriage to Frances Folsom, 224; the scandalous campaign against him, 225; the only ex-President to come back to the White House, 231; his election in 1892, 231, 232; the panic of 1893, 232; repeal of the Silver Purchase Act, 232, 233; Cleveland operated upon for cancer, 232; his refusal to sign tariff bill, 233; putting down a railroad strike, 233; his Venezuelan message, 233; upholding the gold standard, 234; last Jeffersonian leader of Democrats, 362

Colfax, Schuyler, his forced resignation, 180

Colombia, Roosevelt's action in the Panama revolution, 260, 261

Conkling, Roscoe, enraged by President Hayes, 193; in the convention of 1880, 201, 202; his fight with President Garfield, 205, 206; his resignation from the Senate, 206

Constitution, The, alarming rumors that its framers were planning to set up a monarchy, v

Coolidge, President Calvin, antecedents; education; at the bar, 299–302; his marriage to Grace Goodhue and their simple life, 302, 303; his experience and success in politics, 303, 304; in the Boston police strike, 304; unsuccessful candidate for Republican Presidential nomination in 1920, 304, 305; how he was nominated for Vice-President, 305; his accession to the Presidency, 306, 307; "the Coolidge Market" in Wall St., 313; "I do not choose to run," 314–15; in campaign of 1932, 316; wrote autobiography and syndicated articles, 316–17; death, 317

Coolidge, Mrs. Grace Goodhue, marriage to Calvin Coolidge, 302, 303

Coolidge, John C., father of President Coolidge, who administered the Presidential oath at his son's inauguration, 301, 306

Corbin, Gen. Henry C., his choice of Taft for service in the Philippines, 265

Cornwallis, Lord Charles, anecdote of him and Washington at Yorktown, 8

Cranford, William H., in Monroe's Cabinet, 44

Cuba, threat of Pierce administration to take the island from Spain by force, 122; in the Spanish War, 243, 244

Cullom, Shelby M., his remark to President McKinley, 247

Czolgosz, Leon F., his assassination of President McKinley, 248–50

Daugherty, Harry M., sponsor for Warren G. Harding, 287; his prophecy of Harding's nomination for President, 291

Davis, Jefferson, married a daughter of Zachary Taylor, 104, 105; Secretary of War under Pierce, 121; his flight from Richmond, 155; accused of complicity in Lincoln's assassination, 163, 164

Day, William R., opposed annexation of the Philippines, 244

Debs, Eugene V., leading the railroad strike of 1893, 233

Democratic Party, The, its origin, 26

Dewey, Admiral George, in Battle of Manila, 243; under orders from Roosevelt to stop a German landing in Venezuela, 259

Dewey, Thomas E., Republican candidate for President in 1944, 375; defeated again in big upset of 1948, 392–5

Dickinson, Daniel S., narrowly missed the Presidency, 120

Dix, John A., "If any man attempts to haul down the American flag, shoot him on the spot," 131

Dixon-Yates controversy, 418–420

Donelson, Mrs. Andrew Jackson, mistress of the White House in Jackson's administration, sent home by the President on account of Peggy O'Neal, 66

Dorset, The Duke of, his warning to the Adamses at their presentation at the Court of St. James's, 16

Douglas, Stephen A., his slighting reference to President Pierce, 118; author of the repeal of the Missouri Compromise; his debate with Lincoln, 141

Dred Scott Decision, The, 115, 128

Dulles, John Foster, as Secretary of State, 407, 410, 412

Eaton, Mrs. Peggy O'Neal, the tempest over her in Jackson's Cabinet circle, 65, 66

Einstein, Albert, interested Roosevelt in atom bomb experiment, 370

Eisenhower, President Dwight David, military background, 399–400; as presidential timber, 399–400; antecedents and birth, 400; graduates from West Point, 401; marries Marie Geneva (Mamie) Doud, 401; son dies, 401; son John born, 401; as Supreme Commander of AEF, 403; as army Chief of Staff, 403–404; as president of Columbia University, 404; activities for NATO, 404–405; and draft-Eisenhower movement, 405–406; at 1952 Republican National Convention, 406; embarrassed by Joseph R. McCarthy, 406, 420–422; wins election and flies to Korea, 407; dominance of foreign policy in administration of, 407–415; atoms-for-peace plan, 408; Geneva Summit meeting, 408–409; and SEATO, 411; and Formosa, 411–412; Doctrine, 412–413; and Suez Canal crisis, 413; defense policies of, 414–415; anti-depression measures, 416–418; domestic policies, 416–422; and Dixon-Yates controversy, 418–420; relations with Congress, 422–424; White House organization of, 423, 424–425; has heart attack, 425–426; has operation, 426; in 1956 campaign, 426–427; agreement with Nixon, 427–428; and racial discrimination, 428; and Little Rock crisis, 428–429; decline in popularity, 428–429

Eisenhower, Mrs. Marie Geneva (Mamie), marriage to Dwight David Eisenhower, 401

Ellsworth, Oliver, his objection to a limited term in the Presidency, vi

Erskine, Lord, his homage to Washington, 13

Evarts, William M., an anecdote of him at the trial of Andrew Johnson, 168; his jest at the "dry" dinners of Mrs. Hayes, 196

Fairfax, Lord Bryan, employed Washington as surveyor, 3

Fauquier, Governor, entertaining Thomas Jefferson, 21

Federal Reserve Act, The, its passage under Wilson, 275, 276

Federalist Party, The, its origin, 26; its death, 44

Fessenden, William Pitt, voted for the acquittal of Andrew Johnson, 169

Fillmore, Mrs. Abigail Powers, marriage to Millard Fillmore and her inspiration of his ambition, 110; her death, 111

Fillmore, Mrs. Caroline McIntosh,

second wife of Millard Fillmore, 111

Fillmore, Miss Mary Abigail, acted for her mother as mistress of the White House and installed first library there; her death, 111

Fillmore, President Millard, an anecdote of his accession to the Presidency, 109; early life and marriage to Abigail Powers, 110; sent Commodore Perry on Japanese expedition, 111; death of his wife, and marriage to Mrs. Caroline McIntosh, 111; defeated for nomination by the Whigs, 111; defeated four years later as the candidate of Whigs and Know-Nothings, 111; his approval of the Fugitive Slave Act, 114

Finder, Leonard V., 400

Fiske, James, Jr., his attempt to corner gold, 180

Florida, purchased from Spain in the Monroe administration, 44

Floyd, John B., accusation against him as Buchanan's Secretary of War, by Stanton, 131

Foster, Charles, with Garfield at the latter's nomination, 202, 203

France, The President of, contrasted with the American President, v

France, Washington's neutrality in its Revolution, 10, 11; President Adams' preparation for war with and the peace, 18; Jackson's success in collecting the French spoliation claims, 69; at the Washington Conference, 294

Franklin, Benjamin, his prediction that the Presidency would end in a dynasty, ix; on committee with Jefferson and Adams to draft the Declaration, 22; Jefferson's famous reference to, 25

Frémont, Gen. John C., raised the flag over California, 101

Gallatin, Albert, said Lafayette was the only man Washington loved, 12

Garfield, President James A., antecedents, youth and education, 197, 198; his marriage to Lucretia Rudolph, 198; in the Civil War, 199; in Congress, 199, 200; his speech after Lincoln's assassination, 200; his nomination for President and election, 200–204; his inauguration and administration, 204–06; his assassination, 206, 207

Garfield, Mrs. Lucretia Rudolph, her marriage to James A. Garfield, 198; a public fund for her benefit, 207

George III, his interview with John Adams, 16

George, David Lloyd, "A race between Wilson and Hindenburg," 281

Germany, its expedition against Venezuela stopped by Roosevelt, 258, 259; in World War I, 278–84; in World War II, 366; surrender, 387–8

Germany, The President of, contrasted with the American President, v

Gladstone, William E., his tribute to Washington, 13

Gould, Jay, his attempt to corner gold, 180

Grant, Mrs. Julia Dent, marriage to Ulysses S. Grant, 172

Grant, President Ulysses, at Vicksburg and Chattanooga, 153; in the Wilderness, 154; "swinging around the circle" with Johnson, 165, 166; changing his name, 171; at West Point, 171, 172; marriage to Julia Dent, 172; in the Mexican War and his resignation from the army, 172, 173; borrowing money from West Point classmate Simon B. Buckner, 172, 173; hard struggles in civil life, 173; his start in the Civil War, 173, 174; removed from command by Halleck, his arrest suggested by McClellan, 175; his relations with Sherman and Sheridan, 176; nation horrified by slaughter in his campaigns, 176; his meeting with Buckner at Fort Donelson, 176, 177; his conduct at Appomattox, 177; his Presidency, 178–81; accused of Cæsarism, 181; grief at wedding of his daughter, 182; his tour of the world, 182; defeated for a third term, 182; his disastrous experience in Wall Street, 183; writing his "Personal Memoirs," 184; his death, 184, 185

Great Britain, Anglo-American disarmament agreement on the Great Lakes, 44; the Ashburton Treaty, 92; settlement of the boundary dispute in the Northwest, 100; how Cleveland's Venezuelan message opened a new era in Anglo-American relations, 233; dissuaded by Roosevelt from making an expedition against Venezuela, 258; at the Washington Conference, 293, 294

Greeley, Horace, "Let the erring brethren go," 129

Green, John Richard, his tribute to Washington, 13

Greene, Gen. Nathanael, Washington's devotion to, 13

Grimes, James W., voted for the acquittal of Andrew Johnson, 169

Guiteau, Charles J., his assassination of President Garfield, 206, 207

Halleck, Gen. Henry W., removed Grant from his command, 175

Hamilton, Alexander, proposed that the President should serve for life, vi; his assumption of leadership in Adams' administration, 17; his conflict with Jefferson, 26, 27; aided Jefferson's election for President, 27

Hanna, Marcus Alonzo, his management of McKinley's campaign, 241, 242; opposed Roosevelt's nomination for Vice-President, 254

Harding, Mrs. Florence Kling Delong, marriage to Warren G. Harding, 287

Harding, President Warren G., antecedents and marriage to Mrs. Florence Kling Delong, 289; in politics, 289, 290; his nomination for President foretold by Daugherty, 291; his election and inauguration, 292, 293; his foreign policy, 293; the Washington Conference, 293, 294; disruption of Republican majority in Congress, 295, 296; his last tour and death, 296–98

Harrison, Mrs. Anna Symes, wife of William Henry Harrison, 87

Harrison, President Benjamin, his life and administration, 227–30

Harrison, Mrs. Caroline Scott, first wife of Benjamin Harrison, 228–30

Harrison, Frederic, his tribute to Washington, 13

Harrison, Mrs. Mary Lord, second wife of President Benjamin Harrison, 230

Harrison, President William Henry, campaigning against the Indians with Mad Anthony Wayne, 82; territorial delegate in Congress, 82; governor of the territory of Indiana, 82; at the battle of Tippecanoe, and in the War of 1812, 82, 83; in the House and Senate, 84; minister to Colombia, 84; clerk of a county court, 85; candidate for President in "Hard Cider and Log Cabin campaign," 85; his inaugural censored by Webster, 86; quarreling with Clay, 87; death, 87, 88

Hawthorne, Nathaniel, his life-long friendship with President Pierce, 117

Hay, Mrs. Eliza Monroe, her friendship with Queen Hortense, 42, 43

Hay, John, his picture of Lincoln, 151; reference to Garfield, 205; his declaration for "the open door" in China, 246

Hayes, Mrs. Lucy Webb, under whom the White House "went dry" for the first time, 195, 196

Hayes, President Rutherford B., his remarks about a Napoleon in the White House, x; surprise of the country at his nomination for President, 186, 187; his birth and education, 187; his services in war and peace, 188; why he was nominated, 189; his disputed election, 189–93; his appointments, 193; his efforts at civil service reform thwarted by Congress, 193, 194; his abandonment of the reconstruction policy of his party, 194, 195; his resistance to silver coinage, 195

Henry, Prince, of Prussia, his American tour, 259

Henry, Patrick, his dread of a Presidential tyrant, ix

Hitler, Adolf, 366, 402

Hoar, George F., presiding over the convention of 1880, 202; his opposition to Philippine annexation, 247

Hooker, Gen. Joseph, overruled in military plan by Lincoln, 153

Hoover, President Herbert, career before entering politics, 318–21; Chairman Belgian war relief and Food Administrator, 321–23; dropped middle name, 323; supported Wilson in 1918, 323; Secretary of Commerce, 324; elected President, 325–26; good will tour of South America, 326; the "Hoover Doctrine," 326; sticking to prohibition, 327; Wall St. crash, 327; fighting great depression, 328–32; moratorium, 330; dealing with Bonus Expeditionary Force, 332; losing campaign and defeat, 332–33; on missions for President Truman and Chairman of Commission on Reorganization of Executive Departments, 388–9

Hortense, Queen, her friendship with Eliza Monroe, 42, 43

Hughes, Charles E., Republican nominee for President in 1916, 269; his startling proposal to the Washington Conference, 293

Hull, Cordell, Secretary of State, 372

"Hunkers," The, a New York political faction, 107

Ingersoll, Robert G., his "plumed knight" speech, 188

Irving, Washington, his description of White House reception under the Madisons, 37

Italy, in World War II, 366

Jackson, President Andrew, his denunciation of Adams and Clay, 51; first President born in a log cabin, 57; in the Revolution at 14 and taken prisoner, 58; judge of the Supreme Court of Tennessee, 59; married Mrs. Rachel Donelson Robards, 59; his duels and altercations, 59, 60; in the War of 1812, 60–62; elected to the Senate and resigned, 62; elected President, 63; Jacksonian revolution, 63–6; scenes of his inauguration described by Justice Story, 64; anecdote of Buchanan and Jackson, 64; introduction of the Spoils System, 64; the tempest in the Cabinet circle over Peggy O'Neal, 65, 66; death of Mrs. Jackson, 66; his overthrow of the U.S. Bank, 66, 67; his challenge to Southern nullification, 67, 68; his honorary degree from Harvard censured by John Quincy Adams, 69; his success in collecting the French spoliation claims, 69; his "Kitchen Cabinet," 70; his introduction of the national convention, 71; how Van Buren became his political heir, 71, 72

Jackson, Mrs. Rachel Donelson Robards, her marriage to Andrew Jackson, 59; death, 66

Japan, anecdote of Commodore Perry's expedition, vi; President Fillmore's gifts to Japanese government, 111; its peace with Russia under Roosevelt's guidance, 260; its naval competition with the United States led to the calling of the Washington Conference, 293, 294; its attack on Pearl Harbor, 371–2; last stand at Okinawa, 379; surrendered, 388

Jefferson, Mrs. Martha Wales Skelton, her marriage to Thomas Jefferson, 21; death and last wish, 24, 25

Jefferson, President Thomas, his defiance of a subpoena by Chief Justice Marshall, viii; his anecdote of Washington, x; resigned from Washington's Cabinet, 10; through mediation of Mrs. Adams, reconciled to John Adams, 19; born on the frontier, 20; at William and Mary College, 21; frequent guest of Gov. Fauquier, 21; at the bar, 21; the building of Monticello, 21; marriage to Mrs. Martha Wales Skelton, 21; listening to Patrick Henry's patriotic oratory, 22; writing the Declaration of Independence, 22, 23; remaking the laws of Virginia, 23, 24; his view of slavery, 24; his flight from the British, 24; death of his wife, and her last wish, 24, 25; introducing the dollar into our currency, 25; minister to France and his famous remark about Franklin, 25; in Washington's Cabinet, 25; origin of our political parties, 26; defeated for the Presidency and elected Vice-President, 27; chosen President in an exciting election, 27; the fable of his inauguration, 27; introduction of Jeffersonian simplicity, 28; his course in the Napoleonic Wars, 28; purchase of Louisiana, 29; only President to remain leader of his party in retirement, 29; dispatched Lewis and Clark and Capt. Pike on exploring expeditions in new territory, 29; mentor of Madison and Monroe, 29; his versatility, 30; impoverished in old age, 30, 31; building the University of Virginia, 30, 31; death, 31; his self-made epitaph, 32; his repudiation of an English treaty negotiated by Monroe, 43

Johnson, President Andrew, always at odds with the slaveholding aristocracy, 160; a penniless youth and a runaway apprentice, 160; tailoring his only private occupation, 161; his marriage to Eliza McCardle, who became his teacher, 161; his official services, 161; author of the Homestead Act, 161, 162; only Southern Senator to remain when South seceded, 162; military governor of Tennessee and Vice-President, 162, 163; rejoicing of the radicals at his succession to the Presidency, 163, 164; his adoption of Lincoln's reconstruction policy and its defeat, 164–67; his struggle to remove Stanton, 167; his impeachment and acquittal, 167–69; his election to the Senate, his death, 169, 170

Johnson, Mrs. Eliza McCardle, her marriage to Andrew Johnson, who became her pupil, 161

Johnson, Hiram W., unsuccessful candidate for Republican Presidential nomination, 291

Johnston, Mrs. Harriett Lane, one of the most admired mistresses of the White House, and her monument to her uncle, President Buchanan, 126

Jusserand, Ambassador Jules, sent to Washington by France, 259

Kansas, the real beginning of the Civil War, 122

Khrushchev, Nikita S., 409

Killian, James R., 415

Know-Nothing Party, The, defeated in 1856, 111; started to divert public attention from slavery, 114

Knox, Frank, Secretary of Navy, 368

Knox, Gen. Henry, affection for, by Washington, 13

Knox, Philander C., introduced to public life under McKinley, 247

Lafayette, Marquis de, alarmed by fear of an Adams dynasty, ix; said to be the only man Washington loved, 12

Lawrence, Abbott, an incendiary suggestion against the Van Buren administration, 79

League of Nations, The, President Wilson's view of its importance, 284, 285

Lee, Henry, his famous tribute to Washington, 13

Lee, Gen. Robert E., at Antietam, 147; at Chancellorsville and Gettysburg, 153; at Appomattox, 177

Lewis and Clark Expedition, dispatched by Jefferson to explore the Northwest, 29

Lincoln, President Abraham, his exercise of the autocratic power of the Presidency, viii; birth and youth, 133–35; took stand against slavery and for woman suffrage, 136; marriage to Mary Todd, 137, 138; his homely habits, 137, 138; life on the old circuit, 138; retired from Congress after criticizing Mexican War, 139; aroused by the repeal of the Missouri Compromise and joined the Republican Party, 139, 140; his debate with Douglas, 140, 141; nominated for President, 141, 142; elected, 142; his attitude toward the seceding states, 142, 143; his superstitious presentiments, 143, 144; his journey to Washington, 144, 145; his decision to fight for the Union, 145, 146; Seward's remarkable proposal to him, 146; early disappointments in the war, 147; his emancipation proclamation, 147; his success in winning the border states, 148; stories of him in the White House, 149–52; death of his son Willie and his dependence on Tad, 152; his reception of the news from Gettysburg and Vicksburg, 153; "Don't swap horses while crossing the river," 154; re-elected, 154; at Hampton Roads Conference, 155; his second inaugural, 155; entering Richmond, 155; working for reunion, 156, 157; his magnanimous sentiments, 157; his dream, 157; his last words and assassination, 157–59; rejoicing of radicals when Johnson replaced him, 163, 164; adoption of his policy by Johnson and its defeat, 164–67; its ultimate triumph under Hayes, 194, 195

Lincoln, Mrs. Mary Todd, her marriage to Abraham Lincoln, 137, 138; her dark forebodings, 155

Lodge, Henry Cabot, Jr., 406

Longworth, Mrs. Alice Roosevelt, daughter of Theodore Roosevelt, 261

Louis Philippe, King, his diplomatic hint to Jackson, 69

Louisiana Purchase, negotiated under Jefferson, 29; Jefferson's dispatch of Lewis and Clark and Captain Pike on exploration expedition in new territory, 29; Monroe one of the negotiators of the Purchase, 42

Lowden, Frank O., unsuccessful candidate for Republican Presidential nomination, 291

Lowell, James Russell, his reference to Grant in Europe, 182; called "a dashed literary feller" by Simon Cameron, 193; tribute to Grover Cleveland, 221, 222

Lyons, Lord, his quotation of Sec. Seward's remark regarding the power of the Presidency, vii

McClellan, Gen. George B., his Peninsular campaign, 147; defeated as the Democratic candidate against Lincoln, 154; suggested Grant's arrest, 175

McElroy, Mrs. Mary Arthur, mistress of the White House in Arthur's term, 211

McKinley, Mrs. Ida Saxton, her marriage to William McKinley and their married life, 238, 239; President McKinley's Pacific Coast tour interrupted by her illness, 247; her dying husband's consideration for her, 248, 249

McKinley, President William, twice declined nomination for President, 235; defeated for speakership, 236; author of the McKinley bill, 237; his Civil War record, 237; youth and young manhood, 237, 238; his marriage to Ida Saxton and their married life, 238, 239; his campaign for Presidency and election, 239–42; Spanish War, 243, 244; annexation of the Philippines, 244, 245; expedition to Pekin and declaration for "the open door" in China, 245, 246; a notable group of men whom he introduced to public life, 247; abandonment of Pacific Coast tour on account of wife's illness, 247; his last speech at Buffalo, 247, 248; his assassination by Leon F. Czolgosz at Buffalo, 248–50; his reluctant appointment of Roosevelt as Assistant Secretary of the Navy, 253; his opposition to his nomination for Vice-President, 254

Madison, Mrs. Dolly Payne Todd, marriage to James Madison, 35; her popularity as mistress of the White House, 36; Washington Irving's description of one of her receptions, 37; impoverished old age and death, 39

Madison, President James, under Jefferson's tutorship, 29; personal appearance, 33; overstudying at Princeton, 33; in Virginia legislature, 34; "Father of the Constitution," 34; in the first Congress, 35; marriage to Mrs. Dolly Payne Todd, 35; description of him by Washington Irving, 37; forced into the War of 1812, 37; driven from the White House by the British, 38; his view of secession, 39; impoverished old age and death, 39

Maine, settlement of Anglo-American dispute by Ashburton treaty, 92

Marshall, Gen. George C., as Secretary of State announced plan for aiding European recovery, 390

Marshall, John, his summons of Jefferson ignored, viii

Mellon, Andrew W., Secretary of the Treasury, aiding Wall St. boom, 313

Milburn, John G., in whose house President McKinley died, 249

Missouri Compromise, The, made in the Monroe administration, 44; converted slavery question into a football of politics, 113; its repeal, 114

Monroe, Mrs. Elizabeth Kortright, marriage to James Monroe, 42; her daughter's friendship with Queen Hortense, 42; her amendments of Jeffersonian simplicity in the White House, 45

Monroe, President James, under Jefferson's tutorship, 29; at college, his varied public services and his personal qualities, 40, 41; at the National Convention in the French Revolution, 41; protecting Thomas Paine, 42; recalled, 42; one of the negotiators of the Louisiana Purchase, 42; marriage to Elizabeth Kortright, 42; his negotiation of an English treaty repudiated by Jefferson, 43; Secretary of State and in charge of the War Department also, 43; President, 43; Anglo-American disarmament on the Great Lakes negotiated in his administration, 44; purchase of Florida, 44; proclaimed Monroe Doctrine, 44; the Missouri Compromise, 44; "The Era of Good Feeling," 44; Monroe's strong Cabinet, 44; last President to wear knee breeches and sword, personal description, 45; an impoverished old age and his death, 46

Monroe Doctrine, The, proclaimed, 44; Cleveland's assertion of the doctrine in Venezuelan message, 233

Morgan, J. Pierpont, appealed to by Presidents Cleveland and Roosevelt in financial crises, 276

Morley, John, his estimate of Roosevelt, 259

Morris, Gouverneur, favored a life tenure in the Presidency, vi

Morse, Samuel F. B., still regarded as an impostor by many when he received telegraphic report in Washington of the Baltimore convention in 1844, 98

"Mugwumps," The, 218

"Mulligan Letters," The, 217, 218

Mussolini, Benito, seizure of Italian government, 366

Nasser, Gamal, 413

New Hampshire, in the inner councils of the Democratic Party before the Civil War, 119

New Mexico, all its territory east of the Rio Grande claimed by Texas, 108

New York, mother of Vice-Presidents and its disappointed ambitions for the Presidency, 110

Nixon, Richard M., Senator and Vice-President, 407, 427–428

Oregon, settlement of Anglo-American boundary dispute, 100

"Ostend Manifesto," The, 122

Paine, Thomas, his denunciation of Washington, 11; protected by Monroe in the French Revolution, 42

Panama, Roosevelt's action in its secession from Colombia, 260, 261

Panama Canal, its construction begun under Roosevelt, 260, 261

Pendergast, Boss Tom, gave Truman political start, in prison, death, 385–6

Perry, Commodore Matthew C., anecdote concerning his expedition to Japan, vi; presenting gifts of President Fillmore to Japanese government, 111

Philippine Islands, their annexation to the United States, 244, 245

Pierce, President Franklin, student days at Bowdoin College and his lifelong friendship with Hawthorne, 116, 117; his official service and in the Mexican War, 117, 118; surprise of country at his nomination for President, 118, 119; tragic death of his son, 120, 121; his election and administration, 121, 122; defeated for renomination, 123; his letter to Jefferson Davis in 1860, 123; his position in the Civil War, 123

Pierce, Mrs. Jane Means, her aversion to public life, 118; tragic death of her son and her belief that it was due to an act of God, 120, 121

Pike, Captain Zebulon M., dispatched by Jefferson on an exploring expedition in the West, 29

Pinkerton, Allan, accompanied Lincoln to Washington, 144, 145

Platt, Thomas C., his resignation from Senate, 206; his alarm over Roosevelt's progressiveness, 254; nominating Roosevelt for Vice-President to get rid of him, 254

Polk, President James K., the first dark horse, 96; youth and education, 96, 97; at the bar, in Congress, speaker, governor, 97; defeated Van Buren for the nomination, 97; the first nomination that was reported by telegraph, 98; defeated Clay at the polls, 99; settled the Anglo-American boundary dispute in Pacific Northwest, 100; the Mexican War and the annexation of Mexican territory, 101, 102; death, 102

Polk, Mrs. Sarah Childress, her régime as mistress of the White House, 102

Presidency, The, discussions concerning the office in the Constitutional Convention, v–xi; strange delusion under which it was created, vii; intrusted with more power than any king, vii; autocratic power exercised by Lincoln, viii; President's part in annexation of territory, viii; President Hayes' remark about a Napoleon in the White House, x; a title for the President debated in Congress, 10; first Presidential tour, 10; the emoluments of the office, 266; representative character of our Presidents, 271, 272; Wilson's theory of Presidential leadership, 272–75; occupational and geographical statistics, 287–89; prejudice against choosing Presidents from among men long in Washington, 295; the custom and strain of Presidential tours, 297; political experience of Presidents, 303; Vice-Presidents who have acceded to the Presidency, 307

Preston, Mrs. Thomas J., Jr. *See* Mrs. Frances Folsom Cleveland

Quay, Matthew Stanley, "Fry the fat out of the protected industries," 229

Randolph, Edmund, his course as Secretary of State under Washington, 10

Randolph, John, denunciation of Adams and Clay, 51

Rawlins, Gen. John A., his relations with Grant, 179

Reed, Thomas B., sarcastic references to Benjamin Harrison, 229, 230; the "billion-dollar Congress," 230; defeated McKinley for speaker, 236, 237

Republican Party, The, its birth, 122; its description in 1912, 265–68

Robinson, Theodore Douglas, 338

Roosevelt, Mrs. Alice Lee, first wife of Theodore Roosevelt, 261

Roosevelt, Mrs. Edith Kermit Carow, her marriage to Theodore Roosevelt, 261, 262

Roosevelt, Eleanor, niece of T. R. and wife of F. D., 335; her "new deal" in the White House, 349

Roosevelt, President Franklin D., called a maverick by T. R., Jr., 334; antecedents and youth, 334–37; marriage, 335; fighting Tammany in state Senate, 337–38; Assistant Secretary of Navy, 338; defeated for Vice-President, 338–39; stricken by infantile paralysis, 339–40; christened Alfred E. Smith the "Happy Warrior," 340–41; elected governor, 341; campaign for President and election, 341–43; attempted assassination, 345; inauguration, 344–48; emergency actions, 346–49; his "golden voice" on the radio, 349; the New Deal, 352–61; Supreme Court and New Deal, 357–58; second election, 1936, 362; Democratic and Republican parties changed sides, 362; sit down strikes, 1937, 363; Court Plan and defeat, 363–4; Supreme Court sustained New Deal, 365; F.D.R. challenged Hitler and Mussolini in Quarantine speech, 366; broke third term tradition, 367–9; appointed Stimson and Knox, Republicans, to Cabinet, 368; rushed guns to Britain and transferred destroyers in exchange for bases in British islands, 368–9; first peace time draft, 369; "psychopathic hatred" of "That Man," 369; four freedoms, 370; Lend-Lease, 370; race for atom bomb, 370; Atlantic Charter, 370; launched United Nations, 372; as war leader, 372–4; bipartisan foreign policy, 375; fourth election, 375; most traveled President, 376–7; National Foundation for Infantile Paralysis and March of Dimes, 378; last days and death, 377–81; personal characteristics, 378; second millionaire in the Presidency, 380; ranking Presidents, 380–81; Roosevelt first in hearts of the burden bearers, 381

Roosevelt, Henry Latrobe, 338

Roosevelt, James, father of Franklin D., 335

Roosevelt, Quentin, his death in World War I, 270

Roosevelt, Sara Delano, mother of Franklin D., 335; at his inauguration, 346

Roosevelt, President Theodore, his youth and education, 251, 252; ranching in the Wild West, 252; entering politics, 252, 253; Civil Service commissioner and police commissioner, 253; Assistant Secretary of the Navy and with the Rough Riders in the Spanish War, 253, 254; governor and Vice-President, 254; his succession to President McKinley, 254, 255; his adoption of progressive policies, 255, 256; settlement of coal strike, 256; our wealthiest President, 256; the campaign of slander against him, 256; methods and manners, 257; his election, 257; how he made the Kaiser back down, 258, 259; John Morley's estimate of him, 259; interest of foreign governments in him, 259, 260; stopping the Russo-Japanese War, 260; received the Nobel Prize, 260; his part in the Panama revolution, 261; digging the Panama Canal, 261; life in the White House, 261, 262; his two marriages, 261; first President since Jackson to choose his successor, 263; how he forced Taft's nomination, 263, 264; his hunting expedition in Africa and its trophies, 267; disruption of the Republican Party in his absence, 267, 268; his candidacy for nomination against Taft, 268; "My hat is in the ring," 268; defeated by the Old Guard, 268; "We stand at Armageddon," 268; running on the Progressive ticket, 268; shot while campaigning, 269; his expedition to Brazil, 269; supported Hughes in 1916, 269; his position in World War I, 269; his desire to enter the war overruled by Wilson, 269;

death of his son, Quentin, in battle, 270; death, 270

Roosevelt, Theodore, Jr., called F. D. a maverick, 334; Assistant Secretary of Navy, 338

Root, Elihu, drawn into political life by McKinley, 247

Russia, its peace with Japan under Roosevelt's guidance, 260; its collapse in World War I, 280, 281; F. D. Roosevelt's last efforts to unite her with West, 379–80; Cold War, 390

Sartoris, Mrs. Nellie Grant, her White House wedding, 182

Scott, Gen. Winfield, ordered to South Carolina by Jackson at time of nullification, 68; in the Mexican War, 101; "Wayward sisters, depart in peace," 129

Seward, William H., his remark concerning the power of the Presidency, viii; defeated by Lincoln for the Republican nomination, 141; his remarkable proposal to Lincoln, 146

Sherman, John, his candidacy in 1880, 200, 201

Sherman, William T., at West Point with Grant, 171, 172; with him in Civil War, 175

Slavery Question, The, how parties and politicians were wrecked by trying to dodge it, 112–15

Smith, Alfred E., Democratic candidate for President, 325; christened "Happy Warrior" by F. D. Roosevelt, 340–41; in "Stop Roosevelt" movement, 341–42

South Carolina, its attempt to nullify a Federal law, 68

Southey, Robert, his tribute to Washington, 13

Spain, sold Florida to the United States, 44; threat of "Ostend Manifesto" to take Cuba from her by force, 122; war with the United States, 243, 244

Stalin, Josef, Russian dictator's tribute to Lend Lease, 370

Stanton, Edwin M., in Buchanan's Cabinet, 130, 131; "Now he belongs to the ages," 158; turned the War Department into a fort against President Johnson, 167

Stevens, Robert T., 421

Stevenson, Governor Adlai E., 406, 426

Stewart, A. T., disqualified for Secretary of the Treasury under Grant, 179

Stimson, Henry L., Secretary of War, 368

Story, Joseph, describes scene at Jackson's inauguration, 64

Sumner, Charles, started discussion of forcing President Johnson to resign, 164; Grant's retort to him, 178, 179

Taft, Mrs. Helen Herron, wife of William H. Taft, 263

Taft, Senator Robert A., 405, 406

Taft, President William H., introduced to political life by McKinley, 247; how his nomination for President was forced by Roosevelt, 263, 264; a judicial rather than an executive mind, 264; his services in the Philippines and in the Cabinet, 265; his lack of leadership in the Presidency, 265; his defeat, 265, 266; appointed Chief Justice by Harding, 266

Taylor, Mrs. Margaret Smith, her preference for the simple life to White House formality, 105

Taylor, President Zachary, entering the Mexican War, 101; his youth, 103; anecdote of his army service, 104; his daughter married Jefferson Davis, 104, 105; ridiculed proposal to make him President, 105; his nomination by the Whigs, 105, 106; denounced by Webster and disliked by Clay, 106; his opposition to the Compromise of 1850, 108; his death in office, 108

Texas, its annexation, 93; the boundary dispute that led to the Mexican War, 101; its claim of all of New Mexico, east of the Rio Grande, 108

Tilden, Samuel J., his election to the Presidency announced by the press, 190; how he lost it, 190–93; on Grover Cleveland, 221

Thackeray, William M., his estimate of Washington, 13

Thompson, Jacob, arraigned as Secretary of the Interior by Stanton, 131; his arrest, 157, 163

Truman, President Harry S., slow rise of unambitious man, 381–6; connection with Boss Pendergast and rise to fame as head of Truman Committee, 385–6; nominated for Vice-President, 386; humility on becoming President, 387; in World War I, 384; married, 384; failure of his store, 385; surrender of Germany, 388; Truman at San Francisco Conference and with Big Three at Potsdam, 388; broke news of atom bomb and surrender of Japan, 388; recalled Hoover to public service, 388–9; election of Republican Congress, 390; Truman Doctrine, Marshall Plan and Cold War, 390; Wallace out of Cabinet, 390–1; Civil Rights Message, 391; Truman's party split by Wallace Progressives and Dixiecrats, 391–2; nominated by spiritless convention but aroused it by fighting speech, 392; in hardest campaigning on record, won in biggest election upset, 393–7; thwarted in new Democratic Congress by coalition of Republicans and southern Conservatives, 397; Atlantic Pact, 397

Trumbull, Lyman, voted for the acquittal of Andrew Johnson, 169

Tyler, President John, first Vice-President to succeed to the Presidency, 89, 90; his education and official services, 90; a political revolution on his accession, 91, 92; resignation of the Whig Cabinet, 92; the Ashburton treaty, 92; his policy that led to the annexation of Texas, 93; death of his wife, Letitia Christian, and his remarriage to Julia Gardiner, 94; a tragedy on a warship, 94; chairman of the Peace Conference in Washington in 1861, 95; member of the Confederate Congress, and death, 95

Tyler, Mrs. Julia Gardiner, second wife of John Tyler, 94

Tyler, Mrs. Letitia Christian, first wife of John Tyler, 94

United States Bank, overthrown by Jackson, 66, 67

Van Buren, Mrs. Angelica, mistress of the White House in her father-in-law's term, 80

Van Buren, Mrs. Hannah Hoes, wife of Martin Van Buren, 73

Van Buren, John, a familiar election-day slogan coined by him, 80

Van Buren, President Martin, how he became the political heir of Jackson, 71, 72; first President born under the American flag, 73; success at the bar, 73; early political honors, 74; an anecdote of his evasiveness, 74, 75; the first national campaign manager, 75; in Jackson's Cabinet, and minister to England, 75, 76; made Washington Irving his secretary of legation, 76; his nomination as minister rejected by Senate, 76; elected Vice-President, 77; an anecdote of him and Clay, 77; his administration as President wrecked by the panic of 1837, 78, 79; established the subtreasury system, 79; accused of extravagance in the White House, 80; defeated, 80; defeated for nomination in 1844, 97–9; nominated by the Free Soilers in 1848, 107

Vanderbilt, William H., his loan to Grant, 183, 184

Venezuela, Cleveland's intervention in dispute with England, 233; Roosevelt's intervention to stop German expedition, 258, 259

Victoria, Queen, sent first message by Atlantic cable, 128, 129

Wade, Benjamin F., his rejoicing over Johnson's succession to Lincoln, 164; expected to supplant Johnson on latter's impeachment, 168, 169

Wallace, Henry A., out of Truman's Cabinet and Progressive candidate for President, 390–2.

Wallace, Gen. Lew, wrote campaign biography of Benjamin Harrison, 227

War of 1812, forced upon President Madison, 37; its dismal record, the capture and burning of Washington and final victory at New Orleans, 38; Harrison's campaign, 82, 83

War, The Civil, when and how it started, 112–15, 121–23, 127–32; secession of the southern states, 142, 143, 145, 146; the opening of the conflict, 146; dark days for the Union, 147, 148; the turn in the tide, 153–55; Lincoln's work for reconstruction, 156, 157; Johnson's adoption of Lincoln's reconstruction policy and its failure, 163–67

War with Mexico, origin, campaigns and annexation of territory, 100, 101.

War with Spain, 243, 244

War, World, I, entry of the United States into the war, 278–81; Wilson's moral leadership, 281–83; his part in the overthrow of the German and Austrian emperors, 283; the peace-making, 283–86

War, World, II, armies of Hitler and Mussolini overrunning Europe when third term tradition was broken by election of Roosevelt, 366–9; Pearl Harbor, 371–2; numbers in American uniform, 374; Allies landed in North Africa, 374; landed in Normandy, 374; Germany surrendered, 387; Japan surrendered, 387

Washburne, Elihu B., Secretary of State under Grant, 179

Washington, settlement of Anglo-

American boundary dispute, 100.

Washington, President George, his indignation under charge of usurpation, x; had less schooling than any other President in first forty years, 2; his modest ancestry, 2; as a boy surveyor on the frontier, 3; inherited Mount Vernon, 4; personal appearance, 4; as a sportsman, 4; disappointed in love, 5; married Mrs. Martha Dandridge Custis, 5; in the Seven Years' War, 5, 6; read prayers at burial of Gen. Braddock, 5; differences with English officers, 6; his appointment as commander-in-chief in the Revolution, 6, 7; his services in war, 7, 8; his reported toast at Yorktown, 8; heavy financial sacrifices, 8; his inauguration as President, 9; his tour of the country, 10; his challenge to the Whisky Rebellion, 10; set first example of neutrality, 10; quarrels in his Cabinet, 10; denounced by John Adams and Thomas Paine, 10, 11; the victim of mud-slinging and his anger, 11; financial loss in the Presidency, 11; retired to Mount Vernon, 11; the value of his estate, 12; land-poor, 12; his expenses in the Presidency, 12; his large family, 12; freeing his slaves, 12; his valet and his war horse, 12; Lafayette said to be the only man he loved, 12; his expression of affection for Gen. Knox and his devotion to Gen. Greene, 13; his consideration of others as he was dying, 13; English tributes to his memory, 13; familiar tribute to him by Henry Lee, 13

Washington, Mrs. Martha Custis, marriage to George Washington, 5

Watterson, Henry, his anecdote of President Pierce, 118; on Garfield's assassination, 207

Webster, Daniel, his assistance to Dolly Madison in her impoverished old age, 39; censoring Harrison's inaugural, 86; Secretary of State under Harrison and Tyler, 92; negotiated Ashburton treaty, 92; his denunciation of President Taylor, 106; his ridicule of Van Buren as a Free Soiler, 107; sponsored the Fugitive Slave Act, 114

Webster, Ezekiel, his criticism of John Quincy Adams, 52

Wenzell, Adolphe H., 419

Whig Party, The, wrecked on the slavery question, 112–15

Whisky Rebellion, The, challenged by Washington, 10

"Whisky Ring," 180

White House, The, Abigail Adams its first mistress, and her amusing description of the place, 18; introduction of Jeffersonian simplicity, 28; Washington Irving's description of a reception under the Madisons, 37; burned by the British in 1814, 38; Mrs. Monroe's amendments of Jeffersonian simplicity, 45; scandal created by John Quincy Adams when he installed a billiard table and furnished the East Room, 52, 53; the name "White House" first bestowed in derision by Jackson's critics, 64; campaign stories of extravagance under Van Buren, 80; Mrs. Polk's strait-laced régime, 102; Miss Fillmore installed first library,

111; "went dry" for the first time under Mrs. Hayes, 195, 196; Roosevelt's idea of it and its remodelling in his term, 261, 262; changes between Cleveland and Hoover, 350–52.

Wilhelm II, Kaiser, forced to back down by Roosevelt, 258, 259; his overthrow in World War I, 282, 283

Willkie, Wendell, Republican candidate for President, 368; endorsed Roosevelt's foreign policy, 368–9; tour of his "one world," 369.

Wilson, Mrs. Edith Bolling Galt, her marriage to Woodrow Wilson, 277

Wilson, Mrs. Ellen Axson, first wife of Woodrow Wilson, 277.

Wilson, James, suggested election of the President by the people, vi

Wilson, President Woodrow, his antecedents, 271, 272; governor, 272; his philosophy of leadership, 272, 273; his lack of popularity, 273, 274; his nomination for President, 273, 274; his revival of custom of delivering messages to Congress in person, 274, 275; the record of his first administration, 275, 276; his

forcing through of the Federal Reserve Act, 275, 276; death of his wife, his remarriage, 277; his re-election, 277; his policy of neutrality in World War I and efforts at peace-making, 278; his War Message and war policies, 278–81; "The world must be made safe for democracy," 282; his moral leadership, 281–83; his part in the overthrow of the German and Austrian emperors, 283; defeat of his leadership at home in the election of 1918, 283; President and Congress deadlocked between the parties, 283, 284; his two trips to Paris, his part in the Peace Conference, and the failure of the League of Nations in the Senate, 283–85; his physical collapse on speaking tour and his paralysis, 285; his retirement and death, 285, 286

Wood, Gen. Leonard, unsuccessful candidate for Republican Presidential nomination, 291

Woodbury, Levi, slated to succeed President Van Buren, but death intervened, 119

Wormley's Hotel Conference, 192

Zwicker, General Ralph W., 421

Date Due			
APR 6	2 JAN		
MAY 1 8	FEB 1		
JUL 2 8	APR 1 0		
AUG 8	JUL 15		
DEC 7	JUL 2 6		
JAN 1 6	AUG 3		
APR 1 1	MAR 2 0		
MAY 7	MY 1		
MAY 2 3	JUL 2 0		
JUL 1 9	JUL 3 1		
AUG 3			
JAN 9			

Morgan, James.
Our presidents, 2d enl. ed.